TOEFL
Complete Guide

시원스쿨 LAB

ETS 토플 공식 파트너
TOEFL Complete Guide
시원스쿨 토플 이론서

초판 1쇄 발행 2025년 12월 1일

지은이 시원스쿨어학연구소
펴낸곳 (주)에스제이더블유인터내셔널
펴낸이 양홍걸 이시원

홈페이지 www.siwonschool.com
주소 서울시 영등포구 영신로 166 시원스쿨
교재 구입 문의 02)2014-8151
고객센터 02)6409-0878

ISBN 979-11-7550-033-4 13740
Number 1-110505-26269920-09

이 책은 저작권법에 따라 보호받는 저작물이므로 무단복제와 무단전재를 금합니다. 이 책 내용의 전부 또는 일부를 이용하려면 반드시 저작권자와 ㈜에스제이더블유인터내셔널의 서면 동의를 받아야 합니다.

머리말

미국 ETS(Educational Testing Service)는 2026년 1월 21일부터 TOEFL iBT 시험을 전면 개정한다고 공식 발표했습니다. 1964년 첫 시행 이후, TOEFL은 전 세계 수험생들이 영어 실력을 입증하기 위한 가장 권위 있는 국제 영어 시험으로 자리매김해 왔습니다. 그러나 그동안 시험이 상위권 대학, 특히 미국 명문대 입학 기준에 초점을 두고 있다는 지적도 꾸준히 제기되어 왔습니다. 이에 따라 ETS는 보다 폭넓은 수준의 대학에서 요구하는 현실적 영어 능력을 평가하고, 수험생에게는 더 간결하고 효율적인 시험 경험을 제공하기 위해 시험 구조와 문항 유형을 대대적으로 개편하기로 결정했습니다.

개정 TOEFL의 주요 변화는 다음과 같습니다.

❶ Reading(읽기)과 Listening(듣기) 영역은 다단계 적응형(multistage adaptive) 형식으로 바뀌어, 응시자의 실력에 따라 시험 난이도가 실시간으로 조정됩니다. 또한, 특정 전공 지식이나 배경지식이 필요한 지문은 축소되고, 캠퍼스 생활, 이메일, 공지문, 웹사이트 등 실제적이고 현대적인 상황을 반영한 내용이 추가됩니다.

❷ Writing(쓰기)과 Speaking(말하기) 영역 또한 큰 폭의 변화를 맞습니다. 기존의 통합형(integrated) 과제는 모두 폐지되며, 준비 시간 없이 바로 응답해야 하는 짧은 문항 중심으로 구성됩니다. 특히 Writing 영역에서는 2023년에 도입된 토론형 과제가 유지되는 한편, 문장 만들기 및 이메일 쓰기 등 실용적인 과제가 새롭게 추가됩니다.

❸ 시험 결과 발표 기간은 기존의 5일 내외에서 72시간 이내로 단축되며, 점수 체계 또한 기존의 0–120점 방식에서 CEFR(the Common European Framework of Reference for Languages 유럽공통참조기준) 연동 1–6 밴드(0.5 단위) 체계로 전환됩니다.

❹ 형식은 간소화되었지만, TOEFL의 핵심 철학인 실력 기반 평가 원칙은 더욱 강화됩니다. 난이도 조정 시스템을 통해 수험자의 실제 언어 능력이 보다 정밀하게 측정되며, 고득점을 위해서는 '운'이 아닌 정확하고 탄탄한 영어 실력이 요구됩니다.

이 책은 이러한 개정 TOEFL의 새로운 방향성을 충실히 반영하여 구성되었습니다. 실용적인 영어 능력을 기르는 데 중점을 두고 있으며, 각 영역별 최신 출제 경향과 학습 전략을 구체적으로 안내합니다. 특히 ETS 공식 파트너 시원스쿨은 공신력 있는 ETS 문제를 수록하여 수험생들이 시험의 구조와 요구 사항을 정확하고 확실하게 이해할 수 있도록 하였습니다.

이 책이 변화하는 시험에 효과적으로 대비하고, 자신의 영어 실력을 정확히 진단하며 한 단계 성장할 수 있는 든든한 길잡이가 되길 바랍니다.

시원스쿨어학연구소

- 머리말 03
- 목차 04
- 이 책의 구성과 특징 06
- 개정 TOEFL에 대한 모든 것 08
- 학습 플랜 10

Reading
1. Complete the Words 14
2. Read in Daily Life 28
3. Read an Academic Passage 36

Listening
1. Listen and Choose a Response 52
2. Listen to a Conversation 64
3. Listen to an Announcement 72
4. Listen to an Academic Talk 80

Writing
1. Build a Sentence 94
2. Write an Email 104
3. Write for an Academic Discussion 112

Speaking
1. Listen and Repeat 122
2. Take an Interview 136

ETS Practice Tests

1. Test 1 — 145
2. Test 2 — 197
3. Test 3 — 250

Answers

1. Reading — 304
2. Listening — 316
3. Writing — 334
4. Speaking — 343
5. ETS Practice Tests — 350

음원(MP3), Script for ETS Practice Tests(PDF), Answers(PDF) 다운로드
lab.siwonschool.com 접속 ▶ 교재/MP3 탭 클릭 ▶ 해당 도서 검색 ▶ 다운로드

이 책의 구성과 특징

1 영역별 분석 및 문제 해결법 제시

2026년부터 적용되는 시험 개정 내용을 철저히 분석하여, 각 영역(Reading, Listening, Writing, Speaking)마다 「출제 경향 분석」→「유형별 문제 풀이 전략」→「실전 문제 연습」의 3단계 구성으로, 체계적인 학습이 가능하도록 설계했습니다.

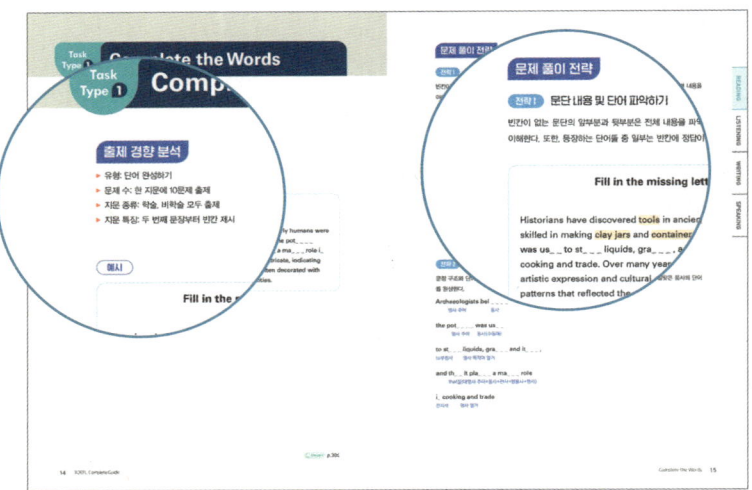

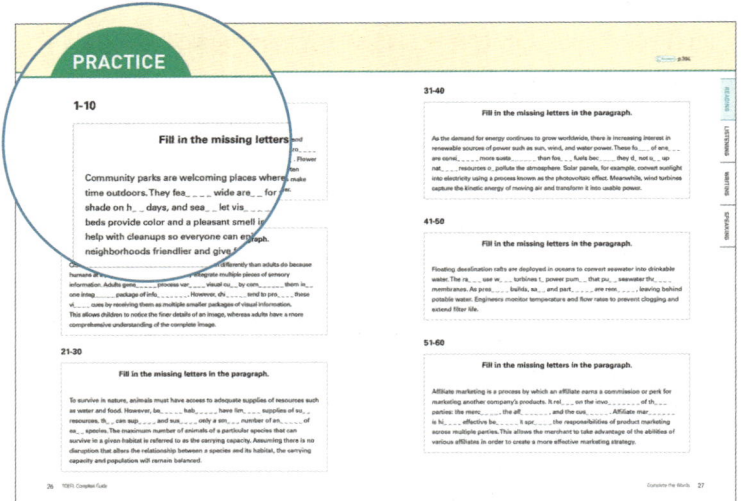

2 Writing & Speaking 최신 유형 집중 훈련

가장 큰 변화가 있는 Writing과 Speaking 영역에서는, 개정된 ETS 채점 기준에 따른 모범 답안과 채점 기준 포인트를 통해 자가 점검이 가능하도록 하였습니다.

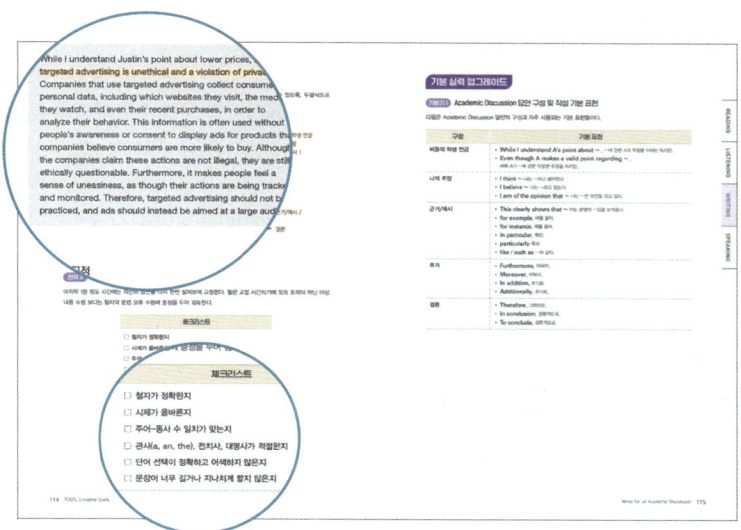

3 ETS 제공 문제를 통한 개정 시험 완벽 준비

ETS 제공 실전모의고사 3세트를 직접 풀어보면서 개정 토플 시험을 완벽하게 대비합니다. 특히 실제 시험 화면 구성을 최대한 지면에 반영하여 수험생들이 보다 쉽게 시험에 적응할 수 있도록 돕습니다.

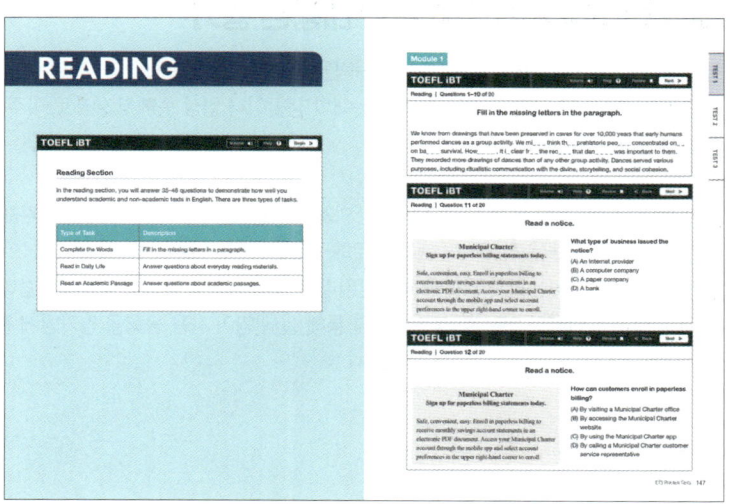

개정 TOEFL에 대한 모든 것

2026년 1월 21일부터 시행되는 개정 TOEFL iBT는 다음과 같은 특징을 갖고 있습니다.

1 두 개의 모듈과 더미 문항이 출제되는 Reading과 Listening

Reading 영역은 두 개의 모듈(세트)로 구성되어 있습니다. 먼저 첫 번째 모듈을 모두 풀면, 두 번째 모듈이 자동으로 제시되며, 이때 두 번째 모듈의 난이도는 수험자의 첫 번째 모듈 성적에 따라 조정됩니다.

Listening 영역 또한 Reading과 동일하게 두 개의 모듈로 구성되며, 응시자의 실력 수준에 따라 두 번째 모듈의 난이도가 달라집니다.

또한, 각 모듈에는 2023년 7월 개정 이후 한동안 제외되었던 더미(dummy) 문항이 다시 포함됩니다. 더미 문항은 점수 산정에 반영되지 않는 문항으로, 실제 시험 중에는 어느 문항이, 몇 문항이 더미인지 구별하기 어렵습니다. 따라서 수험자는 모든 문항을 실제 시험 문항이라 생각하고 성실히 응시해야 합니다.

2 Writing과 Speaking 시험 순서 변경

개정 이전에는 Listening 영역이 종료된 직후 Speaking 영역이 바로 이어지는 구조였습니다. 이로 인해 Listening을 늦게 마치는 수험생들은 시험장 내에서 다른 수험생들의 Speaking 답변 소리에 방해를 받아 집중하기 어려운 불편함을 겪기도 했습니다.

이러한 문제를 개선하기 위해 개정된 TOEFL에서는 Listening 영역이 끝난 뒤 Writing 영역이 이어지도록 시험 순서가 조정되었습니다. 이로써 수험생들은 보다 조용하고 안정적인 환경에서 시험을 치를 수 있게 되었습니다.

3 학문적 내용은 감소하고 실생활 기반 내용은 증가

개정 TOEFL은 실생활과 밀접한 상황에서의 영어 사용 능력을 중점적으로 평가합니다. 기존 시험이 비교적 장문의 학문적 지문으로 구성되었던 것과 달리, 개정 시험에서는 대학 생활이나 일상 속에서 실제로 마주할 수 있는 상황을 다룬 짧고 실용적인 내용이 주를 이룹니다.

특히, 기존 Writing 및 Speaking 영역에 출제되던 통합형 과제(Integrated Task)는 긴 학술적 주제를 바탕으로 한 지문과 강의 내용을 정리한 뒤 답변을 작성해야 했기 때문에, 노트테이킹이 필수적이었습니다. 그러나 개정 TOEFL에서는 이러한 형식이 사라지고, 실생활과 밀접하게 연관된 짧고 실용적인 문항으로 대체되었습니다. 수험자는 별도의 준비 시간 없이 즉시 응답해야 하는 형태의 과제를 통해 실제 영어 사용 능력을 평가받게 됩니다.

주요 변화	개정 전	개정 후
점수 체계	• 0-120점	• CEFR 연동 1-6 밴드(0.5 단위)
점수 발표	• 약 5일 이후	• 72시간 이후
Reading (읽기 영역)	• 600-700 단어의 학술적 지문 읽기	• 단어 완성하기(Complete the Words) • 실용문 읽기(Read in Daily Life) • 200-300 단어의 학술적 지문 읽기 (Read an Academic Passage)
Listening (듣기 영역)	• 긴 대화 및 강의 듣기	• 듣고 적절한 응답 고르기 (Listen and Choose a Response) • 대화 듣기 (Listen to a Conversation) • 공지 듣기 (Listen to an Announcement) • 강연 듣기 (Listen to an Academic Talk)
Writing (쓰기 영역)	• 학술적 지문과 강의를 요약하는 통합형 과제(Integrated Task) • 학술적 토론을 위한 글쓰기 (Write for an Academic Discussion)	• 문장 만들기(Build a Sentence) • 이메일 쓰기(Write an Email) • 학술적 토론을 위한 글쓰기 (Write for an Academic Discussion)
Speaking (말하기 영역)	• 질문에 대한 나의 의견을 답변하는 독립형 과제(Independent Task) • 짧은 지문, 대화 또는 강의를 요약하는 통합형 과제 (Integrated Task)	• 듣고 따라 말하기(Listen and Repeat) • 면접 보기(Take an Interview)

학습 플랜

- 자신의 레벨에 맞게 다음의 학습 진도를 참조하여 매일 학습합니다.
- 문제를 풀 때에는 시간제한을 두고 실제 시험처럼 풀어 봅니다. 문제를 푼 뒤에는 오답은 물론, 문제를 풀면서 궁금했던 사항들을 반드시 확인하기 바랍니다.
- 교재를 끝까지 한 번 읽고 나면 2회독에 도전합니다. 두 번째 읽을 때는 훨씬 빠르게 끝낼 수 있습니다. 같은 교재를 여러 번 읽을수록 훨씬 효과가 좋으니 다독하기를 권장합니다.
- 혼자서 학습하기 어렵다면, 시원스쿨랩 홈페이지(lab.siwonschool.com)에서 유명 토플 선생님의 강의를 들으며 보다 쉽고 재미있게 공부할 수 있습니다.

초고속 7일 완성 학습 플랜

▶ 영어 실력이 좋은 수험생 대상
▶ 이미 기존 TOEFL 시험 준비를 어느 정도 끝마친 수험생 대상
▶ 시험이 얼마 남지 않은 상태에서 짧은 시간 내에 최종 정리를 원하는 수험생 대상

1일	2일	3일	4일	5일
Reading	Listening	Writing	Speaking	ETS Practice Tests (Test 1)

6일	7일
ETS Practice Tests (Test 2)	ETS Practice Tests (Test 3)

입문자 30일 완성 학습 플랜

▶ TOEFL 시험이 처음인 수험생 대상
▶ 개정 TOEFL을 체계적으로 학습하기를 원하는 수험생 대상

1일	2일	3일	4일	5일
Reading 1. Complete the Words - Practice 전	**Reading** 1. Complete the Words - Practice	**Reading** 2. Read in Daily Life - Practice 전	**Reading** 2. Read in Daily Life - Practice	**Reading** 3. Read an Academic Passage - Practice 전
6일	**7일**	**8일**	**9일**	**10일**
Reading 3. Read an Academic Passage - Practice	**Listening** 1. Listen and Choose a Response - Practice 전	**Listening** 1. Listen and Choose a Response - Practice	**Listening** 2. Listen to a Conversation - Practice 전	**Listening** 2. Listen to a Conversation - Practice
11일	**12일**	**13일**	**14일**	**15일**
Listening 3. Listen to an Announcement - Practice 전	**Listening** 3. Listen to an Announcement - Practice	**Listening** 4. Listen to an Academic Talk - Practice 전	**Listening** 4. Listen to an Academic Talk - Practice	**Writing** 1. Build a Sentence - Practice 전
16일	**17일**	**18일**	**19일**	**20일**
Writing 1. Build a Sentence - Practice	**Writing** 2. Write an Email - Practice 전	**Writing** 2. Write an Email - Practice	**Writing** 3. Write for an Academic Discussion - Practice 전	**Writing** 3. Write for an Academic Discussion - Practice
21일	**22일**	**23일**	**24일**	**25일**
Speaking 1. Listen and Repeat - Practice 전	**Speaking** 1. Listen and Repeat - Practice	**Speaking** 2. Take an Interview - Practice 전	**Speaking** 2. Take an Interview - Practice	**ETS Practice Tests** Test 1 Reading/Listening
26일	**27일**	**28일**	**29일**	**30일**
ETS Practice Tests Test 1 Writing/Speaking	**ETS Practice Tests** Test 2 Reading/Listening	**ETS Practice Tests** Test 2 Writing/Speaking	**ETS Practice Tests** Test 3 Reading/Listening	**ETS Practice Tests** Test 3 Writing/Speaking

READING

1. Complete the Words
2. Read in Daily Life
3. Read an Academic Passage

Overview

문제 수	35-48 문제
시험 시간	약 27분
문제 유형	총 3개 ☑ Complete the Words ☑ Read in Daily Life ☑ Read an Academic Passage
문제 세트	총 2 모듈(세트) 출제 ☑ 첫 번째 모듈에서 높은 점수를 받으면 두 번째 모듈에서도 아카데믹 지문 유형이 출제되지만, 반대로 낮은 점수를 받으면 두 번째 모듈에서 아카데믹 지문 유형이 출제되지 않음
더미 문제	두 모듈에 더미 문제(성적에 반영되지 않는 실험용 문제)가 랜덤으로 들어가 있음

Type of Task 1: Complete the Words

출제 경향 분석

- 유형: 단어 완성하기
- 문제 수: 한 지문에 10문제 출제
- 지문 종류: 학술, 비학술 모두 출제
- 지문 특징: 두 번째 문장부터 빈칸 제시

예시

Fill in the missing letters in the paragraph.

Historians have discovered tools in ancient settlements that reveal early humans were skilled in making clay jars and containers. Archaeologists bel_ _ _ _ the pot_ _ _ _ was us_ _ to st_ _ _ liquids, gra_ _ _ , and it_ _ _ , and th_ _ it pla_ _ _ a ma_ _ _ role i_ cooking and trade. Over many years, the designs became more intricate, indicating artistic expression and cultural exchange. These artifacts were often decorated with patterns that reflected the values and beliefs of their communities.

Answers p.304

문제 풀이 전략

전략 1   문단 내용 및 단어 파악하기

빈칸이 없는 문단의 앞부분과 뒷부분은 전체 내용을 파악할 수 있게 도와주므로, 먼저 이 문장들을 해석하며 내용을 이해한다. 또한, 등장하는 단어들 중 일부는 빈칸에 정답이 되기도 한다.

Fill in the missing letters in the paragraph.

Historians have discovered **tools** in ancient settlements that reveal **early humans** were skilled in making **clay jars** and **containers**. Archaeologists bel_ _ _ _ the pot_ _ _ _ was us_ _ to st_ _ _ liquids, gra_ _ _ , and it_ _ _ , and th_ _ it pla_ _ _ a ma_ _ _ role i_ cooking and trade. Over many years, the **designs** became more intricate, indicating artistic expression and cultural exchange. These **artifacts** were often decorated with patterns that reflected the values and beliefs of their communities.

→ 첫 문장에서 도구의 발견과 초기 인류가 점토 항아리와 용기 제작한 내용을, 마지막 두 문장에서 디자인과 유물들의 특징에 대한 내용을 확인

전략 2   문법에 유의하며 빈칸 품사 유추하기

문장 구조와 단어 형태를 고려하여, 명사, 동명사, 동사, 조동사, 형용사, 부사, 전치사, 접속사 등 알맞은 품사의 단어를 완성한다.

Archaeologists bel _ _ _ _
    명사 주어   동사

the pot_ _ _ _ was us_ _
    명사 주어   동사(수동태)

to st_ _ _ liquids, gra_ _ _ and it_ _ _ ,
to부정사   명사 목적어 열거

and th_ _ it pla_ _ _ a ma_ _ _ role
   that절(대명사 주어+동사+관사+형용사+명사)

i_ cooking and trade
전치사   명사 열거

Complete the Words

전략 3 내용과 문법을 고려하여 빈칸 단어 유추하기

전체 지문 내용과 어울리는 빈칸 단어를 유추하는데, 문장 구조와 단어 형태를 고려하여 알맞은 단어를 완성한다. 중간에 모르는 빈칸은 건너뛰고 아는 단어부터 채운 후, 문장을 해석하면서 빠진 빈칸을 다시 유추한다.

Archaeologists bel i e v e the pot_ _ _ _ was use d to st o r e liquids, gra i n s, and it_ _ _, and tha t it play e d a ma j o r role i n cooking and trade.

고고학자들은 이 pot_ _ _ _ 가 액체, 곡물 및 it_ _ _을 보관하는 데 사용되었으며, 요리 및 무역에서 중요한 역할을 했다고 믿는다.

pot_ _ _ _
→ 첫 문장에 나온 clay jars and containers를 지칭하는 pottery(도자기류) 유추 가능

it_ _ _
→ 액체, 곡물과 같이 pottery에 담는 물품들(items) 유추 가능

Fill in the missing letters in the paragraph.

Historians have discovered tools in ancient settlements that reveal early humans were skilled in making clay jars and containers. Archaeologists belie v e the pot t e r y was use d to st o r e liquids, gra i n s and ite m s, and tha t it play e d a majo r role i n cooking and trade. Over many years, the designs became more intricate, indicating artistic expression and cultural exchange. These artifacts were often decorated with patterns that reflected the values and beliefs of their communities.

→ 빈칸을 채우고 제대로 문장이 완성되고 해석되는지 반드시 최종 확인

기본 실력 업그레이드

기본기1 문장 구조 분석 능력

단어 일부가 빈칸으로 제시되는 문제에서 문맥과 문법 구조를 통해 빈칸 단어를 완성해야 하므로, 어휘력뿐만 아니라 문장 구조 분석 능력이 매우 중요하다.

❶ 주어(Subject) - 동사(Verb) 관계
주어와 동사의 일치 여부(수일치)를 알아야 빈칸에 들어갈 단어의 형태를 정확히 완성할 수 있다.

- **단수/복수 일치: 주어가 단수면 단수 동사, 복수면 복수 동사**
  - 예 The discovery was unexpected.
    그 발견은 예상치 못했다.

- **형식 주어 there: 동사 형태 결정은 실제 주어를 기준**
  - 예 There were several factors.
    여러 요인들이 있었다.

- **주어와 동사가 떨어져 있을 때: 수식어에 흔들리지 않기**
  - 예 The number of people who participated in the experiments provides reliable results.
    그 실험들에 참여한 사람들의 수는 믿을 만한 결과를 제공한다.

❷ 품사 구별
빈칸 앞뒤 단어와 문장 구조를 보고 해당 단어가 명사, 동사, 형용사, 부사 중 무엇인지 판단해야 한다.

- **명사 자리: 관사(a, an, the), 소유격(my, his, their), 형용사, 전치사 뒤**
  - 예 The researcher made an important discovery.
    조사자는 중요한 발견을 했다.

- **동사 자리: 주어 뒤, 조동사 뒤, 시제 변화를 받는 자리**
  - 예 They investigated the cause of the accident.
    그들은 그 사건의 원인을 조사했다.

- **형용사 자리: 명사 앞(수식) 또는 be동사 뒤**
  - 예 The results were significant.
    그 결과들은 중요했다.

- **부사 자리: 동사, 형용사, 다른 부사를 수식**
  - 예 The theory was widely accepted.
    그 이론은 널리 받아들여졌다.

Complete the Words

③ 절, 구 파악
빈칸이 절(clause) 또는 구(phrase) 안에 있는지 파악하면 품사와 동사의 형태 결정이 쉽다.

- 절: 주어와 동사가 모두 있는 문장 단위로, 혼자서 완전한 문장이 되는 독립절과 접속사나 관계사 뒤에 나오는 종속절로 구분

  예 People did not believe his theory because his experiment had failed.
  그의 실험은 실패했기에 사람들은 그의 이론을 믿지 않았다.

- 구: 주어나 동사가 하나라도 없는 단어 뭉치로, 전치사와 명사로 이루어진 전명구(in the library), 명사 중심의 명사구(a remarkable discovery), 동명사 중심의 동명사구(analyzing the data), to부정사 중심의 to부정사구(to improve efficiency)가 있음

  예 The retrieved samples were stored in a refrigerator to prevent decay.
  그 회수된 샘플들은 부패를 방지하기 위해 냉장고에 보관되었다.

  예 Discovering new elements significantly enhances our understanding of the world.
  새로운 원소를 발견하는 것은 세상에 대한 우리의 이해를 크게 향상시킨다.

④ 시제 구분
동사 자리 빈칸에 시제가 잘못되면 무조건 오답 처리되며, 실제 시험에서 시제 함정을 통해 정답률을 떨어뜨리므로 시제를 유의하며 빈칸을 채워야 한다.

- 시간 부사와의 일치: yesterday, currently, recently와 같은 시간에 유의하여 시제를 결정

  예 The researchers finished the project last month.
  그 연구자들은 지난 달에 그 프로젝트를 끝마쳤다.

- 문장 내 시제 일관성: 같은 문장/절 안에서 시제를 흐름에 맞추기

  예 The team was confident they could win the contract.
  그 팀은 그들이 계약을 따낼 수 있을 거라고 자신했다.

- 완료형: 과거부터 현재까지의 경험/완료/결과를 나타냄

  예 The scientist has published several papers on the topic since 2010.
  그 과학자는 2010년부터 해당 주제에 관한 여러 논문을 발표해 왔다.

⑤ 수동/능동 여부 판단
동사 자리 빈칸이 수동태인지 능동태인지 파악하여 동사를 그에 맞게 변형해야 한다.

- 형태: be동사 + p.p. (이때 be 동사의 시제에 유의)

  예 The new policy was approved by the committee last week.
  새로운 정책이 지난 주 위원회에 의해 승인되었다.

기본기 2 어휘 패턴 인식 능력

단어의 일부분(접두사, 어근, 접미사, 철자 패턴)만 보고 나머지를 빠르게 유추하는 능력으로, Complete the Words 문제는 단어의 철자 암기력보다는 단어의 형태·의미 패턴을 인식하는 능력을 중시한다.

❶ 접두사(Prefix)
단어의 앞부분에 나오는 접두사를 통해 단어의 의미가 갖는 방향성이 결정된다.

접두사	빈출 접두사별 단어 리스트	접두사	빈출 접두사별 단어 리스트
co- 함께, 같이	coherent 일관성 있는 coincide 일치하다 colleague 동료 collection 수집품, 무리 cooperate 협력하다, 협동하다 coordinate 조직화하다, 편성하다 corporation 기업, 단체	em-/en- ~이 되게 하다	embarrass 당황스럽게 만들다 embrace 수용하다, 포옹하다 empower 권한을 주다 enable 가능하게 하다 encouraging 격려하는 enhance 향상시키다 enlarge 확대하다 enlighten 이해시키다, 계몽하다
com- 함께, 같이	combination 조합 common 공통의, 흔한 communication 의사소통 community 공동체 companion 동반자 compassion 동정심, 연민 compose 구성하다 composition 구성	ex- 이전, 밖, 무(無), ~로부터	exchange 교환하다 exclusively 독점적으로 exhale 내쉬다, 내뿜다 exit 출구 explore 탐구하다 exposure 노출, 폭로 expressed 표현된 extinction 멸종 extract 뽑아내다, 발췌하다 extrovert 외향적인 (사람)
dis- 부정, 반대	disability 장애 disagree 동의하지 않다 disarray 혼란 discharge 해고하다, 방출 discomfort 불편 disillusioned 환멸을 느낀 dismount (탈 것에서) 내리다 disorder 무질서 disputable 반론의 여지가 있는 dispute 반박하다, 분쟁	il-/ir- 부정, 반대	illegal 불법의 illogical 비논리적인, 불합리한 illusion 오해, 착각 irrational 비이성적인 irregular 불규칙의, 불법의 irrelevant 관계없는, 부적절한 irresponsible 무책임한 irreversible 되돌릴 수 없는

접두사	빈출 접두사별 단어 리스트	접두사	빈출 접두사별 단어 리스트
im-/in- 부정, 반대, 안, 속	impatient 참지 못하는 impractical 터무니없는, 비현실적인 improper 부적절한, 부당한 inaction 활동 부재 induce 유발하다, 초래하다 influence 영향을 미치다, 영향력 injustice 불공정, 부당 insinuate 넌지시 말하다 invisible 볼 수 없는	over- 위에, 과도한	overcharge 바가지를 씌우다 overcome 극복하다 overestimate 과대평가하다 overflow 넘치다 overlap 겹치다, 포개지다 overlook 간과하다 overly 너무, 몹시 overreact 과잉 반응 보이다 overweight 과체중의
inter- 속, 사이, 상호	interact 상호 작용하다, 교류하다 interchange 교환하다, 교체하다 interference 간섭, 개입 interlude 사이, 중간, 막간 intermediate 중간의 international 국제적인, 국가 간 interpersonal 대인관계에 관련된 interrogation 질문, 심문 interstate 주와 주간의	pre- 전(前)	precaution 예방, 주의 precedent 전례 precondition 전제 조건 prediction 예측 prelude 전주, 서곡, 머리말, 도입부 premature (예정 보다) 이른 preparation 대비, 준비 previously 미리, 이전에
mis- 나쁜, 잘못	mishap 작은 사고 misinformation 잘못된 정보, 오보 misinterpret 잘못 해석하다, 오역하다 misjudge 잘못 판단하다 mislead 잘못 인도하다 misrepresentation 잘못된 설명 mistakenly 실수로 mistrust 불신, 신뢰하지 않다 misunderstanding 오해 misuse 남용, 남용하다	re- 다시, 새로	recall 기억해 내다, 상기하다 reconstruct 재건하다, 재구성하다 reminiscent 연상시키는 renewable 재생 가능한 reset 다시 맞추다 retrieve 회수하다 revert 복귀하다, 되돌아가다 review 재검토하다, 논평 revise 개정하다, 수정하다 revival 회복, 부활
non- 부정, 반대, 무(無)	nondescript 특징이 없는 nonetheless 그럼에도 불구하고 nonexistent 존재하지 않는 nonfiction 허구가 아닌 전기 또는 역사 nonsense 터무니없는 nonspecific 특이하지 않은, 불특정한 nonviolent 비폭력의	semi- 반, 불완전	semiannual 반년마다 semicircle 반원 semicolon 세미콜론 semiconductor 반도체 semiconscious 의식이 완전치 않은 semiformal 반정장의

접두사	빈출 접두사별 단어 리스트	접두사	빈출 접두사별 단어 리스트
sub- 아래, 하위	subjunction 첨가, 추가(첨가)물 submarine 잠수함, 해저의 submerge 잠수하다 submissive 순종적인 subordinate 종속된 subsequently 그 뒤에, 나중에 substandard 표준 이하의 suburban 교외의	un- 부정, 반대, 무(無)	uncompromising 타협하지 않는 undemanding 힘들지 않은 undeniable 부인할 수 없는 undo 원상태로 돌리다 unlikely ~할 것 같지 않은 unplug 플러그를 뽑다 unproductive 비생산적인 unscrupulous 부도덕한 unstable 불안정한 unwise 현명하지 못한
trans- 이전, 횡단, 초월, 변화	transatlantic 대서양을 횡단하는 transfer 옮기다, 이전하다 transform 바꾸다, 전환하다 transit 수송, 통과 transition 전이, 변화 transitive 과도적인 translation 번역 transport 운송하다	under- 밑, 아래, 불완전	undercut ~보다 저가로 팔다, 약화시키다 underestimate 과소평가하다 underground 지하 underlie ~의 기저를 이루다 undermine 손상시키다, 악화시키다 understated 절제된 undertake 착수하다 undertaker 장의사 underwear 속옷

❷ 접미사(suffix)

단어의 뒷부분에 나오는 접미사를 통해 단어의 품사와 문장에서의 위치가 결정된다.

접미사	빈출 접미사별 단어 리스트	접미사	빈출 접미사별 단어 리스트
–able (형) 할 수 있는, 적합한	adjustable 조정 가능한 capable 할 수 있는 comfortable 편안한 inevitable 불가피한 profitable 수익성이 있는 reasonable 합리적인 reliable 믿을 수 있는 replaceable 바꿀 수 있는 suitable 적합한 valuable 가치 있는	–en (형) ~으로 된, ~특징의 (동) ~로 만들다(되다)	brighten 밝아지다, 밝히다 fasten 고정하다 frighten 놀라게 하다 golden 황금의, 금으로 만든 lessen 줄이다 sharpen 날카롭게 하다 sunken 가라앉은, 움푹 들어간 weaken 약화시키다 wooden 나무로 된, 목재의
–ant/–ent (명) ~하는 사람 (형) ~한 성질의	assistant 조수 attendant 안내원 consultant 상담가 descendant 후손 fragrant 향기로운 observant 관찰력 있는 reluctant 마지못한 significant 중요한 student 학생 vacant 비어있는	–er/–or (명) 사람, 기계	admirer 숭배자 cleaner 청소부, 청소기 contender 경쟁자, 도전자 customer 고객 manufacturer 생산자, 제조업자 supervisor 감독관, 관리자 supporter 후원자, 지지자 thermometer 온도계 visitor 방문객 voter 투표자
–ary (형) ~의, ~에 관한 (명) ~에 관한 사람(사물)	dictionary 사전 elementary 초급의 honorary 명예의 military 군대, 군대의 missionary 선교사 monetary 통화의, 화폐의 planetary 행성의 secretary 비서 sedentary 주로 앉아 있는 voluntary 자발적인, 자원의	–ful (형) 가득한, 많은	bountiful 많은, 풍부한 colorful 다채로운 doubtful 의심스러운 frightful 끔찍한 helpful 도움이 되는 merciful 자비로운 resourceful 자원이 풍부한 rightful 정당한 truthful 정직한, 진실한 useful 유용한
–ed (형) ~의 특징이 있는, 과거분사 (동) 과거형	alleged (증거 없이) 주장된 clichéd 상투적인 extended 연장된 insulted 모욕 당한, 무시 당한 interested 관심 있는 motivated 동기부여가 된 reduced 감소된 related 관련된 sacred 신성한 terrified 무서워하는	–ing (명) 동명사 (동) 진행형 (형) 현재분사	amazing 놀라운, 멋진 depressing 우울한 disputing 논란이 있는, 반박하는 encouraging 격려하는, 장려하는 fascinating 멋진, 매혹적인 humiliating 굴욕적인 intoxicating 취하는 promising 전도 유망한 rewarding 보람 있는 underlying 근본적인

접미사	빈출 접미사별 단어 리스트	접미사	빈출 접미사별 단어 리스트
–ion/ –sion/ –tion (명) 행동, 상태, 과정	allocation 할당 attraction 매력, 명소 confusion 혼란, 혼동 evolution 진화, 발전 extinction 멸종 isolation 고립, 소외 subtraction 공제, 삭감 supervision 감독, 관리 suspension 매달(리)기, 보류 vision 시력, 환영	–ize (동) ~으로 되다, 만들다	emphasize 강조하다 familiarize 익숙하게 하다 industrialize 산업화하다 maximize 극대화하다 minimize 최소화하다 personalize (개인의 필요에) 맞추다 rationalize 합리화하다 standardize 표준화하다
–ism (명) 행동, 결과, 특성, 체계	altruism 이타주의 communism 공산주의 criticism 비판 idealism 이상주의 materialism 물질주의 mechanism 매커니즘, 방법 optimism 낙관론 realism 현실주의, 사실성 utilitarianism 공리주의	–less (형) 없는	aimless 목적 없는 ceaseless 중단 없는 faultless 흠잡을 데 없는 fearless 겁 없는 helpless 무력한 merciless 무자비한 restless 쉼 없는, 안절부절 못하는 thoughtless 생각 없는 valueless 가치 없는
–ity (명) 특성, 상태	capability 능력, 역량 credibility 신뢰성 diversity 다양성 mediocrity 보통 사람, 평범 mortality 사망자수 priority 우선권 proximity 근접 scarcity 부족 validity 유효성, 타당성 vicinity 부근	–ly (부) 상태, 방법	abruptly 갑자기, 불쑥 capriciously 변덕스럽게 consistently 일관되게 incredibly 믿을 수 없이 moderately 적절하게 obstinately 완고하게 preferably 더 좋아하여 readily 손쉽게 sufficiently 충분히 unnecessarily 불필요하게
–ive/–ous (형) 특징	adventurous 모험심이 강한 ambiguous 애매한, 모호한 capricious 변덕스러운 cautious 신중한 corrosive 부식성의 excessive 과도한, 지나친 notorious 악명 높은 outrageous 충격적인 predictive 예측의 voracious 게걸스러운, 열렬한	–ment (명) 동작, 상태, 결과	achievement 업적, 성취 acknowledgement 인정 amusement 즐거움, 오락 contentment 만족 enrollment 등록 involvement 관련, 개입, 연루 movement 운동 requirement 요건 tournament 토너먼트 treatment 치료, 대우

접미사	빈출 접미사별 단어 리스트	접미사	빈출 접미사별 단어 리스트
−ness (명) 성질, 상태	attractiveness 끌어 당기는 힘, 매력 brightness 밝음, 선명함, 현명함 fitness 건강, 적합함 forgiveness 용서, 면제 kindness 친절, 다정 preciseness 정확, 정밀 stubbornness 완강 toughness 단단함, 질김 wickedness 악의 willingness 의지	−th (명) 행동, 과정	aftermath 여파 childbirth 출산 dearth 부족, 결핍 death 죽음 depth 깊이 growth 성장 length 길이 truth 진실 warmth 따뜻함 wealth 부
−ship (명) 상태, 특질, 지위	championship 챔피언 지위, 선수권 citizenship 시민권 friendship 우정 hardship 고난 ownership 소유 partnership 동반자 관계, 동업 relationship 관계		

③ 어근(root)
단어의 중심이 되는 어근을 통해 단어의 의미를 파악할 수 있다.

어근	빈출 단어	어근	빈출 단어
audi / aud 듣다	audible 들리는 audience 청중 auditorium 강당	spec / spect 보다	inspect 검사하다 perspective 관점 spectator 구경꾼
bene 좋은	benefit 이익 benevolent 자비로운 benign 온화한	struct 세우다	construct 건설하다 destruct 파괴하다 infrastructure 기반 시설
dict 말하다	contradict 반박하다 dictate 지시하다 predict 예측하다	tele 멀리	telegraph 전신 telephone 전화기 telescope 망원경
port 나르다	import/export 수입/수출 portable 휴대용의 transport 운송하다	vid / vis 보다	evidence 증거 supervise 감독하다 visible 눈에 보이는
scrib / script 쓰다	describe 묘사하다 inscription 비문, 새긴 글 manuscript 원고	voc / vok 부르다	advocate 옹호하다, 변호사 provoke 도발하다 vocal 목소리의

Complete the Words

PRACTICE

1-10

> **Fill in the missing letters in the paragraph.**
>
> Community parks are welcoming places where people can relax, play, and spend time outdoors. They fea_ _ _ _ wide are_ _ for wal_ _ _ _ and pla_ _ _ _. Trees pro_ _ _ _ shade on h_ _ days, and sea_ _ let vis_ _ _ _ _ sit and ta_ _ with one an_ _ _ _ _. Flower beds provide color and a pleasant smell in spring and summer. Volunteers often help with cleanups so everyone can enjoy the grounds. These shared spaces make neighborhoods friendlier and give families an easy way to be active together.

11-20

> **Fill in the missing letters in the paragraph.**
>
> Children aged 12 and under perceive visual information differently than adults do because humans at a young age lack the ability to fully integrate multiple pieces of sensory information. Adults gene_ _ _ _ _ process var_ _ _ _ visual cu_ _ by com_ _ _ _ _ _ them in_ _ one integ_ _ _ _ _ package of info_ _ _ _ _ _ _. However, chi_ _ _ _ _ tend to pro_ _ _ _ these vi_ _ _ _ cues by receiving them as multiple smaller packages of visual information. This allows children to notice the finer details of an image, whereas adults have a more comprehensive understanding of the complete image.

21-30

> **Fill in the missing letters in the paragraph.**
>
> To survive in nature, animals must have access to adequate supplies of resources such as water and food. However, be_ _ _ _ _ hab_ _ _ _ _ have lim_ _ _ _ supplies of su_ _ resources, th_ _ can sup_ _ _ _ and sus_ _ _ _ only a sm_ _ _ number of an_ _ _ _ _ of ea_ _ species. The maximum number of animals of a particular species that can survive in a given habitat is referred to as the carrying capacity. Assuming there is no disruption that alters the relationship between a species and its habitat, the carrying capacity and population will remain balanced.

31-40

Fill in the missing letters in the paragraph.

As the demand for energy continues to grow worldwide, there is increasing interest in renewable sources of power such as sun, wind, and water power. These fo_ _ _ of ene_ _ _ are consi_ _ _ _ _ more susta_ _ _ _ _ _ than fos_ _ _ fuels bec_ _ _ _ they d_ not u_ _ up nat_ _ _ _ resources o_ pollute the atmosphere. Solar panels, for example, convert sunlight into electricity using a process known as the photovoltaic effect. Meanwhile, wind turbines capture the kinetic energy of moving air and transform it into usable power.

41-50

Fill in the missing letters in the paragraph.

Floating desalination rafts are deployed in oceans to convert seawater into drinkable water. The ra_ _ _ use w_ _ _ turbines t_ power pum_ _ that pu_ _ seawater thr_ _ _ _ membranes. As pres_ _ _ _ builds, sa_ _ and part_ _ _ _ _ are rem_ _ _ _, leaving behind potable water. Engineers monitor temperature and flow rates to prevent clogging and extend filter life.

51-60

Fill in the missing letters in the paragraph.

Affiliate marketing is a process by which an affiliate earns a commission or perk for marketing another company's products. It rel_ _ _ on the invo_ _ _ _ _ _ of th_ _ _ parties: the merc_ _ _ _, the aff_ _ _ _ _ _, and the cus_ _ _ _ _. Affiliate mar_ _ _ _ _ _ is hi_ _ _ _ effective be_ _ _ _ _ it spr_ _ _ _ the responsibilities of product marketing across multiple parties. This allows the merchant to take advantage of the abilities of various affiliates in order to create a more effective marketing strategy.

Type of Task 2: Read in Daily Life

출제 경향 분석

▶ 유형: 일상에서 접할 수 있는 짧은 글 읽고 객관식 문제 풀기
▶ 문제 수: Reading 시험 각 모듈에서 보통 2개 지문이 출제되며 짧은 지문은 두 문제, 긴 지문은 세 문제 출제
▶ 지문 종류: 포스터, 공지문, 전단지, 표지판, 메뉴판, 양식, 일정표, 신문 기사, 광고, 송장, 영수증, 웹페이지, 소셜미디어 게시물, 이메일, 문자 메시지 창, 채팅 창 등
▶ 지문 특징: 약식으로 쓰여져 문법적 완전성이 부족하나 짧고 직관적이기에 빠르게 정보를 전달하는 데 효과적이며 일상어로도 쓰여 있기에 원어민이 자주 사용하는 관용 표현(common idiomatic expressions)도 나옴

예시

Read a notice.

Riverside Utility Cooperative
Go green with e-billing!

Skip the mailbox and save a tree. Members of the Riverside Utility Cooperative can now receive monthly electricity statements by e-mail. Signing up is fast and secure—just log into your online account or download the Riverside Utility mobile app and go to "Billing Preferences." Participants will also get a $5 credit after enrolling.

What is the main purpose of the notice?
(A) To announce a change in payment deadlines
(B) To encourage customers to use electronic billing
(C) To introduce a new utility pricing plan
(D) To report an outage in electricity service

What incentive is offered to customers?
(A) A monthly discount
(B) An energy assessment
(C) An electronic device
(D) A financial credit

Answers p.307

문제 풀이 전략

전략1 글의 종류 및 목적 파악하기

Read in Daily Life 유형에서 가장 많이 출제되는 문제는 글을 쓴 목적이다. 따라서 지문을 읽을 때 글 쓴 목적을 생각하며 읽어야 한다. 지문의 종류가 지문 시작 전에 나오는데, 이러한 글의 종류를 미리 확인하면 글의 목적을 파악하는 데 도움이 된다. 또한 글의 제목이나 주제문이 맨 앞에 굵은 글씨로 나오기도 하므로 이러한 부분을 놓치지 말고 읽도록 한다.

Read a notice. ┄┄▶ 무엇인가를 알리는 공지문임을 파악

Riverside Utility Cooperative ┄┄┄┄▶ 리버사이드 유틸리티 조합에서
Go green with e-billing! 전자 청구서로 친환경을
 실천하도록 촉구함

전략2 필요한 정보만 스캐닝하기

Read in Daily Life 유형에서 대부분의 문제는 지문의 세부 내용을 묻는다. 따라서, 먼저 문제를 읽고 문제에서 묻는 세부 내용이 지문의 어디에서 나오는지 찾아야 한다. 이때 지문 전체를 읽을 필요 없이 필요한 정보만 찾아읽는 스캐닝(scanning)으로 정답 단서를 찾는다.

What incentive is offered to customers?
➡ 고객에게 어떤 인센티브가 제공되는지 지문에서 찾기

Skip the mailbox and save a tree. Members of the Riverside Utility Cooperative can now receive monthly electricity statements by e-mail. Signing up is fast and secure—just log into your online account or download the Riverside Utility mobile app and go to "Billing Preferences." Participants will also get a $5 credit after enrolling.

➡ 참가자들은 5달러 크레딧을 받음

(A) A monthly discount
(B) An energy assessment
(C) An electronic device
(D) A financial credit
➡ 정답은 D번, 금전적 크레딧

기본 실력 업그레이드

기본기 1 스키밍(훑어읽기) 스킬

스키밍(skimming)은 글 전체를 빠르게 훑어보면서 대략적인 내용이나 주제를 파악하는 읽기 방법으로, 세부적인 정보보다는 글의 주제나 전반적인 흐름을 파악하는 데 목적이 있다.

❶ 제목과 소제목 반드시 읽기
글의 핵심 내용이 제목과 소제목으로 나타나기에 제목과 소제목은 반드시 읽는다.

❷ 굵은 글씨, 강조된 부분에 집중하여 읽기
제목과 소제목 외 지문 중간중간에 굵은 글씨 등으로 강조된 부분이 나올 수 있는데, 이렇게 강조되는 부분은 글쓴이가 강조하려는 중요 내용이므로 스키밍할 때에도 반드시 읽고 넘어가도록 한다.

❸ 첫 문장과 마지막 문장은 제대로 이해하기
많은 글이 글의 주제 및 핵심 내용이 처음에 나오는 두괄식 또는 마지막에 나오는 미괄식이므로, 첫 문장과 마지막 문장은 제대로 이해해야 한다.

❹ 지문 전체 구조 및 흐름을 생각하며 빠르게 본문을 훑어읽기
전체 지문을 그냥 빠르게 훑어보는 것이 아니라, 지문 전체 구조가 어떻고 내용이 어떻게 흐르는지를 생각하며 읽으면, 빠르게 훑으면서도 지문의 전체적인 윤곽을 파악할 수 있다.

기본기 2 스캐닝(찾아읽기) 스킬

스캐닝(scanning)은 글 전체를 읽지 않고, 특정 정보나 키워드만 빠르게 찾아내는 읽기 방법으로, 세부적인 정보를 묻는 문제를 풀 때 반드시 필요한 스킬이다.

❶ 문제의 키워드 확인
문제에서 묻는 내용과 문제의 키워드를 먼저 파악한다. 특히, 날짜와 금액 같은 숫자, 이름과 장소 같은 고유명사가 나오면 이를 키워드로 체크한다.

❷ 지문에서 유의어 고려하여 키워드 확인
숫자, 고유명사 등의 키워드가 지문에 나온 곳을 빠르게 찾아 이와 관련된 문제의 정답을 찾는다. 또한 키워드는 유의어로, 또는 같은 의미의 다른 표현으로 패러프레이징(paraphrasing)이 되는 경우가 많기에, 완전히 같은 단어만 스캐닝하는 것이 아니라 의미를 생각하면서 유의어도 스캐닝해야 한다.

스키밍 vs 스캐닝

	스키밍(훑어읽기)	스캐닝(찾아읽기)
목적	전체 내용 파악	지문에서 특정 정보 찾기 * 먼저 문제를 읽고 키워드를 파악할 것!
속도	빠름	매우 빠름
초점	주제, 흐름	키워드, 세부 정보

Campus Shuttle Service Update

From **March 15 to April 2**, the Green Line will operate on a modified schedule due to road construction near the South Gate.

Weekdays:
- First bus: 06:40 from North Residence Hall
- Last bus: 22:20 from Library Stop
- South Gate Stop will be closed; passengers should use East Gate Stop instead.

Saturdays:
- First bus: 07:10 from North Residence Hall
- Last bus: 20:00 from Library Stop

No service on Sundays during this period.

√ Passengers traveling after 21:00 must show a valid student ID to board.
√ Normal service will resume on **April 3**.

For full details, visit: transport.campus.edu/greenline.

→ 스키밍: 빠르게 제목, 굵은 글씨, 첫 문장, 마지막 문장을 읽어서 글 전체 내용이, 도로 공사로 인해 특정 기간 대학 셔틀 서비스 일정 변경 공지임을 파악

→ 스캐닝: 지문에 다양한 숫자(요일, 시간)와 고유명사(장소)가 나오므로 문제와 관련된 지문 부분만 읽어서 정답을 선택함
 (예) 언제 서비스가 정상적으로 재개하는지?

PRACTICE

1-2

Read an email.

Date:	August 8
Subject:	Walking Tour Registration Confirmation

Dear Ms. Jonas,

Thank you for registering for the Bayside Historical Walking Tour. Your spot on the tour scheduled for October 17 has been confirmed. The tour will begin promptly at 10:00 A.M. in front of the Heritage Museum. Please wear comfortable shoes and bring a refillable water bottle. Printed maps and tour guides will be provided at the check-in table.

We look forward to seeing you there!

Best regards,

Martin Kim
Bayside History Events Coordinator

When is the walking tour scheduled to take place?
(A) October 8
(B) October 10
(C) October 17
(D) October 27

What should Ms. Jonas bring to the tour?
(A) A city map
(B) A drink container
(C) A proof of payment
(D) A registration form

3-4

Read an email.

To:	amir.haddad@email.com
From:	tickets@mariner-museum.org
Date:	07/09/2025
Subject:	Timed Entry Pickup — Morning Window

Dear Mr. Haddad,

Your timed-entry passes for Sailing the Ice Edge can be collected between 10:00 A.M. and 12:00 P.M. at the Harbor Hall desk on July 15. Please bring a government-issued photo ID; passes are released only to the purchaser listed on the order.

Warm regards,
K. Duarte, Visitor Services

What is the earliest time Mr. Haddad can pick up the passes?
(A) 9:00 A.M.
(B) 10:00 A.M.
(C) 11:00 A.M.
(D) 12:00 P.M.

Why must Mr. Haddad bring photo identification?
(A) To verify he is the named purchaser
(B) To pay a separate entrance fee
(C) To join the museum as a member
(D) To change the time slot

5-7

Read a social media post.

Jim Nicholson

Looking for a fun way to spend your Sunday afternoon? Stop by the Meadowview Community Robotics Fair! It's a family-friendly event packed with interactive exhibits, tech demonstrations, and beginner-friendly coding workshops.

One of the most popular exhibits is the "Battle Bots Arena," hosted by the Ridgeway Robotics Club. These student-built robots compete in friendly matches and are known for their creative designs and impressive engineering. The matches are scheduled early in the day, and seats fill up quickly—so come early if you want a good view!

Local tech businesses also have booths set up with hands-on gadgets, and representatives are there to answer questions about STEM careers. There's even a "Build Your Own Robot" booth where you can take home a small solar-powered machine.

Whether you're a tech enthusiast or just curious, the fair is a great place to learn, play, and be inspired. Come enjoy food trucks, music, and exciting tech fun for the whole community!

👍 Like   💬 Comment

What is the main purpose of the post?
(A) To explain the history of robotics
(B) To describe the activities available at a local tech event
(C) To compare various engineering schools in the area
(D) To offer advice on starting a robotics club

What reason is given for the popularity of the Ridgeway Robotics Club's exhibit?
(A) It provides tutorials for beginners.
(B) It is inexpensive to attend.
(C) It showcases unique robot designs.
(D) It has won national competitions.

Why are visitors encouraged to arrive early at one of the exhibits?
(A) To register for workshops
(B) To receive free refreshments
(C) To secure optimal seating
(D) To avoid paying an entrance fee

8-10

Read an email.

To:	janebookaddict@gmail.com
From:	events@greenleaflibrary.org
Subject:	You're Invited – Join Us for Library Night at Greenleaf!

Dear Ms. Booker,

Please come along to a special evening event this Friday at 6:00 P.M. to mark the reopening of our newly renovated Greenleaf Library on 18 Maple Avenue. The event is a great opportunity to explore our updated reading rooms, new multimedia center, and expanded children's section.

This celebration, held especially for regular library patrons, will feature guided tours, live storytelling, interactive reading stations, and complimentary refreshments. It's the perfect occasion to enjoy the community spirit of Greenleaf and share your love of books with others.

Feel free to bring guests! All attendees will also receive a one-night-only voucher for discounted library merchandise and early access to the fall author talk schedule.

If you have questions or would like to RSVP, please contact our events coordinator at 555-0198.

Warm regards,
Ellen Hart
Greenleaf Public Library

What is the main purpose of the email?
(A) To invite someone to a library celebration
(B) To promote a new book series for children
(C) To request donations for the library renovation
(D) To introduce a new librarian to community members

What can be inferred about Ms. Booker's relationship with the library?
(A) She is a frequent visitor or existing member.
(B) She works at the local public school.
(C) She helped with library renovation work.
(D) She is organizing the author talk schedule.

What are event attendees encouraged to do?
(A) Visit a website
(B) Recommend a book
(C) Bring their friends
(D) Complete a form

Type of Task 3: Read an Academic Passage

출제 경향 분석

▶ 유형: 중·고등 및 대학 교육에서 접할 수 있는 짧은 설명문 읽고 객관식 문제 풀기
▶ 문제 수: Reading 시험 각 모듈에서 보통 1개 지문이 출제되며 한 지문에 5문제 출제
▶ 지문 종류: 역사, 예술, 경영, 경제, 생명과학, 물리학, 사회과학 영역 등의 학술적 지문
▶ 문제 특징: 정보 찾기, 문맥상 어휘, 추론, 문장 또는 문단 간 관계, 문단 또는 전체 지문의 목적 관련한 문제 등 출제

예시

Fossils

Fossils are the preserved remains or traces of organisms from a past geological age. Mostly thought of as massive dinosaur bones, fossils also include footprints and other impressions or the microscopic stone imprints of ancient microbes. Not only do fossils provide fascinating insight into ancient life, but they also help construct the geological timescale. Initially, geologists had hoped that cataloging strata, or layers of rock, would provide an accurate picture of the Earth's geologic history. But as more strata were studied and more layers compared, it became apparent that the type of rock in presumably correlating strata did not match from region to region. Attempting to match strata across separate regions could not denote past ages throughout the world. Even if the types of rock in the strata across regions were identical, conclusive findings were still difficult to make. Unlike organic material, which decays over time, rocks remain the same. Quartz, for example, is atomically identical whether it formed during the Pleistocene or during the Cambrian.

The word "insight" in the passage is closest in meaning to
(A) understanding
(B) imagination
(C) perspective
(D) evidence

Why could information from rock strata not be used to establish a geological timeline?
(A) Because identical layers of rock strata were far apart
(B) Because the organic material in rock decayed too quickly
(C) Because not enough data could be gathered from rock strata
(D) Because the sequences of rock varied in different areas

Answers p.311

문제 풀이 전략

전략 1 문제 읽고 키워드 및 문제 내용 파악

문제를 먼저 읽고 key words를 체크한 후 지문에서 관련 부분을 집중해서 읽어야 시간 절약이 가능하다. 이때 스키밍(skimming)과 스캐닝(scanning) 스킬을 적절하게 활용해야 하는데, 전체 지문의 중심 아이디어 및 구조 관계를 묻는 문제면 스키밍을, 세부 내용을 묻는 문제면 키워드 스캐닝을 하여 해당 지문이 어디인지 파악한다.

Why could information from rock strata not be used to establish a geological timeline?
➡ 세부 내용(왜 암석 지층의 정보가 지질학적 연대표 확립에 사용될 수 없는지) 지문에서 스캐닝

전략 2 오답 선택지 제거

해당 지문을 읽고 나서 문제에 제시된 선택지를 읽는다. 선택지에서 바로 정답을 선택할 수도 있지만 다음과 같이 오답인 선택지들은 먼저 제거함으로써 정답 확률을 높일 수 있다.

– 지문에 없는 내용이 포함된 선택지
– 지문과 다른 내용이 포함된 선택지
– 문제와 관련 없는 지문 내용의 선택지

또한 always, never, all, none 과 같은 절대적 표현이 있는 선택지는 오답으로 나오는 경우가 많기에 유의해야 한다.

(A) Because identical layers of rock strata were far apart
➡ 지문에 없는 내용
(B) Because the organic material in rock decayed too quickly
➡ 문제와 관련 없는 지문 내용
(C) Because not enough data could be gathered from rock strata
➡ 지문에 없는 내용
(D) Because the sequences of rock varied in different areas

전략 3 정답 선택지는 지문 문구 패러프레이징

정답 선택지는 지문의 단어나 문구를 그대로 사용하지 않고, 같은 의미를 다르게 표현한 패러프레이징(paraphrasing)으로 제시되는 경우가 많다.

But as more strata were studied and more layers compared, it became apparent that the type of rock in presumably correlating strata did not match from region to region.
지역마다 상관 관계가 있을 것으로 짐작되었던 지층의 암석 종류가 일치하지 않았다
→ (D) Because the sequences of rock varied in different areas
　　　　　　암석층의 순서는 지역마다 달랐다

기본 실력 업그레이드

기본기 1 지문 정독 연습을 통한 정확한 문장 해석 능력 기르기

대부분의 토플 문제는 스캐닝을 통해 지문에서 언급된 곳을 찾은 후 해당 부분을 제대로 해석할 수 있어야 정답을 선택할 수 있다. 즉, 스캐닝 스킬만으로는 문제를 풀 수 없고 제대로 된 문장 해석을 통해서만 정답을 맞출 수 있다. 따라서 평소에 토플 지문을 한 문장 한 문장 정독하는 연습을 통해 지문 해석 능력을 길러야 한다. 이때, 의미 단위로 끊어서 해석하는 연습을 하면 아무리 문장이 길고 복잡해도 빠르고 정확하게 해석할 수 있게 된다.

Fossils are / the preserved remains / or traces / of organisms / from a past geological age.
화석은 ~이다 / 보존된 유해 / 또는 흔적/ 생물체의 / 과거 지질학적 시대로 부터

Mostly thought of / as massive dinosaur bones, / fossils also include / footprints and other impressions / or the microscopic stone imprints / of ancient microbes.
주로 인식되는데 / 거대한 공룡 뼈로, / 화석은 또한 포함한다 / 발자국과 기타 눌린 자국 / 또는 미세한 돌 자국 / 고대 미생물의

Not only do fossils provide / fascinating insight / into ancient life, / but they also help / construct the geological timescale.
화석은 제공해 줄뿐만 아니라 / 흥미로운 통찰력을 / 고대의 삶에 대한, / 그것들은 도움이 되기도 한다 / 지질학적 연대를 구성하는 데

Initially, / geologists had hoped / that cataloging strata, / or layers of rock, / would provide / an accurate picture / of the Earth's geologic history.
처음에, / 지질학자들은 희망했었다 / 지층을 분류하는 것이, / 또는 암석 층들이 / 제공해 주기를 / 정확한 그림을 / 지구의 지질 역사에 대한

But / as more strata were studied / and more layers compared, / it became apparent / that the type of rock / in presumably correlating strata / did not match / from region to region.
그러나 / 더 많은 지층을 연구하고 / 더 많은 층을 비교할수록, / 명확해졌다 / 암석 종류가 / 상관 관계가 있을 것으로 짐작되었던 지층에서 / 일치하지 않았다 / 지역마다

Attempting to match strata / across separate regions / could not denote past ages / throughout the world.
지층을 맞춰보기 위한 시도는 / 여러 분리된 지역들에 걸친 / 과거의 시대를 보여주지 못했다 / 전 세계에 걸친

Even if the types of rock / in the strata across regions / were identical, / conclusive findings / were still difficult / to make.
설사 암석의 종류가 / 여러 지역에 걸친 지층에서 / 동일하다고 해도, /결정적인 연구결과는 / 여전히 어려웠다 / 만들어 내기가

Unlike organic material, / which decays over time, / rocks remain / the same.
유기 물질과 달리, / 시간이 흐를수록 부패하는, / 암석은 남아 있다 / 동일한 상태로

Quartz, / for example, / is atomically identical / whether it formed / during the Pleistocene / or during the Cambrian.
석영은 / 예를 들어, / 원자적으로 동일하다 / 그것이 형성된 것이든 / 홍적세 동안에 / 아니면 캄브리아기 동안에

기본기 2 다양한 학술적 주제와 연관된 어휘 범위 확장

생물학, 예술, 지구과학, 사회과학 등 다양한 학술적 주제의 지문이 토플 리딩에 출제된다. 따라서 다음과 같이 토플 지문에 자주 등장하는 단어들을 숙지해야 빠르고 정확한 지문 해석이 가능하다.

① 생물학

R_01

단어	뜻	단어	뜻
affinity	관련성, 친밀감	mammal	포유류, 포유동물
aggregation	집단, 집합	mating	짝짓기
algae	해조류	migrate	이주하다
burrow	(서식지로서의) 굴	nest	둥지, 둥지를 틀다
coexist	공존하다	nourish	영양분을 공급하다
contagious	전염성의	organism	생물, 유기체
courtship	구애	population	인구, 개체 수
endangered	멸종 위기에 처한	predator	포식자
evolve	진화하다, 발전하다	prey	먹이
extinct	멸종된	prosper	잘 자라다, 번성하다
fauna	동물군	reproduce	번식하다
flora	식물군	reptile	파충류
forage	먹이를 찾다	resilience	회복력, 탄력성
fungus	균류, 곰팡이류	species	(동식물의) 종
game	사냥감	symbiosis	공생
habitat	서식지	tolerate	~을 견디다
hatch	부화되다, 부화하다	vegetation	초목, 식물
herd	무리, 떼	vertebrate	척추동물
immune	면역성이 있는	vital	(생명 유지에) 필수적인
luminous	야광의, 발광의	vulnerable	취약한

❷ 예술

R_02

단어	뜻	단어	뜻
abstract	추상적인	feature	~을 특징으로 하다
aesthetic	심미적, 미적인, 미학	fragile	깨지기 쉬운
appreciation	감상, 이해, 진가	geometrical	기하학적인
artisan	장인	gloss	광택, 윤
aspiration	열망	hue	색조, 빛깔, 색
arduous	고된, 힘든	inspire	~에 영감을 주다
authentic	진품의, 진짜의	medieval	중세의
carving	조각(술)	object	대상, 물체
cavern	동굴	obsolete	구식의, 쓸모 없는
chamber	방, 공간	patent	~의 특허를 얻다, 특허
coarse	거친, 조잡한, 저급한	portrait	초상화
colossal	거대한	projection	투사, 영사
concrete	구체적인	prolific	다작의, 풍부한
configuration	구성, 형상	reproduction	복제, 재현
contemporary	동시대의, 현대의	scope	범위, 규모
counterfeit	위조의, 모조의	secular	세속적인
duplicate	~을 복제하다, 사본	spacious	널찍한
durable	내구성이 있는	synthesis	종합, 합성
elaborate	정교한	transparent	투명한
eloquent	표현력 있는, 설득력 있는	universal	보편적인, 일반적인

Read an Academic Passage

❸ 지구과학

R_03

단어	뜻	단어	뜻
accumulate	축적되다, ~을 축적하다	harness	~을 이용하다
alteration	변화	humidity	습기, 습도
arid	건조한	insulation	단열, 단열재
barren	척박한, 불모의	irrigation	관개, 물을 댐
cavity	구멍, 빈 부분	landscape	풍경
circulate	순환하다	marginal	주변의, 미미한
crust	(딱딱한) 표면	marine	해양의
decompose	~이 분해되다	peninsula	반도
deposit	~을 두다, 침전시키다	phenomenon	현상
disposal	처리, 폐기	plain	평원
drift	(서서히) 이동하다, 이동	planet	행성
erosion	침식, 부식	precipitation	강우, 강수량
evaporate	증발하다	sediment	퇴적물, 침전물
expedition	탐험	subside	가라앉다
exotic	이국적인	symmetrical	대칭적인
fertile	비옥한	temperature	온도, 기온
fracture	~을 갈라지게 하다, 균열	terrestrial	지구의, 육지의
geothermal	지열의	tropical	열대의
glacier	빙하	wilderness	황야
gravel	자갈	withstand	~을 견디다

42　TOEFL Complete Guide

4 사회과학

R_04

단어	뜻	단어	뜻
adolescent	청소년	intact	온전한
advent	출현, 도래	intricate	복잡한
affluent	부유한	isolated	고립된
boost	~을 증대하다	lavish	사치스러운
capital	자본금, 자금	obstacle	장애(물)
cluster	무리	opulent	호화로운
cognitive	인지의	pagan	이교도의
commodity	상품	parental	부모의
desolate	황폐한	pastoral	전원적인
discipline	수련, 훈육	possession	소유(물), 재산
divine	신의, 신성한	predominant	지배적인
empathy	공감, 감정이입	realm	영역
esteem	존중, 존경	reflection	성찰, 반성
ethnic	민족의	revolution	혁명
facilitate	~을 용이하게 하다	scarce	부족한
feasible	실현 가능한	settlement	정착지
flourish	번영하다	spur	~에 박차를 가하다
foster	~을 발전시키다	subsidize	~에 보조금을 주다
inherited	선천적인	surplus	잉여, 과잉
innate	타고난	worship	예배, 숭배

Read an Academic Passage

PRACTICE

1-5

The Feather Coding Project

Scientists have long been fascinated by the communication systems of birds. While humans use language to convey complex messages, many bird species rely on songs, chirps, and plumage displays. One of the more intriguing discoveries in avian research is the possibility that feather patterns might serve a purpose beyond aesthetics or mating—perhaps even encoding information similar to a visual language.

To investigate this theory, researchers launched what became known as the "Feather Coding Project." They studied the wing patterns of a species called the painted lark. By carefully altering markings using safe, temporary dyes, they observed changes in the behavior of other birds. In some trials, larks with specific patterns were either welcomed or avoided by other birds in the flock, suggesting recognition or communication based on visual cues.

Recent findings expanded the study to parrots and starlings. While parrots showed moderate responses to pattern changes, starlings were particularly sensitive, altering their flocking behavior significantly. This suggests that visual signaling through feather patterns might be more **prevalent**—and more sophisticated—than previously understood.

What is the passage mainly about?
(A) How feathers protect birds from predators
(B) A project studying patterns in bird feathers
(C) The evolution of bird flight techniques
(D) Methods used to track migratory bird species

What was the purpose of applying temporary dyes to bird feathers?
(A) To make the birds easier to photograph
(B) To protect them from ultraviolet light
(C) To test how visual cues affect social behavior
(D) To signal human presence in the study area

According to the passage, all of the following are true about the painted lark EXCEPT:
(A) It is part of the Feather Coding Project.
(B) It responded to changes in wing patterns.
(C) It avoided other birds with altered markings.
(D) It displayed advanced verbal communication.

If further studies confirm these observations, it could transform how scientists understand nonverbal animal communication, particularly in species not previously known for complex social structures.

The word "prevalent" in the passage is closest in meaning to
(A) unusual
(B) temporary
(C) widespread
(D) dangerous

Why does the author mention starlings?
(A) To illustrate that they learn behavior from parrots
(B) To provide an example of birds that ignored pattern changes
(C) To highlight a species highly responsive to visual cues
(D) To suggest that they are easier to train than other birds

6-10

Soundproof Cities: Quiet Pavements and Calmer Streets

Urban planners have begun testing porous asphalt and rubberized concrete to reduce traffic noise. These surfaces absorb tire vibrations and scatter sound, lowering ambient levels without erecting additional barriers. Early trials show modest reductions that become significant when applied across long roadways.

However, materials that dampen noise can age unpredictably. Clogged pores reduce performance, and winter freeze-thaw cycles may break down the concrete. That means street sweeping, drainage design, and replacement schedules are as crucial as the asphalt itself. Neighborhoods closest to freight routes see the biggest benefits, yet they also face the heaviest wear.

To evaluate results, engineers deploy mobile microphones and analyze spectral fingerprints of traffic at rush hour and midnight. International workshops bring road agencies together to share maintenance strategies and model lifecycle costs. These collaborations reveal that quieter streets depend on policy and upkeep as much as on chemistry.

The word "absorb" in the passage is closest in meaning to
(A) take in
(B) amplify
(C) imitate
(D) reflect

In which situation do the materials perform poorly?
(A) When long roadways are resurfaced
(B) When pores become clogged over time
(C) When microphones are mounted on vehicles
(D) When freight routes bypass neighborhoods

What is the relationship between paragraphs 2 and 3?
(A) Paragraph 3 describes methods to measure the challenges noted in paragraph 2.
(B) Paragraph 3 disputes the maintenance issues in paragraph 2.
(C) Paragraph 3 repeats paragraph 2's examples.
(D) Paragraph 3 introduces an unrelated topic.

What do the workshops help agencies do?
(A) Ban freight traffic outright
(B) Share upkeep tactics and cost models
(C) Replace noise maps with crowd surveys
(D) Standardize one concrete recipe worldwide

Why does the author mention spectral fingerprints?
(A) To show a way of distinguishing traffic patterns
(B) To argue that barriers are unnecessary
(C) To compare music recordings and highways
(D) To explain why microphones fail at night

11-15

The Impact of Ambient Noise on Creativity

Recent studies in psychology and neuroscience suggest that a moderate level of background noise can actually enhance creative thinking. While silence is often associated with focus and productivity, complete quiet may not always be ideal for tasks that involve innovation and abstract thinking. Researchers have found that working in environments with moderate ambient sounds—such as a café, library with background murmurs, or a gently humming air conditioner—can promote a level of distraction that stimulates creative problem-solving.

One experiment conducted at a university had participants perform a series of creative tasks, such as inventing new uses for common household items. When the participants were exposed to a moderate noise level (around 70 decibels), their performance significantly improved compared to those who worked in quiet (around 50 decibels) or high-noise (around 85 decibels) environments. The moderate noise seemed to provide just enough distraction to encourage abstract thinking without completely impairing concentration.

Which of the following best states a main idea of the passage?
(A) Creative thinking improves in completely silent environments.
(B) Moderate ambient noise can enhance creativity.
(C) People work best in places with constant noise.
(D) Productivity always decreases with background sound.

What is one result of the university experiment mentioned in the passage?
(A) Participants found it easier to recall factual information.
(B) Higher noise levels improved participants' memory.
(C) Moderate noise levels led to more creative responses.
(D) Complete silence helped participants stay more focused.

Why does the author mention household items in the passage?
(A) To give an example of a common problem in psychology experiments
(B) To demonstrate the types of tasks used to test creativity
(C) To suggest that household tools can inspire new inventions
(D) To show how noise levels affect shopping behavior

This phenomenon is believed to occur because a mild level of background noise creates a slight disruption to the normal thought process. This disruption can prompt individuals to think in less conventional ways, broadening their cognitive processing and leading to more original ideas. However, once noise becomes too loud, it overwhelms the brain's ability to process thoughts effectively, leading to a drop in creativity and productivity.

These findings have implications for the design of workspaces, classrooms, and creative studios. Rather than striving for absolute silence, it may be beneficial to introduce gentle, ambient soundscapes to foster innovation. Businesses and educators alike might consider how the acoustic environment influences performance, especially when creative thinking is essential.

The word "disruption" in the passage is closest in meaning to
(A) delay
(B) increase
(C) repetition
(D) distraction

What can be inferred about the use of ambient sound in workplaces?
(A) It can lower productivity by making people less focused.
(B) It may encourage people to talk more and collaborate.
(C) It could lead to improvements in innovation.
(D) It leads to greater levels of dissatisfaction among workers.

LISTENING

1. Listen and Choose a Response
2. Listen to a Conversation
3. Listen to an Announcement
4. Listen to an Academic Talk

Overview

문제 수	35-45 문제
시험 시간	약 27분
문제 유형	총 4개 ☑ Listen and Choose a Response ☑ Listen to a Conversation ☑ Listen to an Announcement ☑ Listen to an Academic Talk
문제 세트	총 2 모듈(세트) 출제 ☑ 첫 번째 모듈에서 높은 점수를 받으면 두 번째 모듈에서도 아카데믹 토크 유형이 출제되지만, 반대로 낮은 점수를 받으면 출제되지 않음
더미 문제	두 모듈에 더미 문제(성적에 반영되지 않는 실험용 문제)가 랜덤으로 들어가 있음
발음/억양	북미식, 영국식, 호주식, 뉴질랜드식

Type of Task 1: Listen and Choose a Response

출제 경향 분석

- ▶ 유형: 화자의 짧은 말에 가장 알맞은 답변 선택하기
- ▶ 문제 수: 보통 첫 모듈에서 8–12문제, 두 번째 모듈에서 3–8문제 출제
- ▶ 문제 풀이 시간: 음원이 끝나면 정답 선택 시간 20초가 주어짐
- ▶ 내용: 캠퍼스 일상에서 발생하는 내용
- ▶ 음원 길이: 짧은 한 문장의 질문 또는 진술
- ▶ 문제 특징: 문제는 한 번만 들려주며, 정답은 4개의 선택지 중 상대적으로 가장 적합한 것을 선택

예시

Choose the best response.

L1_00

(A) It was moved to a new venue.
(B) I went twice last month.
(C) Yes, admission is free on Sundays.
(D) Let me check the price for you.

Answers p.316

문제 풀이 전략

전략 1 　질문의 키워드 빠르게 파악하기

질문이 한 번만 들리기 때문에, 질문이 정확히 무엇을 묻는지 파악하는 것이 중요하다. 질문 처음에 나오는 의문사와 조동사, 그리고 핵심 단어(주어 + 동사)를 집중해서 들으면 정답을 선택할 확률이 높아진다. 필요하다면 간단한 노트 테이킹을 한다.

How much is the **entry ticket** for the technology expo?
→ 입장권의 가격을 묻는 질문

전략 2 　함정 선택지 소거하기

질문에 사용된 단어나 연상되는 표현을 포함한 선택지는 함정일 가능성이 높다. 소거법을 활용하여 질문이 묻고 있지 않는 내용의 선택지를 제거한다. 질문에 대한 직접적인 답변이 아니라도 상황상 자연스럽게 이어지는 우회 답변이 정답으로 자주 출제된다.

(A) It was moved to a new venue.
→ 장소(where)에 대한 답변으로 오답

(B) I went twice last month.
→ 횟수(how often, how many times) 또는 시간(when)에 대한 답변으로 오답

(C) Yes, admission is free on Sundays.
→ 의문사 의문문을 Yes로 답변하므로 오답

(D) Let me check the price for you.

기본 실력 업그레이드

기본기 1 질문 유형 익히기

Listen and Choose a Response 유형에서 출제되는 질문 유형은 크게 4가지로 분류할 수 있다.

① 의문사 의문문
Who, What, Where, When, Why, How (5W1H 의문사) 의문문
→ 각 의문사에 맞는 정확한 정보 응답(누구인지, 무엇인지, 어디인지, 언제인지, 왜인지, 어떻게/얼마나 ~인지)이 정답이고 Yes, No 선택지는 오답임

예 How do I contact the registrar's office? 등록처에 어떻게 연락하지?
   (A) No, I don't mind. 아니, 난 괜찮아.
   (B) They provide good service. 그들은 좋은 서비스를 제공해.
   (C) Yes, you're allowed to use that. 응, 넌 그것을 사용해도 돼.
   (D) Use the convenient chat feature. 편리한 채팅 기능을 사용해봐. (정답)

② be동사 또는 조동사 의문문
Yes/No 응답 유의
→ Yes/No로 대답하거나, Yes/No가 생략되는 대신 부가적인 설명으로 답변하며, 둘 중 하나를 선택하는 선택의문문 (A or B)에서 Yes, No 선택지는 오답임

예 Didn't I just see you in the student center? 학생 센터에서 내가 방금 너 보지 않았니?
   (A) Yes, you can find it. 맞아, 넌 그걸 찾을 수 있어.
   (B) Actually, I think I can get there a little earlier. 사실, 내가 조금 더 일찍 갈 수 있을 것 같아.
   (C) I don't think I'll have enough time to do that. 난 그걸 할 시간이 충분치 않을 것 같아.
   (D) As a matter of fact, I was checking on some information.
      사실, 난 어떤 정보를 확인하고 있었어. (정답)

③ 제안/요청/명령문
Let's~, Can you~, Would you like~, Would you mind~? 등
→ 제안을 수락하거나 거절 또는 제 3의 대안을 제시하는 답변이 정답으로 빈출

예 Would you like a copy of my notes? 내 노트 복사본 원하니?
   (A) Yes, this coffee is great. 응, 이 커피 훌륭해.
   (B) The break is in an hour. 휴식은 한 시간 후야.
   (C) That would be great. 그거 정말 좋겠네. (정답)
   (D) No, that was mine. 아니, 그건 내 거야.

4 평서문
감탄, 정보 전달, 푸념 등 평서문
→ 공감, 확인, 추가 설명 또는 질문 등으로 답변

예 **If you need more information, contact Ms. Brown.** 만일 추가 정보가 필요하면, 브라운 씨에게 연락해.
   (A) Whom should contact? 누구에게 연락하지?
   (B) I can help with that. 내가 도울 수 있어.
   (C) What is her role in the organization? 조직 내에서 그녀의 역할이 무엇인데? (정답)
   (D) I ask a lot of questions. 내가 많은 질문을 하지.

기본기 2 빈출 정답 선택지 익히기

아래 우회 답변들은 Listen and Choose a Response 유형에서 출제되는 정답이 될 수 있는 만능 답변들이다. '모른다', '확인해 보겠다', '~가 알고 있다', '아직 결정이 안 났다', '나중에 알려주겠다', '~에 달려 있다'는 식의 유형으로 출제된다. 이렇게 의외의 답변이 정답이 되는 상황에 대해 익숙해져야 한다.

유형	빈출 정답
모른다	• I don't know. 모른다. • I'm not sure. 확실치 않다. • I have no idea. 모른다. • We're not sure yet. 우리도 아직 확실치 않다. • Not that I know of. 내가 알기로는 아니다. • Who knows? 누가 알겠어? • I wish I knew. 나도 알았으면 좋겠어. • She hasn't told us yet. 그녀는 아직 얘기해주지 않았어. • I haven't heard about it. 그것에 대해 들은 바가 없어. • He didn't give me a reason. 그는 이유를 알려주지 않았어. • We haven't been notified[informed] yet. 우린 아직 들은 바가 없어. • Sorry. I'm not from around here. 미안. 난 여기 살지 않아. (그래서 모른다) • I'm not in charge of that. 내 담당이 아니야. • I didn't organize the concert. 내가 콘서트 준비를 맡지 않았어. • I was meeting with clients all day. 하루 종일 고객들을 만나고 있었어. • I missed it too. 나도 거기에 못 갔어. • I lost all that paperwork when I moved. 이사할 때 모든 서류를 잃어버렸어. • I forgot about it. 깜빡 잊었어.
확인해 보겠다	• Let me check that out for you. 확인해 줄게. • Let me check my schedule. 내 스케줄을 확인해 볼게. • I'll have to check. 확인해 봐야겠다. • I'll find out today. 오늘 알아볼게. • Let me check and get back to you. 확인하고 다시 연락 줄게.

유형	빈출 정답
~가 알고 있다, ~에게 물어보다, ~을 참조하다	• I'll ask her. 그녀에게 물어볼게. • Jessica would[should, might] know. 제시카가 알고 있을 거야. • Ask the manager. 매니저에게 물어봐. • Check with Mr. Smith. 스미스 씨에게 확인해 봐. • Why don't we ask them? 그들에게 물어보는 게 어때? • Ella's more familiar with that. 엘라가 더 잘 알아. • You'd better call them. 그들에게 전화해 봐. • You'd better ask Ms. Chen. 첸 씨에게 물어 봐. • That information is in the email. 그 정보는 이메일에 있어. • I usually call Support. 난 보통 고객지원팀에 전화해.
아직 결정이 안 났다	• It hasn't been decided yet. 아직 결정되지 않았어. • It hasn't been confirmed yet. 아직 확인되지 않았어. • It hasn't been announced yet. 아직 발표되지 않았어. • We're still deciding. 우린 아직 결정 중이야. • I'm still considering it. 아직 고려 중이야. • I'm still waiting. 아직 (결과를) 기다리고 있어. • It hasn't been discussed yet. 아직 논의되지 않았어. • I haven't decided yet. 난 아직 결정 못했어. • A decision hasn't been made yet. 결정이 아직 안 났어.
나중에 알려주겠다	• I'll show you in a minute. 내가 곧 보여줄게. • They'll call back later today. 그들이 오늘 중 전화를 할 거야.
~에 달려 있다	• It depends on the location. 그건 위치가 어디냐에 달려 있죠. • It's up to the directors to decide. 이사들의 결정에 달려 있죠.

기본기 3 의외의 정답 상황 유의하기

질문에 대한 직접적인 답변 대신, 질문이 요구하는 정보가 아닌 전혀 다른 정보를 제시하여 돌려 답하거나, 질문을 질문으로 대답하는 의외의 정답 상황을 유의하도록 한다.

유형	의외의 정답 상황
돌려 답하기	• Q: Where can I find Dr. Brown's office? A: I'm afraid he's out of town. 질문: 브라운 박사님의 사무실을 어디에서 찾을 수 있지? 답변: 유감스럽게도 그는 지금 여기에 없어. • Q: When will the bus arrive to take us on the company trip? A: There is a train that goes there. 질문: 우리를 사내 야유회로 데려다 줄 버스가 언제 도착하지? 답변: 그곳으로 가는 기차가 있어. • Q: The first band was great, wasn't it? A: I came in just a minute ago. 질문: 첫 번째 밴드가 대단했어, 그렇지 않니? 답변: 나 조금 전에 막 도착했어. • Q: How often do you go back to your hometown to visit? A: None of my family members are there anymore. 질문: 넌 얼마나 자주 고향을 방문하니? 답변: 가족 중에 더 이상 그곳에 있는 사람이 아무도 없어. • Q: How often do you visit the recycling facility? A: There hasn't been a need to for a while. 질문: 넌 얼마나 자주 재활용 시설을 방문하지? 답변: 한동안 그럴 필요가 없었어. • Q: Would you like to try first, or should I? A: I'm not sure how to do it. 질문: 먼저 해 볼래, 아니면 내가 먼저 할까? 답변: 나는 어떻게 그것을 하는지 잘 모르겠어. • Q: Are you ready to perform, or are you still warming up? A: Our concert isn't until 7. 질문: 공연을 할 준비가 되었니, 아니면 여전히 워밍업 중이니? 답변: 콘서트는 7시나 되어야 해. • Q: Will our application get to the committee on time? A: I sent it by express service. 질문: 우리 지원서가 제때 위원회에 도착할까? 답변: 내가 그것을 특급 배송 서비스로 보냈어.

유형	의외의 정답 상황
	• Q: What time does your train leave? 　A: I got a ride today. 　질문: 네 기차가 몇 시에 떠나지? 　답변: 난 오늘 누가 차 태워줬어. • Q: Where's the demonstration being held? 　A: Oh, I didn't think you had the time. 　질문: 시연회가 어디에서 열릴 예정이지? 　답변: 오, 난 네가 시간이 있을 거라고 생각하지 못했어. • Q: Should I grab a blanket? 　A: I'll turn the heat on. 　질문: 담요를 가져 올까? 　답변: 내가 난방기를 틀게. • Q: Didn't we just buy a different keyboard? 　A: Don't tell me it doesn't work either! 　질문: 우리가 다른 키보드를 사지 않았니? 　답변: 그것도 작동되지 않는다고 말하지 마! • Q: Why do you need the Jacobson case? 　A: It's the Jackson case. 　질문: 왜 너는 제이콥슨 사례를 필요로 하니? 　답변: 그건 잭슨 사례야 • Q: Has the repairman fixed the sink on the 6th floor yet? 　A: It was on the 7th floor. 　질문: 수리 기사가 6층에 있는 싱크대를 이미 수리했니? 　답변: 그건 7층이었어. • Q: Are these posters being sold? 　A: Each attendee can take one. 　질문: 이 포스터들은 판매되는 것이니? 　답변: 각 참석자는 1장씩 가져 갈 수 있어. • Q: Do you know what time it is now? 　A: We still have 10 minutes. 　질문: 지금 몇 시인지 알아? 　답변: 아직 10분 더 있어. • Q: Which contractor was selected to renovate the lobby? 　A: We postponed that project. 　질문: 로비 개조 작업을 하는 데 어느 하청업체가 선정되었지? 　답변: 우리 그 프로젝트를 연기했어.

유형	의외의 정답 상황
질문으로 답변하기	• Q: Isn't the pool open today? 　A: Did you want to go for a swim? 　질문: 오늘 수영장 열지 않았니? 　답변: 너 수영 가려고 했어? • Q: Would you like to try the appetizer special? 　A: What is it? 　질문: 애피타이저 특별 메뉴 좀 먹어볼래? 　답변: 그게 뭔데?

기본기 4 쉐도잉(따라 말하기) 훈련

듣기 실력 향상에 가장 좋은 방법인 쉐도잉(shadowing)은 영어 MP3를 들으면서 발음, 속도, 리듬, 호흡을 최대한 원음과 동일하게 따라하는 학습법이다. 많은 학생들이 "많이 듣다 보면 귀가 뚫리겠지"라는 생각으로 영어 MP3를 무작정 반복해 듣지만, 이해하지 못하는 내용과 모르는 단어는 들리지 않는다. 따라서 정확히 이해한 내용을 그대로 따라 말하는 쉐도잉 훈련이 필요하다. "발음할 수 없으면 들을 수 없다"는 사실을 기억하고 다음 단계를 따라 쉐도잉 훈련을 하도록 하자.

❶ 스크립트 이해하기
바로 쉐도잉이 어렵다면 먼저 스크립트를 보며 어려운 단어와 표현을 익히고, 잘 들리지 않는 부분을 반복해서 읽는다.

❷ 스크립트를 보며 따라 읽기
MP3를 들으면서 스크립트를 눈으로 확인하며 따라 읽는다.

❸ 스크립트 없이 따라 말하기
스크립트를 보지 않고 MP3를 들으며 발음과 속도를 똑같이 따라 한다.

❹ 반복하기
완벽하게 따라 할 수 있을 때까지 1~3단계를 반복한다.

Listen and Choose a Response는 문장이 짧기에 쉐도잉이 가장 쉬운 문제 유형이다.
앞으로 학습할 Conversation, Announcement, Academic Talk 모두 쉐도잉을 통해 정복할 수 있다.

PRACTICE

1

L1_01

Choose the best response.

(A) How do I change my password?
(B) What time is the meeting?
(C) I'm always available to help.
(D) I'll get in touch with him.

2

L1_02

Choose the best response.

(A) Just across from the bakery.
(B) I usually drive instead.
(C) Only during rush hour.
(D) I already returned it.

3

L1_03

Choose the best response.

(A) Yes, you can return it anytime.
(B) Why don't you follow the instructions in the manual?
(C) That's a great idea.
(D) No, mine is a different brand.

 p.316

4

 L1_04

Choose the best response.

(A) We meet every two weeks.
(B) Do you want me to take notes for you?
(C) That café has great coffee.
(D) Yes, I'll bring my own copy.

5

 L1_05

Choose the best response.

(A) I don't remember why.
(B) Lisa would know.
(C) Let me check my schedule.
(D) You should try this coffee.

6

 L1_06

Choose the best response.

(A) I don't have your number yet.
(B) No, I didn't sign up for the class.
(C) She should be back from lunch soon.
(D) Do you have any questions?

Listen and Choose a Response

7

L1_07

Choose the best response.

(A) Yes, but only in the mornings.
(B) No, I already made plans with friends.
(C) I hope they will pay you the overtime rate.
(D) It's usually better on Sundays.

8

L1_08

Choose the best response.

(A) I ran out of time.
(B) Yes, it starts next month.
(C) It'll last for about 3 hours.
(D) I'm bringing my camera.

9

L1_09

Choose the best response.

(A) He signed up yesterday.
(B) It hasn't been finalized yet.
(C) Let's attend the science fair.
(D) The fair is scheduled for May.

10

 L1_10

Choose the best response.

(A) Hold on—I'll check the calendar.
(B) Pick your favorite date.
(C) I already finished mine.
(D) Yes, I think we already met it.

11

 L1_11

Choose the best response.

(A) Every semester.
(B) There's a sale on notebooks.
(C) Want me to come with you?
(D) The class starts at five.

12

 L1_12

Choose the best response.

(A) I'm changing majors.
(B) Let's meet later to talk about it.
(C) She dropped the course.
(D) Yes, it's a required course.

Type of Task 2 : Listen to a Conversation

출제 경향 분석

▶ 유형: 두 사람의 짧은 대화를 듣고 이와 관련된 두 개의 객관식 문제를 푸는 유형
▶ 문제 수: 보통 첫 모듈에서 2–4개 대화, 두 번째 모듈에서 2개 대화 출제
▶ 문제 풀이 시간: 음원이 끝나면 각 문제의 정답 선택 시간 20초가 주어짐
▶ 내용: 캠퍼스 일상에서 발생하는 내용
▶ 음원 길이: 2–3번 정도 두 사람의 말이 오고 감(2–3 turns)
▶ 문제 특징: 먼저 음원을 한 번만 들려주고, 다음 화면에서 각각의 문제와 선택지가 제시됨

예시

L2_00

Listen to a conversation.

Why does the man say "I completely lost track of the days"?
(A) He forgot what he needed from a store.
(B) He was confused about a lesson schedule.
(C) He was not sure what day of the week it was.
(D) He did not know the electronics store was open.

Answers p.319

문제 풀이 전략

전략 1 음원을 들을 때 대화 맥락 파악

음원이 다 끝난 후에 화면에 문제가 나오므로, 먼저 음원을 집중해서 들어 다음과 같이 대화 맥락을 이해하는 데 도움이 되는 사항들을 파악하자.

– 대화가 무엇에 관한 내용인지 (예: 물건 구매, 수업 과제, 모임 약속, 행사 또는 공연 등)
– 화자 간 관계가 어떻게 되는지 (예: 친구, 동료, 룸메이트 등)
– 대화의 흐름 (예: 누가 정보를 알려 주는지, 어떤 제안을 하는지, 왜 그렇게 말하는지 등)
– 여자 또는 남자가 무엇이 필요한지

이는 대부분의 문제가 주제, 목적, 문제점, 세부사항(무엇을 했는지, 왜 했는지, 어떻게 했는지, 어디서 했는지, 언제 했는지, 누구와 했는지 등), 제안/요청, 추론, 다음에 할 일 등을 묻기 때문이다. 또한 화자가 한 말의 의미를 묻는 문제도 등장하는데, 관용 어구가 대화에서 어떤 뜻으로 사용되었는지를 묻는 방식으로 자주 출제된다.

전략 2 모르는 단어 또는 관용 어구는 흐름으로 파악

음원에서 자신이 모르는 단어나 관용 어구가 나오는 경우가 있다. 비록 그 단어와 관용 어구를 처음 들어도 음원의 맥락상 파악할 수 있는 경우가 대부분이다. 따라서 자신이 모르는 단어나 관용 어구가 나오더라도 맥락상 자연스러운 흐름으로 이해하도록 한다. TOEFL Listening 문제는 몇몇 단어나 문구의 정확한 의미를 모르더라도 문제를 푸는 데 지장이 없음을 기억하자.

> W: Hey, do you need anything from the electronics store?
> M: Huh? Aren't you giving a guitar lesson in a few minutes?
> W: That's not until tomorrow morning.
> M: Oh wow, I completely lost track of the days. ·········▶ 시간과 날짜 착각에 대한 반응
>   What are you planning to get from the store?
> W: Just some new earbuds, and if they're on sale, maybe a USB drive too. Do you need anything?
> M: No, but thanks!

Why does the man say "I completely lost track of the days"?
(A) He forgot what he needed from a store.
(B) He was confused about a lesson schedule.
(C) He was not sure what day of the week it was.
(D) He did not know the electronics store was open.

Listen to a Conversation

기본 실력 업그레이드

기본기 1 빈출 질문 익히기

비록 질문을 알지 못한 상태로 음원을 듣지만 시험에 나오는 질문은 다음과 같이 정해져 있다. 따라서 미리 빈출 질문을 숙지하면, 음원을 들을 때 자주 질문으로 나오는 부분을 중점적으로 들을 수 있게 된다.

유형	빈출 질문
주제	• What are the speakers mainly discussing? 화자들이 주로 이야기하는 것은? • What event are the speakers planning to attend? 화자들이 참석하려는 행사는?
목적	• Why is the man asking about a place to eat? 남자가 식사할 곳을 묻는 이유는?
문제점	• Why is the woman running late? 여자가 지각하는 이유는? • What problem does the man mention? 남자가 언급하는 문제는?
세부사항	• What did the man do yesterday? 남자가 어제 한 것은? • When will the event begin? 행사가 시작되는 때는? • Where will the conference be held? 회의가 열리는 장소는? • What does the woman say about the place? 여자가 그 장소에 대해 말하는 것은?
제안/요청	• What does the woman suggest the man do? 여자가 남자에게 하도록 제안하는 것은? • What does the woman encourage the man to do? 여자가 남자에게 하도록 권하는 것은?
추론	• What can be inferred about the woman? 여자에 대해 추측할 수 있는 것은?
다음에 할 일	• What will the man probably do next? 남자가 아마도 다음에 할 것은? • What will the man most likely do next? 남자가 다음에 가장 할 것 같은 행동은? • What does the man plan to bring to the event? 남자가 행사에 가져갈 계획인 것은?
말의 의미 (관용 표현)	• What does the man imply when he says, "That was a piece of cake"? 남자가 "그건 식은 죽 먹기였어"라고 말할 때 암시하는 것은?

기본기 2 관용 표현(idiomatic expressions)

Listen to a Conversation 유형에서 이디엄(idiom), 즉 관용 표현(관용구)이 자주 나오는데, 관용 표현이란 단어 하나하나의 뜻만으로는 전체 의미를 알 수 없는 표현을 말한다. 관용구는 하나의 덩어리 표현으로 외우는 것이 좋다. 또한, 단어 하나하나를 해석하기보다는, 전체 의미와 쓰임새를 익히는 것이 중요하다. 문자 그대로 해석하면 의미가 통하지 않는 표현들로, 다음은 영어권 원어민들이 일상적으로 자주 사용하는 말들이다.

관용 표현	의미	예문
act up	말을 안 듣다	My car is acting up again. 내 차가 또 말을 안 들어.
a piece of cake	아주 쉬운 일, 식은 죽 먹기	That exam was a piece of cake. 그 시험은 정말 쉬웠어.
break the ice	어색한 분위기를 깨다	He told a joke to break the ice. 그는 농담을 해서 어색한 분위기를 깨뜨렸다.
burn out	녹초가 되다	Stop working so hard—you'll burn yourself out. 그렇게 열심히 일하지 마 – 녹초가 될 거야.
burn the midnight oil	밤늦게까지 일하다	I burned the midnight oil to finish the report. 나는 보고서를 끝내려고 밤늦게까지 일했다.
cost an arm and a leg	매우 비싸다	That bag cost an arm and a leg! 그 가방은 정말 비쌌어!
hit the nail on the head	정곡을 찌르다	Her analysis hit the nail on the head. 그녀의 분석은 정곡을 찔렀다.
I'd forget my head if it wasn't screwed on	건망증이 심하다, 깜빡 잘한다	I left my wallet at home again—I'd forget my head if it wasn't screwed on. 나는 또다시 지갑을 집에 두고 왔다—(머리가 붙어 있지 않으면 머리를 잊어버릴 정도로) 난 건망증이 심하다.
let the cat out of the bag	비밀을 실수로 말하다	She accidentally let the cat out of the bag about the promotion. 그녀가 승진 소식을 실수로 말해버렸다.
lose track of	~을 놓치다	I have lost track of the number of times you have been late this month. 난 이번 달에 네가 지각한 횟수를 놓쳤어.(몇 번이나 늦었는지 세어보기도 힘들 정도야.)
(be) running behind	뒤쳐지다, 부족하다	We're running behind, so let's skip the coffee break. 시간이 부족하니, 커피 브레이크는 건너뛰자.
(be) running late	늦을 것 같다, 지각일 것 같다	I'm running late for my meeting. 회의에 늦을 것 같아.
spill the beans	비밀을 누설하다	He spilled the beans about the surprise party. 그는 깜짝 파티에 대해 비밀을 누설했다.
swing by (= drop by)	잠깐 들르다	I'll swing by this weekend. 이번 주말에 잠깐 들를게.
(be) torn (between A and B)	(A와 B 사이에서) 고민이다, 갈피를 잡지 못하다	I am torn between accepting the job offer in another city and staying close to my family. 나는 다른 도시의 취업 제안을 받아들일지, 아니면 가족과 가까이 머물지 고민이다.
under the weather	몸이 안 좋다	I'm feeling under the weather today, so I'll stay home. 난 오늘 몸이 안 좋아서 집에 있을 거야.

Listen to a Conversation

PRACTICE

1-2 주의: 음원을 다 듣고 나서 문제를 보시오.

Listen to a conversation.

L2_0102

Why did the woman contact the library staff?
(A) A printer was not working.
(B) A computer was missing.
(C) A phone line was down.
(D) A scanner was giving errors.

What does the woman suggest the man do?
(A) Return to class early
(B) Buy something to eat
(C) Use a different printer
(D) Report the issue again

3-4 주의: 음원을 다 듣고 나서 문제를 보시오.

Listen to a conversation.

L2_0304

What is the man trying to decide between?
(A) A painting class and a hiking trip
(B) A photography club and a hiking club
(C) A writing group and an art club
(D) A cooking class and a fitness class

What reason does the woman give for her suggestion?
(A) The activity costs less.
(B) The club meets more often.
(C) The man enjoys being outside.
(D) The club has more members.

5-6 주의: 음원을 다 듣고 나서 문제를 보시오.

Listen to a conversation.

L2_0506

What problem is the woman experiencing with her clarinet?
(A) It has been misplaced.
(B) It was accidentally damaged.
(C) It is missing some parts.
(D) It will not stay in tune.

What will she most likely do next?
(A) Buy a new instrument
(B) Purchase a different reed
(C) Have an instrument repaired
(D) Give a musical performance

7-8 주의: 음원을 다 듣고 나서 문제를 보시오.

L2_0708

Listen to a conversation.

What problem does the man mention?
(A) He cannot find a print shop.
(B) He is unable to attend an event.
(C) He lost some printed materials.
(D) He has no time to complete a task.

What does the woman imply when she says, "I've got nothing on"?
(A) She will design some event posters.
(B) She is available to help the man.
(C) She does not have enough money.
(D) She would prefer to skip an event.

Type of Task 3: Listen to an Announcement

출제 경향 분석

▶ 유형: 한 사람이 발표하는 짧은 공지사항을 듣고 이와 관련된 두 개의 객관식 문제를 푸는 유형
▶ 문제 수: 보통 첫 모듈에서 2-4개의 공지사항이 출제되는데, 첫 모듈에서 점수가 높으면 두 번째 모듈에서는 Listen to an Announcement 대신 Listen to an Academic Talk만 출제
▶ 문제 풀이 시간: 음원이 끝나면 각 문제의 정답 선택 시간 20초가 주어짐
▶ 내용: 캠퍼스 일상에서 발생하는 내용으로 화자가 직접 대면으로 공지하거나 방송으로 공지하는 형식
▶ 음원 길이: 약 20초
▶ 문제 특징: 먼저 음원을 한 번만 들려주고, 다음 화면에서 각각의 문제와 선택지가 제시됨

예시

L3_00

Listen to an announcement at a university event.

What is the main topic of the announcement?
(A) A change in venue
(B) A donation drive
(C) A charity auction
(D) A year-end ceremony

Answers p.323

문제 풀이 전략

전략 1 음원을 듣기 전 공지사항 장소 파악

Listen to a Announcement 문제 유형은 음원이 시작할 때 화면에 공지사항의 장소가 다음과 같이 나온다.

Listen to an announcement at a university event. → 대학교 행사

장소는 대학 생활과 관련된 장소로, 교실(class), 대학 내 라디오 방송(school radio), 대학 동아리 모임(university club meeting), 대학 행사(university event) 등이 자주 나온다.

전략 2 음원을 들을 때 공지의 목적과 주제 파악

Listen to a Conversation과 마찬가지로 음원이 다 끝난 후에 화면에 문제가 나온다. 따라서 음원을 들을 때, 시험에서 자주 묻는 내용을 중심으로 집중해서 들어야 한다. Listen to an Announcement에서는 공지의 목적과 주제를 묻는 문제가 높은 확률로 출제되기에 음원을 들을 때 반드시 공지의 목적과 주제를 파악하도록 한다.

Good afternoon, everyone. We're excited to share that the university's yearly <mark>charity auction</mark> is scheduled for next Friday at 6 P.M. in the main hall. All funds raised will benefit local charities. We look forward to your participation and appreciate your support.
→ 자선 경매

전략 3 화자가 청자에게 제안 또는 요청하는 사항 확인

공지의 목적과 주제와 함께 가장 많이 나오는 문제는 화자가 청자에게 제안 또는 요청하는 사항이다. 따라서 음원을 들을 때, 공지의 목적과 주제 파악과 함께, 화자가 청자에게 구체적으로 무엇을 하도록 요구하거나 권장하는지 파악하도록 한다.

Good afternoon, everyone. We're excited to share that the university's yearly charity auction is scheduled for next Friday at 6 P.M. in the main hall. All funds raised will benefit local charities. We look forward to <mark>your participation</mark> and appreciate <mark>your support</mark>.
→ 참여와 지원

Listen to an Announcement 73

기본 실력 업그레이드

기본기 1 빈출 질문 익히기

Listen to an Announcement에서 자주 등장하는 질문을 미리 숙지하여, 음원을 들을 때 자주 질문으로 나오는 부분을 중점적으로 듣도록 한다. 두 문제 중 첫 문제로는 공지사항의 목적 또는 주제, 두 번째 문제로는 화자가 청자에게 제안/요청하는 내용을 자주 묻는다.

유형	빈출 질문
목적	• What is the main purpose of the announcement? 공지사항의 주요 목적은?
주제	• What is the main topic of the announcement? 공지사항의 주요 주제는? • What is the announcement about? 공지사항은 무엇에 관한 것인가?
의도	• Why does the speaker mention A? 화자가 A를 언급한 이유는? • What does the speaker imply when he says A? 화자가 A라고 말할 때 암시하는 것은?
세부사항	• Which of the following is true about the program? 프로그램에 대해 사실인 것은? • According to the announcement, what do the students do every day? 공지사항에 따르면, 학생들이 매일 하는 것은?
제안/요청	• What are students advised to do? 학생들에게 하도록 권고되는 것은? • What are students encouraged to do? 학생들에게 하도록 권장되는 것은? • What should students do after the event? 행사가 끝나고 학생들이 해야하는 것은? • What does the speaker hope the listeners will do? 화자가 청자들이 하도록 희망하는 것은? • What does the speaker suggest the listeners do? 화자가 청자들이 하도록 제안하는 것은?

기본기 2 빈출 시나리오 구조 익히기

Listen to an Announcement에서 자주 등장하는 시나리오의 구조를 미리 알고 있으면 음원을 들을 때 내용을 보다 쉽게 이해할 수 있다. 보통 다음과 같이 인사 또는 주목의 말, 공지의 주제 또는 목적 소개, 청자들에게 제안 또는 요청하는 세 단계로 시나리오가 전개된다.

구조	예문
인사/주목	Good afternoon, everyone. 안녕하세요, 여러분.
공지 주제/목적	We're excited to share that the university's yearly charity auction is scheduled for next Friday at 6 P.M. in the main hall. All funds raised will benefit local charities. 대학의 연례 자선 경매가 다음 주 금요일 오후 6시 본관 강당에서 열릴 예정임을 알려드리게 되어 기쁩니다. 모금된 모든 기금은 지역 자선 단체에 기부될 예정입니다.
제안/요청	We look forward to your participation and appreciate your support. 여러분의 참여를 기대하며, 여러분의 지원에 감사드립니다.

PRACTICE

1-2 주의: 음원을 다 듣고 나서 문제를 보시오.

L3_0102

Listen to an announcement in a university cafeteria.

What is the main purpose of the announcement?
(A) To inform students about a cleaning schedule
(B) To advertise new cafeteria items
(C) To introduce a new campus café
(D) To warn students about food shortages

What should students do during the closure?
(A) Eat lunch in the cafeteria early
(B) Avoid using vending machines
(C) Visit other nearby food options
(D) Help clean the cafeteria

3-4 주의: 음원을 다 듣고 나서 문제를 보시오.

🔊 L3_0304

Listen to an announcement at a university club meeting.

Why does the speaker mention traffic jams?
(A) To explain why he was late to a meeting
(B) To advise listeners to leave early
(C) To give an example of a stressful situation
(D) To highlight an environmental issue

What are participants encouraged to do?
(A) Create an online profile
(B) Submit their previous work
(C) Review some meeting notes
(D) Register for a course

5-6 주의: 음원을 다 듣고 나서 문제를 보시오.

 L3_0506

Listen to an announcement at a university event.

What is the main purpose of the announcement?
(A) To advertise a lecture series
(B) To promote a movie night
(C) To announce park renovations
(D) To request new volunteers

What is mentioned about the event?
(A) It takes place outdoors.
(B) Tickets must be purchased in advance.
(C) Free refreshments are available.
(D) It has been postponed to next week.

7-8 주의: 음원을 다 듣고 나서 문제를 보시오.

L3_0708

Listen to an announcement in a classroom.

What is the announcement about?
(A) A special cooking presentation
(B) A food competition for students
(C) A change to a class schedule
(D) A tour of a local restaurant

Why does the speaker mention Chef Lazzari's background?
(A) To encourage students to take cooking more seriously
(B) To explain why attendance is mandatory
(C) To suggest that students consider culinary careers
(D) To highlight his qualifications as a guest speaker

Type of Task 4: Listen to an Academic Talk

출제 경향 분석

- ▶ 유형: 한 명의 교수 또는 전문가가 수업 또는 팟캐스트에서 진행하는 학술 강연을 듣고 이와 관련된 네 개의 객관식 문제를 푸는 유형
- ▶ 문제 수: 첫 모듈에서 보통 1–2개의 강연이 출제되는데, 첫 모듈에서 점수가 높으면 두 번째 모듈에서 2개 강연 출제
- ▶ 문제 풀이 시간: 음원이 끝나면 각 문제의 정답 선택 시간 30초가 주어짐 (cf. 다른 리스닝 문제 유형은 20초 주어짐)
- ▶ 내용: 캠퍼스 역사, 미술, 음악, 생명과학, 물리과학, 경영 및 경제학, 사회과학 등의 분야
- ▶ 음원 길이: 약 1분 30초–2분
- ▶ 문제 특징: 먼저 음원을 한 번만 들려주고, 다음 화면에서 각각의 문제와 선택지가 제시됨

예시

L4_00

Listen to a talk in an art class.

What is the main topic of the talk?
(A) The role of Impressionism in modern art
(B) The popularity of Impressionism in Paris
(C) The famous Impressionists
(D) The development of Impressionism over time

Answers p.327

문제 풀이 전략

전략 1 음원을 듣기 전 강연의 전문 분야 파악

Listen to an Academic Talk 문제 유형은 음원이 시작할 때 화면에 강연의 전문 분야(역사, 미술, 음악, 생명과학, 물리과학, 경영 및 경제학, 사회과학 등)가 다음과 같이 나온다.

→ 미술수업

Listen to a talk in an art class.

전략 2 음원을 들을 때 다음 사항을 노트테이킹

Listen to an Academic Talk의 강연과 같이 내용이 길고 복잡하면 반드시 노트테이킹(노트 필기)을 해야 이후 제시되는 문제를 풀 수 있다. 보통 다음과 같은 사항들이 문제로 나오므로 음원을 들을 때 반드시 노트테이킹을 한다.

– 강연의 목적이나 주제
– 예시: 어떤 예시가 무엇을 설명하기 위해 쓰였는지
– 역접 연결사(however, but) 이후 부분: 새로운 또는 중요한 정보가 제시
– 나열 표현(first, second, finally 등): 주요 포인트 구조화
– 반복: 화자가 되풀이하는 부분으로 강연의 핵심을 강조
– 질문: 단순 질문이 아닌 중요성 강조 가능성 높음

기본 실력 업그레이드

기본기1 올바른 단어 발음 숙지

단어의 철자와 뜻을 알면 리딩 문제는 풀 수 있지만, 리스닝은 발음까지 제대로 알고 있어야 문제를 풀 수 있다. 만일 thesis(논문)를 그동안 [테시스]라고 알고 있었다면 리스닝에 나오는 [θi:sɪs 씨시스]를 알아들을 수 없다.

또한 우리가 알고 있는 외래어가 실제 영어 발음과 다른 경우가 많은데, 예를 들어 흔히 '테마'로 발음하는 theme은 [θi:m 씸]으로, 프랑스 수도 Paris는 [pǽris 패리스]로 발음한다.

다음은 Academic Talk에 자주 나오는 단어들로 우리가 한국식으로 잘못 발음하기 쉬운 몇 가지 예시이다. f, v 발음과 강세에 유의하여 발음하도록 한다.

🔊 L4_01

단어	잘못된 발음 [X]	정확한 영어 발음 [O]
label 상표	[라벨]	[레이블]
capacity 용량, 수용력	[캐파시티]	[커패씨디]
connect 연결하다	[코넥트]	[커넥트]
material 재료	[매테리얼]	[머티리얼]
facility 시설	[팩실리티]	[f어씰리디]
alternative 대안	[알터네이티브]	[알터너티v]
chaos 혼란	[카오스]	[케이아스]
report 보고(서)	[레포트]	[리포트]
recording 녹음(된 것)	[레코딩]	[리코딩]
ultra- 초과의	[울트라]	[얼트러]
model 모델, 모형	[모델]	[마들]
philosophy 철학	[필로소피]	[f일라서f이]
literature 문헌	[리터레이쳐]	[리터러쳐]
phenomenon 현상, 사건, 경이로운 것	[페노메논]	[f어나머넌]
violence 폭력	[바이올렌스]	[v아이얼런스]

기본기 2 | 표시어 인식하기

강연의 흐름은 다음과 같이 표시어(signal words)를 통해 파악할 수 있다. 표시어란 어떠한 내용이 나올지 알려주는 신호가 되는 말을 지칭하는데, 문제 전환 · 핵심 정보 등장을 알려주는 단서로 이러한 시그널 단어 이후에 정답 단서가 나오는 경우가 많다.

따라서 표시어를 유의하여 들으면 음원의 흐름과 맥락을 파악함은 물론, TOEFL Listening 문제의 출제 포인트를 놓치지 않을 수 있다.

유형	표시어
목적 및 주제	• Today's talk is about ~ 오늘 강연은 ~에 관한 것입니다 • I'm here because ~ 제가 이 자리에 선 것은 ~ 때문입니다 • I'm interested in ~ 저는 ~에 관심이 있습니다 • I was wondering if ~ 저는 ~인지 궁금합니다 • I have some questions about ~ 저는 ~에 관한 몇 가지 질문이 있습니다 • Let's continue our study on ~ ~에 대한 학습을 계속해 봅시다 • I'd like to turn your attention to ~ 여러분의 관심을 ~로 돌려보겠습니다 • Why don't we start with ~ ~부터 시작하는 것이 어떨까요
비교	• likewise 마찬가지로 • similar to ~ ~와 유사한 • in comparison to ~ ~와 비교하여
내용 전환	• OK = All right 좋아요 • Anyway 어쨌든 • Now 이제 • Next 다음으로 • When it comes to ~ ~와 관련해서는 • In addition to ~ ~뿐만 아니라 • Let's move on to ~ ~로 넘어가 보겠습니다
제안 및 해결책	• Tell you what 이렇게 하죠 • Let me ~ 제가 ~해 보겠습니다
이유 및 원인	• Since + 절 = Because + 절 ~ 때문에 • Due to + 명사(구) = Because of + 명사(구) ~ 때문에 • That's because ~ 이는 ~ 때문입니다
결과	• So = Therefore 따라서, 그러므로 • Accordingly 그에 따라, 그래서 • As a result 그 결과로, 그래서
강조 및 반복	• In other words 다시 말해서 • What I'd like to point out is ~ 제가 짚고 넘어가려는 것은 ~입니다 • What I mean is ~ 제 말은 ~입니다 • You see = You know 알다시피 • The most important 가장 중요한 것

Listen to an Academic Talk

유형	표시어
예시	• For example = For instance 예를 들어 • Think about ~ ~에 대해 생각해 보세요 • Take ~ ~을 예로 들어보죠 • Let's say ~ ~라고 가정해 봅시다 • One of ~ ~ 중 하나는 • Among them are ~ 그것들 중에 ~이 있습니다 • Something like ~ ~와 같은 것 • In a case study 한 사례 연구에서
순서 및 나열	• First, Second, Third, Finally 첫째, 둘째, 셋째, 마지막으로 • One, Another 하나는, 또 다른 하나는 • Then = Next 그리고 나서, 그 다음에 • There are several things 여러 가지가 있다
역접 및 대조	• But = Yet 그러나 (접속사) • However 그러나 (접속부사) • Whereas = While ~인 반면에 (접속사) • On the other hand 반면에 (접속부사) • On the contrary 반대로 (접속부사) • Actually = In fact 실은 (접속부사)

기본기 3 노트테이킹(노트 필기)

TOEFL Listening은 단 한 번만 들려주기 때문에, 최대한 빠르게 핵심을 기록하는 연습이 필요하다. 모든 문장을 적는 대신 다음과 같이 핵심어 중심의 간략 노트테이킹(notetaking)이 효과적이다.

의미	핵심어	약자/기호	의미	핵심어	약자/기호
역접/전환	but however	△ 또는 b	원인에서 결과로	cause (A) effect (B)	(A) → (B)
상승	increase rise grow	↑	결과	result so therefore	∴
하락	decrease fall drop	↓	긍정	good positive advantage benefit	+
중요	remember important main idea attention note	☆	부정	bad negative disadvantage drawback	−
예시	for example for instance such as	eg 또는 ex	있음/맞음	with yes right	O
비교	compare while	cf	없음/틀림	without not/no wrong	X
같음	same equal	=	이유	because	bc
다름	different unlike	≠	교수	professor	pf
이전	before	bf	학생	student	st
이후	after	af	선생님	teacher	t
장소/시간	at	@	연구	study research	st res

이와 같이 개인만의 약자·기호 체계를 만들어 두면 필기 속도를 크게 단축할 수 있다.

PRACTICE

1-4 주의: 음원을 다 듣고 나서 문제를 보시오.

L4_0104

Listen to a talk on a podcast about nutrition.

What is the topic of the talk?
(A) Strategies for eating on a budget
(B) How hunger affects decision-making
(C) A comparison of two different hungers
(D) The role of breakfast in daily health

What does the speaker say about skipping breakfast?
(A) It caused her to crave food.
(B) It helped her eat healthier later on.
(C) It reduced her appetite overall.
(D) It is part of her normal routine.

Why does the speaker mention cinnamon rolls?
(A) To illustrate how quickly food can be prepared
(B) To show how the brain confuses scent with taste
(C) To explain how habits form around breakfast
(D) To give an example of hedonic hunger

What does the speaker say about hedonic hunger?
(A) It leads to better energy levels.
(B) It can activate the brain's reward system.
(C) It always follows physical hunger.
(D) It is easier to control with exercise.

5-8 주의: 음원을 다 듣고 나서 문제를 보시오.

L4_0508

Listen to a talk in a history class.

What is the main topic of the talk?
(A) The use of clay tablets in ancient architecture
(B) How writing systems influence language pronunciation
(C) The history and significance of the cuneiform writing system
(D) Differences between oral and written traditions in Mesopotamia

Why does the professor mention the *Epic of Gilgamesh*?
(A) To show that cuneiform was used to record famous stories
(B) To illustrate the origins of Mesopotamian religion
(C) To explain how early myths were passed down
(D) To compare cuneiform with Egyptian writing

What does the professor say about the Behistun Inscription?
(A) It contained laws written by the first king of Babylon.
(B) It was used to help scholars translate cuneiform.
(C) It was the first example of bilingual writing in history.
(D) It was uncovered by local farmers in the 1800s.

What will the professor most likely discuss next?
(A) How oral storytelling traditions influenced early religion
(B) The importance of Mesopotamian trade routes
(C) Other ancient writing systems from around the world
(D) How cuneiform spread to Europe in later centuries

9-12 주의: 음원을 다 듣고 나서 문제를 보시오.

L4_0912

Listen to a talk in an urban planning class.

What is the main focus of the talk?
(A) How city parks are created
(B) How gardens can reduce heat
(C) How buildings conserve energy
(D) How plants can survive in cities

What point is made about deeper roof systems?
(A) They never affect drainage.
(B) They always cost less to install.
(C) They eliminate maintenance needs.
(D) They support larger plants and retain more water.

Why does the professor mention special cameras?
(A) To show evidence of cooler surfaces
(B) To explain how storms form
(C) To criticize shallow soil systems
(D) To describe bird surveys

What will the professor most likely discuss next?
(A) How plant species migrate across distances
(B) Noise from rooftop fans
(C) Solar panel chemistry
(D) Suitable plants for different areas

Listen to an Academic Talk

WRITING

1. Build a Sentence
2. Write an Email
3. Write for an Academic Discussion

Overview

문제 수	12 문제
시험 시간	약 23분
문제 유형	총 3개 ☑ Build a Sentence ☑ Write an Email ☑ Write for an Academic Discussion
문제 세트	총 1세트 출제
더미 문제	없음

Type of Task 1: Build a Sentence

출제 경향 분석

- ▶ 유형: 문장 완성하기
- ▶ 문제 수: 10문제
- ▶ 문제 풀이 시간: 총 5분 50초 (한 문제에 30–35초 할당)
- ▶ 문장 종류: 평서문, 의문문
- ▶ 문제 형식: 제시된 단어 또는 구를 사용하여 상대방의 말에 적절한 답변 문장을 만드는 문제
- ▶ 문제 특징: 제시된 단어 또는 구를 모두 사용하는 경우도 있지만 한 개 정도 남는 경우도 있음

예시

Make an appropriate sentence.

 Jane loved the movie you recommended to her.

 _____ she say _____ _____ _____ _____ _____ ?

loved   what   she   part   the best   to be   did

Answers p.334

문제 풀이 전략

전략1 상대방이 말한 문장 확인

빈칸 문장으로 바로 가지 말고 그 위에 상대방이 말한 문장을 통해 내용과 문맥의 흐름에 따라 빈칸 문장을 완성한다.

 Jane loved the movie you recommended to her.
제인이 네가 추천한 영화가 좋았대

전략2 평서문인지 의문문인지 확인

완성해야 하는 문장의 마지막에 있는 마침표 또는 물음표를 확인하여 평서문 또는 의문문을 만들어야 하는지를 먼저 파악한다. 의문문이면 의문사 의문문인지 일반 의문문인지 확인한다.

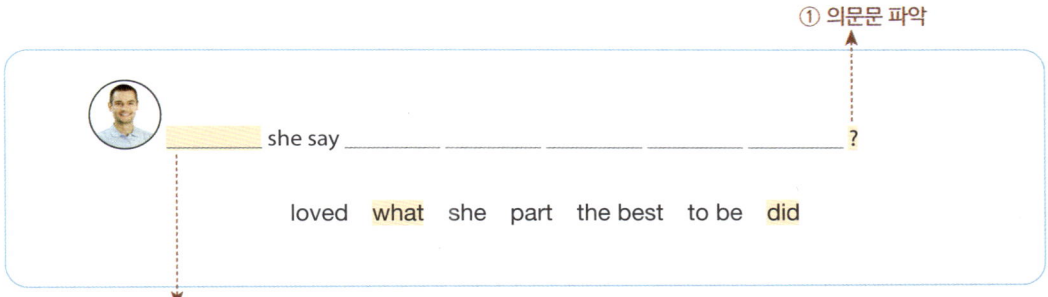

① 의문문 파악

② 의문문은 주어 앞에 의문사 또는 보조 동사(be동사, do, does, did, can, could 등 조동사)가 와야 하는데, 빈칸 문장의 주어(she) 앞에는 빈칸이 하나이므로 빈칸에는 의문사 대신 보조 동사가 와야함

전략3 제시된 단어 또는 구 파악하기

제시된 단어 또는 구에 어떠한 단어가 나왔는지 의미를 파악하고, 특히 명사, 동명사, 동사, 조동사, 형용사, 부사, 전치사, 접속사 등 품사도 확인한다.

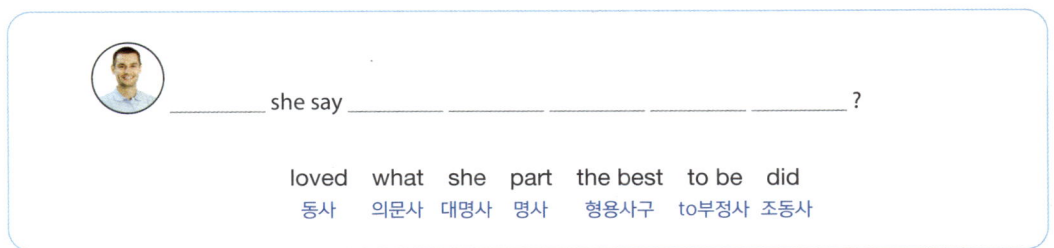

Build a Sentence

전략 4 문장 구조에 맞게 단어 배치

주어-동사-목적어 순서, 전치사 뒤 명사, 절 안에 주어와 동사 등 문장 구조를 고려하여 보기의 단어를 빈칸에 채운다. 문장이 완성되면 문법상 문장이 틀리지 않고 해석이 제대로 되는지 반드시 최종 확인한다.

 Did she say what part she loved the best?

loved | what | she | part | the best | to be | did

기본 실력 업그레이드

기본기 1 평서문 구조 이해

가장 기본적인 어순은 '주어+동사'이다. 동사의 성격에 따라 동사 뒤에 목적어 또는 보어, 목적보어가 추가 된다. 그리고 문장 앞, 뒤, 중간에 수식어가 오기도 한다. 평서문의 기본 구조 및 문장 성분 순서는 다음과 같다.

> 주어 → 동사 → 목적어/보어 → 부사구/수식어

This book 주어 is 동사 interesting 보어.
이 책은 재미있다.

She 주어 studies 동사 English 목적어 every day 수식어.
그녀는 매일 영어를 공부한다.

They 주어 are 동사 not 부정부사 accustomed 보어 to spicy food like that 수식어.
그들은 그런 매운 음식에 익숙하지 않다.
➜ 동사 뒤 부정부사 위치 유의

He 주어 wants 동사 to know what her biggest concerns are 목적어.
그는 그녀의 가장 큰 걱정들이 무엇인지 알기를 원한다.
➜ 목적어 내부 구조 분석: to know (to부정사구), what her biggest concerns are(간접의문문 명사절: 간접의문사+주어+동사)

The tickets you bought last week 주어 will expire 동사 soon 수식어.
그들은 그런 매운 음식에 익숙하지 않다.
➜ 주어 내부 구조 분석: you bought last week(관계절: 주어+동사+부사구)

기본기 2 의문문 구조 이해

일반적으로 의문문은 직접적으로 묻는 직접의문문을 말하며, 의문문은 크게 일반 의문문과 의문사 의문문 두 가지로 나눈다.

❶ 일반 의문문
Yes/No 대답 가능한 의문문으로, 의문문을 만드는 보조동사(do, does, did, can, could, would 등)가 문장 앞에 온다.

> 보조동사 → 주어 → 동사 → 목적어/보어 → 부사구/수식어

Do 보조동사 they 주어 serve 동사 coffee 목적어 all day 부사구?
그들은 하루 종일 커피를 제공하니?

Build a Sentence 97

Can 보조동사 you 주어 find out 동사 why they chose this particular method 목적어?
그들이 왜 이 특정 방법을 선택했는지 알아낼 수 있니?
→ 목적어 내부 구조 분석: why they chose this particular method(간접의문문 명사절: 간접의문사+주어+동사+목적어)

예외적으로 be동사 의문문에서 주어 뒤에 동사가 생략되는 경우가 있다.

be동사 → 주어 → 보어 → 부사구/수식어

Is be동사 the schedule 주어 final 보어?
그 일정이 최종이니?
→ 주어 이후에 동사 생략

❷ 의문사 의문문
Who, What, When, Where, Why, How 등의 의문사로 묻는 의문문으로, 의문사 뒤에 보조동사가 온다. Whose, Which, What은 명사가 따라올 수도 있고, 단독으로 사용 가능하다.

의문사 → 보조동사 → 주어 → 동사 → 목적어/보어 → 부사구/수식어

Why 의문사 are 보조동사 they 주어 running 동사?
그들은 왜 달리고 있니?

Which 의문사 topic 명사 does 보조동사 she 주어 plan 동사 to cover 목적어?
그녀는 어떤 주제를 다룰 계획이지?

What 의문사 did 보조동사 the professor 주어 ask 동사 you 간접목적어(~에게) when you walked into class 수식어?
수업에 들어갔을 때 교수님이 네게 무엇을 물어보셨니?
→ 수식어 내부 구조 분석: when you walked into class(시간 부사절: 부사절접속사+주어+동사+전치사구)

예외적으로, 의문사가 주어 역할을 하면 보조동사가 오지 않는다.

의문사 주어 → 동사 → 목적어/보어 → 부사구/수식어

Who 의문사 주어 broke 동사 the window 목적어?
누가 창문을 깨뜨렸니?

기본기 3 간접의문문 구조 이해

간접의문문은 의문문 내용을 명사절로 바꿔 문장 안에서 주로 목적어나 주어 역할을 하게 만든 것으로 Build a Sentence 유형에서 가장 많이 출제되는 절(clause) 형태이다.

❶ 일반 의문문
일반 의문문은 if/whether를 추가하여 간접의문문을 만든다.

Did she come? 직접의문문 → I wonder **if she came**. 간접의문문
그녀가 왔니?   나는 그녀가 왔는지 궁금해.

The team leader 주어 wanted 동사 to know **whether I plan to make any revisions** 목적어.
조장은 내가 어떤 수정을 할 계획인지 알기를 원했어.
→ 간접의문문 내부 구조 분석: whether I plan to make any revisions(간접의문사+주어+동사+목적어구)

❷ 의문사 의문문
의문사 의문문의 의문사를 사용하여 간접의문문을 만든다.

What did he say? 직접의문문 → I don't know **what he said**. 간접의문문
그가 무엇을 말했지?   나는 그가 무엇을 말했는지 모르겠어.

I 주어 would 보조동사 love 동사 to know **where you went on your last vacation** 목적어.
난 네가 지난 휴가에 어디로 갔는지 정말 알고 싶어.
→ 간접의문문 내부 구조 분석: where you went on your last vacation(간접의문사+주어+동사+수식어구)

PRACTICE

1

Make an appropriate sentence.

Did Mark return the DVD you lent him?

_____ _____ _____ _____ _____ _____ _____ yet.

having   it   has   not   to watch   he   time   had

2

Make an appropriate sentence.

What did your colleagues ask about the new manager?

_____ _____ _____ _____ _____ _____ about _____ .

him   liked   did   to know   I   they wanted   what   best

3

Make an appropriate sentence.

Did you talk to your professor?

Yes. I tried _____ _____ _____ _____ _____ _____ _____ .

wanted   not   I   to explain   the report   finished   had   why

4

Make an appropriate sentence.

 Penny is not here yet.

 _____ you remind _____ _____ _____ _____?

is   her appointment   did   when   her   to be

5

Make an appropriate sentence.

 Why do you need help?

 _____ _____ _____ _____ to me.

clear   did   not   the instructions   were

6

Make an appropriate sentence.

 What did Tina ask you after class?

 She _____ _____ _____ _____ _____ _____ _____.

a part-time job   make   she   apply for   where   wanted to   could   find out

7

Make an appropriate sentence.

Why was everyone in the meeting room?

_____ _____ found out _____ _____ _____ _____ _____.

just   removed   who   was   they   which   being   ingredient

8

Make an appropriate sentence.

Where did Matthew get those shoes?

The shoe store _____ _____ _____ _____ _____ _____ _____.

works   on   the sneakers   he   at   stock   had   in

9

Make an appropriate sentence.

Did you order a desk yet?

No, _____ _____ _____ color _____ _____ _____ _____.

appealing   which   a   I can't   the   figure out   is   most

10

Make an appropriate sentence.

 Did you ask Nicole about the missing file?

 She _____ _____ _____ _____ _____ _____ Sundays.

not   respond   responded   does   on   to   messages

11

Make an appropriate sentence.

 Why did you change the venue?

 _____ _____ _____ at this restaurant to _____ _____ _____ .

comfortable   I   found   be   much more   the atmosphere   do

12

Make an appropriate sentence.

 How may I help you?

 I was hoping _____ _____ _____ _____ _____ I can _____ _____ .

when   with the professor   me   you   could   meet   tell

Type of Task 2: Write an Email

출제 경향 분석

- ▶ 유형: 제시된 시나리오를 읽고 그 내용에 맞게 이메일 작성
- ▶ 문제 수: 1문제
- ▶ 문제 풀이 시간: 7분
- ▶ 시나리오 종류: 대학 또는 일상에서 벌어지는 상황
- ▶ 문제 특징: 문제에 제시되는 세 가지 포인트를 답안에 충실히 작성해야 함
- ▶ 답안 형식: 고득점 답안은 보통 100단어 이상을 작성하고 이메일 형식에 맞추어서 작성

예시

You have recently started working from home, but you have noticed that your internet signal is very weak, and the connection is not reliable. You need to contact your landlord, Ms. Walton, to report the problem and request a repair.

Write an email to Ms. Walton. In your email, do the following:

- Describe the problems you are experiencing with the internet connection.
- Explain how these issues are affecting your work.
- Request a repair and ask when the problem can be fixed.

Write as much as you can and in complete sentences.

Your Response:

To: Ms. Walton
Subject: Internet repair request

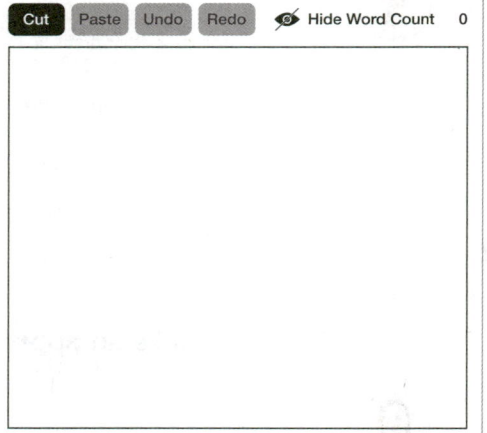

Answers p.336

문제 풀이 전략

전략 1   문제 분석 및 브레인스토밍

1분 이내에 문제에 제시된 시나리오와 답변 포인트 세 가지를 파악한 후 어떻게 이메일을 작성할지 브레인스토밍 한다.

> You have recently started working from home, but you have noticed that your internet signal is very weak, and the connection is not reliable. You need to contact your landlord, Ms. Walton, to report the problem and request a repair. ┄┄▶ 재택 근무 중인데 인터넷이 불안정하여 집주인에게 문제를 알리고 수리 요청을 하는 시나리오
>
> **Write an email to Ms. Walton. In your email, do the following:**
> - Describe the problems you are experiencing with the ┄┄▶ 포인트 1: 경험 중인 인터넷 문제 설명
>   internet connection.
> - Explain how these issues are affecting your work. ┄┄▶ 포인트 2: 이 문제가 일에 미치는 영향 설명
> - Request a repair and ask when the problem can be fixed. ┄┄▶ 포인트 3: 수리 요청과 언제 문제가 해결될지 문의

전략 2   이메일 형식에 맞게 최소 100단어 이상으로 작성하기

약 5분간 이메일 형식에 맞게 최소 100단어 이상으로 작성하고 약 1분의 시간 동안 자신의 답안에 철자와 문법 오류가 없는지 확인하고 수정한다.

> Dear Ms. Walton, ┄┄▶ 받는 사람 이름/직함
>
> I hope this message finds you well. ┄┄▶ 안부
>
> I am writing to report an issue with the internet connection in my ┄┄▶ 이메일 작성 목적
> apartment. The signal is very weak, and the connection ┄┄▶ 포인트 1
> frequently cuts off. When I try to access web pages or make
> video calls, I experience long delays or receive a "failed to
> connect" message. As I work from home, these issues are ┄┄▶ 포인트 2
> affecting my ability to complete tasks efficiently and participate
> in team meetings. They are also making it difficult for me to meet
> an important deadline. Could you please arrange for a repair as ┄┄▶ 포인트 3
> soon as possible and let me know when it is scheduled?
>
> I look forward to your response. ┄┄▶ 마무리
>
> Best regards, ┄┄▶ 맺음말
> Rumi Kim ┄┄▶ 본인 이름

기본 실력 업그레이드

기본기 1 | Email 답안 구성 및 작성 기본 표현

다음은 Write an Email 답안의 구성과 자주 사용되는 기본 표현들이다.

구성	기본 표현
받는 사람 이름/직함	• Hello [이름], / Dear [Mr. 성/ Ms. 성/ 직함], ~에게
안부	• I hope you are doing well. 저는 당신이 잘 지내고 계시길 바랍니다. • I hope this message finds you well. 저는 이 메시지가 당신께 잘 전달되길 바랍니다.
이메일 작성 목적	• [요청] I am writing to ask for / request ~ ~을 요청하기 위해 이메일을 씁니다 • [문의] I am writing to ask about / inquire ~ ~을 문의하기 위해 이메일을 씁니다 • [알림] I am writing to let you know / inform / notify / report ~ 　　　~을 알리기 위해 이메일을 씁니다 • [확인] I am writing to confirm / clarify ~ ~을 확인 / 명확히 하기 위해 이메일을 씁니다 • [제공] I am writing to offer / provide ~ ~을 제공하기 위해 이메일을 씁니다 • [제안] I am writing to suggest / propose ~ ~을 제안하기 위해 이메일을 씁니다 • [사과] I am writing to apologize ~ ~을 사과하기 위해 이메일을 씁니다 • [답변] I am writing to respond to ~ ~에 대해 답변하기 위해 이메일을 씁니다 • [안건] I am writing concerning / with regard to + 명사 ~에 관해 이메일을 씁니다
포인트 답변	• [원인] due to + 명사 ~에 기인하여 　　　as a result of + 명사 ~의 결과로 • [요청] could you please ~ ~해 주시겠어요 　　　I would appreciate it if you could ~ ~해주시면 감사하겠습니다. 　　　I would be grateful if you could ~ ~해주시면 감사하겠습니다. • [계획/예정] be supposed to + 동사원형 ~하기로 되어있습니다. 　　　be expected to + 동사원형 ~하기로 예상됩니다. 　　　be scheduled to + 동사원형 ~하기로 계획되어 있습니다.
마무리	• [답변 요청] I look forward to your response / hearing from you soon. 　　　당신의 답변을 기대하겠습니다 / 곧 연락 주시기를 기대하겠습니다. • [마무리 인사] I hope that you have a wonderful day. 　　　좋은 하루 보내시길 바랍니다.
맺음말	• Best regards, / Kind regards, / Regards, 안녕히 계세요. * 맺음말 바로 밑 줄에 본인 이름을 쓰는데, 앞에서 Hello로 시작했으면 자신의 이름(first name)만, 　Dear로 시작했으면 성(last name)도 같이 적는다.

기본기 2 격식있는 표현

가족이나 친구에게 보내는 이메일은 캐주얼하게 작성하지만, 받는 사람이 Mr. / Ms. / Dr. / Prof. 또는 개인적으로 모르는 어떠한 직책의 특정인(Manager / Editor 등)인 경우에 격식 있는 표현으로 이메일을 작성한다.

의미	일반 표현	격식 표현
곧	soon	shortly
빨리(재촉할 때)	quickly	at your earliest convenience
매우	very, really	significantly, considerably, highly, extremely
많은	a lot of, lots of	many, much, numerous
할 수 없다	cannot	be unable
원하다	want	would like
사과하다	be sorry	apologize
유감이다	be sorry	regret
감사하다	thank	appreciate
받다	get	receive
주다	give	provide
해결하다	fix	resolve, address
알리다	tell me	let me know
희망하다	hope	look forward to
전달하다	pass on	forward
조사하다	look into	investigate
~에 대해 얘기하다	talk about	discuss
~에 대해 생각하다	think about	consider
~에 대해 궁금한	curious about	wondering if
~ 때문에	because of	due to, as a result of

기본기 3 채점 기준에 맞는 글쓰기

Write an Email 유형은 고유의 채점 기준이 있는데, 채점 기준에서 가장 중요한 사항은 다음 네 가지이다.

- 과제에서 요구하는 포인트에 대해 충실한 답변
- 상세한 설명
- 명료하고 정확한 문장
- 다양한 문법과 어휘

5점에서 0점으로 채점이 되고, 5점 채점 기준에 맞춰서 이메일을 작성하도록 연습한다.

점수	채점 기준
5	**완벽히 성공적인 답안** 답안은 효과적이며 명확하게 표현되어 있고, 언어 사용에 있어 일관된 유창성을 보여준다. 전형적인 5점 답안은 다음 특징이 있다: • 이메일 작성 목적을 효과적으로 뒷받침하는 상세한 설명 • 효과적으로 다양한 구문 및 정확한 어휘 사용 • 적절하고 일관성 있는 사회적 관례 (예: 예의, 어체, 정보 구성 및 요청, 거절, 비판 등의 표현) • 시간 제약으로 인해 능숙한 사람이 범할 수 있는 오류를 제외하면(예: there/their 같은 흔한 오타, 철자 오류), 어휘나 문법 오류가 거의 없음
4	**대체로 성공적인 답안** 답안은 대체로 효과적이고 쉽게 이해된다. 언어 사용 능력이 과제에 적합하다. 전형적인 4점 답안은 다음 특징이 있다: • 이메일 작성 목적을 뒷받침하는 적절한 설명 • 다양한 구문과 적절한 어휘 선택 • 대체로 적절한 사회적 관례 • 어휘나 문법 오류가 거의 없음
3	**부분적으로 성공한 답안** 답안은 대체로 과제를 달성한다. 언어 사용 능력의 한계로 인해 메시지의 일부가 완전히 명확하거나 효과적이지 않을 수 있다. 전형적인 3점 답안은 다음 특징이 있다: • 이메일 작성 목적을 부분적으로 뒷받침하는 설명 • 적당한 수준의 구문과 어휘 • 구조, 단어 형태, 어휘 사용 및/또는 사회적 관례에서 눈에 띄는 오류가 일부 있음
2	**대체로 실패한 답안** 답안은 과제를 해결하려는 시도를 반영하지만, 대부분 효과적이지 않다. 메시지가 제한적이거나 해석하기 어려울 수 있다. 전형적인 2점 답안은 다음 특징이 있다: • 제한적이거나 관련 없는 설명 • 일부 연결된 문장 수준의 언어 사용, 제한된 구문 및 어휘 범위 • 문장 구조 및/또는 언어 사용에 오류가 누적됨
1	**실패한 답안** 답안은 과제를 해결하려는 시도를 보여준다. 메시지는 이해할 수 없을 정도로 제한적일 수 있다. 전형적인 1점 답안은 다음 특징이 있다: • 설명 내용이 거의 없거나 전혀 없음 • 매우 제한된 어휘 및 언어(즉, 짧고/또는 연결되지 않은 구와 문장) • 언어 사용에 심각한 오류가 빈번히 발생함 • 독창적인 언어 사용이 거의 없음; 일관된 언어는 대부분 제시문에서 차용됨
0	답안이 공백이거나, 주제를 거부하거나, 영어가 아니거나, 제시문을 완전히 복사했거나, 제시문과 전혀 관련이 없거나, 임의의 키 입력으로 구성되어 있다.

PRACTICE

1

You are a university student and a member of the International Students' Club. The club is organizing a potluck to celebrate food from around the world. The event organizer, Luigi, has asked members to participate.

Write an email to Luigi. In your email, do the following:

- Offer to make a popular dish from your country.
- Provide details about what the dish is.
- Ask Luigi how else you could help with the event.

Write as much as you can and in complete sentences.

2

You are planning to study abroad, and you would like to get a part-time job while you are studying to support yourself financially. You want to ask your friend Chelsea, who already lives there, for advice.

Write an email to Chelsea. In your email, do the following:

- Explain why you want to get a part-time job.
- Mention what kind of work you want to do.
- Ask for her advice on how to find a job.

Write as much as you can and in complete sentences.

Your Response:

To: Chelsea

Subject: Advice for getting a part-time job

Type of Task 3: Write for an Academic Discussion

출제 경향 분석

▶ 유형: 토론 주제에 대한 나의 의견을 논리적으로 작성
▶ 문제 수: 1문제
▶ 문제 풀이 시간: 10분
▶ 토론 종류: 대학 수업의 마케팅, 도시 계획, 경제, 경영, 사회학, 문화인류학 등 다양한 전공
▶ 문제 특징: 담당 교수가 수업과 관련된 토론 질문을 온라인 게시판에 하고, 두 학생이 토론에 참여하여 의견을 제시함
▶ 답안 형식: 토론에 기여하는 나의 의견을 최소 100단어 이상으로 작성

예시

Your professor is teaching a class on marketing. Write a post responding to the professor's question.

In your response, you should do the following:

- Express and support your opinion.
- Make a contribution to the discussion in your own words.

An effective response will contain at least 100 words.

Dr. Brown

We have recently been discussing the concept of a new advertising strategy called targeted advertising, which involves directing advertisements to consumers with certain traits or interests instead of creating ads for a general audience. Some believe that targeted advertising is ethical. Others argue that it violates privacy. What is your opinion on this?

Justin

I do not think there are any ethical problems with targeted advertising. If we do not want to receive targeted ads, we can simply change our privacy settings. Also, businesses can save money by reaching people who have interests that are relevant to their products or services, which would lower prices for customers.

Kelly

I think targeted advertising violates people's privacy. While the strategy can be effective, websites should not be allowed to keep track of people's personal information and use it for their own purposes. Instead, companies should make advertisements that would appeal to a large audience.

[Cut] [Paste] [Undo] [Redo]   👁 Hide Word Count   0

Answers p.339

문제 풀이 전략

전략 1 · 문제 분석 및 브레인스토밍

시험 화면 좌측에 있는 교수의 토론 질문을 분석하고, 화면 우측에 두 학생의 글은 빠르게 읽으며 자신이 동의할 학생, 비동의할 학생, 또는 자신이 제3의 의견을 펼칠지 정한다. (약 1분 소요)

Your professor is teaching a class on marketing. Write a post responding to the professor's question.

In your response, you should do the following:

- Express and support your opinion.
- Make a contribution to the discussion in your own words.

An effective response will contain at least 100 words.

Dr. Brown

We have recently been discussing the concept of a new advertising strategy called targeted advertising, which involves directing advertisements to consumers with certain traits or interests instead of creating ads for a general audience. Some believe that targeted advertising is ethical. Others argue that it violates privacy. What is your opinion on this?

Justin

I do not think there are any ethical problems with targeted advertising. If we do not want to receive targeted ads, we can simply change our privacy settings. Also, businesses can save money by reaching people who have interests that are relevant to their products or services, which would lower prices for customers.

Kelly

I think targeted advertising violates people's privacy. While the strategy can be effective, websites should not be allowed to keep track of people's personal information and use it for their own purposes. Instead, companies should make advertisements that would appeal to a large audience.

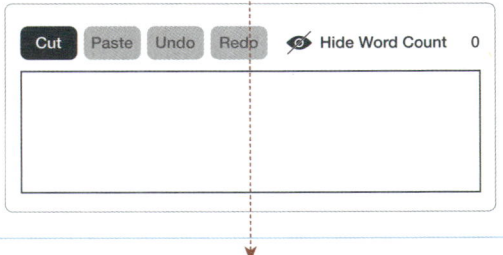

↓ 토론 질문 분석

↓ 두 학생 입장 빠르게 확인

오프 토픽(off-topic)이 발생하지 않도록 질문을 제대로 이해하는 것이 가장 중요하고, 자신의 의견을 어떻게 뒷받침할지 근거 및 예시도 체계적으로 브레인스토밍해야 한다. 브레인스토밍 시 유의할 사항을 정리하면 다음과 같다.

- 나의 주장이 명확하게 드러나도록
- 나의 주장을 뒷받침하는 충분한 근거/예시가 있도록
- 반복되는 내용은 없도록
- 논리적 흐름(원인 → 결과, 주장 → 근거 등)이 자연스럽도록

전략 2   자신의 의견을 논리적으로 기술하며 토론에 기여

약 7–8분간 최소 100단어 이상으로 작성한다. 이때 나의 의견이 명확하게 처음부터 나올 수 있도록, 두괄식으로 작성한다.

While I understand Justin's point about lower prices, **I think targeted advertising is unethical and a violation of privacy.** Companies that use targeted advertising collect consumers' personal data, including which websites they visit, the media they watch, and even their recent purchases, in order to analyze their behavior. This information is often used without people's awareness or consent to display ads for products that companies believe consumers are more likely to buy. Although the companies claim these actions are not illegal, they are still ethically questionable. Furthermore, it makes people feel a sense of uneasiness, as though their actions are being tracked and monitored. Therefore, targeted advertising should not be practiced, and ads should instead be aimed at a large audience.	→ 비동의 학생 언급 → 나의 주장 → 근거/예시 1 → 근거/예시 2 → 결론

전략 3   교정

마지막 1분 정도 시간에는 자신의 답안을 다시 한번 살펴보며 교정한다. 짧은 교정 시간이기에 오프 토픽이 아닌 이상 내용 수정 보다는 철자와 문법 오류 수정에 중점을 두어 검토한다.

체크리스트

- ☐ 철자가 정확한지
- ☐ 시제가 올바른지
- ☐ 주어–동사 수 일치가 맞는지
- ☐ 관사(a, an, the), 전치사, 대명사가 적절한지
- ☐ 단어 선택이 정확하고 어색하지 않은지
- ☐ 문장이 너무 길거나 지나치게 짧지 않은지

기본 실력 업그레이드

기본기 1 Academic Discussion 답안 구성 및 작성 기본 표현

다음은 Academic Discussion 답안의 구성과 자주 사용되는 기본 표현들이다.

구성	기본 표현
비동의 학생 언급	• While I understand A's point about ~ , ~에 관한 A의 주장을 이해는 하지만, • Even though A makes a valid point regarding ~ , 비록 A가 ~에 관한 타당한 주장을 하지만,
나의 주장	• I think ~ 나는 ~라고 생각한다 • I believe ~ 나는 ~라고 믿는다 • I am of the opinion that ~ 나는 ~한 의견을 갖고 있다
근거/예시	• This clearly shows that ~ 이는 분명히 ~임을 보여준다 • for example, 예를 들어, • for instance, 예를 들어, • in particular, 특히, • particularly 특히 • like / such as ~와 같이
추가	• Furthermore, 더욱이, • Moreover, 더욱이, • In addition, 추가로, • Additionally, 추가로,
결론	• Therefore, 그러므로, • In conclusion, 결론적으로, • To conclude, 결론적으로,

기본기 2 채점 기준에 맞는 글쓰기

Write for an Academic Discussion 유형 역시 고유의 채점 기준이 있는데, 채점 기준에서 가장 중요한 사항은 다음 네 가지이다.

— 명확한 자신의 의견을 기술하여 온라인 토론에 기여
— 자신의 의견에 대한 상세한 설명, 예시, 세부 내용 제시
— 명료하고 정확한 문장
— 다양한 문법과 어휘

5점에서 0점으로 채점이 되고, 5점 채점 기준에 맞춰서 토론 주제에 대한 나의 의견을 논리적으로 작성하는 연습을 한다.

점수	채점 기준
5	**완벽히 성공적인 답안** 답안은 명확하게 온라인 토론에 기여를 하는 내용이며, 언어 사용에 있어 일관된 유창성을 보여준다. 전형적인 5점 답안은 다음 특징이 있다: • 관련성 있는, 충분히 상세한 설명, 예시, 세부 내용 • 효과적으로 다양한 구문 및 정확한 어휘 사용 • 시간 제약으로 인해 능숙한 사람이 범할 수 있는 오류를 제외하면(예: there/their 같은 흔한 오타, 철자 오류), 어휘나 문법 오류가 거의 없음
4	**대체로 성공적인 답안** 답안은 온라인 토론에 기여를 하는 내용이며, 언어 사용 능력의 능숙함으로 인해 작성자의 생각이 쉽게 이해된다. 전형적인 4점 답안은 다음 특징이 있다: • 관련성 있는, 적절히 상세한 설명, 예시 및/또는 세부 내용 • 다양한 구문과 적절한 어휘 선택 • 어휘나 문법 오류가 거의 없음
3	**부분적으로 성공한 답안** 답안은 대체로 온라인 토론에 기여를 하고 이해 가능한 내용이며, 언어 사용 능력에 어느 정도 능숙함이 있다. 전형적인 3점 답안은 다음 특징이 있다: • 설명, 예시 또는 세부 내용의 일부가 누락되거나 불분명하거나 관련성이 없을 수 있는 전개 • 어느 정도 다양한 구문 구조와 적절한 어휘 사용 • 문장 구조, 단어 형태 또는 단어 사용에 있어 눈에 띄는 어휘 및 문법 오류가 일부 존재
2	**대체로 실패한 답안** 답안은 온라인 토론에 기여하려는 시도를 반영하지만, 언어 사용의 한계로 아이디어를 이해하기 어렵다. 전형적인 2점 답안은 다음 특징이 있다: • 상세하지 못하고 부분적으로만 관련성이 있는 아이디어 • 제한된 구문 구조 및 어휘 범위 • 문장 구조, 단어 형태 또는 사용에 오류가 누적됨
1	**실패한 답안** 답안은 온라인 토론에 기여하려는 시도가 효과적이지 못함을 반영하며, 언어 사용의 한계로 아이디어를 표현하기 어렵다. 전형적인 1점 답안은 다음 특징이 있다: • 과제를 해결하려는 시도를 보이지만, 일관된 아이디어가 거의 또는 전혀 없는 단어와 구문 • 매우 제한된 구문 구조 및 어휘 • 언어 사용에 심각한 오류가 빈번히 발생함 • 독창적인 언어 사용이 거의 없음; 일관된 언어는 대부분 제시문에서 차용됨
0	답안이 공백이거나, 주제를 거부하거나, 영어가 아니거나, 제시문을 완전히 복사했거나, 제시문과 전혀 관련이 없거나, 임의의 키 입력으로 구성되어 있다.

PRACTICE

1

Your professor is teaching a class on political science. Write a post responding to the professor's question.

In your response, you should do the following:

- Express and support your opinion.
- Make a contribution to the discussion in your own words.

An effective response will contain at least 100 words.

Dr. Robinson

We have been discussing the concept of health taxes in our class as a solution to the rise in preventable diseases. Some argue that taxing unhealthy products, such as sugary drinks and junk food, is essential for improving public health, while others believe it is not effective. Do you think taxing unhealthy products is a good idea? Why or why not?

Julie

I think taxing unhealthy products is a good idea. When the prices of items like soda and snacks increase, people are more likely to be discouraged from buying them. Over time, this can help them develop the habit of making healthier choices.

Paul

I believe putting taxes on unhealthy products will not be effective. People's tastes are hard to change, and they often continue buying what they enjoy regardless of higher prices. Sugary drinks and junk food are deeply ingrained in daily habits, so taxes alone will not significantly reduce consumption.

2

Your professor is teaching a class on education. Write a post responding to the professor's question.

In your response, you should do the following:

- Express and support your opinion.
- Make a contribution to the discussion in your own words.

An effective response will contain at least 100 words.

Dr. Smith

We have recently been discussing the concept of extracurricular activities in education. Some argue that student organizations and clubs, such as sports teams, student governments, and religious groups, are beneficial. Others believe that they are distracting and that universities should primarily be places of learning. What are your thoughts on student organizations?

Brad

I believe that academic achievement is the most important aspect of attending university. However, club activities oftentimes distract students from their studies since some student organizations require a large amount of time and commitment. This can take away precious study time, resulting in lower grades.

April

I think extracurricular activities are beneficial because they allow students to enjoy their university lives. Universities are not just places to study; forming friendships and interacting with a variety of people is a key part of the university experience. Student organizations and clubs are a great way to do this.

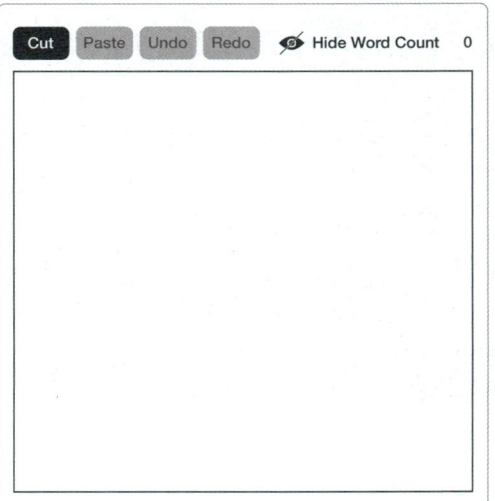

SPEAKING

1. Listen and Repeat
2. Take an Interview

Overview

문제 수	11 문제
시험 시간	약 8분
문제 유형	총 2개 ☑ Listen and Repeat ☑ Take an Interview
문제 세트	총 1세트 출제
더미 문제	없음

Type of Task 1: Listen and Repeat

출제 경향 분석

▶ 유형: 문장을 듣고 따라 말하는 유형
▶ 문제 수: 총 7문제
▶ 내용: 도서관, 박물관, 미술관, 공원, 동물원, 식물원, 체육관, 유적지, 대학 캠퍼스 등 특정 장소 시설 설명
▶ 답변 시간: 보통 처음 두 문제는 8초, 다음 세 문제는 10초, 마지막 두 문제는 12초가 각각 주어짐
▶ 문제 특징: 첫 화면에서 전체 문제의 시나리오와 해당 장소에 대한 흑백 이미지가 제시되고, 이후 각 문제에 해당되는 곳은 칼러로 표시되면서 문제의 문맥을 확인할 수 있도록 제공

예시

You are being trained to assist new students during the college orientation. Listen to your supervisor and repeat what she says. Repeat only once.

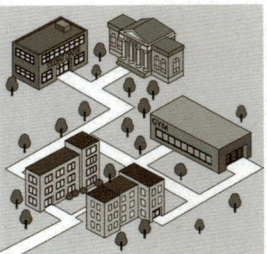

S_00

Listen and repeat only once.

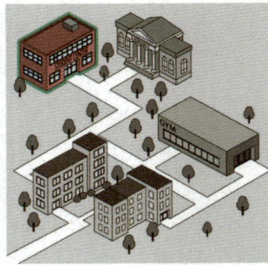

RESPONSE TIME
🎤 00:00:08

Answers p.343

문제 풀이 전략

전략1   시나리오 파악 및 이미지 분석

첫 화면에 나오는 시나리오 내용을 파악하고 이미지를 미리 분석하면 이후 나올 음원을 보다 잘 이해할 수 있다.

시나리오 파악: 대학 오리엔테이션 기간 신입생을 돕기 위한 교육을 받고 있는 상황으로, 슈퍼바이저가 교육 내용을 말할 예정

You are being trained to assist new students during the college orientation. Listen to your supervisor and repeat what she says. Repeat only once.

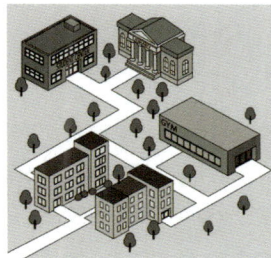

이미지 분석: 다양한 대학 건물과 시설

전략2   음원 경청하기

듣기 기회는 단 한 번이기에, 집중하여 음원을 경청해야 한다.

전략3   시간을 갖고 따라 말하기

답변 녹음 기회는 한 번이므로 바로 말하지 말고 주어진 답변 시간을 최대한 활용하여 머릿속으로 연습 후 말한다. 이때, 너무 빠르지도, 너무 느리지도 않게, 음원에 나온 톤을 따라하며 문장을 말한다.

기본 실력 업그레이드

기본기 1 청킹(의미 단위 덩어리) 익히기

청킹(chunking)은 언어 정보를 덩어리(chunk) 단위로 묶어서 익히는 방법으로, 단어 하나하나가 아니라, 의미 단위 덩어리로 묶어 기억하는 것이다. 이때, 청크 단위 구분의 정답은 없으며, 시험에서는 음원의 화자가 말하는 청크 단위로 기억하고 말하면 된다.

> 예 Free snacks and drinks / are available / in the main lobby.
> (또는) Free snacks and drinks are available / in the main lobby.

기본기 2 쉐도잉(따라 말하기) 훈련

청크 단위로 말할 수 있으면, 이제 청크를 이어서 문장 전체를 말하는 연습이 중요한데, 이를 위해 쉐도잉(shadowing) 훈련이 필요하다. Listening 스킬 훈련법 중 가장 유용한 쉐도잉은 Speaking 학습에서도 가장 중요한 훈련법으로, 쉐도잉을 통해 영어 발음, 리듬, 억양을 동시에 익힐 수 있다. 반복 훈련을 통해 반응 속도를 자연스럽게 끌어올리면 큰 도움이 된다. (훈련 방법은 Listen and Choose a Response 내용 참고)

기본기 3 패턴 학습

대부분의 청크는 패턴(pattern)으로 나타나는데, 패턴이란 자주 반복되어 쓰이는 문장 구조나 틀을 말한다. 익숙한 패턴의 문장은 기억하기 쉬운 반면, 익숙하지 않은 패턴은 기억하기 어렵기에, 패턴을 많이 알수록 Listen and Repeat에서 고득점을 맞을 수 있다. 다음은 Listen and Repeat에서 자주 등장하는 기본 문장 구조이다.

❶ 수동태
시험에서 '주어+be동사+p.p+수식어구' 구조의 수동태 문장이 자주 나온다.

> 예 Various classes are held in the activity rooms.
> 다양한 수업이 활동실에서 열립니다.

❷ 명령문
Listen and Repeat에서는 시설 책임자(supervisor)나 교육 책임자(trainer)가 음원의 청자에게 해야 할 일과, 하지 말아야 할 일들을 알려주는 경우가 많은 만큼, 명령, 요청, 지시, 제안 등을 표현하는 문장이 자주 등장한다. 주어가 생략되어 동사 원형으로 시작하는 문형이 보통 출제되며, 부정형(Don't+동사원형), Please를 사용한 공손한 형태, Let's/Let me/Let us 등의 제안도 출제된다.

> 예 Go to the reception desk for help.
> 도움을 받으려면 안내 데스크로 가세요.

> 예 Please make sure to sign your name.
> 꼭 서명해 주시기 바랍니다.

> 예 Let us direct you to your assigned classroom.
> 당신의 지정된 교실로 안내해 드리겠습니다.

❸ 두 개 이상의 절이 들어간 복문
6번, 7번 문제처럼 문장이 길어질수록 'If절 + 주절'과 같은 부사절, 또는 전치사절, 명사절이 올 확률이 높다.

> 예 If you want to explore the exhibits at your own pace, you can take a self-guided tour.
> 전시물을 자신의 속도에 맞춰 둘러보고 싶다면, 셀프 가이드 투어를 이용하실 수 있습니다.

> 예 Before the tour begins, please check that you have all your belongings with you.
> 투어 시작 전에 소지품을 모두 챙기셨는지 확인해 주세요.

기본기 4 빈출 주제 및 단어 익히기

익숙하지 않은 주제나 모르는 단어가 나오면 들어도 바로 잊게 된다. 따라서 Listen and Choose a Response에 자주 나오는 주제 및 단어를 미리 숙지하도록 한다.

S_00_1

❶ 학교/프로그램

단어	뜻	단어	뜻
activity room	활동실, 활동 공간	flyer	전단지
class	수업, 학급	hall	안쪽 현관, 안쪽 복도, 홀 (큰 방 또는 건물)
community center	주민센터	notice board	게시판
course	강좌, 과정, 수업	session	시간
dormitory	기숙사	under renovation	보수 공사 중
facility	시설	upcoming event	다가오는 행사
fitness program	운동 프로그램	workshop	워크숍, 작업장, 연수회

② 전시/공연

S_00_2

단어	뜻
abstract	추상적인, 추상화
announcement	공지, 알림
artifact	공예품, 인공 유물
artwork	예술품
auditorium	강당, 객석
a wide range of (=a wide selection of)	폭넓은, 다양한
brochure	책자
classic(al)	고전(의)
contemporary	동시대의, 현대의
exhibit	전시품
exhibition	전시(회)
family-friendly	가족 친화적인

단어	뜻
gift shop (=souvenir shop)	기념품 가게
lobby	로비
modern	현대의
painting	그림
piece	작품
private tour	개인 투어
reception desk (=front desk)	안내소, 접수처
sculpture	조각(품)
self-guided tour	자유 여행
self-portrait	초상화
ticket counter (=kiosk)	매표소
wing	(중심 건물에서 옆으로 늘인) 부속 건물

③ 숙박/대여

S_00_3

단어	뜻
agreement	동의서, 계약서
inspection	검사, 조사
for free (=no extra charge)	무료로, 공짜로
identification	신분(증)
rental	대여
reservation	예약

단어	뜻
special promotion	특별 판촉(할인)
station	역
transportation	교통
unit	하나의 장치나 시설
vehicle	차량
workshop	워크숍, 작업장, 연수회

기본기 5 채점 기준에 맞는 말하기

Listen and Repeat 유형은 5점에서 0점으로 채점이 되고, 5점 채점 기준에 맞춰서 한 번 듣고 정확히 따라 말할 수 있도록 연습한다.

점수	채점 기준
5	**답변은 음원을 정확하게 따라 한다.** 전형적인 답변은 다음과 같은 특징을 보인다: • 응답은 완전히 이해 가능하며 음원을 정확히 따라 한다.

4	**답변은 음원에서 표현된 의미를 포착하지만, 정확히 따라하지는 않는다.**
	전형적인 답변은 다음과 같은 특징을 보인다:
	• 음원의 의미를 크게 바꾸지 않는 단어 또는 문법의 사소한 변경이 존재한다.
	  예를 들어: • 한두 개의 기능어가 누락되거나 변경될 수 있으며,
	           • (긴 음원의 경우) 내용어가 누락되거나 관련 단어로 대체될 수 있으며,
	           • 시제/방향/수 등의 표시나 특징이 누락되거나 부정확할 수 있으며,
	           • 두 단어가 위치가 바뀔 수 있다.
	• 한두 개의 내용어가 발음 불명확으로 인해 모호할 수 있다. 응시자가 스스로 수정할 수 있지만, 답변을 성공적으로 끝마친다.

3	**답변은 본질적으로 완전하지만, 원문의 의미를 정확히 포착하지 못한다.** 전형적인 답변은 다음과 같은 특징을 보인다: • 답변에는 음원의 내용어 또는 아이디어 대부분이 포함된다. • 여러 기능어가 변경되거나 누락될 수 있으며, 하나 이상의 내용어가 누락되거나 실질적으로 변경될 수 있다. • 답변은 완전한 문장이다. • 경우에 따라, 이해 가능성 문제로 인해 가끔 의미를 파악하기 어려울 수 있다. 응시자가 단어나 구를 발음하는 데 어려움을 겪거나 단어를 연결하여 발음함으로써 이해도를 떨어뜨릴 수 있다.
2	**답변은 음원의 상당 부분을 누락하고 있거나 매우 부정확하다.** 전형적인 답변은 다음과 같은 특징을 보인다: • 음원의 상당 부분이 누락되어 중요한 원본 의미가 생략된다. • 응시자가 문장의 첫 부분을 반복할 수 있다. 이후 응시자는 멈추거나 부정확한 내용으로 채우거나 마지막 몇 단어를 포함할 수 있다. • 답변은 독립된 문장이 아니며 의미가 단편적이다. • 이해도가 낮다. 음원을 모르는 청취자에게는 답변 내용을 이해하기 어려울 것이다.
1	**답변은 음원의 내용을 거의 반영하지 않거나 대부분 알아들을 수 없다.** 전형적인 답변은 다음과 같은 특징을 보인다: • 몇 단어에 불과한 최소한의 답변만 이루어지며, 음원의 대부분이 누락된다. • 답변이 음원을 반복하려는 시도로 인식되지만, 대부분 알아들을 수 없다.
0	답변이 없거나 답변이 완전히 알아들을 수 없거나 답변에 영어가 전혀 포함되어 있지 않거나 답변 내용이 음원과 전혀 관련이 없거나("모르겠다"와 같은 문구로만 구성되어 있다).

PRACTICE

1-7

You are preparing to welcome visitors to an art gallery. Listen to your supervisor and repeat what she says. Repeat only once.

S1_01

Listen and repeat only once.

RESPONSE TIME
00:00:08

S1_02

Listen and repeat only once.

RESPONSE TIME
00:00:08

S1_03

Listen and repeat only once.

RESPONSE TIME
00:00:10

 S1_04

Listen and repeat only once.

RESPONSE TIME
00:00:10

 S1_05

Listen and repeat only once.

RESPONSE TIME
00:00:10

S1_06

Listen and repeat only once.

RESPONSE TIME
00:00:12

S1_07

Listen and repeat only once.

RESPONSE TIME
00:00:12

8-14

You are being trained to assist customers at a storage unit rental agency. Listen to your trainer and repeat what he says. Repeat only once.

 S1_08

Listen and repeat only once.

RESPONSE TIME
00:00:08

 S1_09

Listen and repeat only once.

RESPONSE TIME
00:00:08

 S1_10

Listen and repeat only once.

RESPONSE TIME
00:00:10

Listen and Repeat

S1_11

Listen and repeat only once.

RESPONSE TIME
00:00:10

S1_12

Listen and repeat only once.

RESPONSE TIME
00:00:10

S1_13

Listen and repeat only once.

RESPONSE TIME
00:00:12

S1_14

Listen and repeat only once.

RESPONSE TIME
00:00:12

Listen and Repeat 135

Type of Task 2: Take an Interview

출제 경향 분석

- ▶ 유형: 사전 녹화된 면접관의 질문에 답변하는 문제 유형
- ▶ 문제 수: 총 4문제
- ▶ 시나리오: 특정 주제에 대한 리서치 또는 연구에 참여하여 질문을 받는 상황
- ▶ 답변 시간: 각 질문에 대해 45초의 답변 시간 주어짐
- ▶ 문제 특징: 초반 질문은 보통 사실적 정보와 개인적 경험에 초점을 맞춰 질문하는 반면, 후반 질문은 더 광범위한 문제에 대한 의견을 밝히고 이를 뒷받침하도록 요구함

예시

You have volunteered for a research study about playing sports. You will have a short online interview with a researcher. The researcher will ask you some questions.

 S2_00

Please answer the interviewer's questions.

RESPONSE TIME
00:00:45

Answers p.345

문제 풀이 전략

전략 1 앞으로 나올 질문 주제 파악하기

처음 화면에 나오는 시나리오에서 질문 주제를 파악하여, 앞으로 나올 4개의 질문에 미리 대비한다.

주제: 스포츠 활동

> You have volunteered for a research study about **playing sports**. You will have a short online interview with a researcher. The researcher will ask you some questions.

전략 2 경청하며 질문의 핵심 파악하기

질문은 한 번만 들려주기에 경청이 중요한데, 특히 질문의 핵심을 파악하여 오프 토픽(off-topic)이 발생하지 않도록 해야 한다.

Thank you for taking the time to speak with me about playing sports. When you play sports, do you **prefer individual sports**, like tennis, **or team sports**, like basketball?

➔ 개인 스포츠를 선호하는지, 팀 스포츠를 선호하는지?

전략 3 3단 구성으로 답변하기

45초 답변 시간을 꽉 채운다는 생각으로, 두괄식의 3단 구성(답변-근거-마무리)으로 답변한다.

Between the two, my preference is to play sports in a team rather than alone. ┈┈┈▶ 답변: 질문에 대한 직접적인 답변을 처음에 하는 두괄식 답변

The main reason is that I find playing sports with team ┈┈┈▶ 근거: 앞의 답변에 대한 근거로 members to be more exciting. An occasion I clearly remember 이유, 예시, 경험 등 제시
is playing soccer with my high school team against another school. We worked together, encouraged each other during the game, and celebrated every point together. Although we lost the match, it was still very fun thanks to my teammates.

Overall, I think playing team sports is more preferable. ┈┈┈▶ 마무리: 답변의 중요 포인트 다시 언급하며 끝내기

전략 4 전달력을 생각하며 정확하게 말하기

답변을 할 때는 전달력을 생각하면서 명확하고 정확하게 말한다.

기본 실력 업그레이드

기본기 1) 인터뷰 답변에 자주 사용하는 표현 익히기

Take an Interview에서는 자신의 의견, 선호, 예측, 방법, 이유, 예시 및 경험 등을 자연스럽게 표현할 수 있는 다양한 문장 시작어(Sentence Starters)를 활용함으로써, 말하고자 하는 문장의 목적을 명확히 드러내고 보다 안정적이고 논리적인 답변을 할 수 있다.

구성	기본 표현
의견	• In my opinion, 제 생각에는, • I (tend to) think / believe (that ~) 저는 (~라고) 생각합니다 / 믿습니다(경향이 있습니다) • While the idea that ~ has its merits, I think (that ~) 　~한 생각이 장점이 있지만, (~라고) 생각합니다 • I agree / disagree with the statement that 저는 ~라는 진술에 동의합니다 / 동의하지 않습니다
선호	• I would (much) prefer 저는 ~을 (훨씬) 선호합니다 • Given the choice, I would choose A over B 선택한다면, 저는 B보다 A를 선택하겠습니다 • Between the two, my preference is A rather than B 　둘 중에서, 제가 선호하는 것은 B보다 A입니다
예측	• I predict (that ~) 저는 (~라고) 예상합니다 • It is likely that A will become B in the future A는 앞으로 B가 될 가능성이 높습니다 • There is a chance that A will become B in the coming years 　A는 앞으로 B가 될 가능성이 있습니다
방법	• One effective way/method is ~ 한 가지 효과적인 방법은 ~입니다 • A good way to A is ~ A에 좋은 방법은 ~입니다 • One practical approach is to부정사 한 가지 실용적인 접근법은 ~하는 것입니다
이유	• This is because ~ 이는 ~때문입니다 • One reason is (that ~) / Another reason is (that ~) 　한 가지 이유는 ~입니다 / 또 다른 이유는 ~입니다 • The (main) reason is (that ~) 그 (주된) 이유는 ~입니다 • The primary reason for A is (that ~) A에 대한 주된 이유는 ~입니다
예시 및 경험	• For example, / For instance, 예를 들면, • In fact, 실제로, • To give an (a personal) example, (개인적인) 예를 들자면, • One experience that comes to mind is ~ 한 가지 생각나는 경험은 ~입니다 • An occasion I clearly remember is 제가 생생하게 기억하는 경험(사건)은 ~입니다
마무리	• Overall, / All in all, 전반적으로, • In conclusion, 결론적으로, • In the end, 결국, • To sum up, / In summary, 요약하면, • For this reason, / For these reasons, 이런 이유로,

기본기 2 채점 기준에 맞는 말하기

Take an Interview 유형의 5점 채점 기준에 맞게, 질문에 맞는 상세한 답변을 정확한 언어(문법 및 어휘)와 발음으로 유창하게 말할 수 있도록 연습한다.

점수	채점 기준
5	**완벽히 성공적인 답변** 답변은 완전하게 문제를 다루며, 분명하고 유창하다. 전형적인 답변은 다음과 같은 특징을 보인다: • 답변은 주제와 관련이 있으며 상세히 잘 설명되어 있다. • 적절하고 자연스러운 멈춤을 통해 대화 속도를 잘 유지하고 있다. • 발음이 이해하기 쉽고, 리듬과 억양이 의미를 효과적으로 전달한다. • 다양하고 정확한 문법과 어휘로 정확한 의미를 명확하게 표현한다.
4	**대체로 성공적인 답변** 답변은 문제를 다루며, 상당히 분명하다. 전형적인 답변은 다음과 같은 특징을 보인다: • 답변은 주제와 관련이 있고 상세히 설명되었으나, 효과적인 문장 연결어가 부족할 수 있다. • 대체로 적절한 말하기 속도를 유지하며, 흐름에 미미한 영향을 줄 수 있는 멈춤이 간혹 있다. • 발음, 리듬, 억양으로 인해 이해도나 의미 전달에 지장이 없으나, 가끔 특정 단어나 구절을 이해하는 데 약간의 노력이 필요할 수 있다. • 문법과 어휘는 대부분의 경우 일반적인 의미를 표현하기에 충분하다.
3	**부분적으로 성공한 답변** 답변은 문제를 다루나 제한된 상술과 명료함을 지닌다. 전형적인 답변은 다음과 같은 특징을 보인다: • 답변은 대체로 주제와 관련이 있으나, 상세 설명이 상대적으로 제한적일 수 있다. • 잦은 또는 긴 멈춤으로 인해 흐름이 끊기며, 채움말(필러)이 빈번하다. • 단어 수준의 발음이나 강세/리듬의 부정확성으로 인해 가끔 알아듣기 어렵다. • 문법과 어휘의 제한된 범위와 정확성은 의미의 정확성과 명확성을 현저히 제한한다.
2	**대체로 실패한 답변** 답변은 문제를 다루려는 시도를 반영하나, 의미 있고/또는 이해 가능한 방식으로 뒷받침되지 않고 있다. 전형적인 답변은 다음과 같은 특징을 보인다: • 답변은 인터뷰 질문과 최소한으로 연관되어 있으며, 관련성 있는 설명이 거의 없거나 전혀 없고, 또는 질문에서 나온 표현으로 주로 구성되어 있다. • 이해도가 제한적이며, 응시자가 의도한 의미를 파악하기 어려운 경우가 많다. • 답변은 매우 제한된 범위의 문법과 어휘를 보여준다.
1	**실패한 답변** 답변은 최소한으로 문제를 다루며, 언어의 매우 제한된 사용 능력을 보여준다. 전형적인 답변은 다음과 같은 특징을 보인다: • 답변은 인터뷰 질문에 사용된 언어와 단지 희미하게 연관되어 있을 뿐이다. • 답변은 대부분 알아들을 수 없다. • 답변은 주로 단편적인 단어나 구로 이루어져 있다.
0	답변이 없거나 답변이 완전히 알아들을 수 없거나 답변에 영어가 전혀 포함되어 있지 않거나 답변 내용이 질문과 전혀 관련이 없거나("모르겠다"와 같은 문구로만 구성되어 있다).

PRACTICE

1-4

You have agreed to participate in a research study about traveling for leisure. You will have a short online interview with a researcher. The researcher will ask you some questions.

S2_01

Please answer the interviewer's questions.

RESPONSE TIME
00:00:45

S2_02

Please answer the interviewer's questions.

RESPONSE TIME
00:00:45

 S2_03

Please answer the interviewer's questions.

RESPONSE TIME
00:00:45

 S2_04

Please answer the interviewer's questions.

RESPONSE TIME
00:00:45

5-8

You have volunteered for a research study about eating habits. You will have a short online interview with a researcher. The researcher will ask you some questions.

 S2_05

Please answer the interviewer's questions.

RESPONSE TIME 00:00:45

 S2_06

Please answer the interviewer's questions.

RESPONSE TIME 00:00:45

S2_07

Please answer the interviewer's questions.

RESPONSE TIME
00:00:45

S2_08

Please answer the interviewer's questions.

RESPONSE TIME
00:00:45

ETS
Practice Tests

Test 1

Answers p.350

READING

TOEFL iBT

Reading Section

In the reading section, you will answer 35-48 questions to demonstrate how well you understand academic and non-academic texts in English. There are three types of tasks.

Type of Task	Description
Complete the Words	Fill in the missing letters in a paragraph.
Read in Daily Life	Answer questions about everyday reading materials.
Read an Academic Passage	Answer questions about academic passages.

Module 1

TOEFL iBT

Reading | Questions **1–10** of 20

Fill in the missing letters in the paragraph.

We know from drawings that have been preserved in caves for over 10,000 years that early humans performed dances as a group activity. We mi_ _ _ think th_ _ prehistoric peo_ _ _ concentrated on_ _ on ba_ _ _ survival. How_ _ _ _, it i_ clear fr_ _ the rec_ _ _ that dan_ _ _ _ was important to them. They recorded more drawings of dances than of any other group activity. Dances served various purposes, including ritualistic communication with the divine, storytelling, and social cohesion.

TOEFL iBT

Reading | Question **11** of 20

Read a notice.

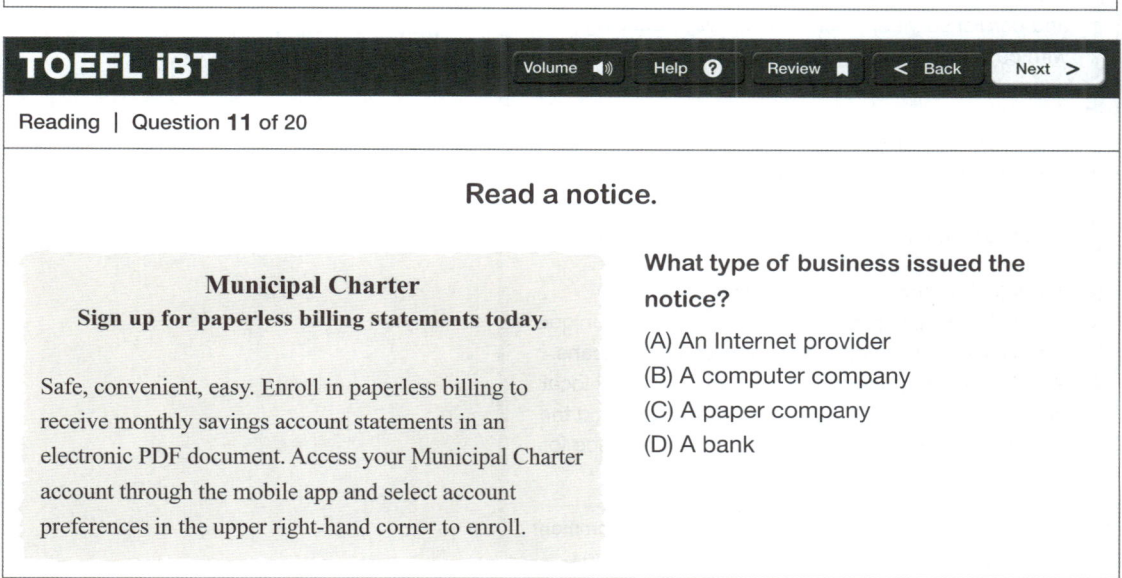

Municipal Charter
Sign up for paperless billing statements today.

Safe, convenient, easy. Enroll in paperless billing to receive monthly savings account statements in an electronic PDF document. Access your Municipal Charter account through the mobile app and select account preferences in the upper right-hand corner to enroll.

What type of business issued the notice?

(A) An Internet provider
(B) A computer company
(C) A paper company
(D) A bank

TOEFL iBT

Reading | Question **12** of 20

Read a notice.

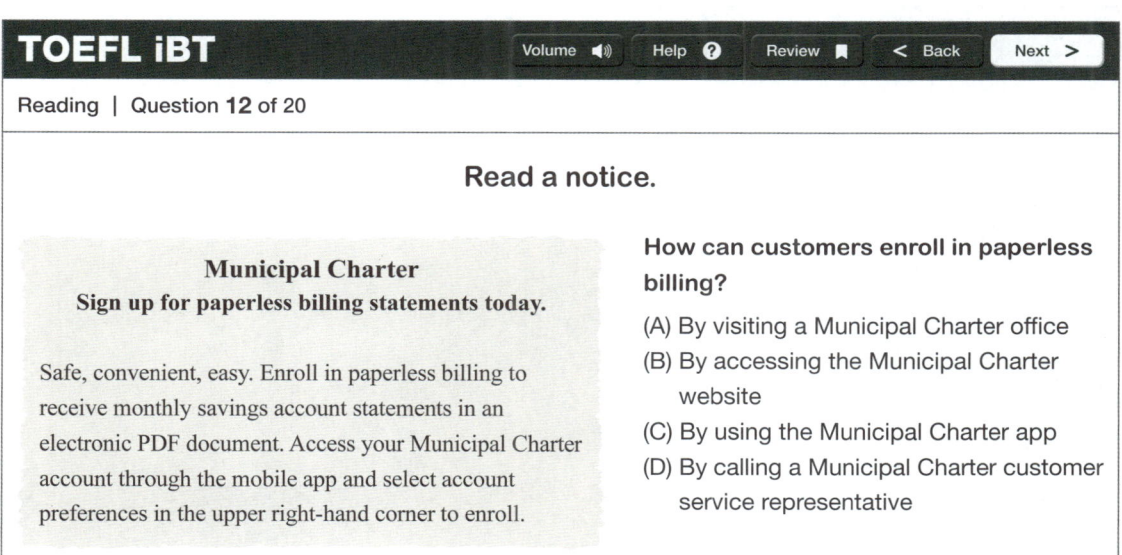

Municipal Charter
Sign up for paperless billing statements today.

Safe, convenient, easy. Enroll in paperless billing to receive monthly savings account statements in an electronic PDF document. Access your Municipal Charter account through the mobile app and select account preferences in the upper right-hand corner to enroll.

How can customers enroll in paperless billing?

(A) By visiting a Municipal Charter office
(B) By accessing the Municipal Charter website
(C) By using the Municipal Charter app
(D) By calling a Municipal Charter customer service representative

Read a social media post.

Sofia Baker

Every Saturday, our local farmer's market is the place to be! Fresh fruits, veggies, homemade goodies, and unique crafts await you. The Thompson family's organic produce is a must-try, known for its quality and cordial service. Their stall is always bustling with customers eager to buy fresh, pesticide-free vegetables from the welcoming staff.

Don't miss the bakery stall—get there early for the best bread and pastries, including gluten-free and vegan options. The smell of freshly baked goods fills the air, and these treats sell out fast!

In addition to food, the market sells handmade crafts like jewelry, pottery, and textiles. These unique items make perfect gifts and support local artisans. Plus, enjoy live music while you shop. Talented local musicians help create a vibrant atmosphere, and the community spirit makes it a delightful experience for all. See you there!

👍 Like   💬 Comment

What is the main purpose of the post?

(A) To explain the benefits of organic farming
(B) To describe the variety of products available at the farmer's market
(C) To compare different farmer's markets in the area
(D) To offer advice on starting a stall at the farmer's market

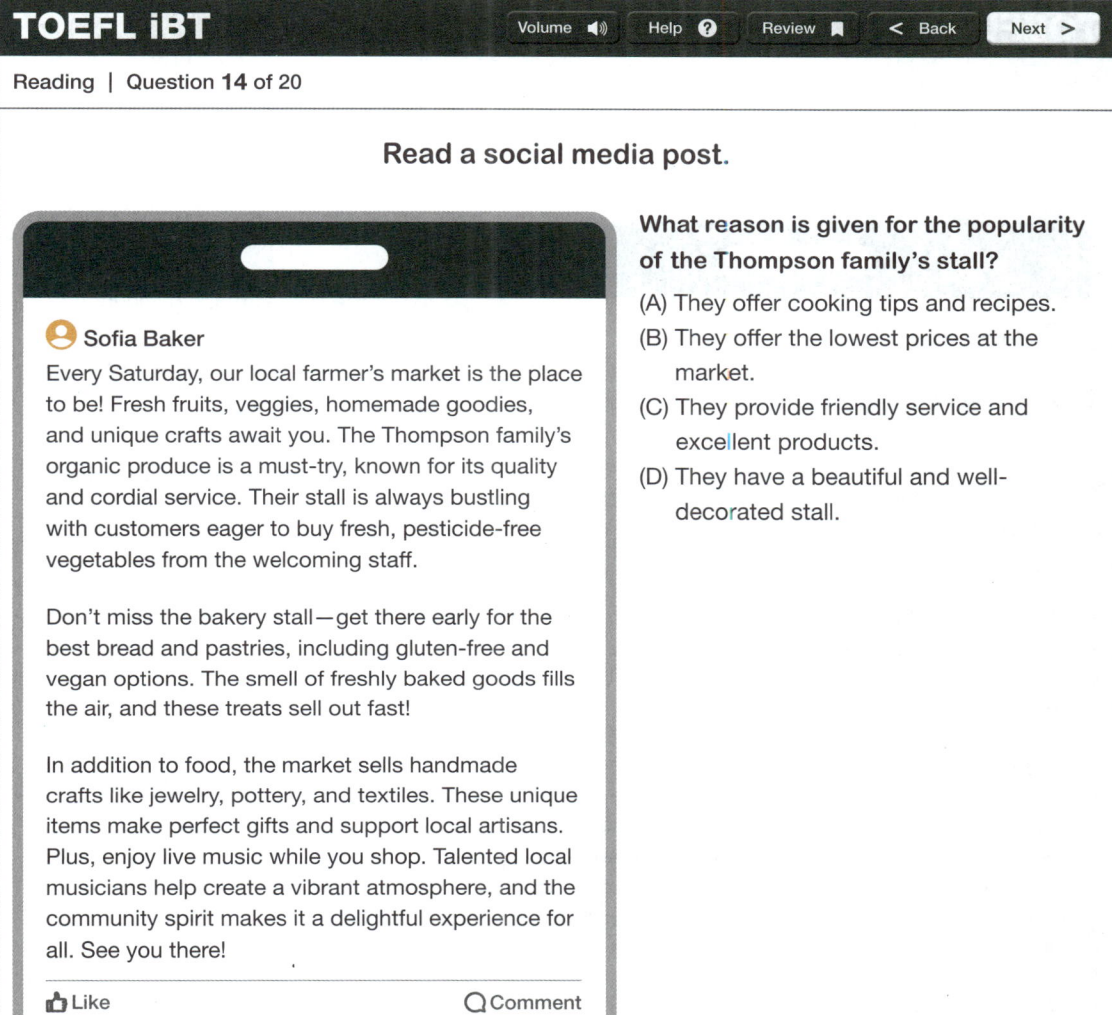

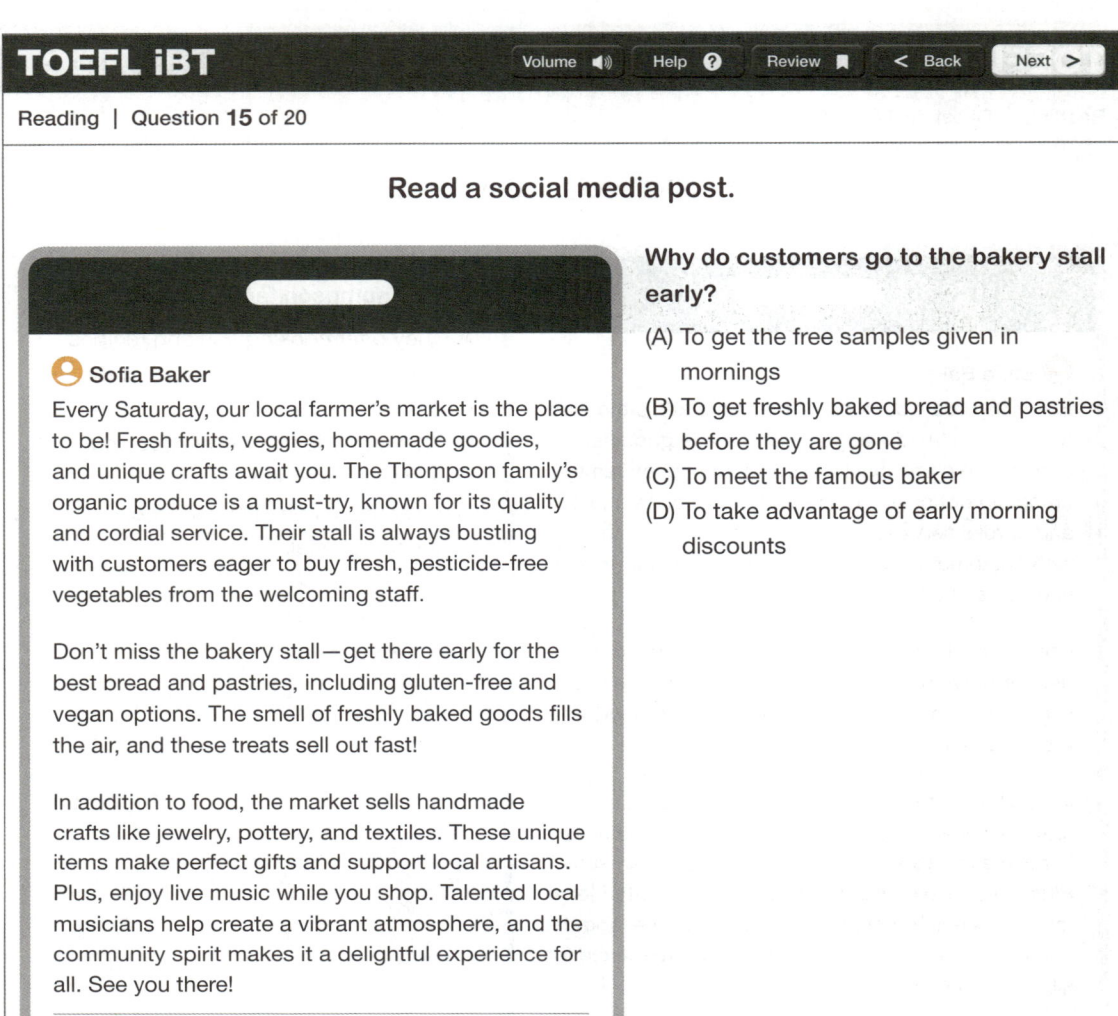

The Mirror Test

Very young children cannot recognize themselves in a mirror; they usually achieve this milestone around 18 months of age. The ability to recognize oneself in the mirror is considered to be a key component of self-awareness and consciousness for humans. But what about animals?

For many years, scientists have known that members of the great ape family could recognize themselves in mirrors. They measured this by the "mirror test," which involved putting a colored mark on an ape's body, and then showing the ape its reflection in a mirror. If the ape tried to remove the mark on its own body, the scientists knew that the ape was recognizing its reflection.

Apes are close relatives of humans, but in recent years, scientists have discovered that other animals also pass the "mirror test." Elephants and dolphins have shown signs of self-recognition. These, like apes, are highly intelligent animals. But in a more recent experiment, a type of fish called the cleaner fish tried to scrape a mark off its body when it saw itself in the mirror. This suggests that even less intelligent animals may possess more self-awareness than previously suspected.

What is the passage mainly about?

(A) Stages of early childhood development
(B) Research on animal cognition
(C) Differences between apes, elephants, and dolphins
(D) Recent experiments on fish

The Mirror Test

Very young children cannot recognize themselves in a mirror; they usually achieve this milestone around 18 months of age. The ability to recognize oneself in the mirror is considered to be a key component of self-awareness and consciousness for humans. But what about animals?

For many years, scientists have known that members of the great ape family could recognize themselves in mirrors. They measured this by the "mirror test," which involved putting a colored mark on an ape's body, and then showing the ape its reflection in a mirror. If the ape tried to remove the mark on its own body, the scientists knew that the ape was recognizing its reflection.

Apes are close relatives of humans, but in recent years, scientists have discovered that other animals also pass the "mirror test." Elephants and dolphins have shown signs of self-recognition. These, like apes, are highly intelligent animals. But in a more recent experiment, a type of fish called the cleaner fish tried to scrape a mark off its body when it saw itself in the mirror. This suggests that even less intelligent animals may possess more self-awareness than previously suspected.

The word "milestone" in the first sentence is closest in meaning to

(A) accomplishment
(B) distance
(C) weight
(D) discovery

The Mirror Test

Very young children cannot recognize themselves in a mirror; they usually achieve this milestone around 18 months of age. The ability to recognize oneself in the mirror is considered to be a key component of self-awareness and consciousness for humans. But what about animals?

For many years, scientists have known that members of the great ape family could recognize themselves in mirrors. They measured this by the "mirror test," which involved putting a colored mark on an ape's body, and then showing the ape its reflection in a mirror. If the ape tried to remove the mark on its own body, the scientists knew that the ape was recognizing its reflection.

Apes are close relatives of humans, but in recent years, scientists have discovered that other animals also pass the "mirror test." Elephants and dolphins have shown signs of self-recognition. These, like apes, are highly intelligent animals. But in a more recent experiment, a type of fish called the cleaner fish tried to scrape a mark off its body when it saw itself in the mirror. This suggests that even less intelligent animals may possess more self-awareness than previously suspected.

Why did scientists put colored marks on animals' bodies?

(A) It made it possible to track the animals' movements.
(B) It helped them determine whether the animals recognized themselves.
(C) It made it easier to tell the animals apart.
(D) It showed whether some animals can detect color differences.

The Mirror Test

Very young children cannot recognize themselves in a mirror; they usually achieve this milestone around 18 months of age. The ability to recognize oneself in the mirror is considered to be a key component of self-awareness and consciousness for humans. But what about animals?

For many years, scientists have known that members of the great ape family could recognize themselves in mirrors. They measured this by the "mirror test," which involved putting a colored mark on an ape's body, and then showing the ape its reflection in a mirror. If the ape tried to remove the mark on its own body, the scientists knew that the ape was recognizing its reflection.

Apes are close relatives of humans, but in recent years, scientists have discovered that other animals also pass the "mirror test." Elephants and dolphins have shown signs of self-recognition. These, like apes, are highly intelligent animals. But in a more recent experiment, a type of fish called the cleaner fish tried to scrape a mark off its body when it saw itself in the mirror. This suggests that even less intelligent animals may possess more self-awareness than previously suspected.

According to the passage, all of the following are true about elephants EXCEPT:

(A) They can recognize themselves in mirrors.
(B) They are highly intelligent animals.
(C) They possess qualities in common with apes.
(D) They understand certain signs from other animals.

The Mirror Test

Very young children cannot recognize themselves in a mirror; they usually achieve this milestone around 18 months of age. The ability to recognize oneself in the mirror is considered to be a key component of self-awareness and consciousness for humans. But what about animals?

For many years, scientists have known that members of the great ape family could recognize themselves in mirrors. They measured this by the "mirror test," which involved putting a colored mark on an ape's body, and then showing the ape its reflection in a mirror. If the ape tried to remove the mark on its own body, the scientists knew that the ape was recognizing its reflection.

Apes are close relatives of humans, but in recent years, scientists have discovered that other animals also pass the "mirror test." Elephants and dolphins have shown signs of self-recognition. These, like apes, are highly intelligent animals. But in a more recent experiment, a type of fish called the cleaner fish tried to scrape a mark off its body when it saw itself in the mirror. This suggests that even less intelligent animals may possess more self-awareness than previously suspected.

Why does the author mention cleaner fish?

(A) To suggest that a wide range of animals may possess self-awareness
(B) To imply that ocean animals are highly intelligent
(C) To demonstrate a flaw in a recent experiment
(D) To provide an example of an animal that does not recognize itself

Module 2

TOEFL iBT

Volume | Help | Review | Next

Reading | Questions **1–10** of 20

Fill in the missing letters in the paragraph.

The human brain is a complex organ responsible for controlling all bodily functions and enabling thought, emotion, and memory. It i_ divided in_ _ several reg_ _ _ _ , each wi_ _ specific ro_ _ _ . The cerebrum, i_ _ largest pa_ _ , is invo_ _ _ _ in cogn_ _ _ _ _ functions su_ _ as reasoning, planning, and language. The cerebellum coordinates movement and balance, while the brainstem controls vital bodily functions like breathing and heart rate. Together, they enable the brain to perform its various tasks.

TOEFL iBT

Volume | Help | Review | < Back | Next

Reading | Question **11** of 20

Read an email.

To:	edward56L@dmail.com
From:	artforeveryone@dmail.com
Date:	10/09/2025
Subject:	Art Workshop Reservation Confirmation

Dear Ms. Edwards,

The reservation for the art workshop that you made on September 10th has been confirmed. The workshop will take place on September 20th at 3:00 PM. All necessary arts supplies will be provided, but please bring your own apron or smock.

Best regards,
Laura Bennett

When is the date of the art workshop?

(A) September 10th
(B) September 12th
(C) September 20th
(D) September 30th

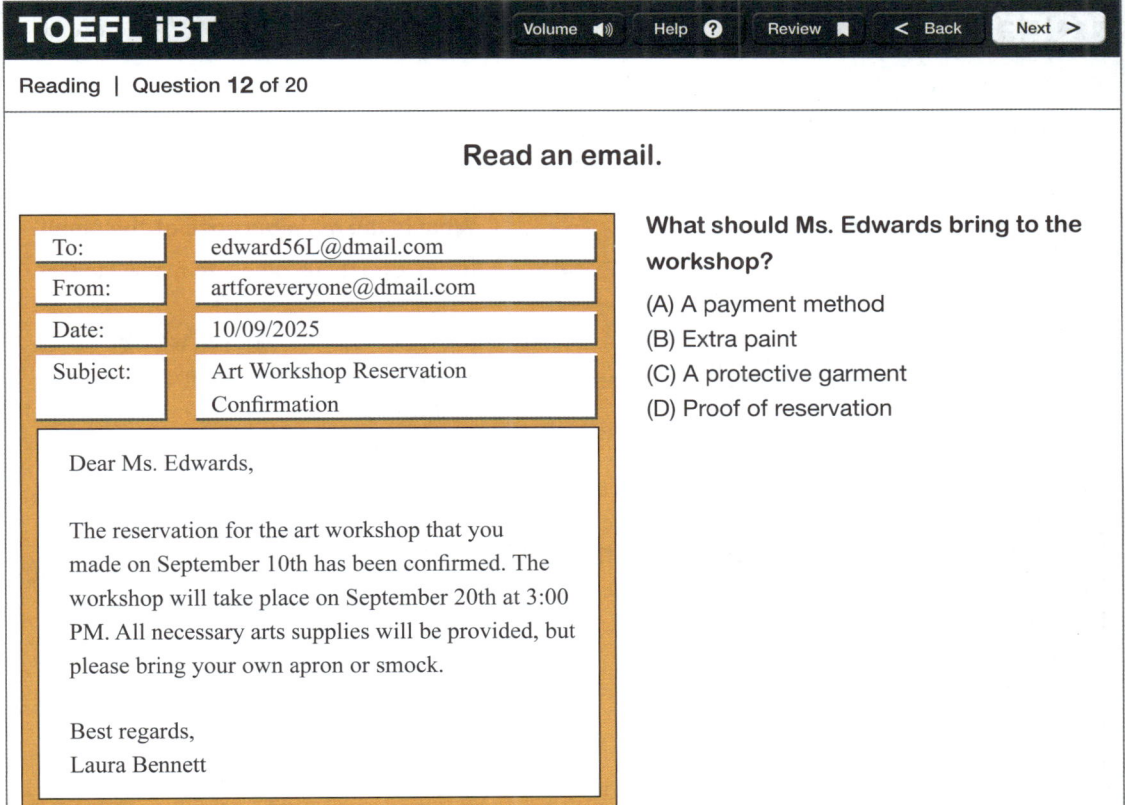

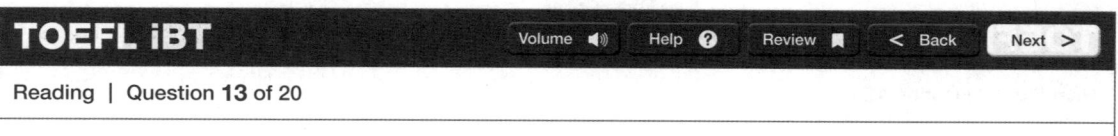

Read an email.

To:	nguyenbooklover@dmail.com
From:	part.gymworkers@dmail.com
Subject:	You're Invited - Bring Friends & Family to Our Grand Opening!

Dear Ms. Nguyen,

We're excited to invite you—and your friends and family—to the grand opening of our new branch at 25 Orchid Street, happening next Monday. This event is a great opportunity to explore our state-of-the-art facility, featuring top-tier equipment, energizing group classes, and expert personal training.

This celebration, exclusively for our valued members and their guests, will include guided tours, live fitness demonstrations, and complimentary refreshments. It's the perfect chance to experience our community-focused approach to wellness and introduce others to a space designed for all fitness levels.

Bring your friends and family! We're offering a special one-day-only discount on memberships for all attendees.

For questions or to RSVP, contact our customer service team at 555-1234.

Warm regards,
John Parker

What is the main purpose of the email?

(A) To attract customers to a new fitness center
(B) To provide Ms. Nguyen with an opportunity to provide expert personal training
(C) To celebrate Ms. Nguyen's achievements in wellness
(D) To announce a discount available to fitness-center members

Read an email.

To:	nguyenbooklover@dmail.com
From:	part.gymworkers@dmail.com
Subject:	You're Invited - Bring Friends & Family to Our Grand Opening!

Dear Ms. Nguyen,

We're excited to invite you—and your friends and family—to the grand opening of our new branch at 25 Orchid Street, happening next Monday. This event is a great opportunity to explore our state-of-the-art facility, featuring top-tier equipment, energizing group classes, and expert personal training.

This celebration, exclusively for our valued members and their guests, will include guided tours, live fitness demonstrations, and complimentary refreshments. It's the perfect chance to experience our community-focused approach to wellness and introduce others to a space designed for all fitness levels.

Bring your friends and family! We're offering a special one-day-only discount on memberships for all attendees.

For questions or to RSVP, contact our customer service team at 555-1234.

Warm regards,
John Parker

What can be inferred about Ms. Nguyen's relationship with the fitness center?

(A) She helps the fitness center to organize activities.
(B) She has already explored the new facility.
(C) She is a member at one of the fitness center's other locations.
(D) She is new to using fitness centers and exercise equipment.

Read an email.

To:	nguyenbooklover@dmail.com
From:	part.gymworkers@dmail.com
Subject:	You're Invited - Bring Friends & Family to Our Grand Opening!

Dear Ms. Nguyen,

We're excited to invite you—and your friends and family—to the grand opening of our new branch at 25 Orchid Street, happening next Monday. This event is a great opportunity to explore our state-of-the-art facility, featuring top-tier equipment, energizing group classes, and expert personal training.

This celebration, exclusively for our valued members and their guests, will include guided tours, live fitness demonstrations, and complimentary refreshments. It's the perfect chance to experience our community-focused approach to wellness and introduce others to a space designed for all fitness levels.

Bring your friends and family! We're offering a special one-day-only discount on memberships for all attendees.

For questions or to RSVP, contact our customer service team at 555-1234.

Warm regards,
John Parker

The new fitness center is intended for use by which of the following groups of people?

(A) Expert personal trainers
(B) Top-tier athletes
(C) Existing fitness-center members
(D) Community members of all fitness levels

The Paradox of Choice

The paradox of choice, a concept popularized by psychologist Barry Schwartz, suggests that more options can lead to less satisfaction. While the freedom to choose is fundamental to consumer culture, an overabundance of choices—from groceries to electronics—can overwhelm individuals, causing anxiety and decision fatigue. This paradox implies that the vast array of possibilities available today might actually diminish consumer contentment, as the fear of making the wrong choice looms large.

Research supports this notion. In an experiment, psychologist Sheena Iyengar found that shoppers were more likely to purchase jam when offered 6 varieties instead of 24. The limited selection eased the decision process, reducing the pressure to find the 'perfect' option and making the experience more enjoyable. This phenomenon reveals that fewer choices can sometimes make consumers happier, which is a valuable insight for marketers and retailers aiming to boost satisfaction by curating their offerings.

The paradox also has broader implications. In individualistic cultures, where personal choice is highly valued, the burden of decision-making can be significant. Conversely, collectivist cultures, which often provide fewer choices, report higher levels of contentment. This dynamic suggests that understanding cultural differences in consumer psychology can help businesses optimize their product strategies and enhance overall well-being.

Which of the following best states a main idea of the passage?

(A) Effective marketing strategies focus on increasing product options.
(B) Modern consumer culture is driven by a demand for fewer products.
(C) Individualism enhances consumer contentment.
(D) Limiting consumer choices can lead to higher satisfaction.

The Paradox of Choice

The paradox of choice, a concept popularized by psychologist Barry Schwartz, suggests that more options can lead to less satisfaction. While the freedom to choose is fundamental to consumer culture, an overabundance of choices—from groceries to electronics—can overwhelm individuals, causing anxiety and decision fatigue. This paradox implies that the vast array of possibilities available today might actually diminish consumer contentment, as the fear of making the wrong choice looms large.

Research supports this notion. In an experiment, psychologist Sheena Iyengar found that shoppers were more likely to purchase jam when offered 6 varieties instead of 24. The limited selection eased the decision process, reducing the pressure to find the 'perfect' option and making the experience more enjoyable. This phenomenon reveals that fewer choices can sometimes make consumers happier, which is a valuable insight for marketers and retailers aiming to boost satisfaction by curating their offerings.

The paradox also has broader implications. In individualistic cultures, where personal choice is highly valued, the burden of decision-making can be significant. Conversely, collectivist cultures, which often provide fewer choices, report higher levels of contentment. This dynamic suggests that understanding cultural differences in consumer psychology can help businesses optimize their product strategies and enhance overall well-being.

What is one effect of decision fatigue as mentioned in the passage?

(A) Desire to make the same choices as other consumers
(B) Anxiety about making the wrong choice
(C) Preference for consumer cultures
(D) Enhanced freedom to choose

The Paradox of Choice

The paradox of choice, a concept popularized by psychologist Barry Schwartz, suggests that more options can lead to less satisfaction. While the freedom to choose is fundamental to consumer culture, an overabundance of choices—from groceries to electronics—can overwhelm individuals, causing anxiety and decision fatigue. This paradox implies that the vast array of possibilities available today might actually diminish consumer contentment, as the fear of making the wrong choice looms large.

Research supports this notion. In an experiment, psychologist Sheena Iyengar found that shoppers were more likely to purchase jam when offered 6 varieties instead of 24. The limited selection eased the decision process, reducing the pressure to find the 'perfect' option and making the experience more enjoyable. This phenomenon reveals that fewer choices can sometimes make consumers happier, which is a valuable insight for marketers and retailers aiming to boost satisfaction by curating their offerings.

The paradox also has broader implications. In individualistic cultures, where personal choice is highly valued, the burden of decision-making can be significant. Conversely, collectivist cultures, which often provide fewer choices, report higher levels of contentment. This dynamic suggests that understanding cultural differences in consumer psychology can help businesses optimize their product strategies and enhance overall well-being.

Why does the author mention Sheena Iyengar's experiment?

(A) To highlight the effectiveness of marketing strategies
(B) To explain the methodology used in consumer psychology
(C) To provide evidence supporting the paradox of choice
(D) To criticize the abundance of products in modern markets

The Paradox of Choice

The paradox of choice, a concept popularized by psychologist Barry Schwartz, suggests that more options can lead to less satisfaction. While the freedom to choose is fundamental to consumer culture, an overabundance of choices—from groceries to electronics—can overwhelm individuals, causing anxiety and decision fatigue. This paradox implies that the vast array of possibilities available today might actually diminish consumer contentment, as the fear of making the wrong choice looms large.

Research supports this notion. In an experiment, psychologist Sheena Iyengar found that shoppers were more likely to purchase jam when offered 6 varieties instead of 24. The limited selection eased the decision process, reducing the pressure to find the 'perfect' option and making the experience more enjoyable. This phenomenon reveals that fewer choices can sometimes make consumers happier, which is a valuable insight for marketers and retailers aiming to boost satisfaction by curating their offerings.

The paradox also has broader implications. In individualistic cultures, where personal choice is highly valued, the burden of decision-making can be significant. Conversely, collectivist cultures, which often provide fewer choices, report higher levels of contentment. This dynamic suggests that understanding cultural differences in consumer psychology can help businesses optimize their product strategies and enhance overall well-being.

The word "curating" in the passage is closest in meaning to

(A) eliminating
(B) organizing
(C) increasing
(D) changing

The Paradox of Choice

The paradox of choice, a concept popularized by psychologist Barry Schwartz, suggests that more options can lead to less satisfaction. While the freedom to choose is fundamental to consumer culture, an overabundance of choices—from groceries to electronics—can overwhelm individuals, causing anxiety and decision fatigue. This paradox implies that the vast array of possibilities available today might actually diminish consumer contentment, as the fear of making the wrong choice looms large.

Research supports this notion. In an experiment, psychologist Sheena Iyengar found that shoppers were more likely to purchase jam when offered 6 varieties instead of 24. The limited selection eased the decision process, reducing the pressure to find the 'perfect' option and making the experience more enjoyable. This phenomenon reveals that fewer choices can sometimes make consumers happier, which is a valuable insight for marketers and retailers aiming to boost satisfaction by curating their offerings.

The paradox also has broader implications. In individualistic cultures, where personal choice is highly valued, the burden of decision-making can be significant. Conversely, collectivist cultures, which often provide fewer choices, report higher levels of contentment. This dynamic suggests that understanding cultural differences in consumer psychology can help businesses optimize their product strategies and enhance overall well-being.

What can be inferred about consumers in collectivist cultures?

(A) They tend to report lower levels of satisfaction.
(B) They are more affected by the paradox of choice.
(C) They generally have fewer choices available.
(D) They prefer individual decision-making.

LISTENING

TOEFL iBT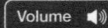

Listening Section

In the listening section, you will answer 35 to 45 questions to demonstrate how well you understand spoken English. There are three types of tasks.

Type of Task	Description
Listen and Choose a Response	Select the best response to the question or statement.
Conversations	Answer questions about short conversations.
Announcements and Academic Talks	Answer questions about announcements and academic talks.

You WILL NOT be able to return to previous questions.

Module 1

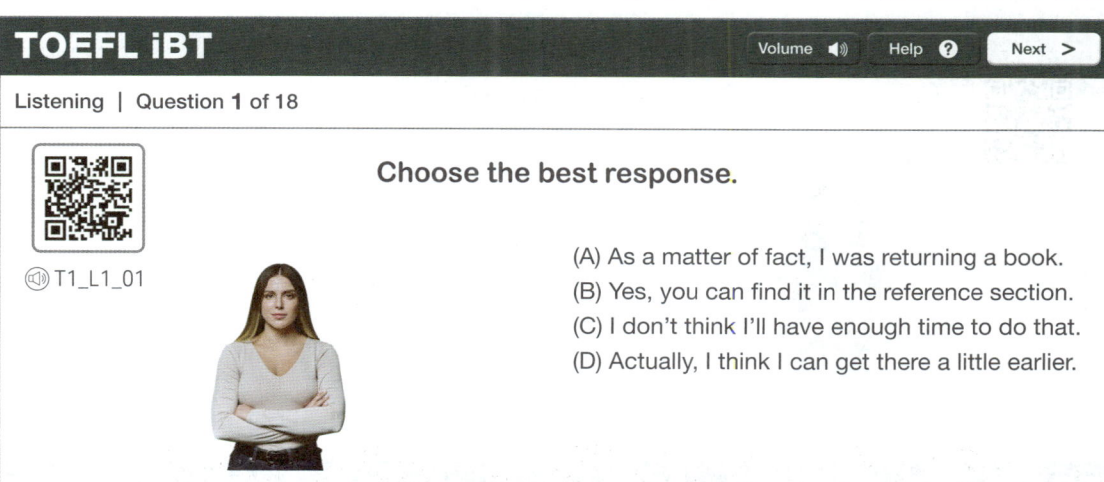

Listening | Question **1** of 18

🔊 T1_L1_01

Choose the best response.

(A) As a matter of fact, I was returning a book.
(B) Yes, you can find it in the reference section.
(C) I don't think I'll have enough time to do that.
(D) Actually, I think I can get there a little earlier.

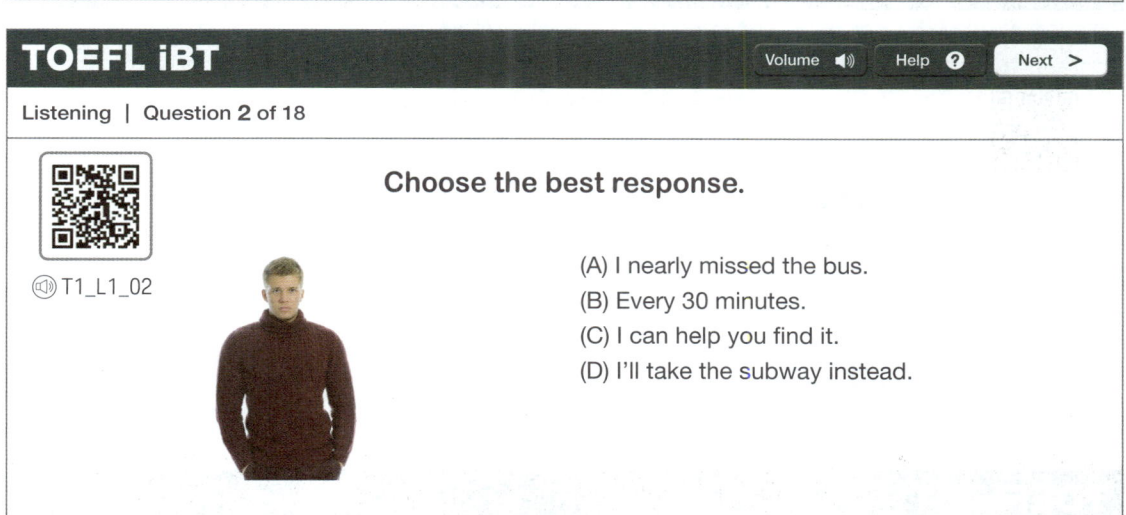

Listening | Question **2** of 18

🔊 T1_L1_02

Choose the best response.

(A) I nearly missed the bus.
(B) Every 30 minutes.
(C) I can help you find it.
(D) I'll take the subway instead.

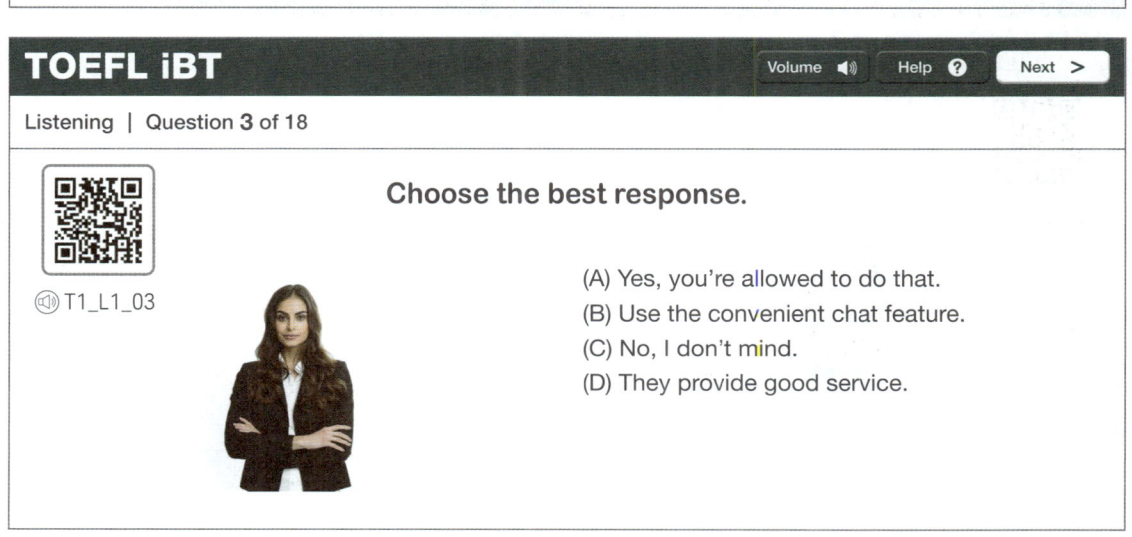

Listening | Question **3** of 18

🔊 T1_L1_03

Choose the best response.

(A) Yes, you're allowed to do that.
(B) Use the convenient chat feature.
(C) No, I don't mind.
(D) They provide good service.

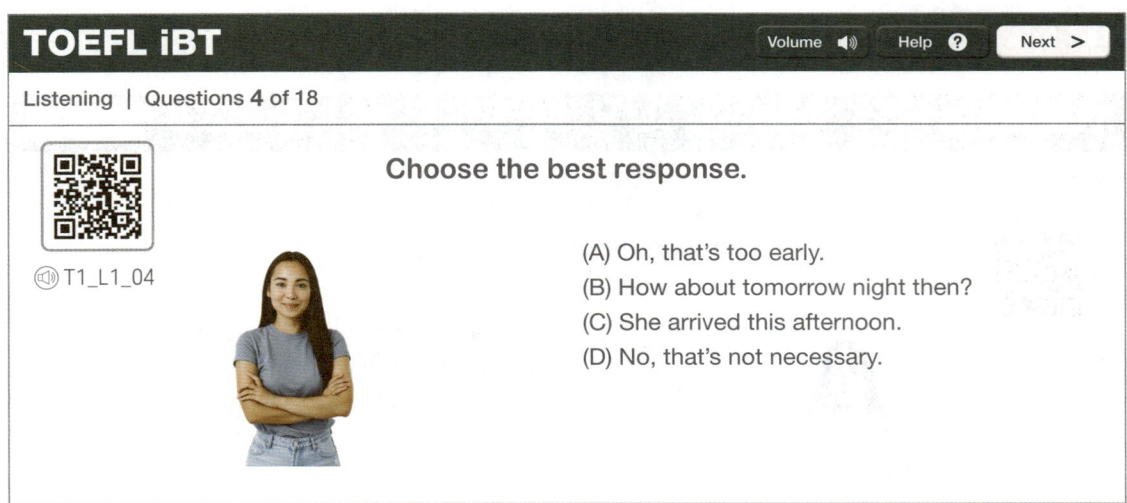

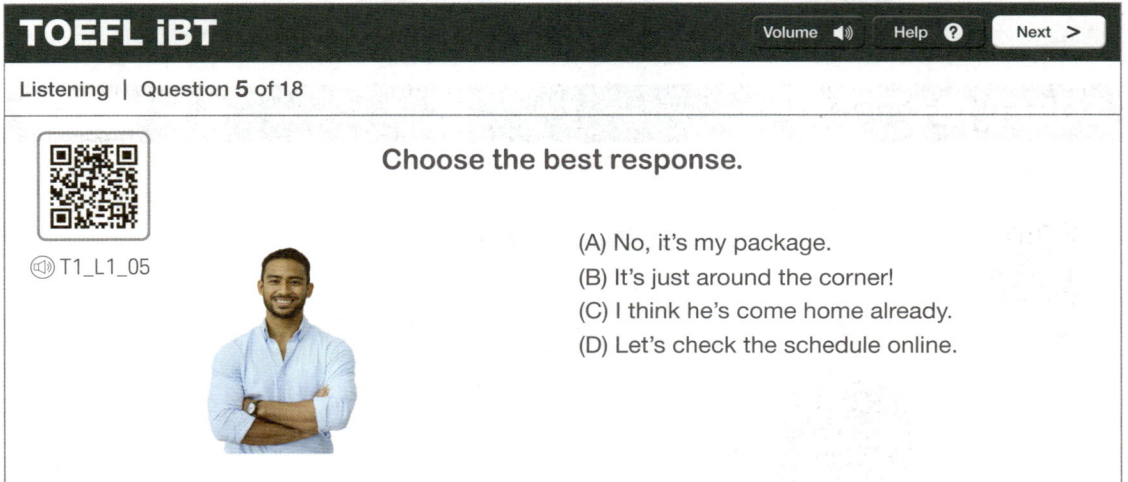

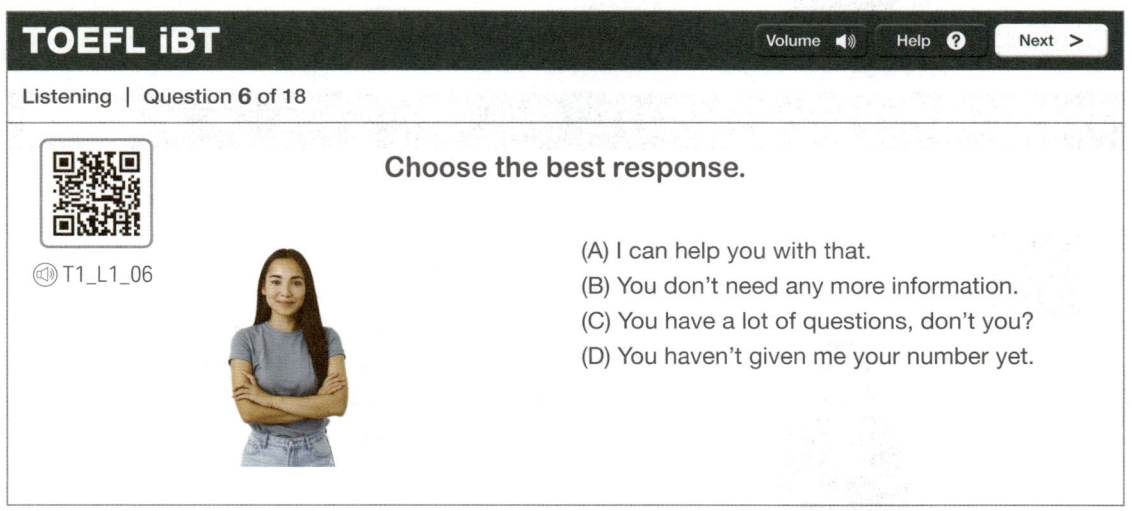

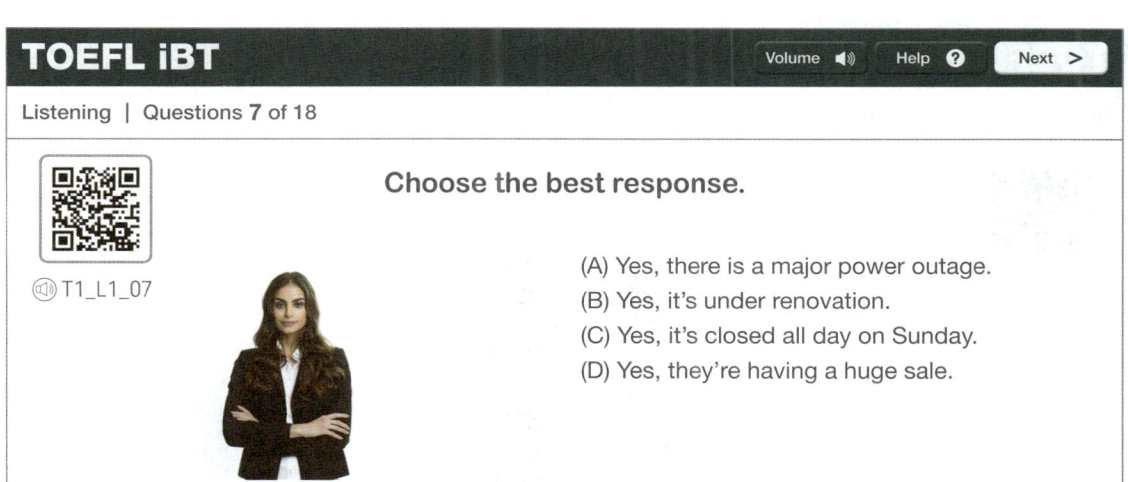

Choose the best response.

(A) Yes, there is a major power outage.
(B) Yes, it's under renovation.
(C) Yes, it's closed all day on Sunday.
(D) Yes, they're having a huge sale.

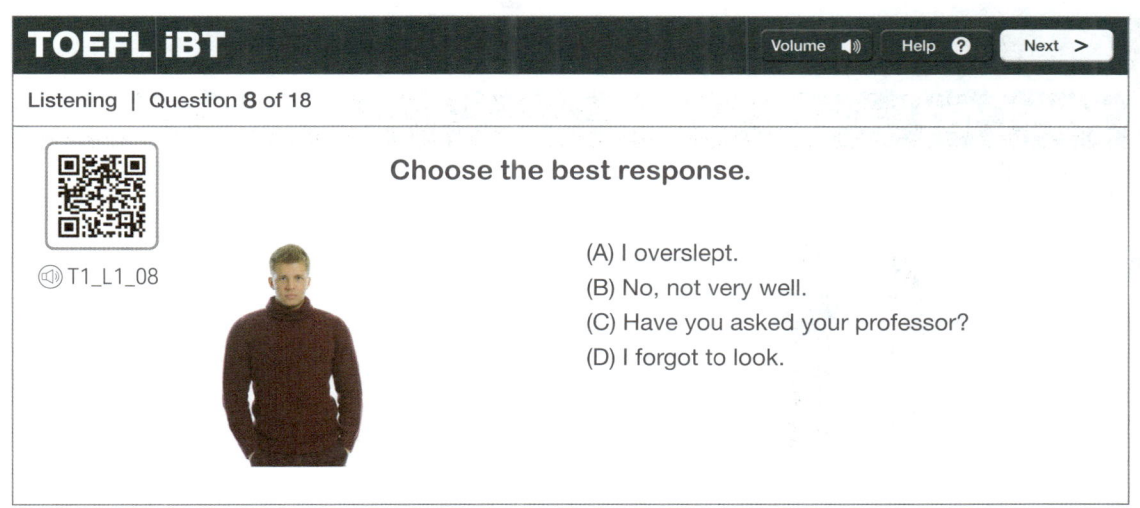

Choose the best response.

(A) I overslept.
(B) No, not very well.
(C) Have you asked your professor?
(D) I forgot to look.

TOEFL iBT

Listening | Questions **9–10** of 18

T1_L1_0910

Listen to a conversation.

TOEFL iBT

Listening | Question **9** of 18

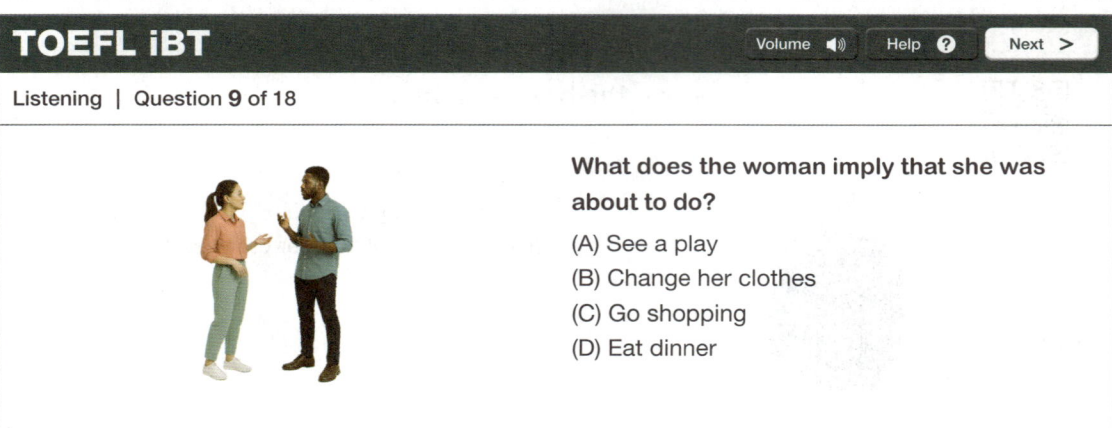

What does the woman imply that she was about to do?

(A) See a play
(B) Change her clothes
(C) Go shopping
(D) Eat dinner

TOEFL iBT

Listening | Question **10** of 18

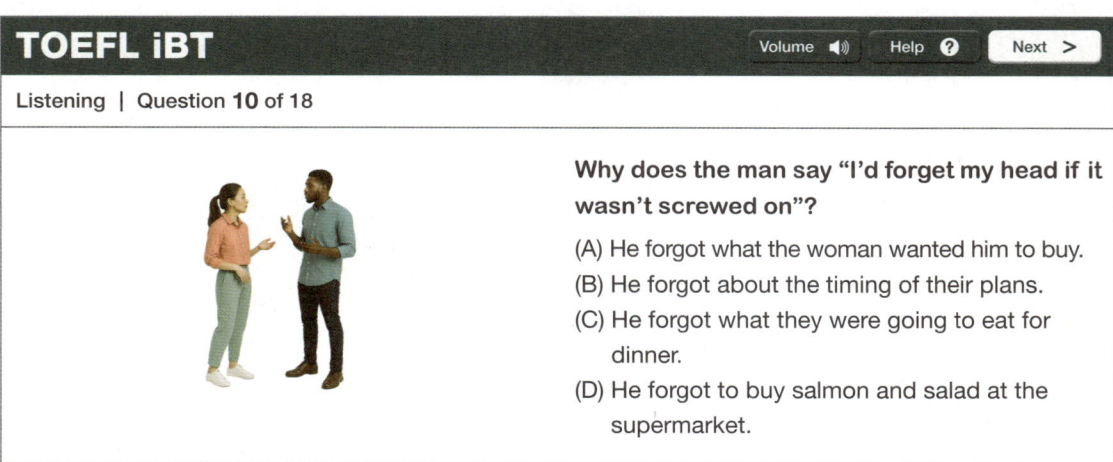

Why does the man say "I'd forget my head if it wasn't screwed on"?

(A) He forgot what the woman wanted him to buy.
(B) He forgot about the timing of their plans.
(C) He forgot what they were going to eat for dinner.
(D) He forgot to buy salmon and salad at the supermarket.

TOEFL iBT

Listening | Questions **11–12** of 18

Listen to a conversation.

T1_L1_1112

TOEFL iBT

Listening | Question **11** of 18

Why did the woman call a technician?

(A) An air-conditioner is leaking.
(B) A room is too hot.
(C) An elevator needs maintenance.
(D) A window will not open.

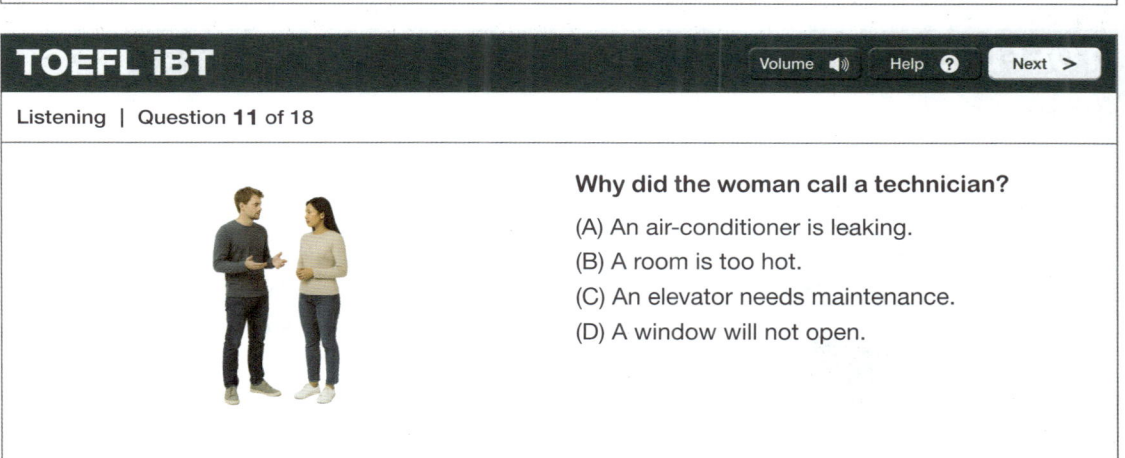

TOEFL iBT

Listening | Question **12** of 18

What does the woman suggest the man do?

(A) Finish an assignment early
(B) Wait for a service agent
(C) Open a door
(D) Take a break early

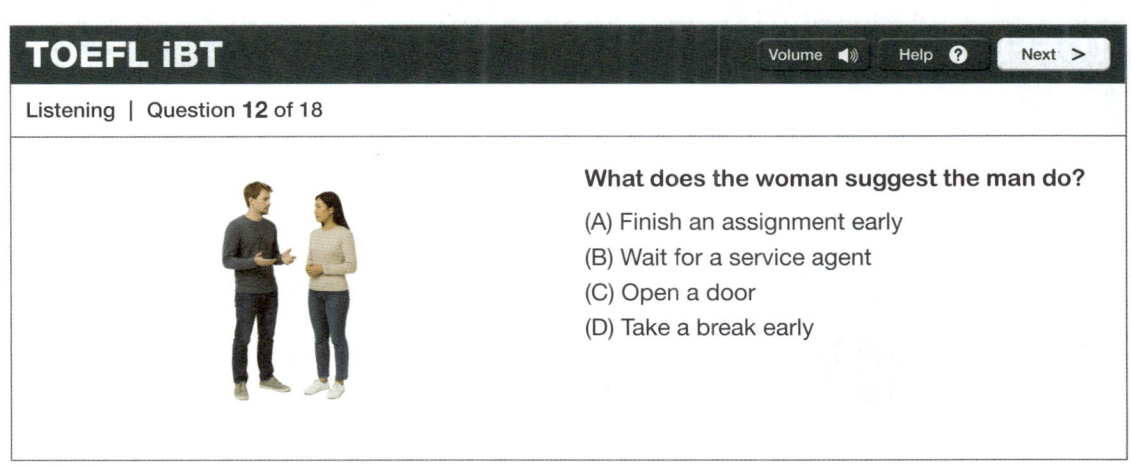

TOEFL iBT

Listening | Questions 13–14 of 18

Listen to an announcement in a classroom.

T1_L1_1314

TOEFL iBT

Listening | Question 13 of 18

What is the announcement about?

(A) A guest lecture
(B) A different location for a class
(C) Requirements for a class
(D) A new university science course

TOEFL iBT

Listening | Question 14 of 18

Why does the professor mention Dr. Palmer's popularity?

(A) To encourage students to read her work
(B) To indicate why she was invited to the university
(C) To compare her to other invited experts
(D) To explain why students should arrive early

TOEFL iBT

Listening | Questions 15–18 of 18

Listen to a talk on a podcast about psychology.

T1_L1_1518

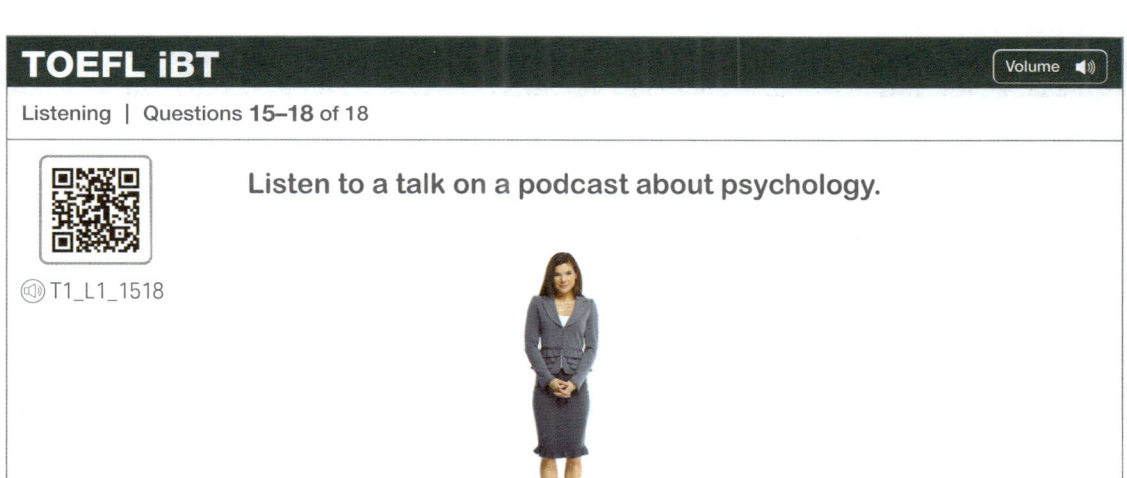

TOEFL iBT

Listening | Question 15 of 18

What is the topic of the talk?

(A) How psychologists study attention
(B) How to keep the mind focused
(C) Two types of fascination
(D) The benefits of hard fascination

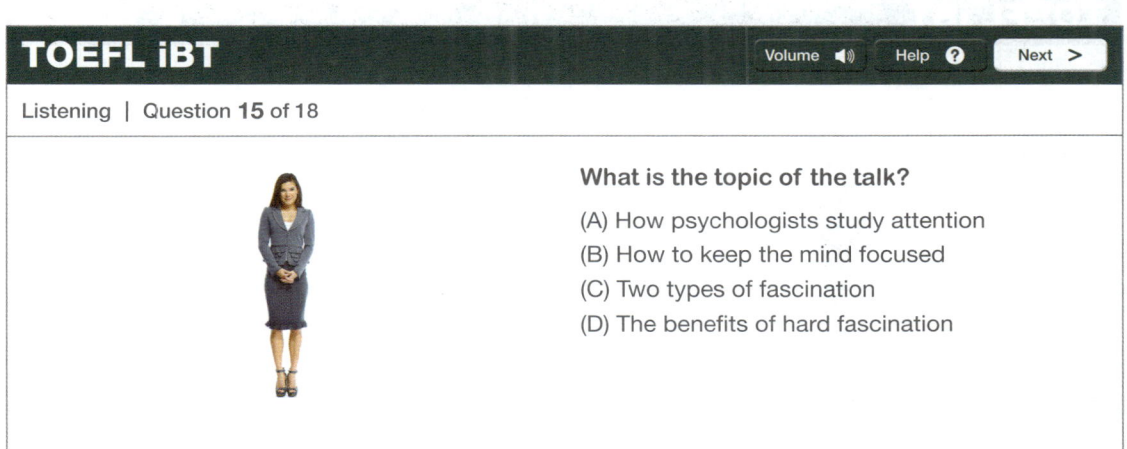

TOEFL iBT

Listening | Question 16 of 18

Why does the speaker mention a movie?

(A) To compare different types of movies
(B) To introduce a concept in psychology
(C) To explain how movies affect emotions
(D) To encourage listeners to watch more movies

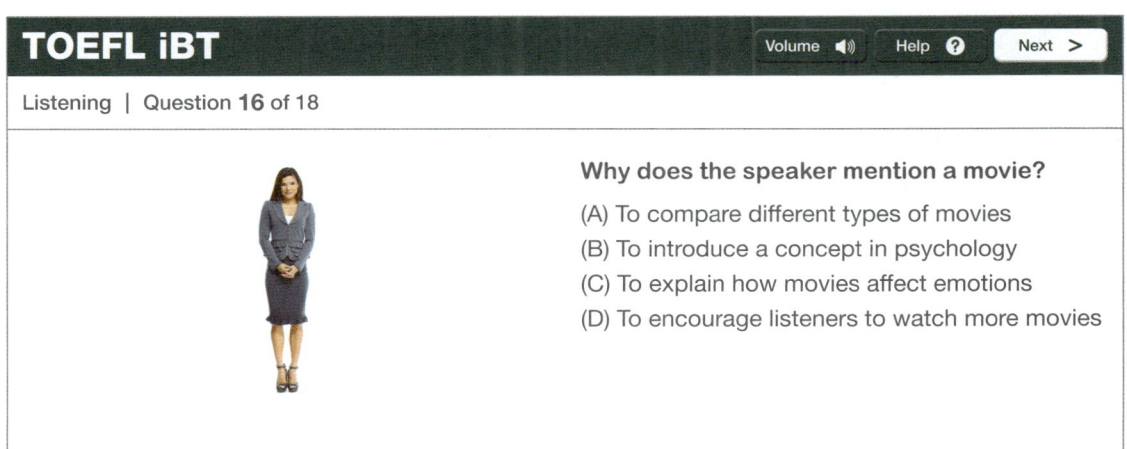

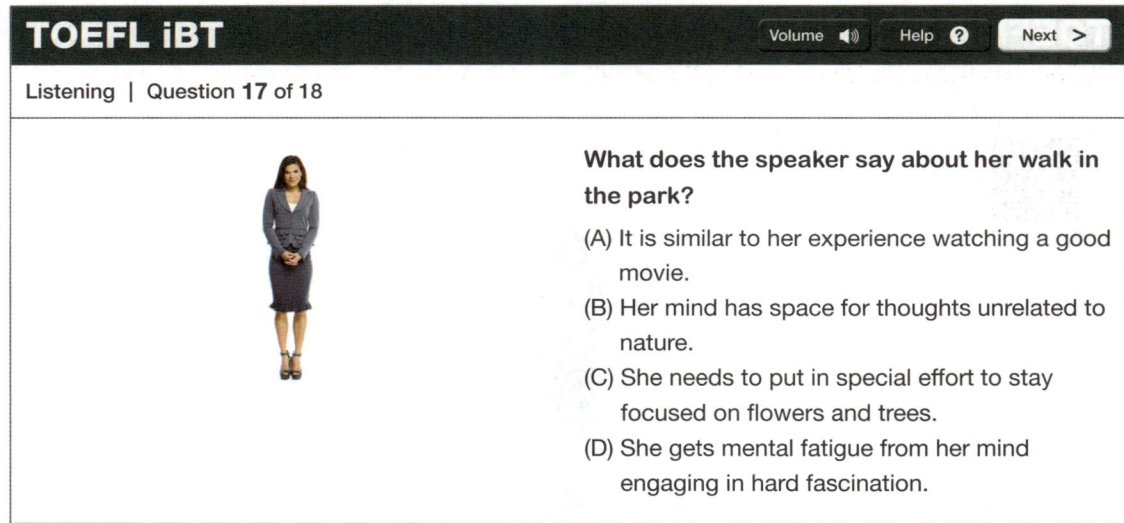

What does the speaker say about her walk in the park?

(A) It is similar to her experience watching a good movie.
(B) Her mind has space for thoughts unrelated to nature.
(C) She needs to put in special effort to stay focused on flowers and trees.
(D) She gets mental fatigue from her mind engaging in hard fascination.

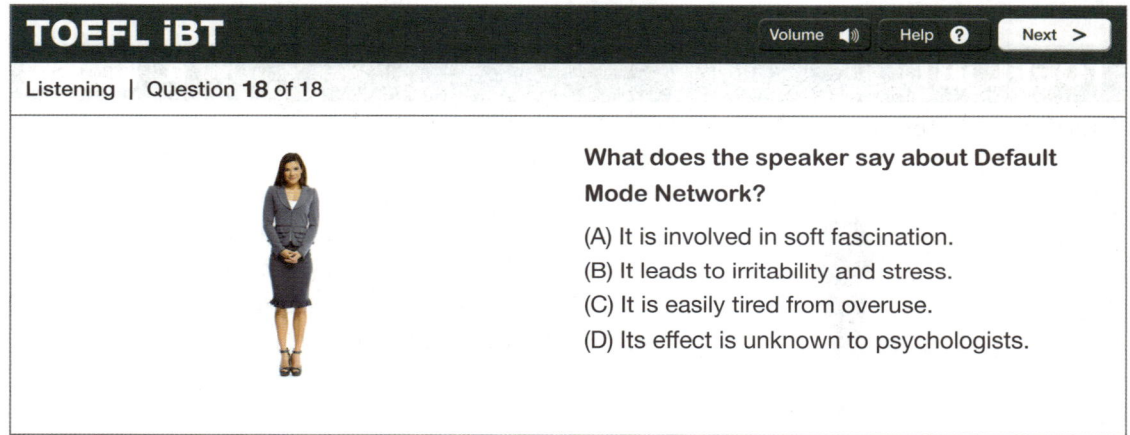

What does the speaker say about Default Mode Network?

(A) It is involved in soft fascination.
(B) It leads to irritability and stress.
(C) It is easily tired from overuse.
(D) Its effect is unknown to psychologists.

Module 2

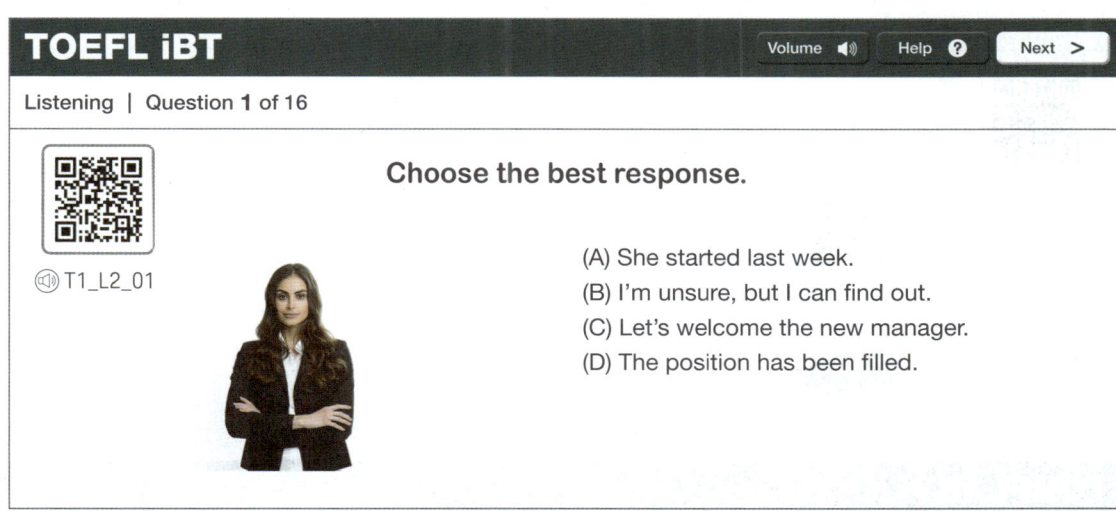

Listening | Question 1 of 16

T1_L2_01

Choose the best response.

(A) She started last week.
(B) I'm unsure, but I can find out.
(C) Let's welcome the new manager.
(D) The position has been filled.

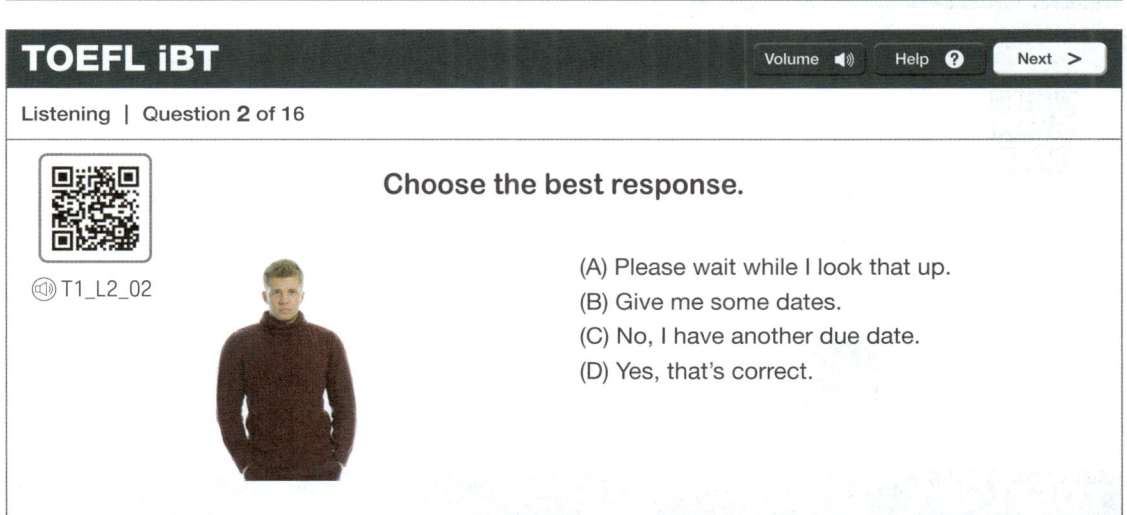

Listening | Question 2 of 16

T1_L2_02

Choose the best response.

(A) Please wait while I look that up.
(B) Give me some dates.
(C) No, I have another due date.
(D) Yes, that's correct.

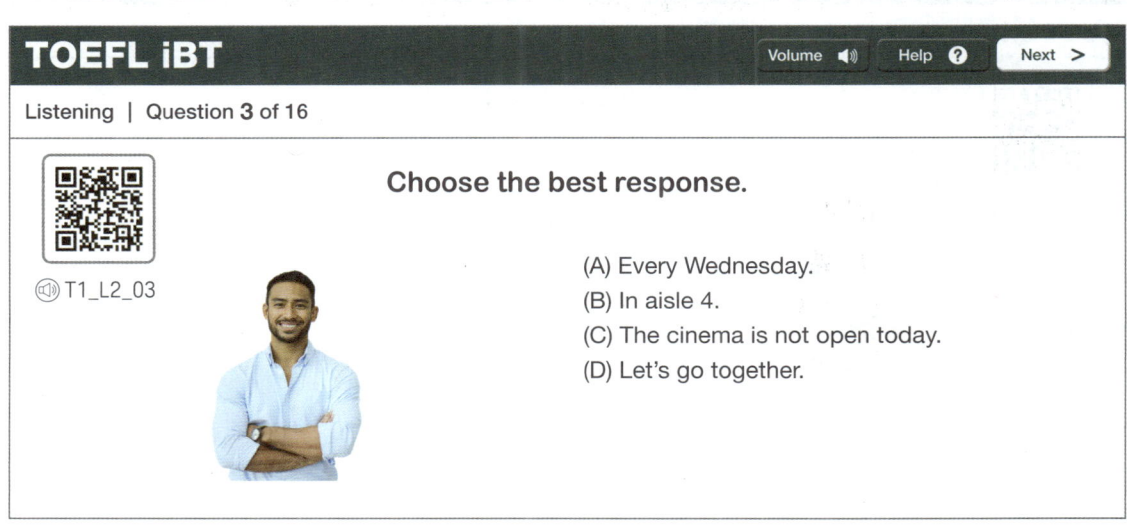

Listening | Question 3 of 16

T1_L2_03

Choose the best response.

(A) Every Wednesday.
(B) In aisle 4.
(C) The cinema is not open today.
(D) Let's go together.

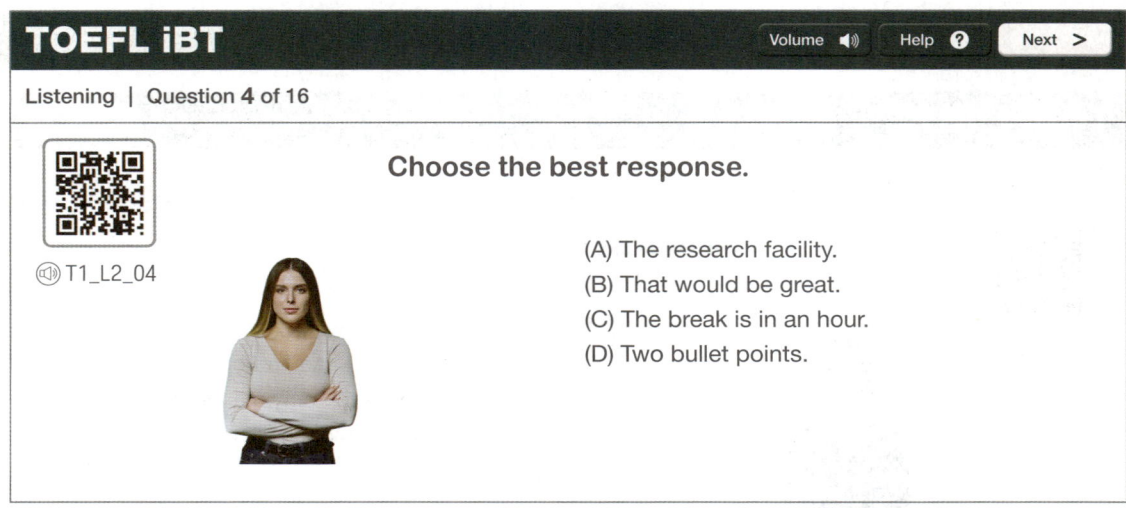

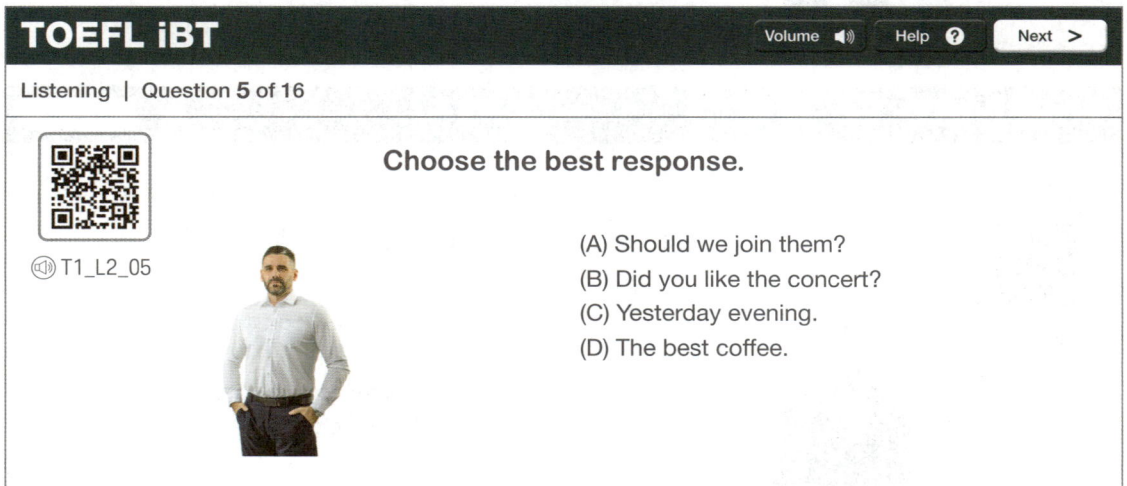

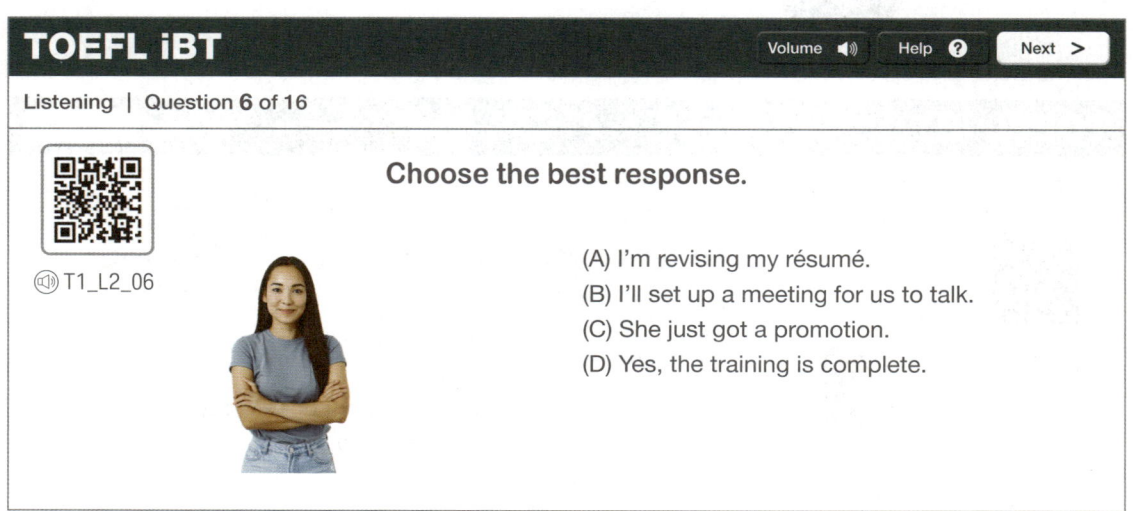

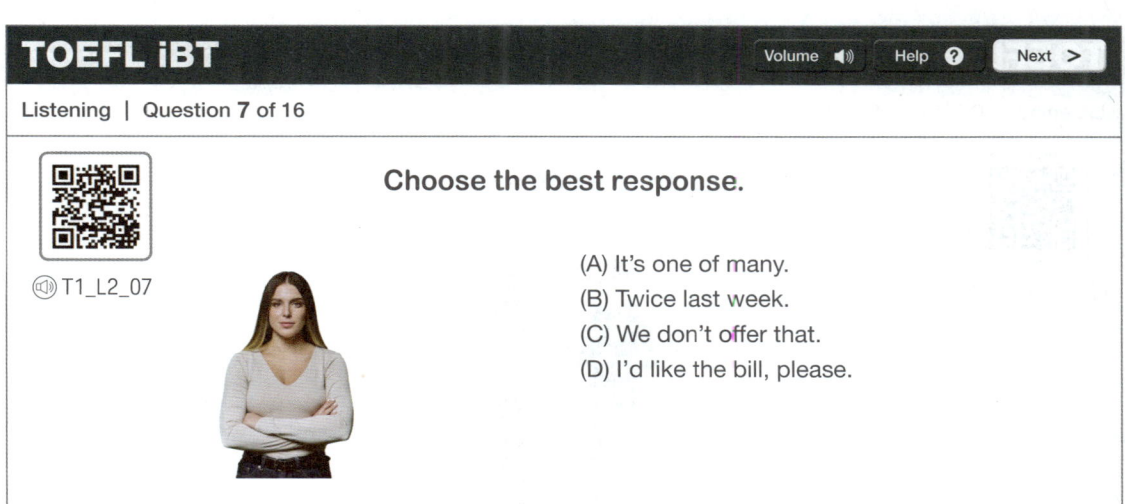

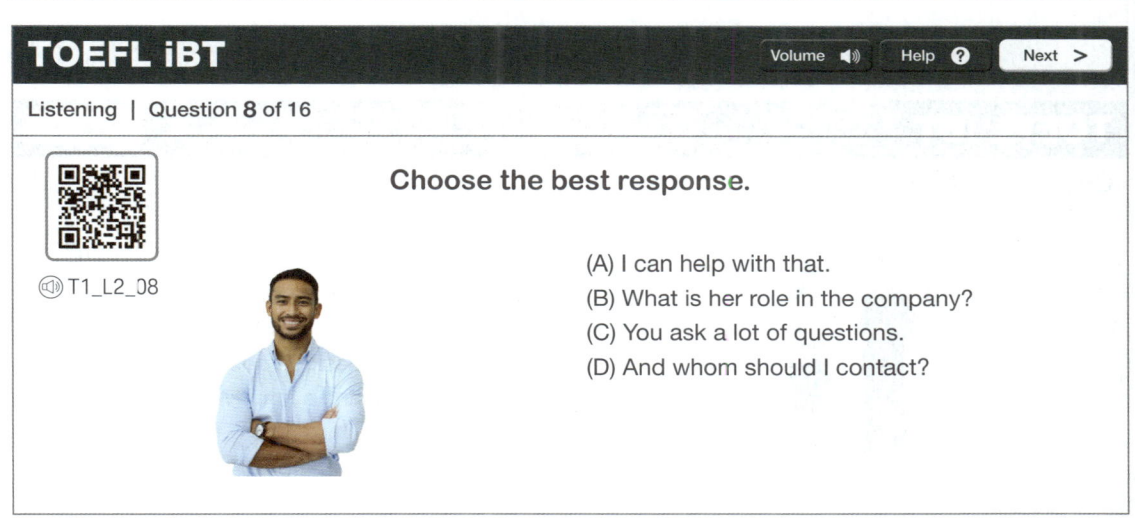

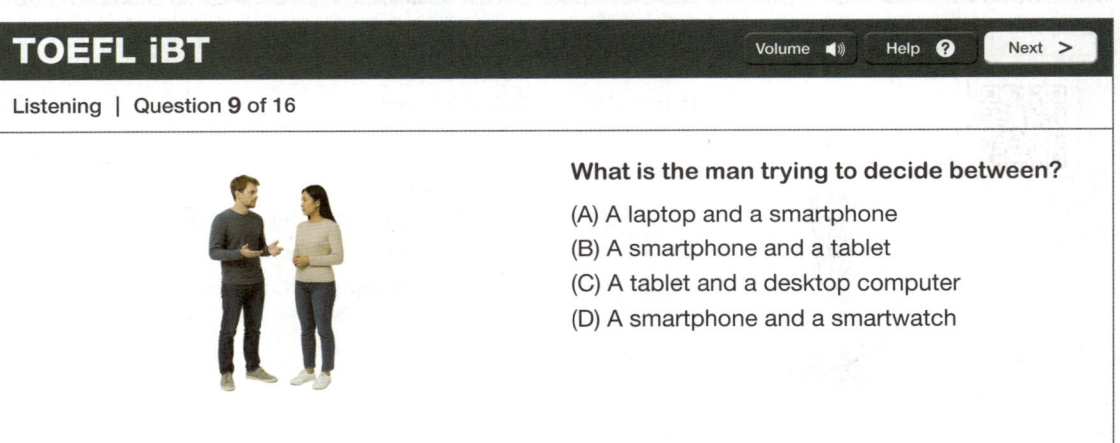

What is the man trying to decide between?

(A) A laptop and a smartphone
(B) A smartphone and a tablet
(C) A tablet and a desktop computer
(D) A smartphone and a smartwatch

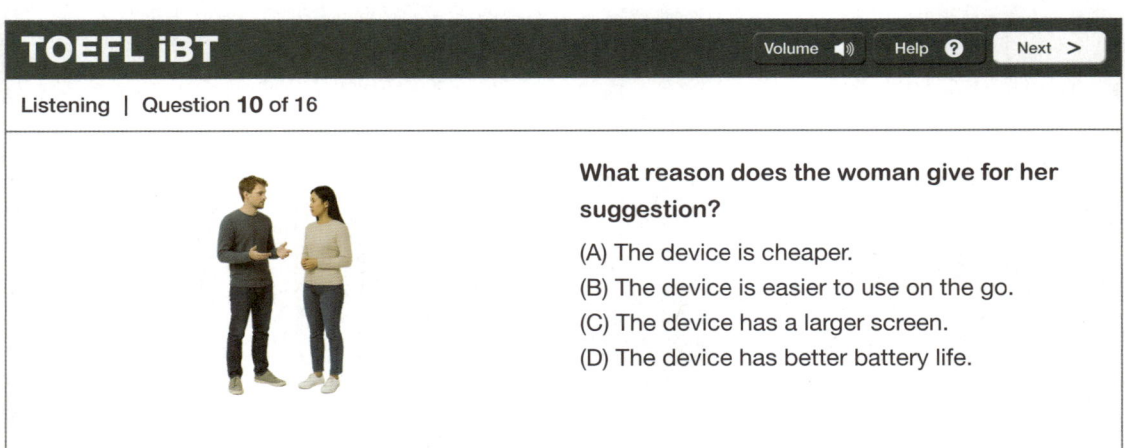

What reason does the woman give for her suggestion?

(A) The device is cheaper.
(B) The device is easier to use on the go.
(C) The device has a larger screen.
(D) The device has better battery life.

TOEFL iBT

Listening | Questions **11–12** of 16

Listen to an announcement in a student lounge.

T1_L2_1112

TOEFL iBT

Listening | Question **11** of 16

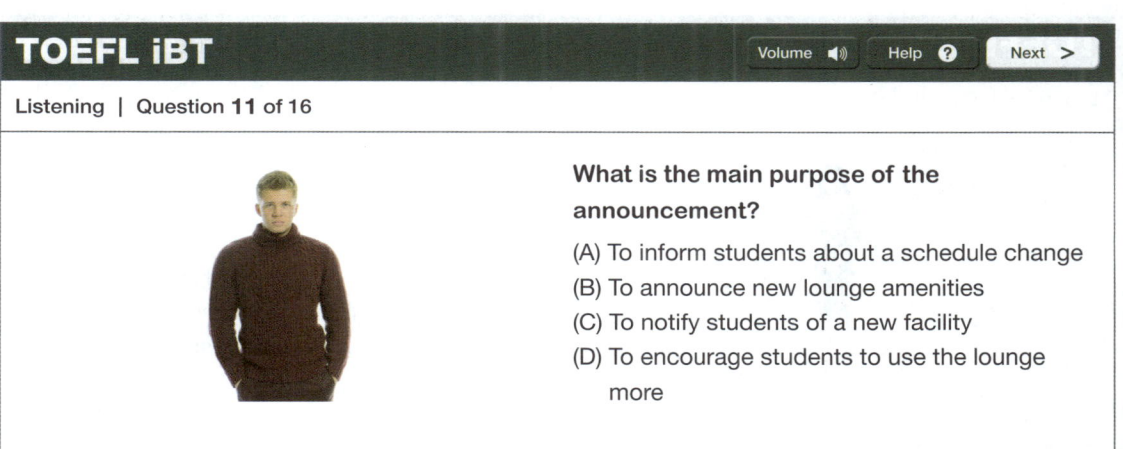

What is the main purpose of the announcement?

(A) To inform students about a schedule change
(B) To announce new lounge amenities
(C) To notify students of a new facility
(D) To encourage students to use the lounge more

TOEFL iBT

Listening | Question **12** of 16

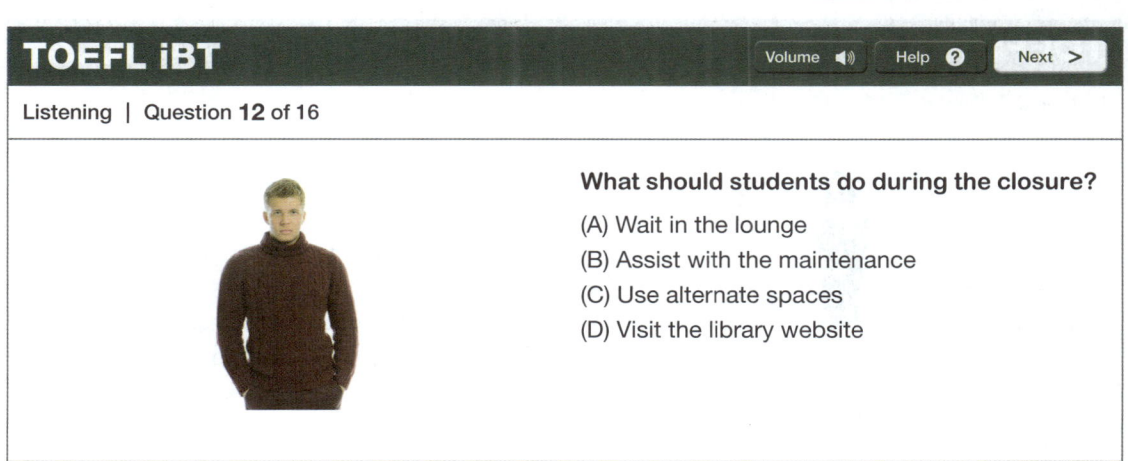

What should students do during the closure?

(A) Wait in the lounge
(B) Assist with the maintenance
(C) Use alternate spaces
(D) Visit the library website

TOEFL iBT

Listening | Questions **13–16** of 16

Listen to a talk in an environmental science class.

T1_L2_1316

TOEFL iBT

Listening | Question **13** of 16

What is the main topic of the talk?

(A) Changes in consumption in societies over time
(B) A measure of environmental impact
(C) Environmentally damaging activities
(D) The role of governments in sustainability

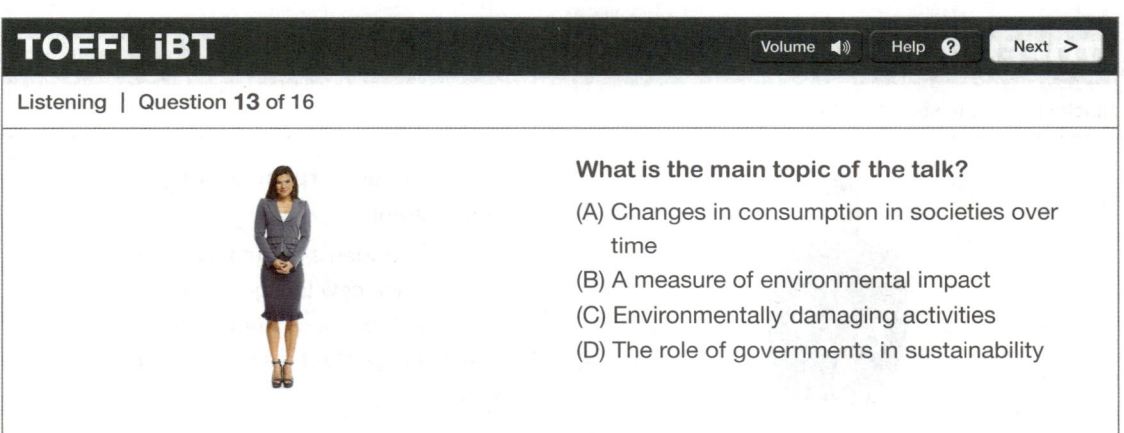

TOEFL iBT

Listening | Question **14** of 16

Why does the speaker mention developed and developing countries?

(A) To contradict a theory related to the ecological footprint
(B) To show that resource depletion can be similar regardless of lifestyle
(C) To illustrate the usefulness of comparing ecological footprints
(D) To point out that production efficiency reduces the ecological footprint

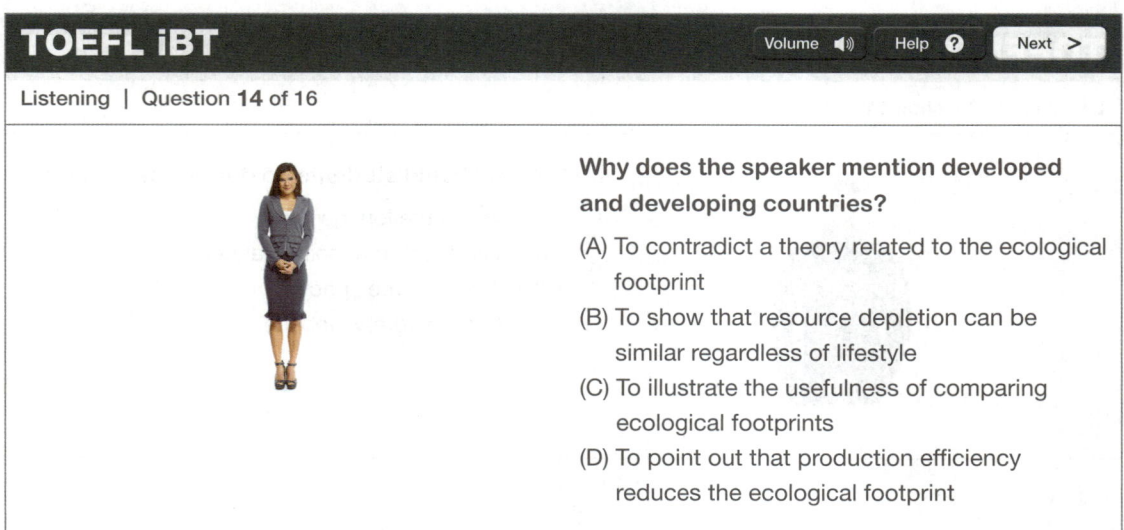

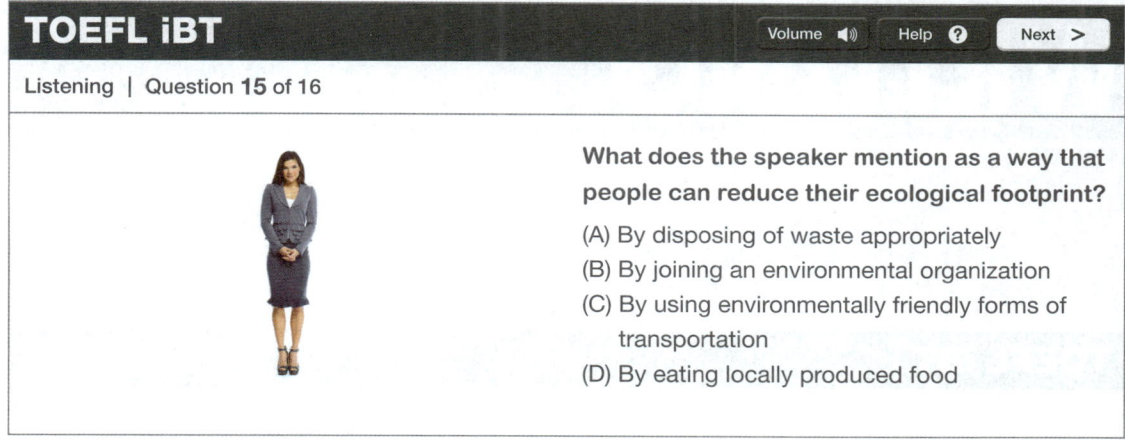

What does the speaker mention as a way that people can reduce their ecological footprint?

(A) By disposing of waste appropriately
(B) By joining an environmental organization
(C) By using environmentally friendly forms of transportation
(D) By eating locally produced food

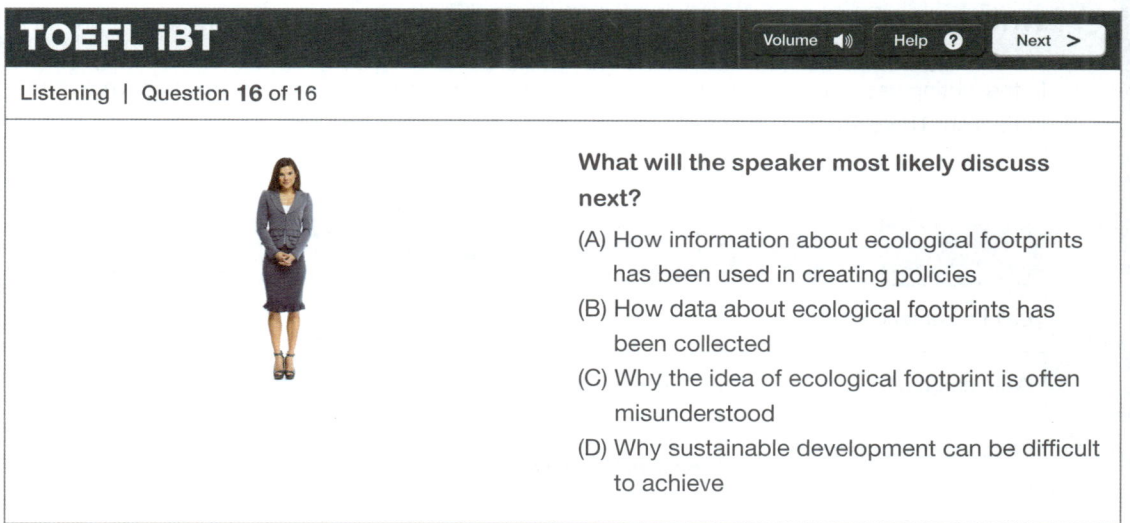

What will the speaker most likely discuss next?

(A) How information about ecological footprints has been used in creating policies
(B) How data about ecological footprints has been collected
(C) Why the idea of ecological footprint is often misunderstood
(D) Why sustainable development can be difficult to achieve

WRITING

TOEFL iBT

Writing Section

In the writing section, you will answer 12 questions to demonstrate how well you can write in English. There are three types of tasks.

Type of Task	Description
Build a Sentence	Create a grammatical sentence.
Write an Email	Write an email using information provided.
Write for an Academic Discussion	Participate in an online discussion.

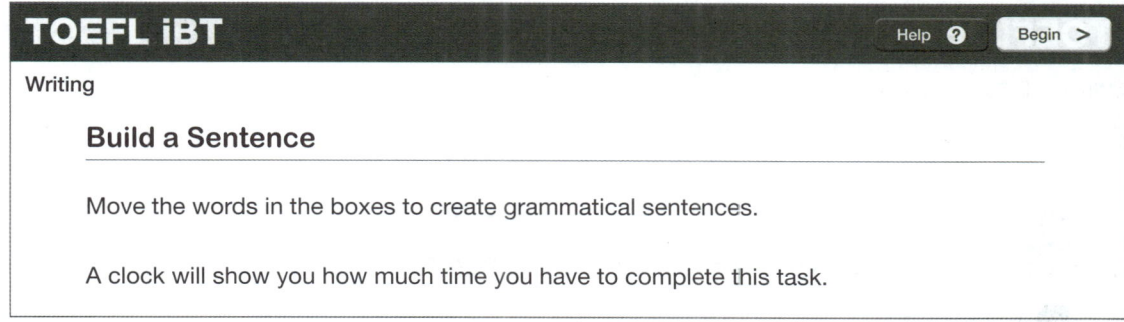

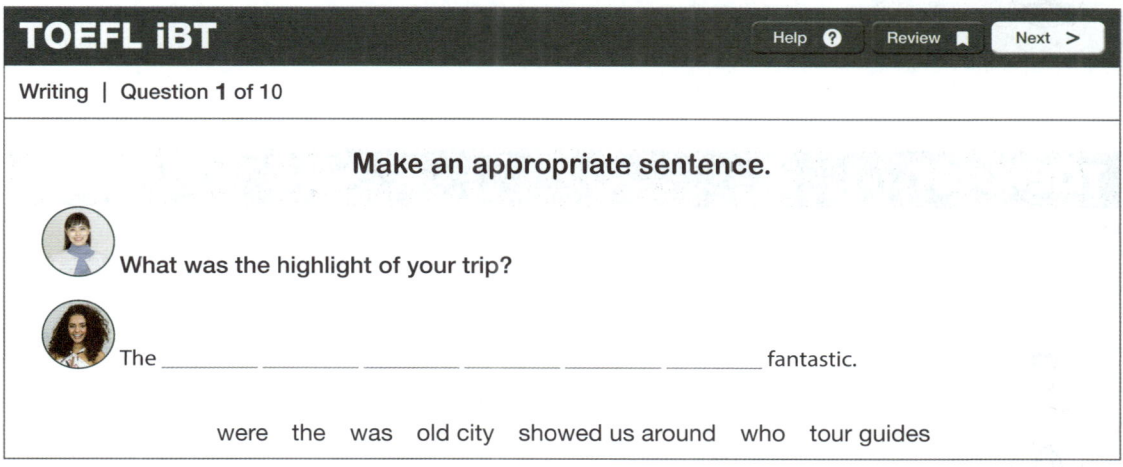

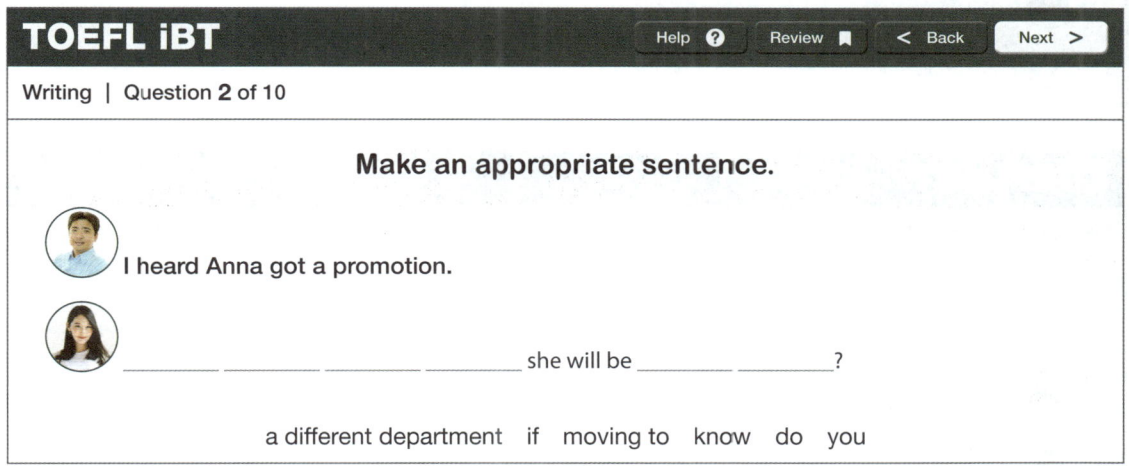

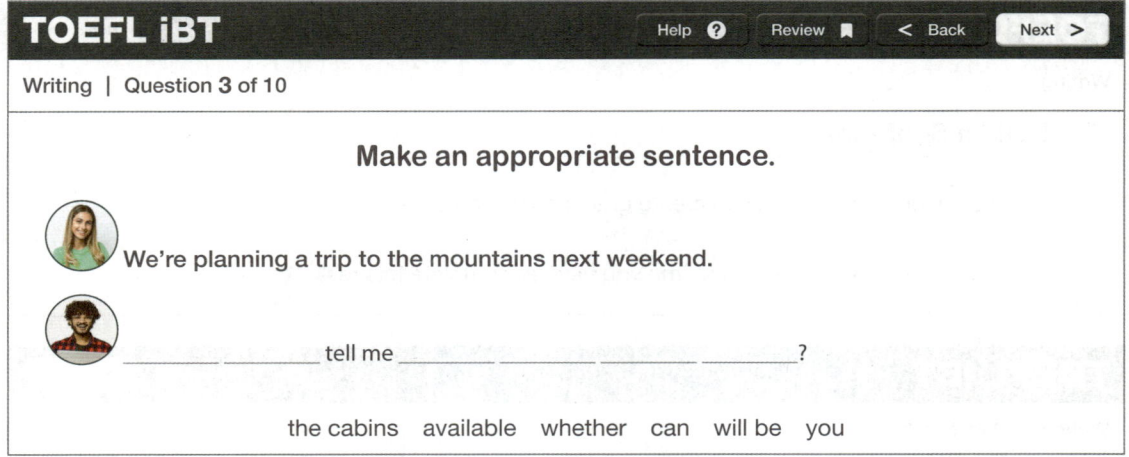

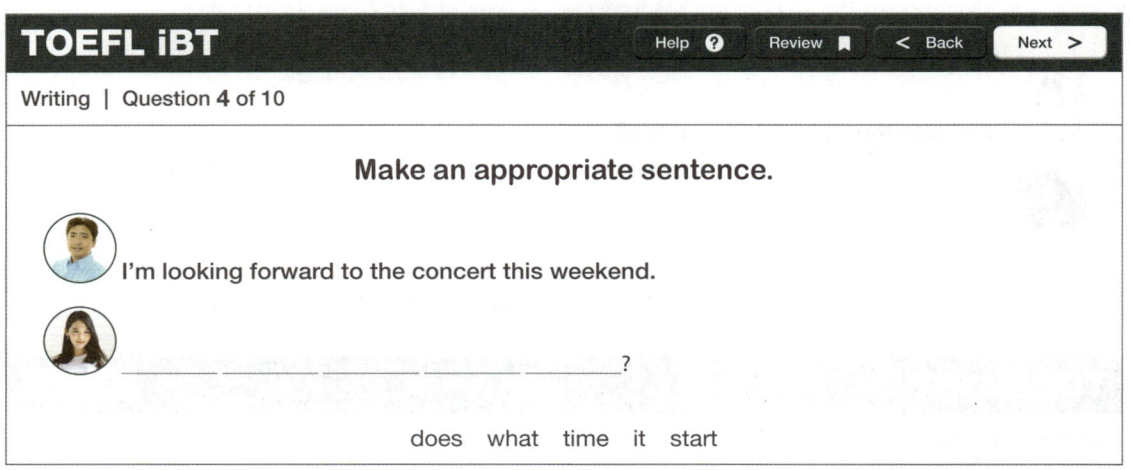

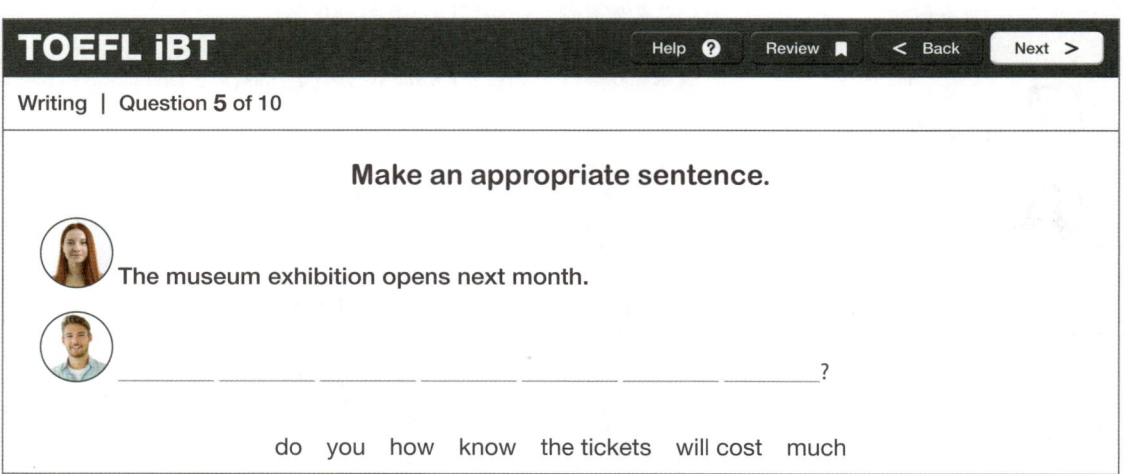

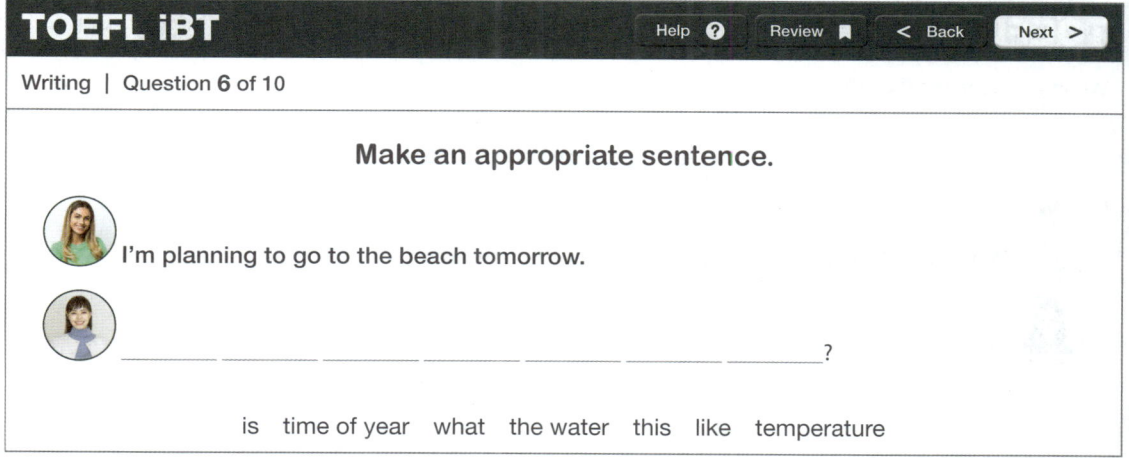

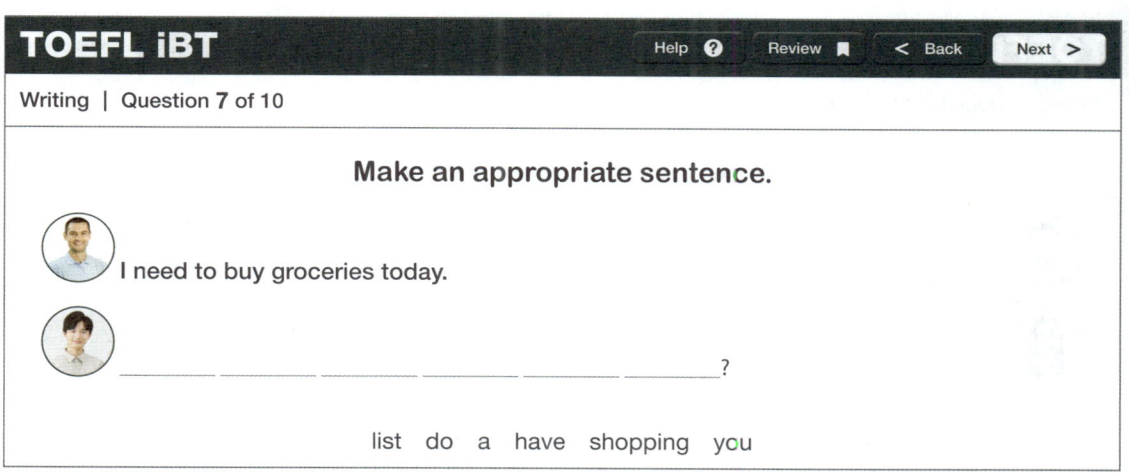

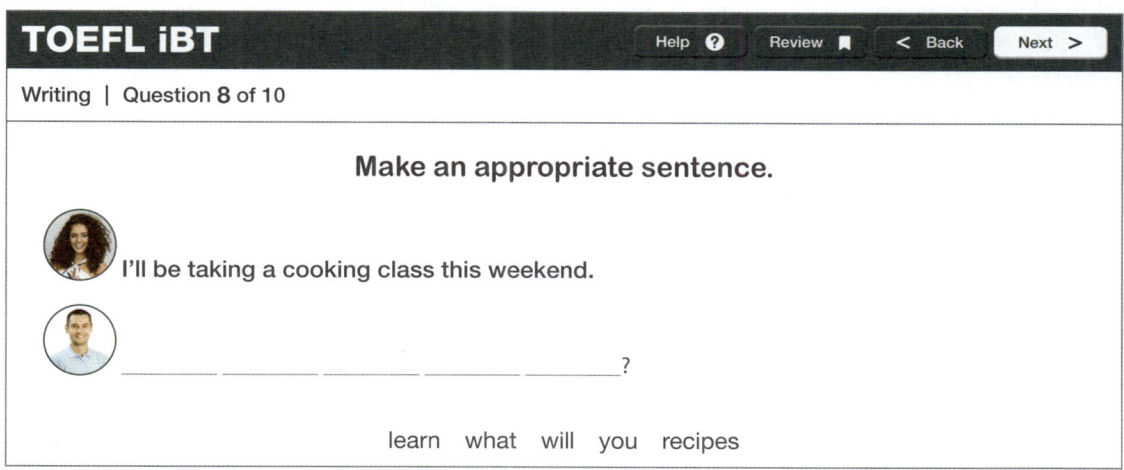

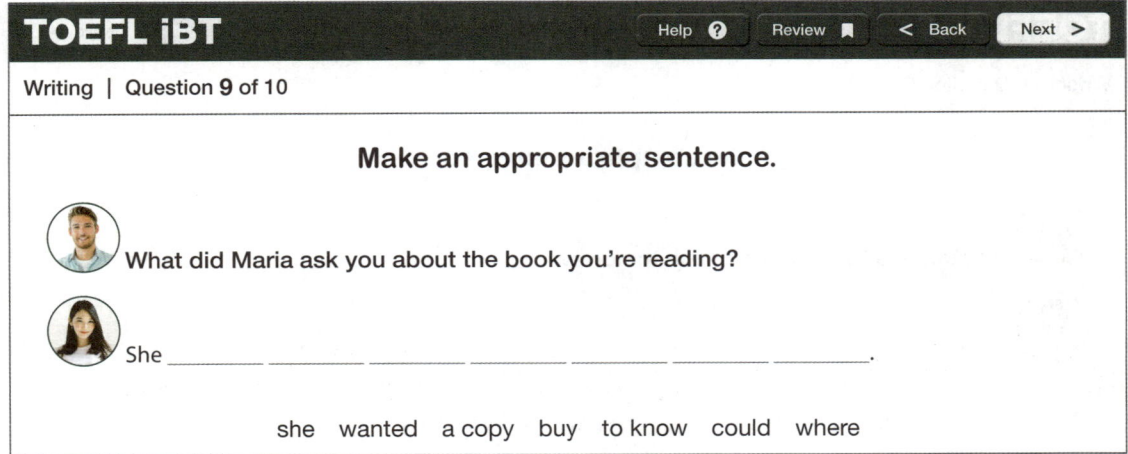

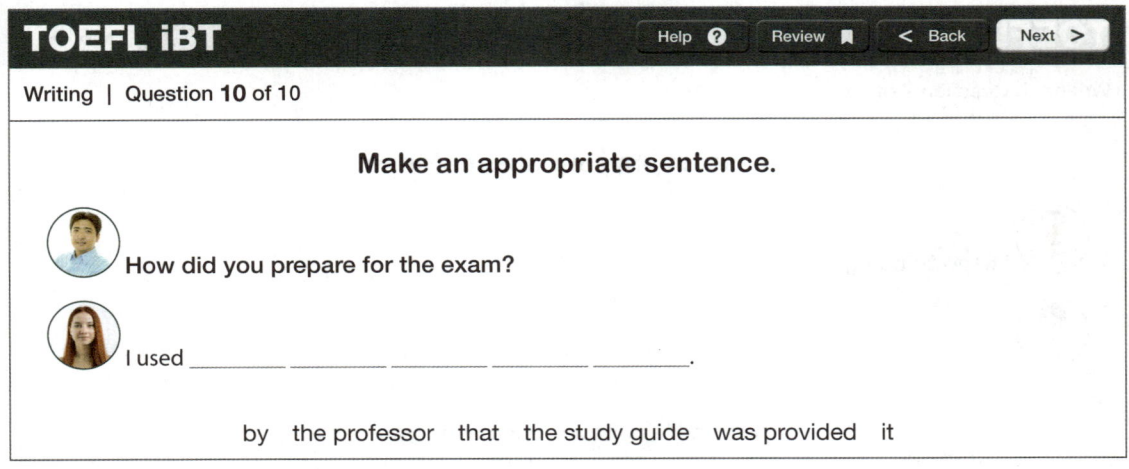

TEST 1
TEST 2
TEST 3

TOEFL iBT

Help ? Begin >

Writing

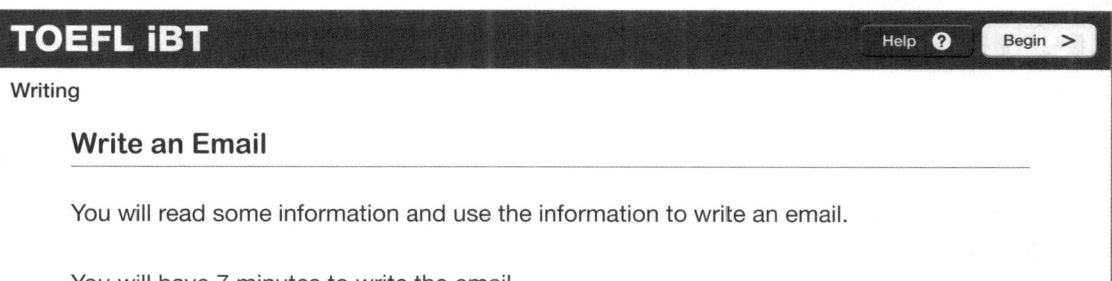

Write an Email

You will read some information and use the information to write an email.

You will have 7 minutes to write the email.

TOEFL iBT

Help ? Next >

Writing

A new poetry magazine has asked its readers for submissions, and you decided to submit two of your poems. However, you had a problem using the online submission form, and you are not certain that your submissions were received.

Write an email to the editor of the magazine. In your email, do the following:

- Tell the editor what you like about the new magazine.
- Describe the problem you experienced.
- Ask about the status of your submissions.

Write as much as you can and in complete sentences.

Your Response:

To: editor@sunshinepoetrymagazine.com

Subject: Problem using submission form

Cut Paste Undo Redo Hide Word Count 0

TOEFL iBT

Help   Begin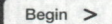

Writing

Write for an Academic Discussion

A professor has posted a question about a topic and students have responded with their thoughts and ideas. Make a contribution to the discussion.

You will have 10 minutes to write.

TOEFL iBT

Help   Next

Writing

Your professor is teaching a class on social studies. Write a post responding to the professor's question.

In your response, you should do the following:

- Express and support your opinion.
- Make a contribution to the discussion in your own words.

An effective response will contain at least 100 words.

Dr. Gupta

Volunteerism refers to the act of offering your time and service without financial compensation to benefit a community, organization, or cause. While many people volunteer mainly to help others, some institutions have mandatory volunteer programs. High schools are one example, where students may be required to complete a certain number of volunteer hours to graduate. What do you think? Should high school students be required to do volunteer work? Why or why not?

Jessica

Yes, I think high schools should require volunteer hours because it helps students build a sense of civic responsibility. Many teenagers don't naturally think about helping others, and this requirement can introduce them to the idea that their time and effort can make a real difference in the lives of others.

Mike

I don't think volunteer hours should be required because many students already have limited free time. Some have part-time jobs or take care of younger siblings after school. Adding a mandatory volunteer requirement could create extra stress and make it harder for those students to balance their existing responsibilities.

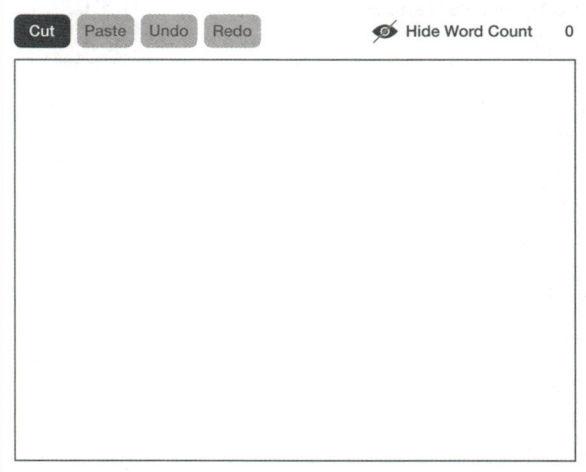

SPEAKING

Speaking Section

In the speaking section, you will answer 11 questions to demonstrate how well you can speak English. There are two types of tasks.

Type of Task	Description
Listen and Repeat	Listen and repeat what you heard.
Take an Interview	Answer questions from the interviewer.

TOEFL iBT

Speaking

Listen and Repeat

You will listen as someone speaks to you. Listen carefully and then repeat what you have heard. The clock will indicate how much time you have to speak.

No time for preparation will be provided.

TOEFL iBT

Speaking

You are learning to welcome visitors to the zoo. Listen to your manager and repeat what she says. Repeat only once.

TOEFL iBT

Speaking | Question **1** of 11

T1_S_01

Listen and repeat only once.

RESPONSE TIME
00:00:08

TOEFL iBT

Speaking | Question **2** of 11

T1_S_02

Listen and repeat only once.

RESPONSE TIME
00:00:08

TOEFL iBT

Speaking | Question **3** of 11

T1_S_03

Listen and repeat only once.

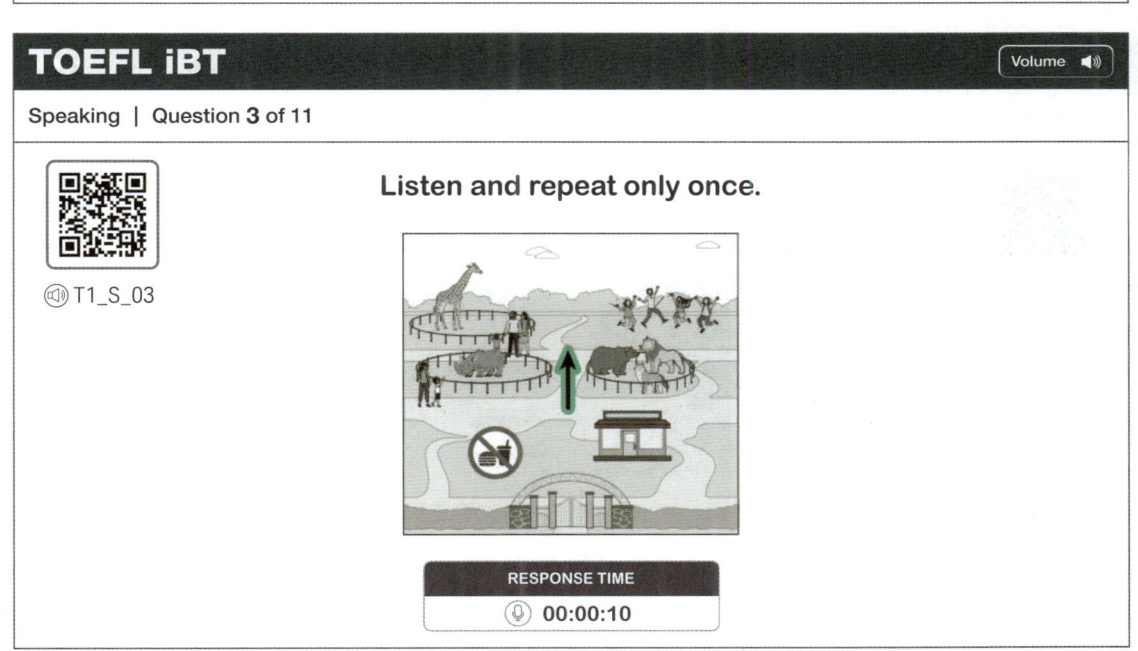

RESPONSE TIME
00:00:10

TOEFL iBT

Speaking | Question **6** of 11

T1_S_06

Listen and repeat only once.

RESPONSE TIME
00:00:12

TOEFL iBT

Speaking | Question **7** of 11

T1_S_07

Listen and repeat only once.

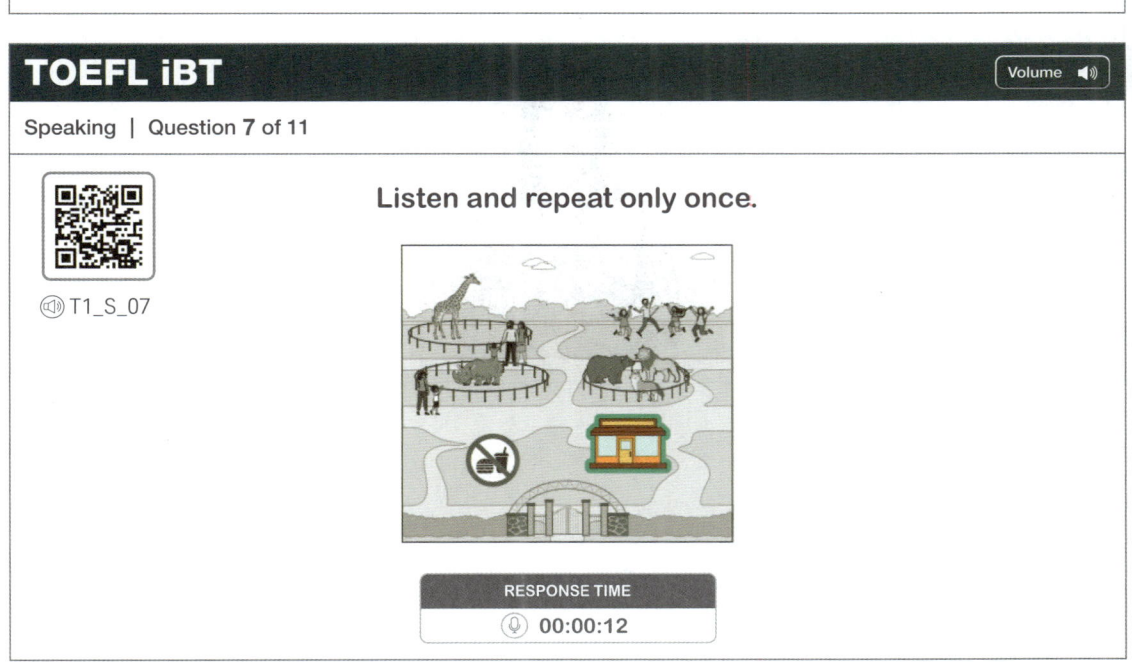

RESPONSE TIME
00:00:12

TOEFL iBT

Speaking

Take an Interview

An interviewer will ask you questions. Answer the questions and be sure to say as much as you can in the time allowed.

No time for preparation will be provided.

TOEFL iBT

Speaking

You have agreed to take part in a research study about urban life. You will have a short online interview with a researcher. The researcher will ask you some questions.

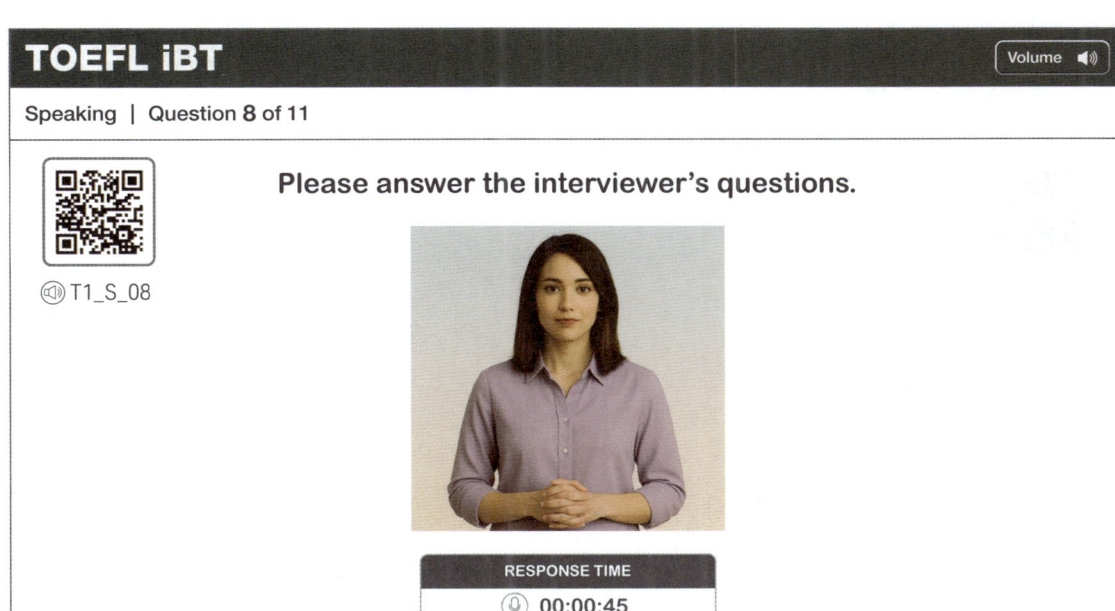

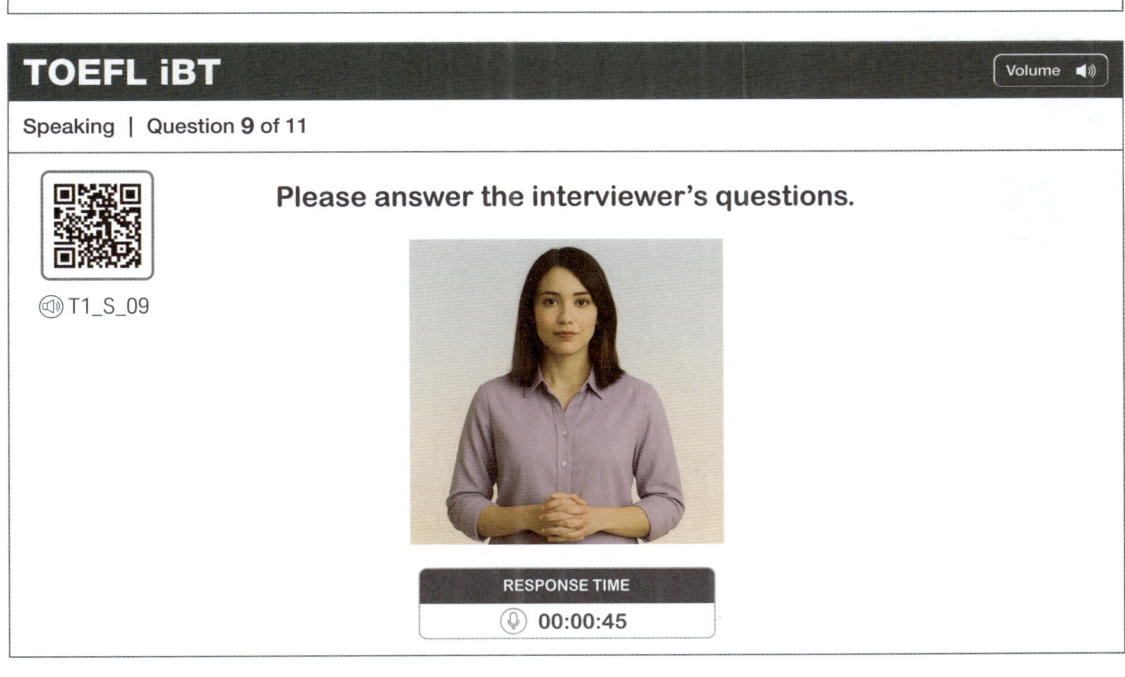

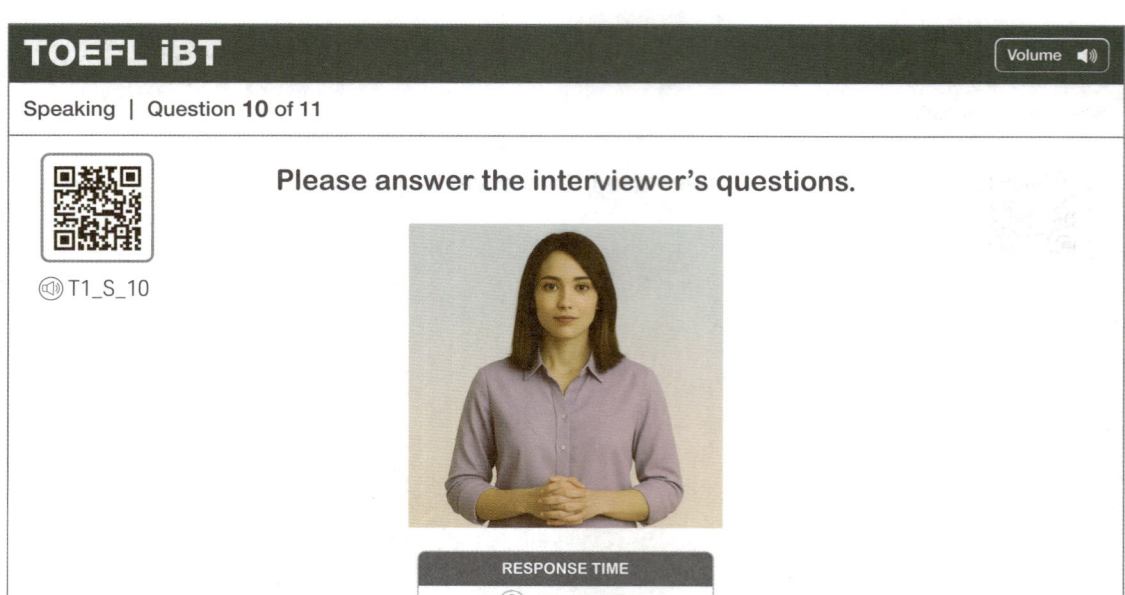

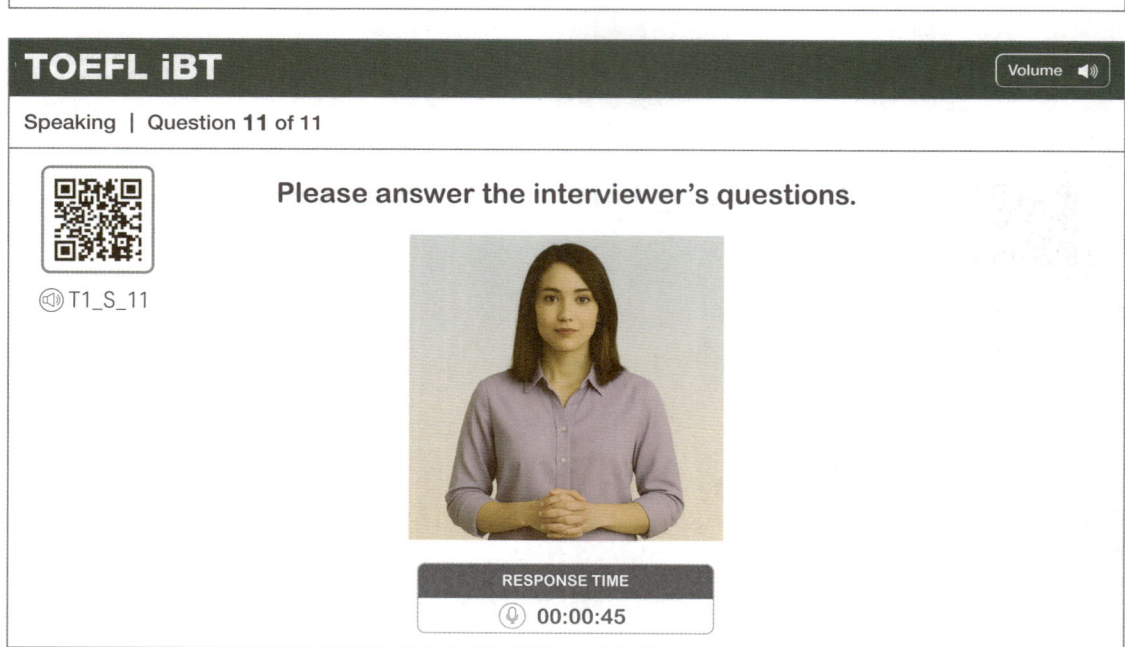

Test 2

READING

TOEFL iBT

Reading Section

In the reading section, you will answer 35-48 questions to demonstrate how well you understand academic and non-academic texts in English. There are three types of tasks.

Type of Task	Description
Complete the Words	Fill in the missing letters in a paragraph.
Read in Daily Life	Answer questions about everyday reading materials.
Read an Academic Passage	Answer questions about academic passages.

Module 1

TOEFL iBT

Volume | Help | Review | Next >

Reading | Questions **1–10** of 20

Fill in the missing letters in the paragraph.

Maps are tools that help us understand the world around us. They sh_ _ the loca_ _ _ _ _ of pla_ _ _ like cit_ _ _ , rivers, a_ _ mountains. Th_ _ _ visual gu_ _ _ _ can al_ _ display different ty_ _ _ of infor_ _ _ _ _ _ , such as climate or population. There are many kinds, including physical, political, and thematic versions. The study of maps and cartography, the process by which they are made, can teach us about the geography of our planet and how people live in different regions.

TOEFL iBT

Volume | Help | Review | < Back | Next >

Reading | Question **11** of 20

Read an email.

To:	brownchocolover@dmail.com
From:	santos.apartments@dmail.com
Date:	05/22/2025
Subject:	Maintenance Request

Dear Mr. Brown,

Your maintenance request has been received. Our technician will visit your apartment on June 10th between 1:00 PM and 3:00 PM. You must be present during that time, as our policy is that only the primary tenant can let the technician in.

Best regards,
Maria Santos

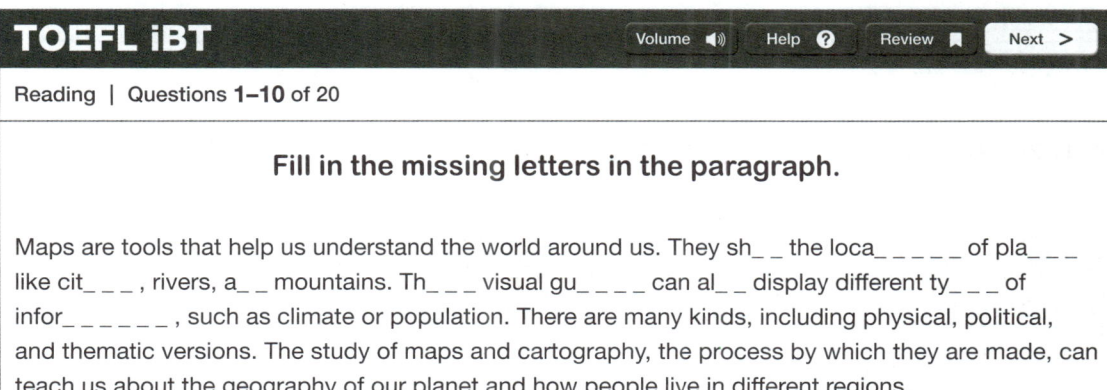

What is the earliest time of day that the technician will arrive?

(A) 10:00 AM
(B) 11:00 AM
(C) 1:00 PM
(D) 3:00 PM

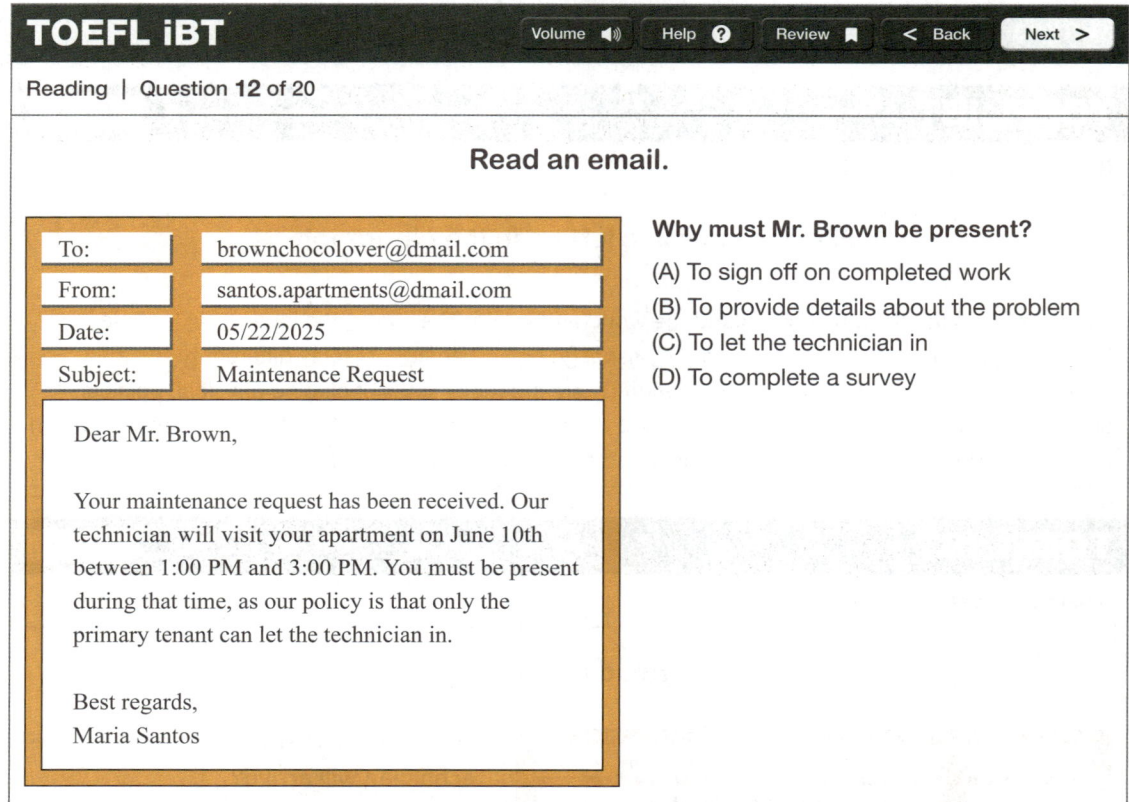

Read an email.

To:	miyazakisuzuki@dmail.com
From:	rogersemily.branscomb.services@dmail.com
Date:	03/23/2025
Subject:	Audit

Dear Mr. Suzuki,

Branscomb Technology's annual inventory audit will be performed on Thursday, April 19, beginning promptly at 8:00 a.m. in the warehouse on Kramer Boulevard. All department heads like yourself are required to attend and assist with the audit process. Please ensure that all inventory logs from your department are updated and will be readily accessible two days prior to the event. Because the audit is expected to take the entire day, we will be providing lunch from Beasly Bistro for participants. Please look over the attached menu and submit your selection to Fran Paloma in the HR department. We ask that you avoid scheduling any meetings on the morning of April 20 in the event that we need additional time to complete the process.

Regards,
Emily Rogers

Why did Ms. Rogers send the email to Mr. Suzuki?

(A) To assist him with an audit process
(B) To remind him to update inventory logs every day
(C) To inform him of an upcoming event
(D) To request his input on how to revise a process

Read an email.

To:	miyazakisuzuki@dmail.com
From:	rogersemily.branscomb.services@dmail.com
Date:	03/23/2025
Subject:	Audit

Dear Mr. Suzuki,

Branscomb Technology's annual inventory audit will be performed on Thursday, April 19, beginning promptly at 8:00 a.m. in the warehouse on Kramer Boulevard. All department heads like yourself are required to attend and assist with the audit process. Please ensure that all inventory logs from your department are updated and will be readily accessible two days prior to the event. Because the audit is expected to take the entire day, we will be providing lunch from Beasly Bistro for participants. Please look over the attached menu and submit your selection to Fran Paloma in the HR department. We ask that you avoid scheduling any meetings on the morning of April 20 in the event that we need additional time to complete the process.

Regards,
Emily Rogers

Why should Mr. Suzuki contact Ms. Paloma?

(A) To provide her with his meal preference
(B) To obtain some information from the HR department
(C) To share a list of employees who have experience with audits
(D) To send her an updated inventory log

Read an email.

To:	miyazakisuzuki@dmail.com
From:	rogersemily.branscomb.services@dmail.com
Date:	03/23/2025
Subject:	Audit

Dear Mr. Suzuki,

Branscomb Technology's annual inventory audit will be performed on Thursday, April 19, beginning promptly at 8:00 a.m. in the warehouse on Kramer Boulevard. All department heads like yourself are required to attend and assist with the audit process. Please ensure that all inventory logs from your department are updated and will be readily accessible two days prior to the event. Because the audit is expected to take the entire day, we will be providing lunch from Beasly Bistro for participants. Please look over the attached menu and submit your selection to Fran Paloma in the HR department. We ask that you avoid scheduling any meetings on the morning of April 20 in the event that we need additional time to complete the process.

Regards,
Emily Rogers

What is indicated about the morning of April 20?

(A) The audit might continue then.
(B) Mr. Suzuki might have several meetings then.
(C) A menu might be updated then.
(D) Employees might have free time then.

The Impact of Sports on Social Integration

Sports can promote social integration by bridging gaps between people of various backgrounds. Participation in sports can lead to increased social cohesion and improved relationships among diverse groups.

For example, community soccer leagues often bring together people from different ethnicities, creating an environment where cultural differences are celebrated and mutual respect is cultivated. However, the impact of sports on social integration is not without challenges. Competitive environments can sometimes exacerbate social tensions, particularly when favoritism or exclusionary practices are present.

Despite these issues, many initiatives aim to use sports as a platform for social change. One such initiative is the Sport for Peace program, which focuses on conflict resolution through team-building activities and collaborative sports events. The role of sports in social integration extends beyond participation. Spectatorship and fandom also play significant roles in uniting people. Major international sports events like the Olympics or the World Cup serve as opportunities for nations to come together and share common goals. The visibility of athletes from diverse backgrounds during these events fosters a sense of global harmony. These events often highlight stories of athletes overcoming adversity, inspiring spectators and fostering a collective sense of achievement.

The word "cohesion" in the passage is closest in meaning to

(A) diversity
(B) awareness
(C) unity
(D) celebration

The Impact of Sports on Social Integration

Sports can promote social integration by bridging gaps between people of various backgrounds. Participation in sports can lead to increased social cohesion and improved relationships among diverse groups.

For example, community soccer leagues often bring together people from different ethnicities, creating an environment where cultural differences are celebrated and mutual respect is cultivated. However, the impact of sports on social integration is not without challenges. Competitive environments can sometimes exacerbate social tensions, particularly when favoritism or exclusionary practices are present.

Despite these issues, many initiatives aim to use sports as a platform for social change. One such initiative is the Sport for Peace program, which focuses on conflict resolution through team-building activities and collaborative sports events. The role of sports in social integration extends beyond participation. Spectatorship and fandom also play significant roles in uniting people. Major international sports events like the Olympics or the World Cup serve as opportunities for nations to come together and share common goals. The visibility of athletes from diverse backgrounds during these events fosters a sense of global harmony. These events often highlight stories of athletes overcoming adversity, inspiring spectators and fostering a collective sense of achievement.

In which of the following situations can sports have an especially negative impact on social integration?

(A) When people from different ethnicities are brought together
(B) When participants are unreasonably strict about the rules of competition
(C) When the social environment is not favorable to competition
(D) When social tensions are heightened by favoring or excluding certain participants

The Impact of Sports on Social Integration

Sports can promote social integration by bridging gaps between people of various backgrounds. Participation in sports can lead to increased social cohesion and improved relationships among diverse groups.

For example, community soccer leagues often bring together people from different ethnicities, creating an environment where cultural differences are celebrated and mutual respect is cultivated. However, the impact of sports on social integration is not without challenges. Competitive environments can sometimes exacerbate social tensions, particularly when favoritism or exclusionary practices are present.

Despite these issues, many initiatives aim to use sports as a platform for social change. One such initiative is the Sport for Peace program, which focuses on conflict resolution through team-building activities and collaborative sports events. The role of sports in social integration extends beyond participation. Spectatorship and fandom also play significant roles in uniting people. Major international sports events like the Olympics or the World Cup serve as opportunities for nations to come together and share common goals. The visibility of athletes from diverse backgrounds during these events fosters a sense of global harmony. These events often highlight stories of athletes overcoming adversity, inspiring spectators and fostering a collective sense of achievement.

What is the relationship between paragraphs 2 and 3?

(A) Paragraph 3 discusses ways of addressing a problem mentioned in paragraph 2.
(B) Paragraph 3 contradicts a theory proposed in paragraph 2.
(C) Paragraph 3 provides evidence for an idea presented in paragraph 2.
(D) Paragraph 3 introduces a new challenge related to paragraph 2.

The Impact of Sports on Social Integration

Sports can promote social integration by bridging gaps between people of various backgrounds. Participation in sports can lead to increased social cohesion and improved relationships among diverse groups.

For example, community soccer leagues often bring together people from different ethnicities, creating an environment where cultural differences are celebrated and mutual respect is cultivated. However, the impact of sports on social integration is not without challenges. Competitive environments can sometimes exacerbate social tensions, particularly when favoritism or exclusionary practices are present.

Despite these issues, many initiatives aim to use sports as a platform for social change. One such initiative is the Sport for Peace program, which focuses on conflict resolution through team-building activities and collaborative sports events. The role of sports in social integration extends beyond participation. Spectatorship and fandom also play significant roles in uniting people. Major international sports events like the Olympics or the World Cup serve as opportunities for nations to come together and share common goals. The visibility of athletes from diverse backgrounds during these events fosters a sense of global harmony. These events often highlight stories of athletes overcoming adversity, inspiring spectators and fostering a collective sense of achievement.

What does the passage suggest about the Sport for Peace program?

(A) Its main goal is to eliminate favoritism in sports.
(B) It primarily targets professional athletes.
(C) It uses team-building exercises to address conflicts.
(D) It is only effective in local communities.

The Impact of Sports on Social Integration

Sports can promote social integration by bridging gaps between people of various backgrounds. Participation in sports can lead to increased social cohesion and improved relationships among diverse groups.

For example, community soccer leagues often bring together people from different ethnicities, creating an environment where cultural differences are celebrated and mutual respect is cultivated. However, the impact of sports on social integration is not without challenges. Competitive environments can sometimes exacerbate social tensions, particularly when favoritism or exclusionary practices are present.

Despite these issues, many initiatives aim to use sports as a platform for social change. One such initiative is the Sport for Peace program, which focuses on conflict resolution through team-building activities and collaborative sports events. The role of sports in social integration extends beyond participation. Spectatorship and fandom also play significant roles in uniting people. Major international sports events like the Olympics or the World Cup serve as opportunities for nations to come together and share common goals. The visibility of athletes from diverse backgrounds during these events fosters a sense of global harmony. These events often highlight stories of athletes overcoming adversity, inspiring spectators and fostering a collective sense of achievement.

Why does the author mention major international sports events like the Olympics and the World Cup?

(A) To argue that these events have little impact on social integration
(B) To illustrate how sports can unite people globally
(C) To suggest that these events mainly benefit athletes
(D) To highlight the competitive nature of these events

Module 2

TOEFL iBT

Reading | Questions **1–10** of 20

Fill in the missing letters in the paragraph.

Elephants are social animals that live in groups called herds. They commu_ _ _ _ _ using sou_ _ _, gestures, a_ _ touch. These ani_ _ _ _ are kn_ _ _ for th_ _ _ strong fam_ _ _ bonds and of_ _ _ help ea_ _ other i_ times of need. They can remember the locations of water sources and food, which helps them survive in their natural environment. These highly intelligent creatures play an important role in their ecosystems, shaping the landscape, creating access to moisture, and spreading seeds.

TOEFL iBT

Reading | Question **11** of 20

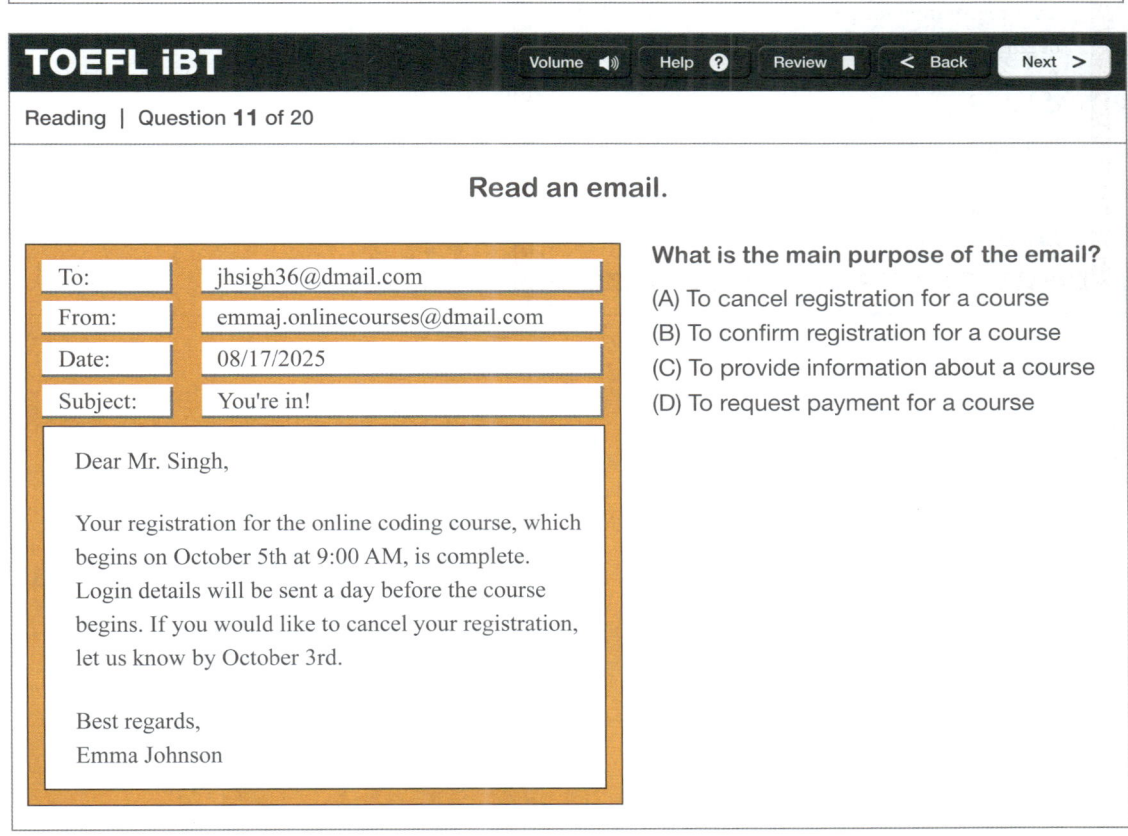

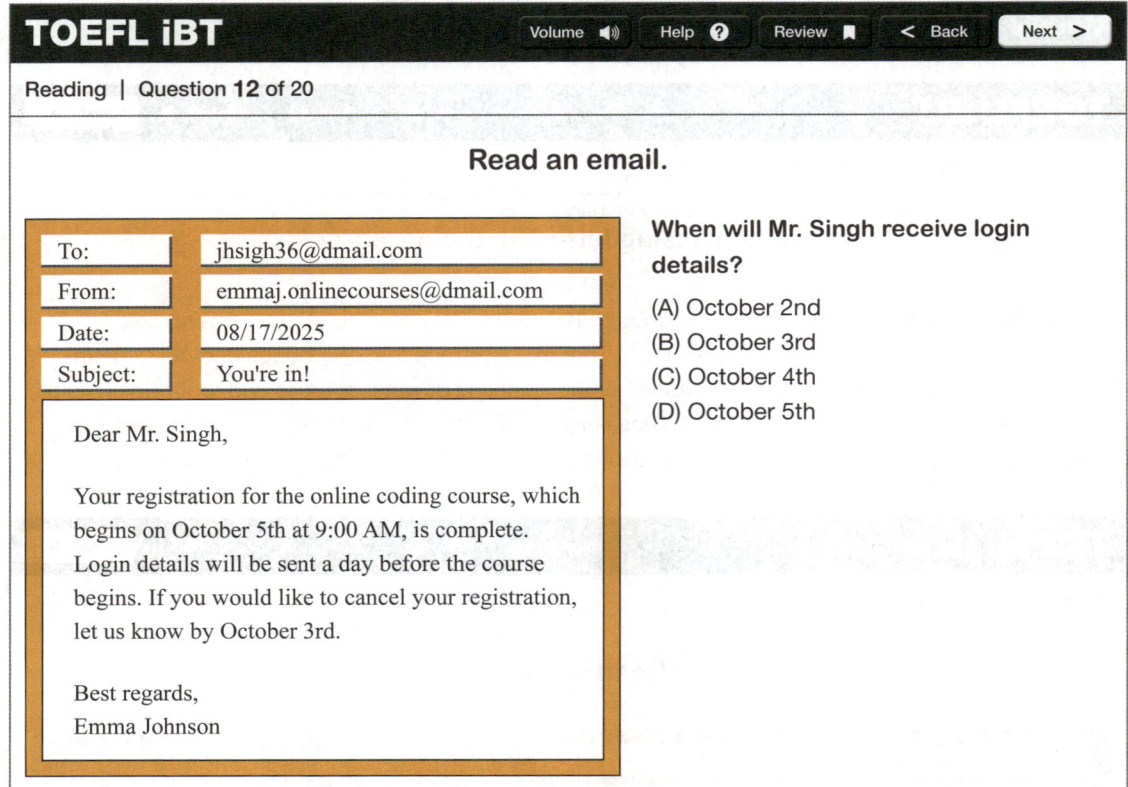

Read an email.

To: gardnerjardinero@dmail.com
From: thompson.building.co@dmail.com
Subject: Upcoming Heating System Maintenance - Tuesday, May 27

Dear Ms. Gardner,

I hope you're doing well. I'm writing to inform you of a scheduled maintenance procedure on the office heating system, set to take place on Tuesday, May 27, from 8:00 A.M. to 5:00 P.M. This essential work is part of our seasonal inspection and efficiency upgrade initiative to ensure optimal performance during the colder months.

Please note that the heating system will be offline throughout the day, and indoor temperatures will drop noticeably. We recommend dressing in warm layers and advising your team to do the same. If any team members are particularly sensitive to cooler environments, remote work arrangements may be considered.

Additionally, as external technicians will be on-site, please ensure all confidential materials are secured appropriately.

Should you have any questions, contact the maintenance team at 555-7264.

Warm regards,
Robert Thompson

What is indicated about the office heating system?

(A) It failed an inspection.
(B) It will not be functioning during maintenance.
(C) It is not working properly.
(D) It performs optimally.

Read an email.

To:	gardnerjardinero@dmail.com
From:	thompson.building.co@dmail.com
Subject:	Upcoming Heating System Maintenance - Tuesday, May 27

Dear Ms. Gardner,

I hope you're doing well. I'm writing to inform you of a scheduled maintenance procedure on the office heating system, set to take place on Tuesday, May 27, from 8:00 A.M. to 5:00 P.M. This essential work is part of our seasonal inspection and efficiency upgrade initiative to ensure optimal performance during the colder months.

Please note that the heating system will be offline throughout the day, and indoor temperatures will drop noticeably. We recommend dressing in warm layers and advising your team to do the same. If any team members are particularly sensitive to cooler environments, remote work arrangements may be considered.

Additionally, as external technicians will be on-site, please ensure all confidential materials are secured appropriately.

Should you have any questions, contact the maintenance team at 555-7264.

Warm regards,
Robert Thompson

What can be inferred about the weather on May 27?

(A) It will be cooler than the temperature at which the office is normally kept.
(B) It will be unusual for the season.
(C) It will require office workers to stay home rather than go to the office.
(D) It will change throughout the day.

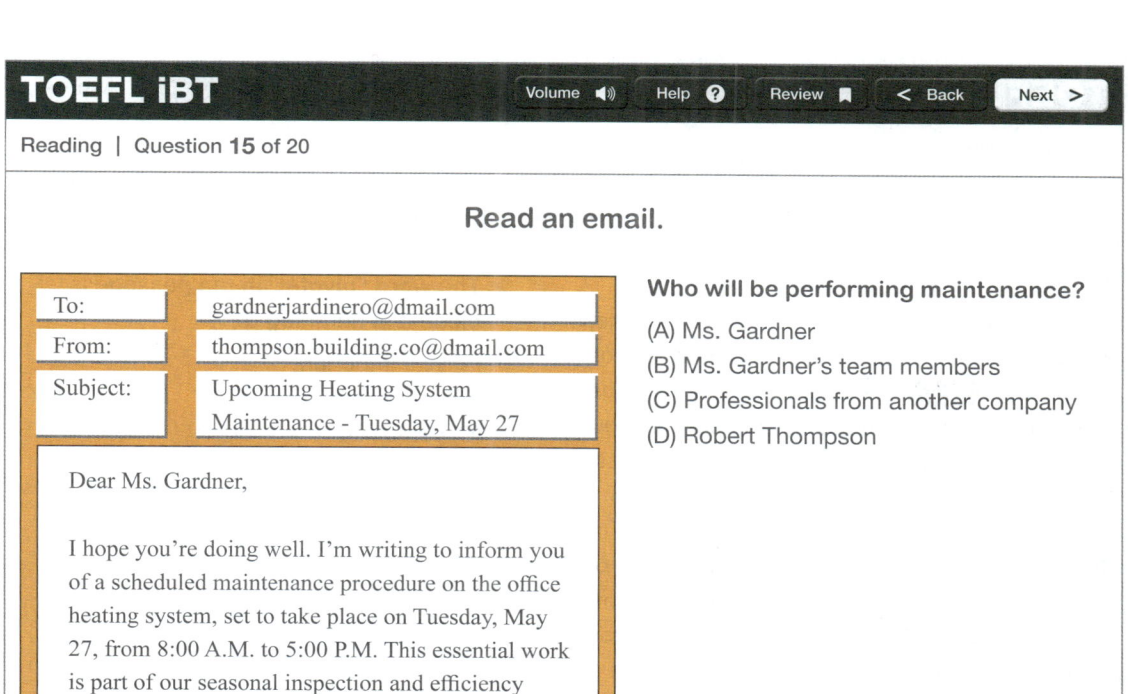

The Human Microbiome

The human microbiome consists of trillions of microorganisms living in and on our bodies. These include bacteria, viruses, fungi, and other microbes. They play a pivotal role in functions such as digestion, immunity, and mood regulation. For instance, gut bacteria help break down food and produce essential vitamins.

Recent studies show that the microbiome can be influenced by diet, lifestyle, and medication. Antibiotics, while effective against harmful bacteria, can disrupt the balance of beneficial microbes. This disruption can lead to health issues like digestive problems and weakened immunity. Researchers are exploring the connection between the microbiome and mental health. Certain gut bacteria produce neurotransmitters affecting brain function. An imbalance in these bacteria may be linked to conditions like depression and anxiety.

Maintaining a healthy microbiome involves eating a varied diet rich in fiber, reducing stress, and avoiding unnecessary antibiotics. Bacteria that aid digestion, known as probiotics and prebiotics, are also beneficial. As understanding of the microbiome grows, it may lead to breakthroughs in treating diseases and improving health.

The word "pivotal" in the passage is closest in meaning to

(A) very important
(B) possible
(C) combined
(D) unwelcome

The Human Microbiome

The human microbiome consists of trillions of microorganisms living in and on our bodies. These include bacteria, viruses, fungi, and other microbes. They play a pivotal role in functions such as digestion, immunity, and mood regulation. For instance, gut bacteria help break down food and produce essential vitamins.

Recent studies show that the microbiome can be influenced by diet, lifestyle, and medication. Antibiotics, while effective against harmful bacteria, can disrupt the balance of beneficial microbes. This disruption can lead to health issues like digestive problems and weakened immunity. Researchers are exploring the connection between the microbiome and mental health. Certain gut bacteria produce neurotransmitters affecting brain function. An imbalance in these bacteria may be linked to conditions like depression and anxiety.

Maintaining a healthy microbiome involves eating a varied diet rich in fiber, reducing stress, and avoiding unnecessary antibiotics. Bacteria that aid digestion, known as probiotics and prebiotics, are also beneficial. As understanding of the microbiome grows, it may lead to breakthroughs in treating diseases and improving health.

What is one way antibiotics can affect humans?

(A) They enhance the production of neurotransmitters.
(B) They can weaken immunity by harming beneficial microbes.
(C) They can help relieve digestive problems.
(D) They make it easier to produce essential vitamins.

The Human Microbiome

The human microbiome consists of trillions of microorganisms living in and on our bodies. These include bacteria, viruses, fungi, and other microbes. They play a pivotal role in functions such as digestion, immunity, and mood regulation. For instance, gut bacteria help break down food and produce essential vitamins.

Recent studies show that the microbiome can be influenced by diet, lifestyle, and medication. Antibiotics, while effective against harmful bacteria, can disrupt the balance of beneficial microbes. This disruption can lead to health issues like digestive problems and weakened immunity. Researchers are exploring the connection between the microbiome and mental health. Certain gut bacteria produce neurotransmitters affecting brain function. An imbalance in these bacteria may be linked to conditions like depression and anxiety.

Maintaining a healthy microbiome involves eating a varied diet rich in fiber, reducing stress, and avoiding unnecessary antibiotics. Bacteria that aid digestion, known as probiotics and prebiotics, are also beneficial. As understanding of the microbiome grows, it may lead to breakthroughs in treating diseases and improving health.

What connection are researchers exploring regarding the microbiome?

(A) The link between gut bacteria and immunity
(B) The role of fungi in mood regulation
(C) The role of viruses in digestion
(D) The link between gut bacteria and mental health

The Human Microbiome

The human microbiome consists of trillions of microorganisms living in and on our bodies. These include bacteria, viruses, fungi, and other microbes. They play a pivotal role in functions such as digestion, immunity, and mood regulation. For instance, gut bacteria help break down food and produce essential vitamins.

Recent studies show that the microbiome can be influenced by diet, lifestyle, and medication. Antibiotics, while effective against harmful bacteria, can disrupt the balance of beneficial microbes. This disruption can lead to health issues like digestive problems and weakened immunity. Researchers are exploring the connection between the microbiome and mental health. Certain gut bacteria produce neurotransmitters affecting brain function. An imbalance in these bacteria may be linked to conditions like depression and anxiety.

Maintaining a healthy microbiome involves eating a varied diet rich in fiber, reducing stress, and avoiding unnecessary antibiotics. Bacteria that aid digestion, known as probiotics and prebiotics, are also beneficial. As understanding of the microbiome grows, it may lead to breakthroughs in treating diseases and improving health.

All of the following help to maintain a healthy microbiome EXCEPT

(A) eating a varied diet rich in fiber
(B) lowering stress levels
(C) avoiding sources of bacteria
(D) reducing the use of antibiotics

The Human Microbiome

The human microbiome consists of trillions of microorganisms living in and on our bodies. These include bacteria, viruses, fungi, and other microbes. They play a pivotal role in functions such as digestion, immunity, and mood regulation. For instance, gut bacteria help break down food and produce essential vitamins.

Recent studies show that the microbiome can be influenced by diet, lifestyle, and medication. Antibiotics, while effective against harmful bacteria, can disrupt the balance of beneficial microbes. This disruption can lead to health issues like digestive problems and weakened immunity. Researchers are exploring the connection between the microbiome and mental health. Certain gut bacteria produce neurotransmitters affecting brain function. An imbalance in these bacteria may be linked to conditions like depression and anxiety.

Maintaining a healthy microbiome involves eating a varied diet rich in fiber, reducing stress, and avoiding unnecessary antibiotics. Bacteria that aid digestion, known as probiotics and prebiotics, are also beneficial. As understanding of the microbiome grows, it may lead to breakthroughs in treating diseases and improving health.

What is the relationship between paragraphs 2 and 3?

(A) Paragraph 3 challenges the ideas proposed in paragraph 2.
(B) Paragraph 3 provides examples of the disruptions mentioned in paragraph 2.
(C) Paragraph 3 specifies how to achieve a healthy microbiome based on the factors mentioned in paragraph 2.
(D) Paragraph 3 elaborates on the benefits of antibiotics mentioned in paragraph 2.

LISTENING

TOEFL iBT

Listening Section

In the listening section, you will answer 35 to 45 questions to demonstrate how well you understand spoken English. There are three types of tasks.

Type of Task	Description
Listen and Choose a Response	Select the best response to the question or statement.
Conversations	Answer questions about short conversations.
Announcements and Academic Talks	Answer questions about announcements and academic talks.

You WILL NOT be able to return to previous questions.

Module 1

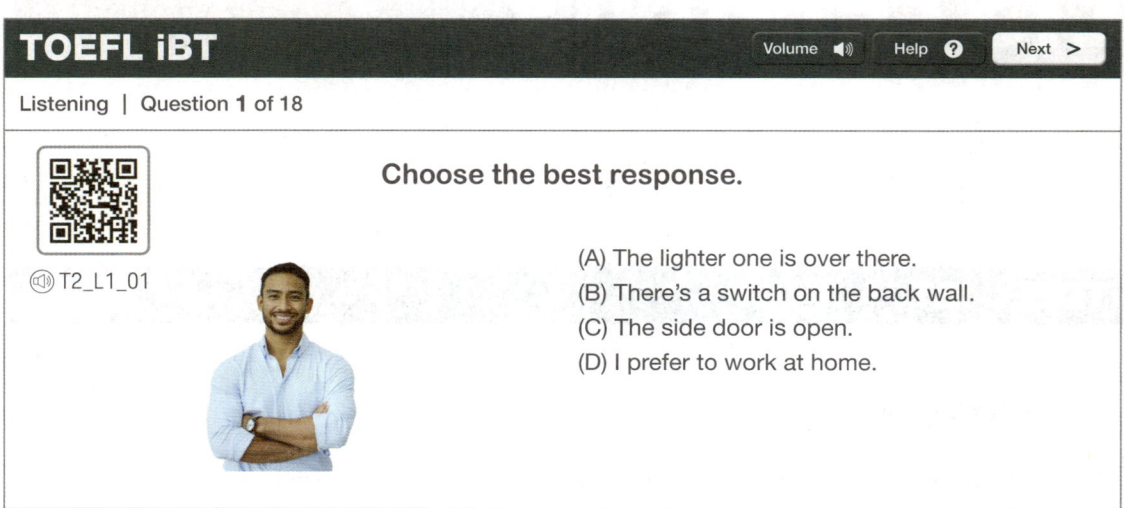

TOEFL iBT

Listening | Question **1** of 18

🔊 T2_L1_01

Choose the best response.

(A) The lighter one is over there.
(B) There's a switch on the back wall.
(C) The side door is open.
(D) I prefer to work at home.

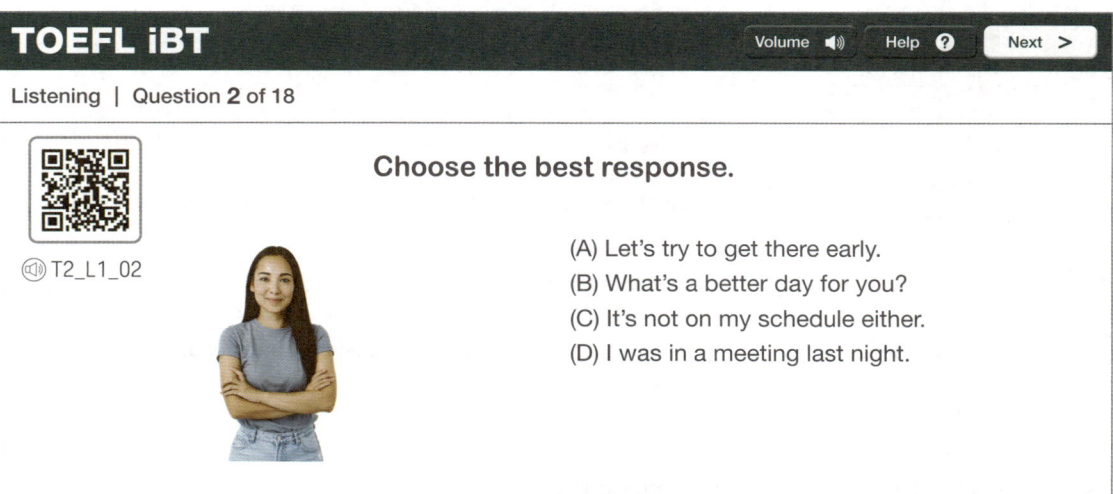

TOEFL iBT

Listening | Question **2** of 18

🔊 T2_L1_02

Choose the best response.

(A) Let's try to get there early.
(B) What's a better day for you?
(C) It's not on my schedule either.
(D) I was in a meeting last night.

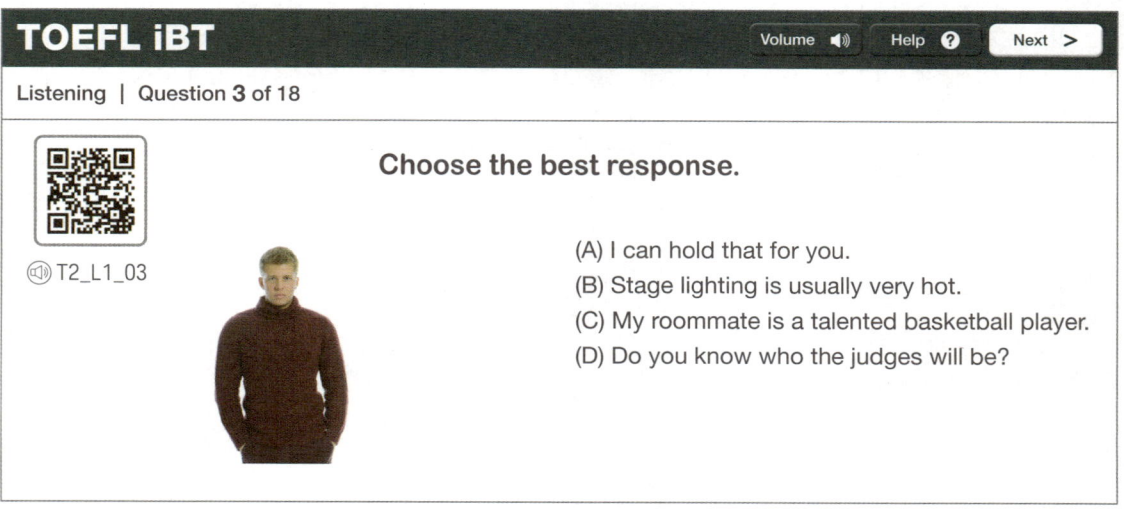

TOEFL iBT

Listening | Question **3** of 18

🔊 T2_L1_03

Choose the best response.

(A) I can hold that for you.
(B) Stage lighting is usually very hot.
(C) My roommate is a talented basketball player.
(D) Do you know who the judges will be?

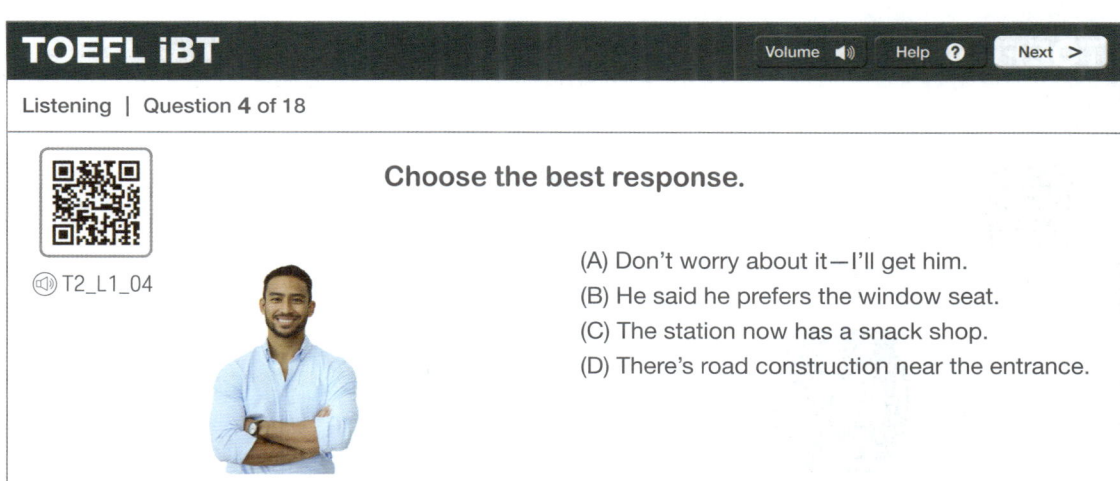

Choose the best response.

(A) Don't worry about it—I'll get him.
(B) He said he prefers the window seat.
(C) The station now has a snack shop.
(D) There's road construction near the entrance.

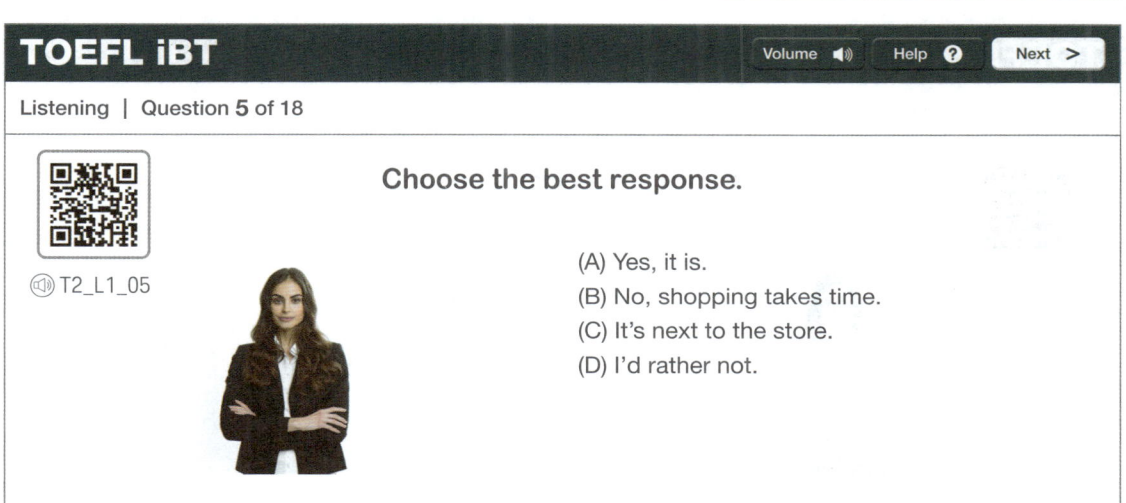

Choose the best response.

(A) Yes, it is.
(B) No, shopping takes time.
(C) It's next to the store.
(D) I'd rather not.

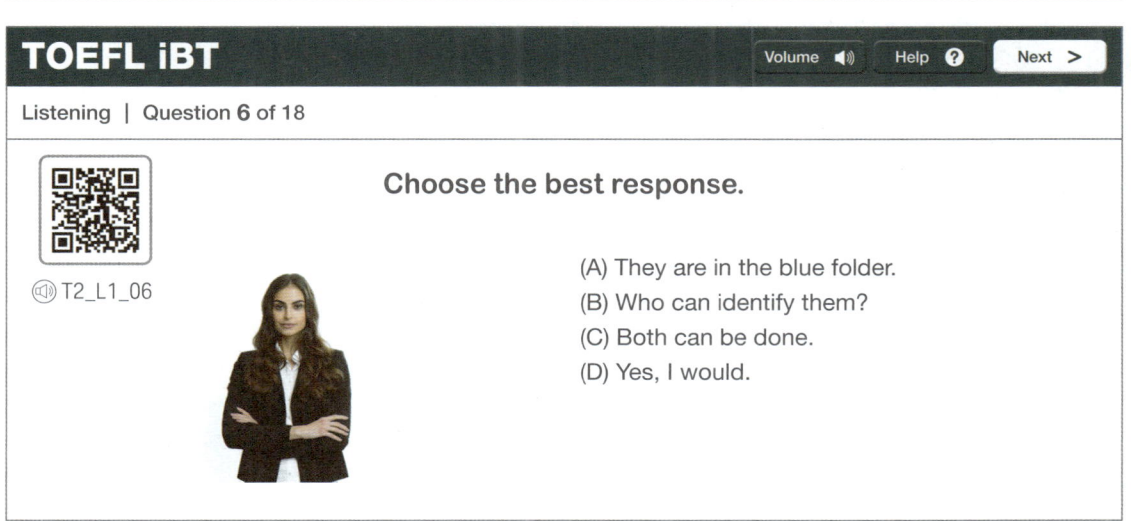

Choose the best response.

(A) They are in the blue folder.
(B) Who can identify them?
(C) Both can be done.
(D) Yes, I would.

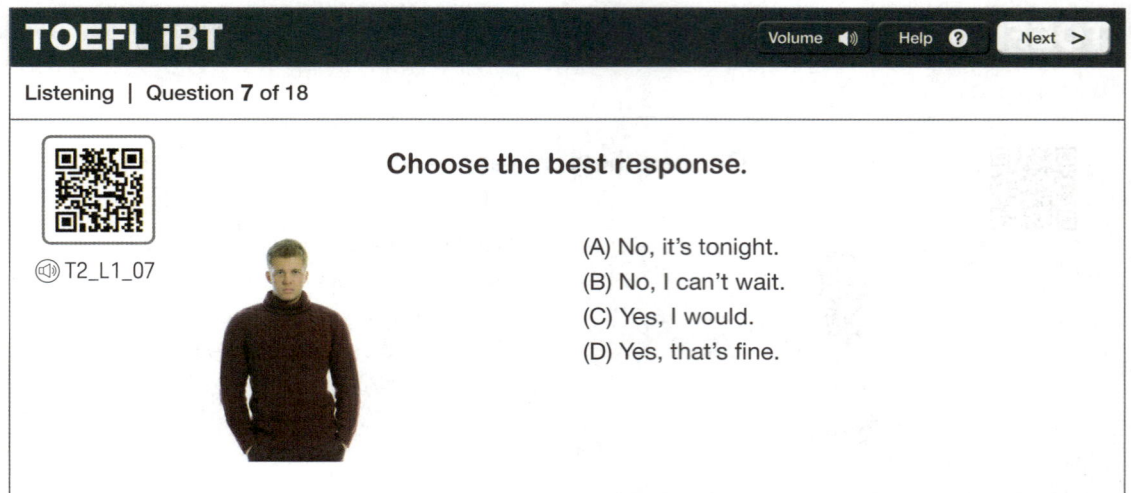

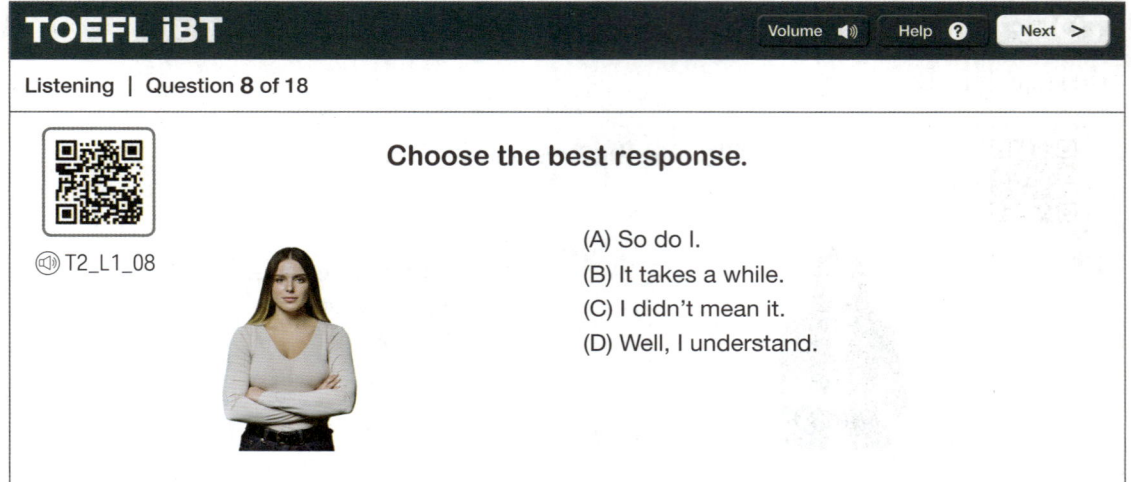

TOEFL iBT

Listening | Questions 9–10 of 18

Listen to a conversation.

T2_L1_0910

TOEFL iBT

Listening | Question 9 of 18

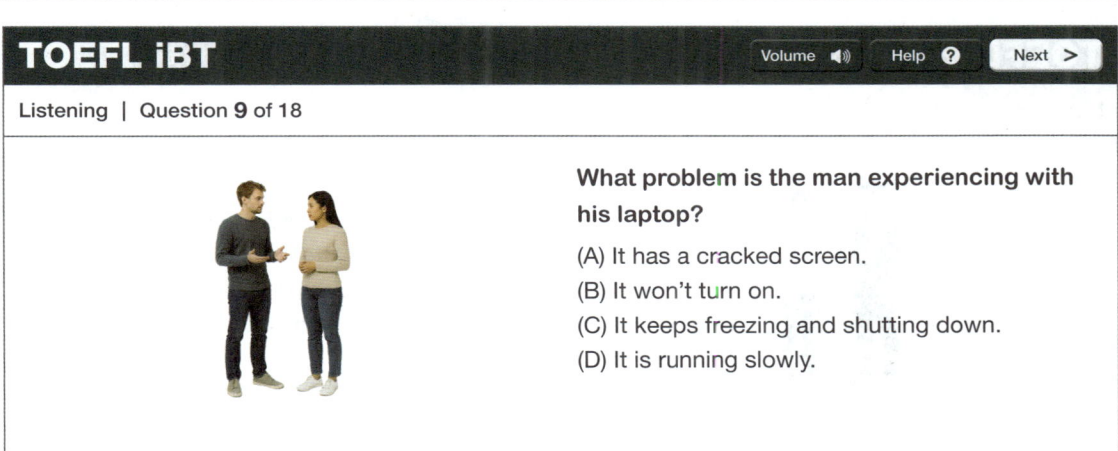

What problem is the man experiencing with his laptop?

(A) It has a cracked screen.
(B) It won't turn on.
(C) It keeps freezing and shutting down.
(D) It is running slowly.

TOEFL iBT

Listening | Question 10 of 18

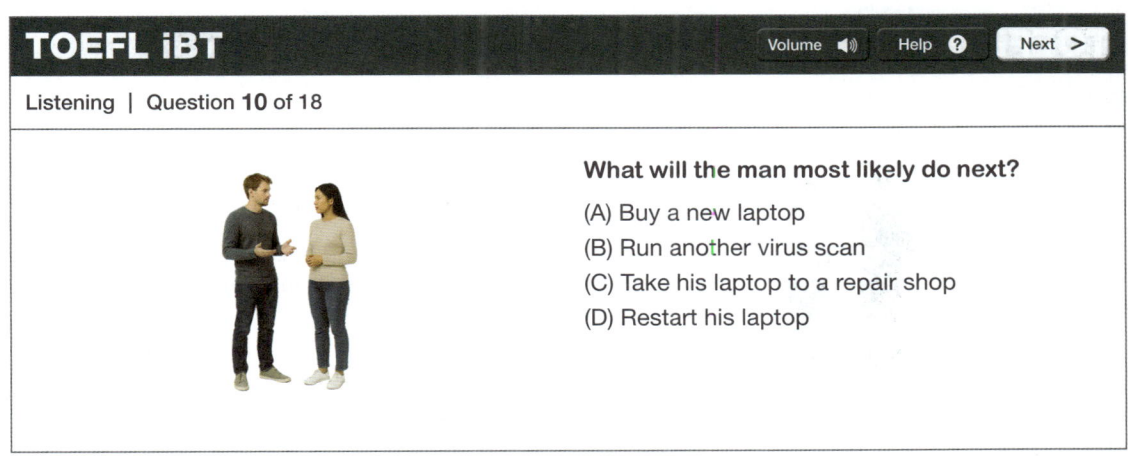

What will the man most likely do next?

(A) Buy a new laptop
(B) Run another virus scan
(C) Take his laptop to a repair shop
(D) Restart his laptop

Listening | Questions 11–12 of 18

Listen to a conversation.

T2_L1_1112

Listening | Question 11 of 18

What is the man's problem?

(A) He has nothing to eat for lunch.
(B) He is unable to attend a meeting.
(C) He forgot about an obligation at work.
(D) He needs more resources to finish a project.

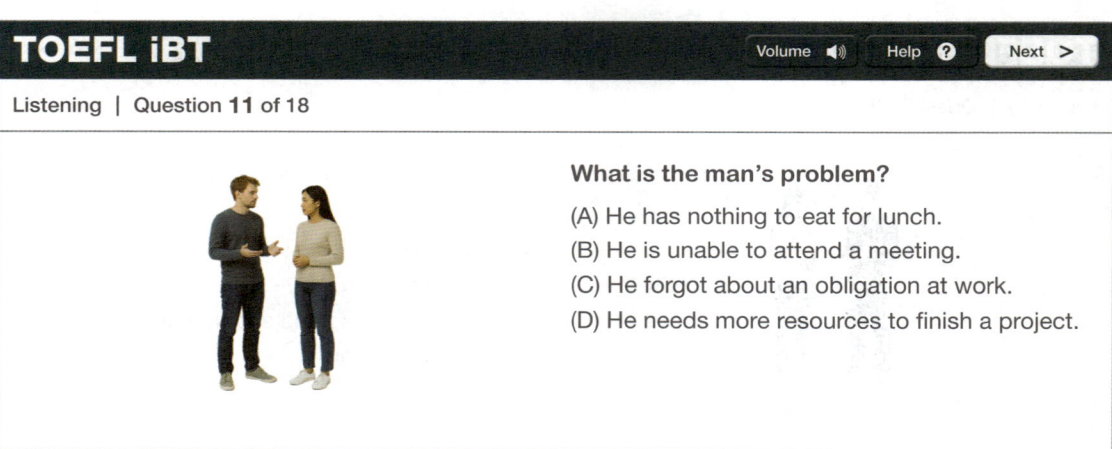

Listening | Question 12 of 18

What does the woman imply when she says, "I stocked up yesterday"?

(A) She does not plan to go to work tomorrow.
(B) She will provide the man with drinks for his meeting.
(C) The supermarket has plenty of drinks available.
(D) The man will not need extra time to finish his project.

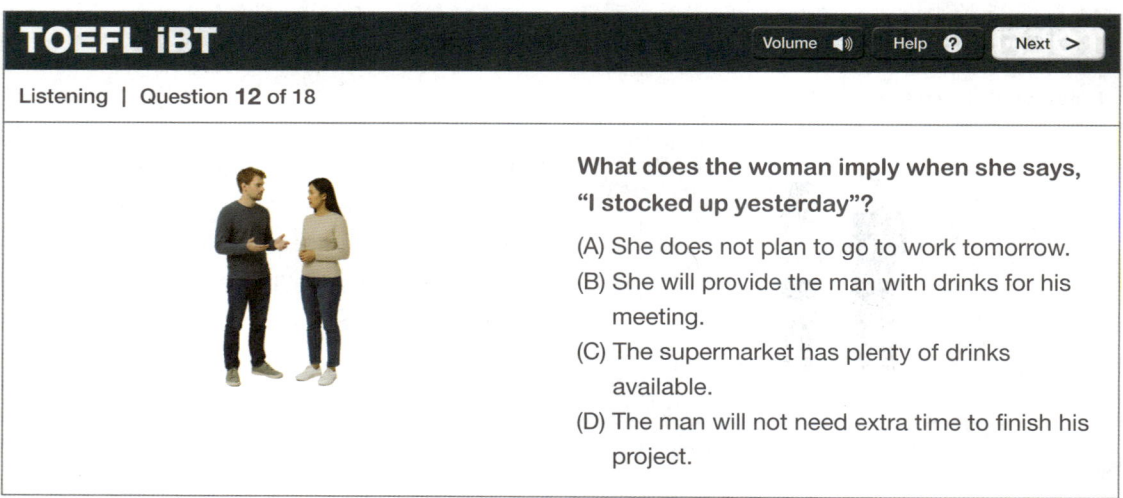

Listening | Questions **13–14** of 18

Listen to an announcement at a university club meeting.

T2_L1_1314

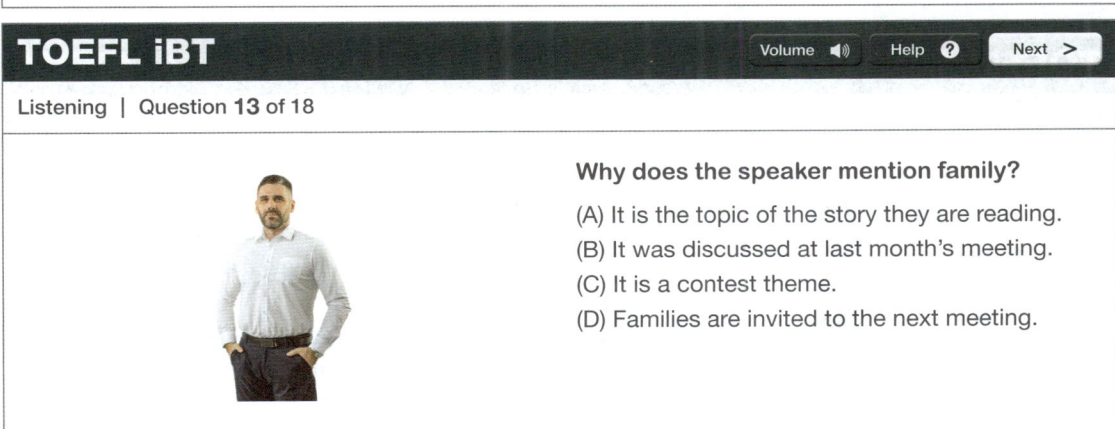

Listening | Question **13** of 18

Why does the speaker mention family?

(A) It is the topic of the story they are reading.
(B) It was discussed at last month's meeting.
(C) It is a contest theme.
(D) Families are invited to the next meeting.

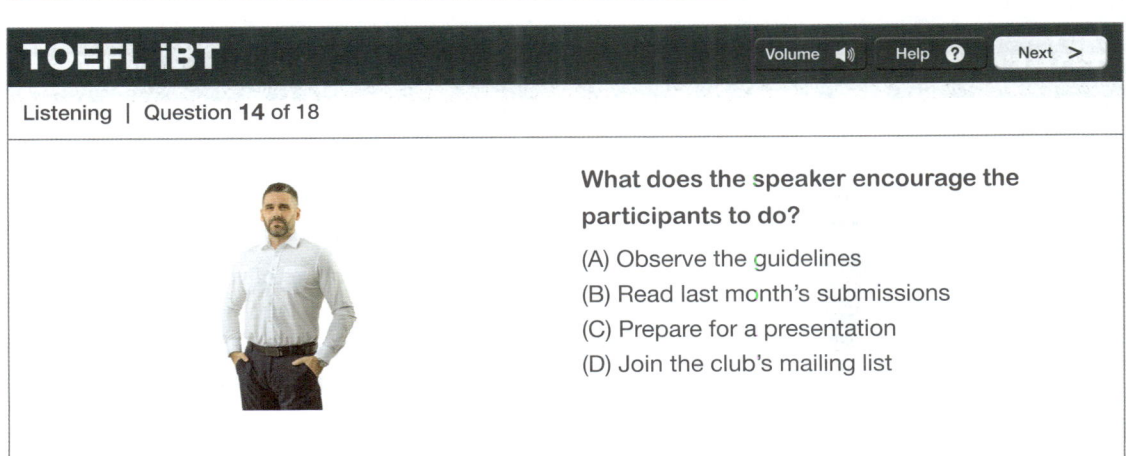

Listening | Question **14** of 18

What does the speaker encourage the participants to do?

(A) Observe the guidelines
(B) Read last month's submissions
(C) Prepare for a presentation
(D) Join the club's mailing list

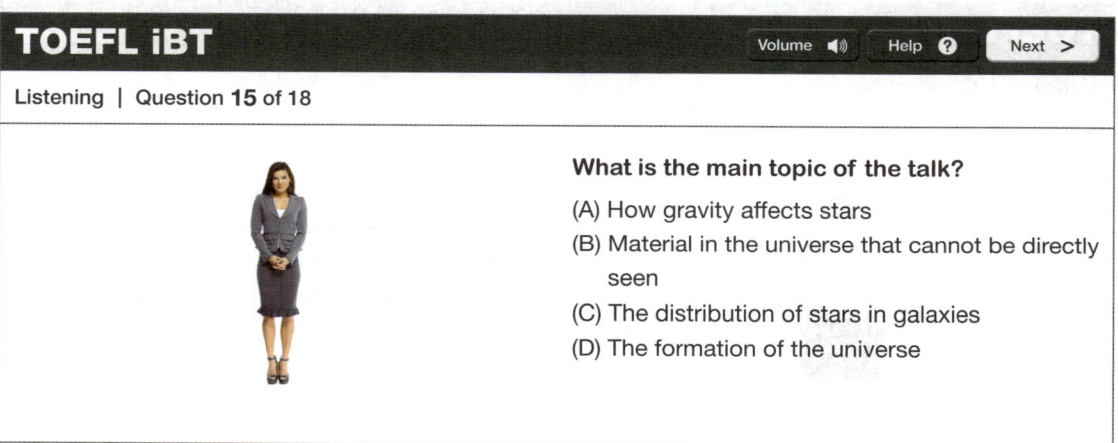

What is the main topic of the talk?

(A) How gravity affects stars
(B) Material in the universe that cannot be directly seen
(C) The distribution of stars in galaxies
(D) The formation of the universe

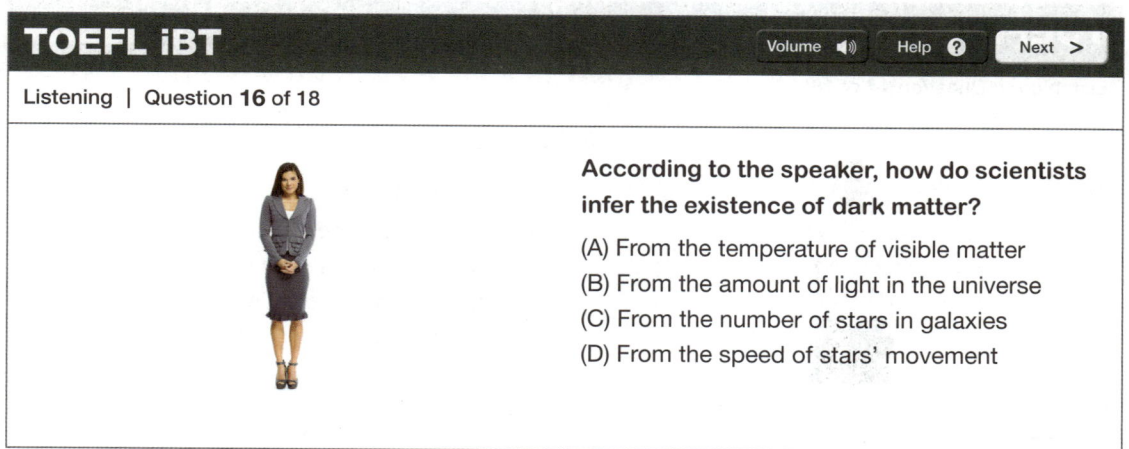

According to the speaker, how do scientists infer the existence of dark matter?

(A) From the temperature of visible matter
(B) From the amount of light in the universe
(C) From the number of stars in galaxies
(D) From the speed of stars' movement

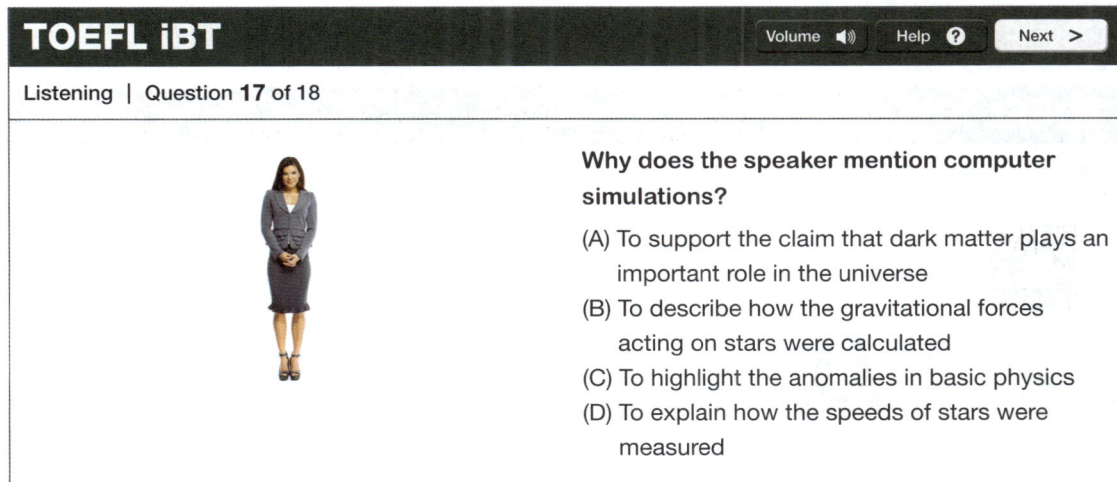

Why does the speaker mention computer simulations?

(A) To support the claim that dark matter plays an important role in the universe
(B) To describe how the gravitational forces acting on stars were calculated
(C) To highlight the anomalies in basic physics
(D) To explain how the speeds of stars were measured

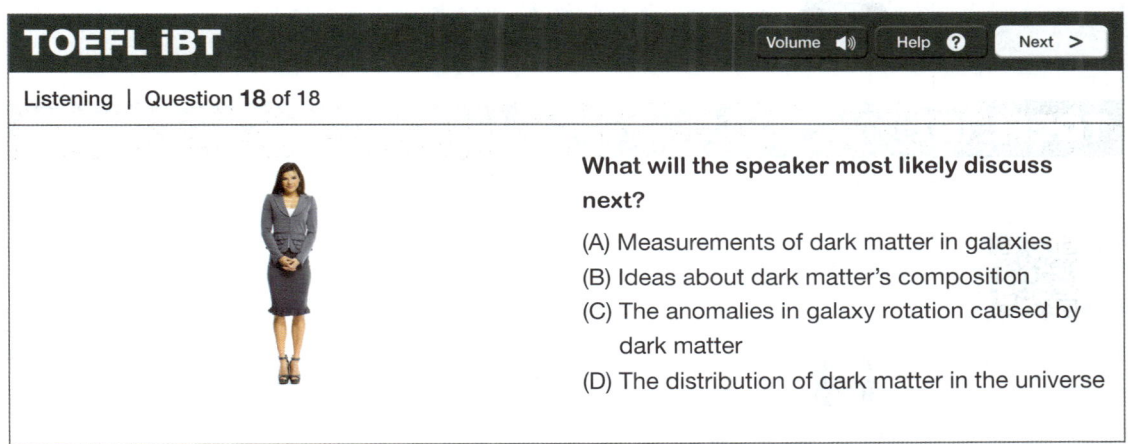

What will the speaker most likely discuss next?

(A) Measurements of dark matter in galaxies
(B) Ideas about dark matter's composition
(C) The anomalies in galaxy rotation caused by dark matter
(D) The distribution of dark matter in the universe

Module 2

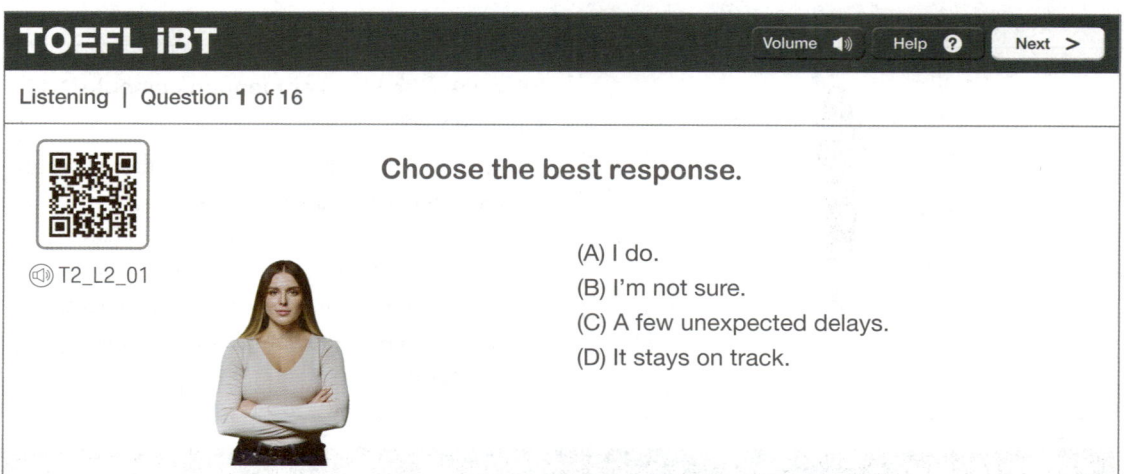

Listening | Question 1 of 16

Choose the best response.

(A) I do.
(B) I'm not sure.
(C) A few unexpected delays.
(D) It stays on track.

T2_L2_01

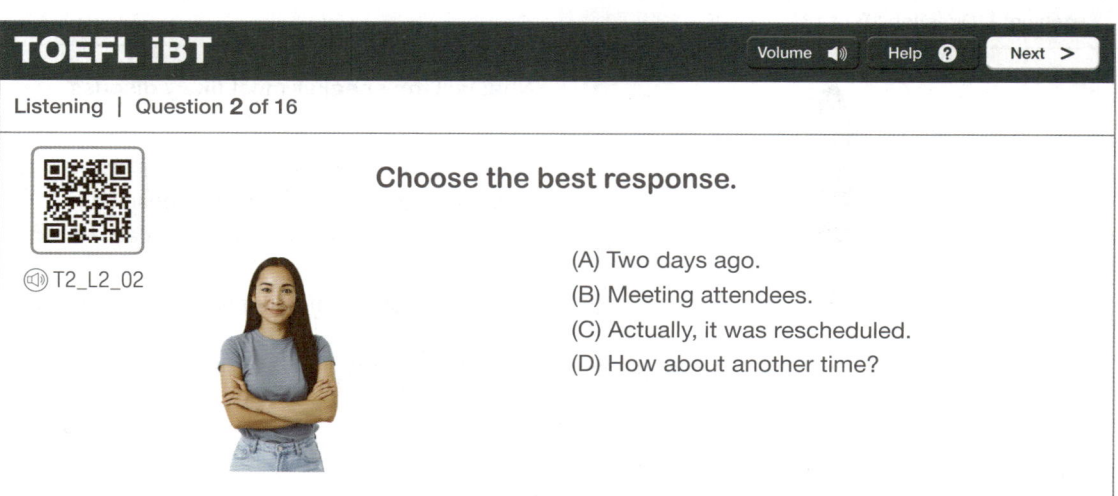

Listening | Question 2 of 16

Choose the best response.

(A) Two days ago.
(B) Meeting attendees.
(C) Actually, it was rescheduled.
(D) How about another time?

T2_L2_02

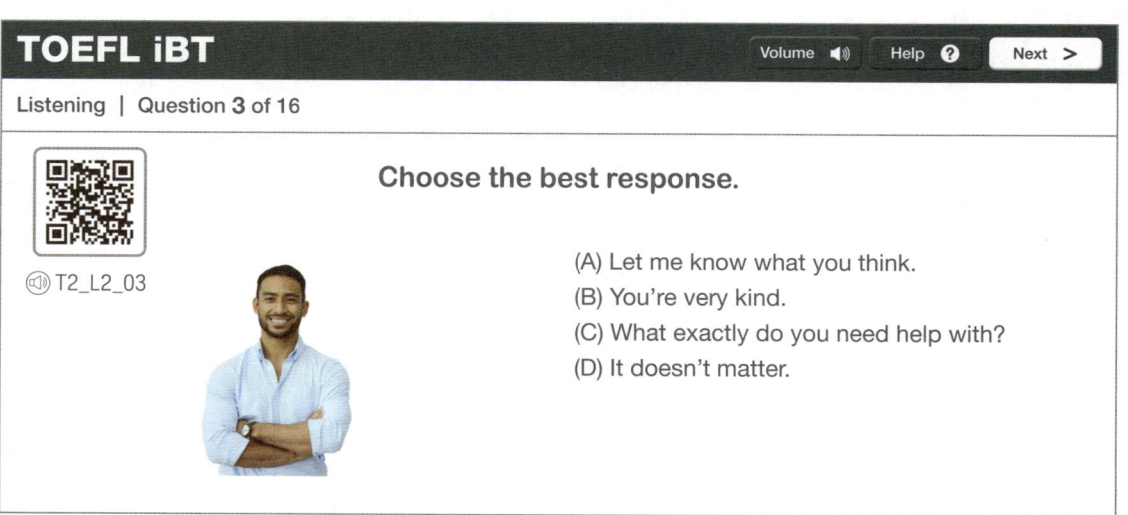

Listening | Question 3 of 16

Choose the best response.

(A) Let me know what you think.
(B) You're very kind.
(C) What exactly do you need help with?
(D) It doesn't matter.

T2_L2_03

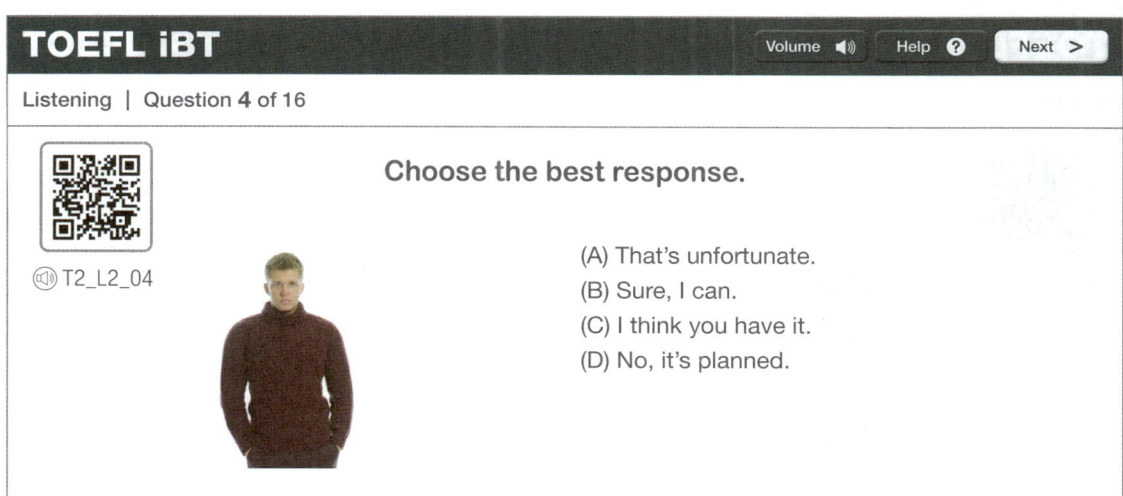

Listening | Question 4 of 16

T2_L2_04

Choose the best response.

(A) That's unfortunate.
(B) Sure, I can.
(C) I think you have it.
(D) No, it's planned.

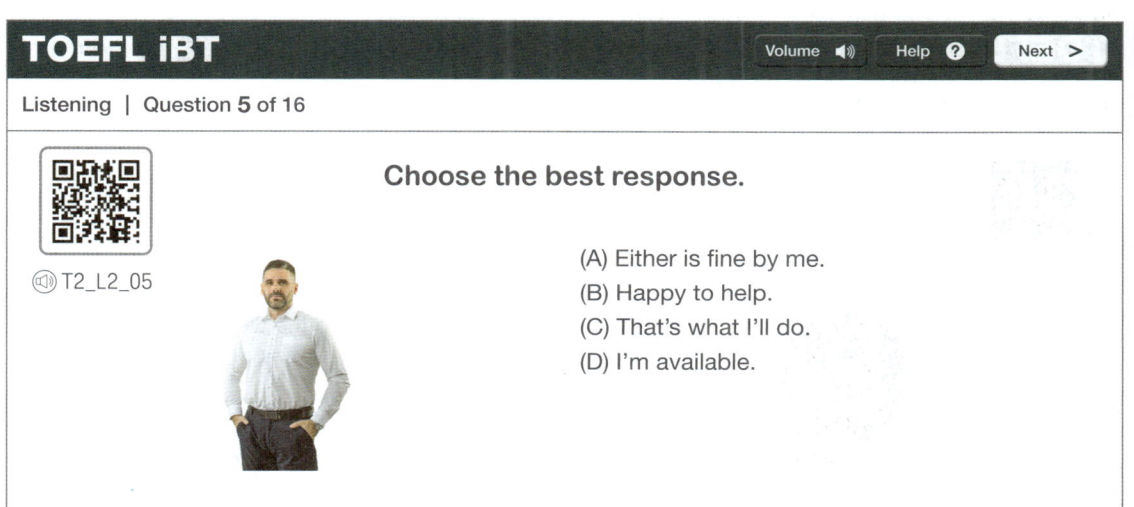

Listening | Question 5 of 16

T2_L2_05

Choose the best response.

(A) Either is fine by me.
(B) Happy to help.
(C) That's what I'll do.
(D) I'm available.

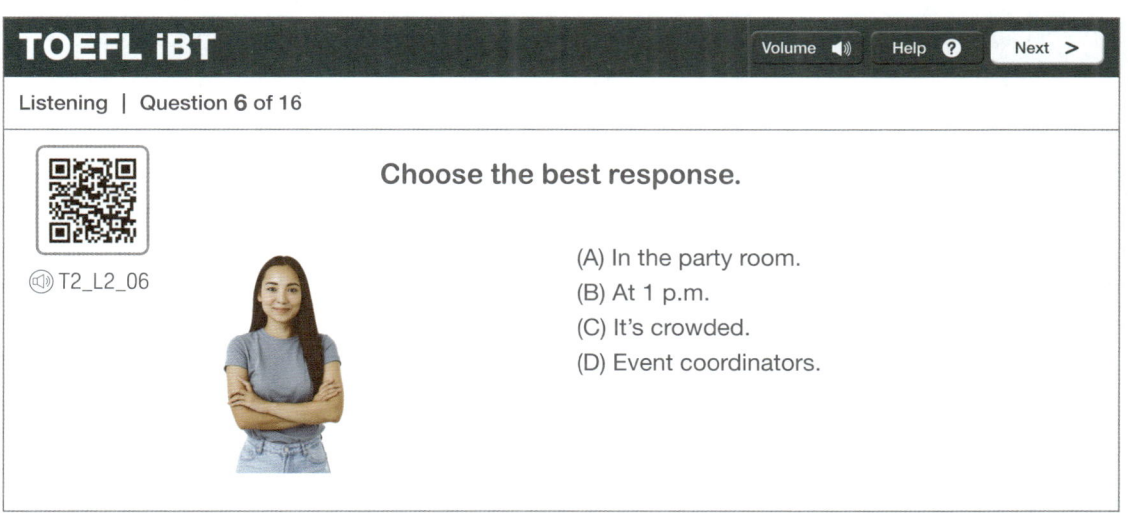

Listening | Question 6 of 16

T2_L2_06

Choose the best response.

(A) In the party room.
(B) At 1 p.m.
(C) It's crowded.
(D) Event coordinators.

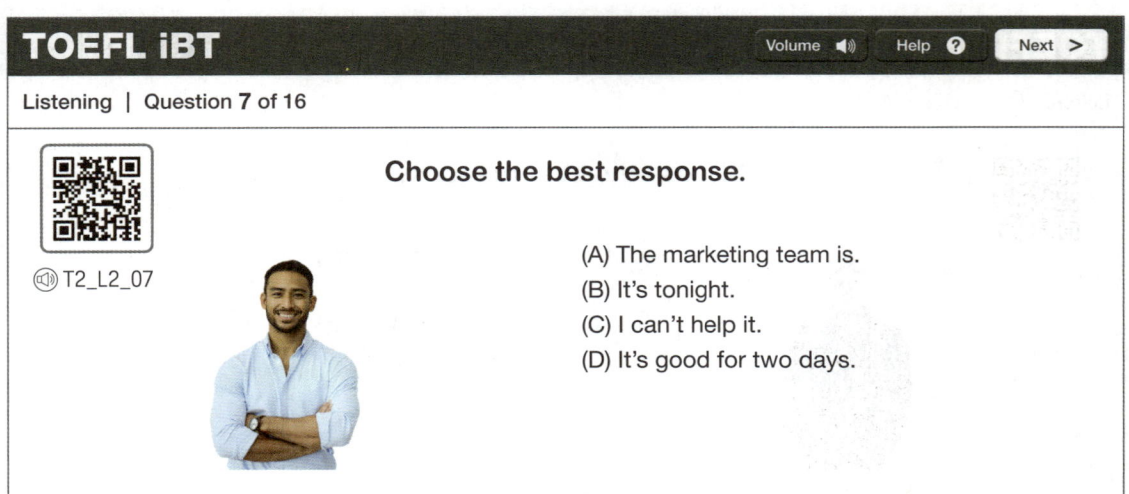

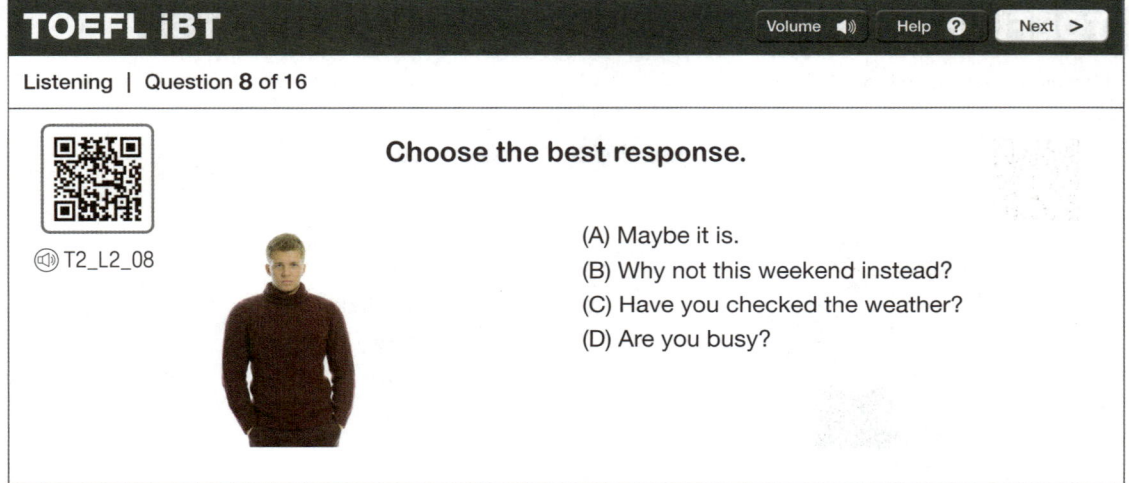

Listen to a conversation.

T2_L2_0910

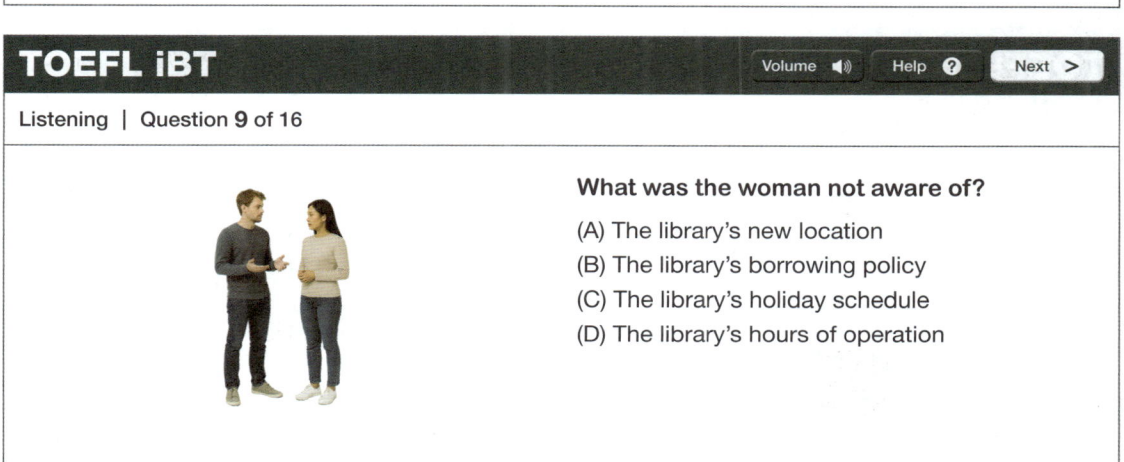

What was the woman not aware of?

(A) The library's new location
(B) The library's borrowing policy
(C) The library's holiday schedule
(D) The library's hours of operation

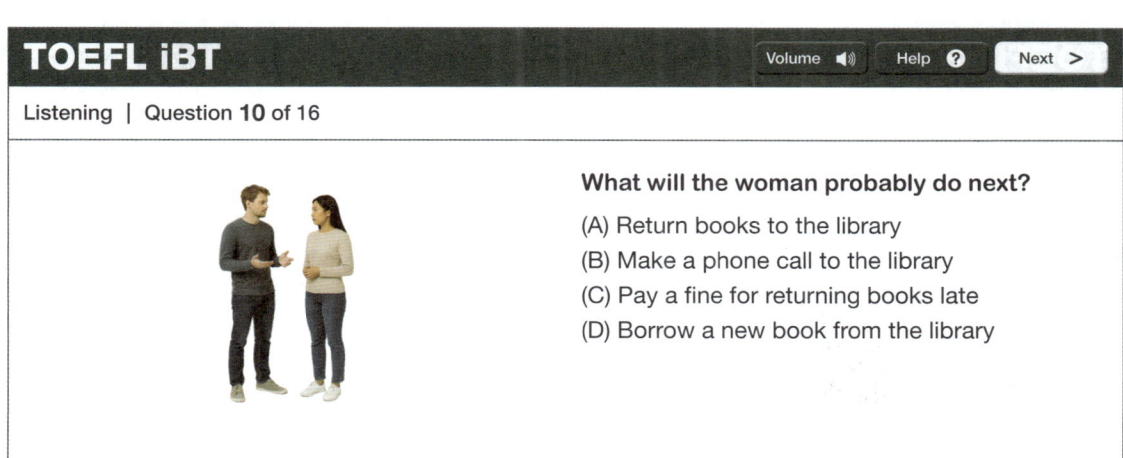

What will the woman probably do next?

(A) Return books to the library
(B) Make a phone call to the library
(C) Pay a fine for returning books late
(D) Borrow a new book from the library

TOEFL iBT

Listening | Questions 11–12 of 16

Listen to an announcement on the campus radio station.

T2_L2_1112

TOEFL iBT

Listening | Question 11 of 16

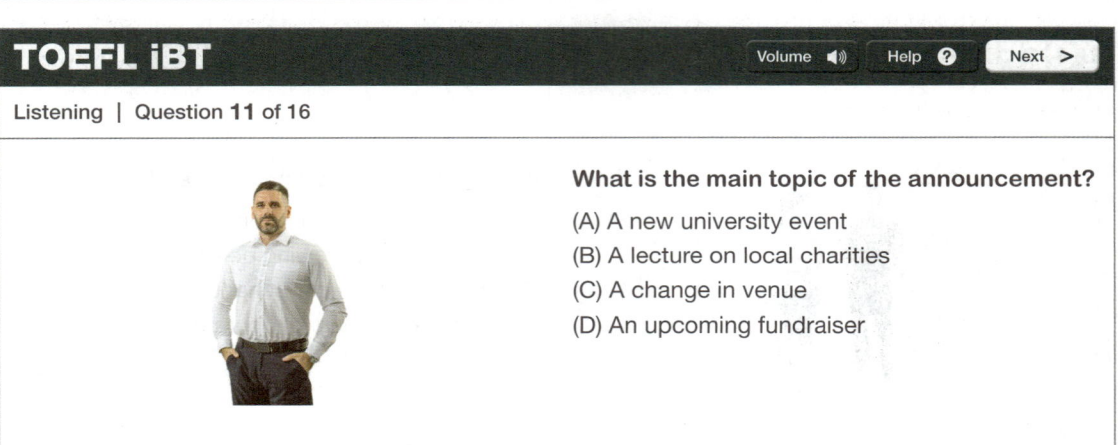

What is the main topic of the announcement?

(A) A new university event
(B) A lecture on local charities
(C) A change in venue
(D) An upcoming fundraiser

TOEFL iBT

Listening | Question 12 of 16

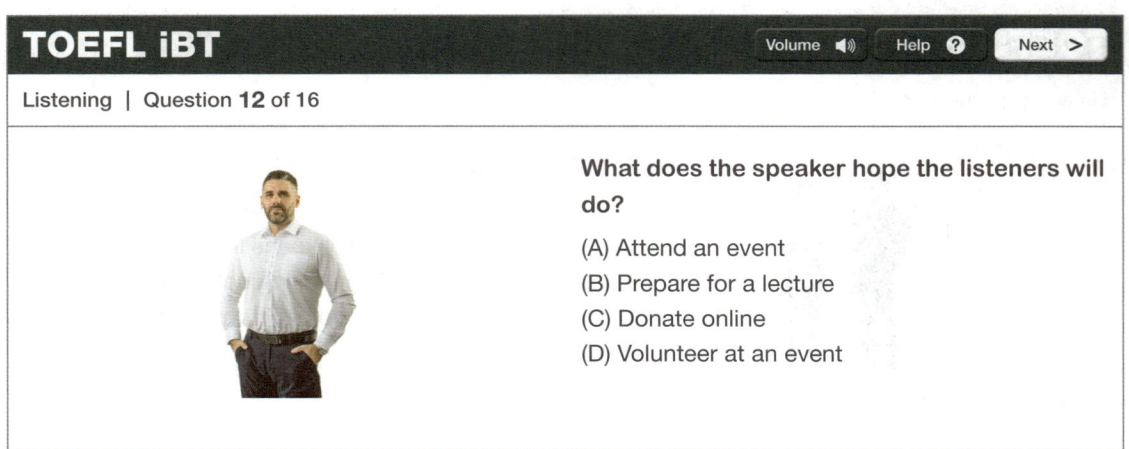

What does the speaker hope the listeners will do?

(A) Attend an event
(B) Prepare for a lecture
(C) Donate online
(D) Volunteer at an event

TOEFL iBT

Listening | Questions 13–16 of 16

Listen to a talk in an environmental science class.

T2_L2_1316

TOEFL iBT

Listening | Question 13 of 16

What is the talk mainly about?

(A) Ways in which humans use natural materials in clothing and architecture

(B) Hiding strategies of different animals

(C) New methods of using renewable energy

(D) Examples of how humans imitate nature for practical purposes

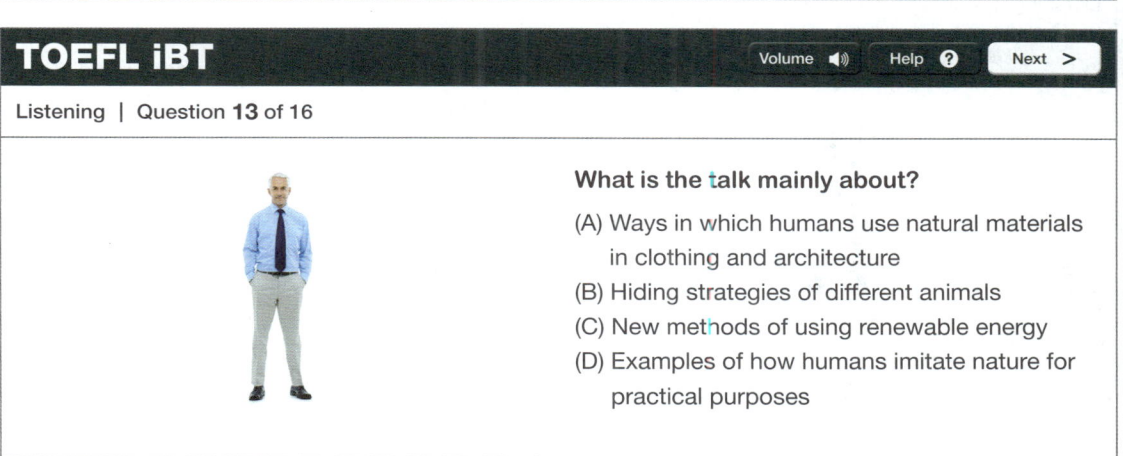

TOEFL iBT

Listening | Question 14 of 16

Why does the speaker mention a dog?

(A) To illustrate how an inventor copied animal behavior

(B) To compare its efficiency in movement with that of humpback whales

(C) To explain how a structure found in plants inspired an invention

(D) To show the close bond between scientists and animals

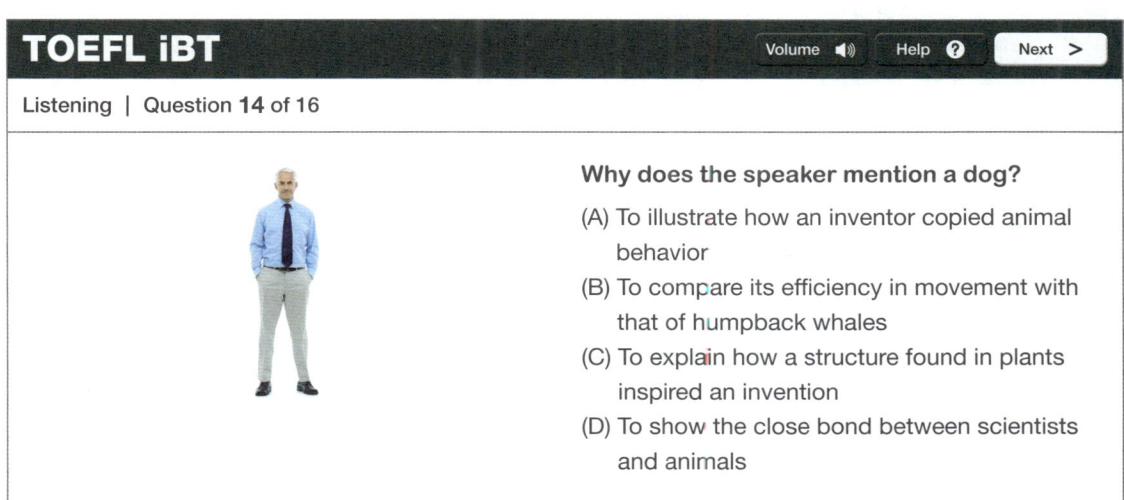

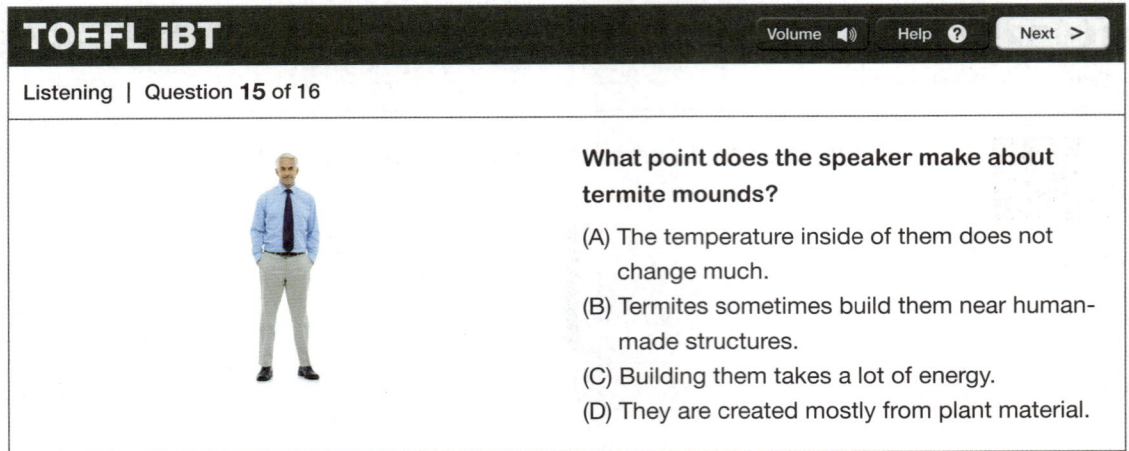

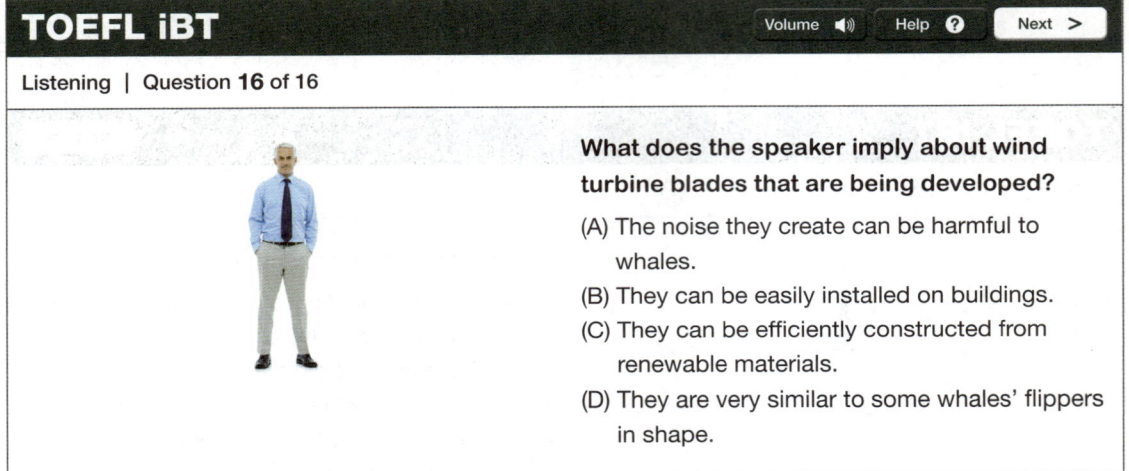

WRITING

TOEFL iBT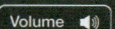

Writing Section

In the writing section, you will answer 12 questions to demonstrate how well you can write in English. There are three types of tasks.

Type of Task	Description
Build a Sentence	Create a grammatical sentence.
Write an Email	Write an email using information provided.
Write for an Academic Discussion	Participate in an online discussion.

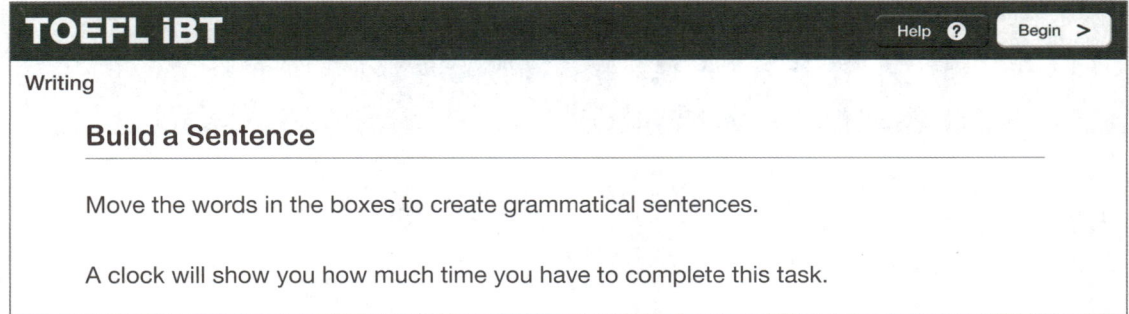

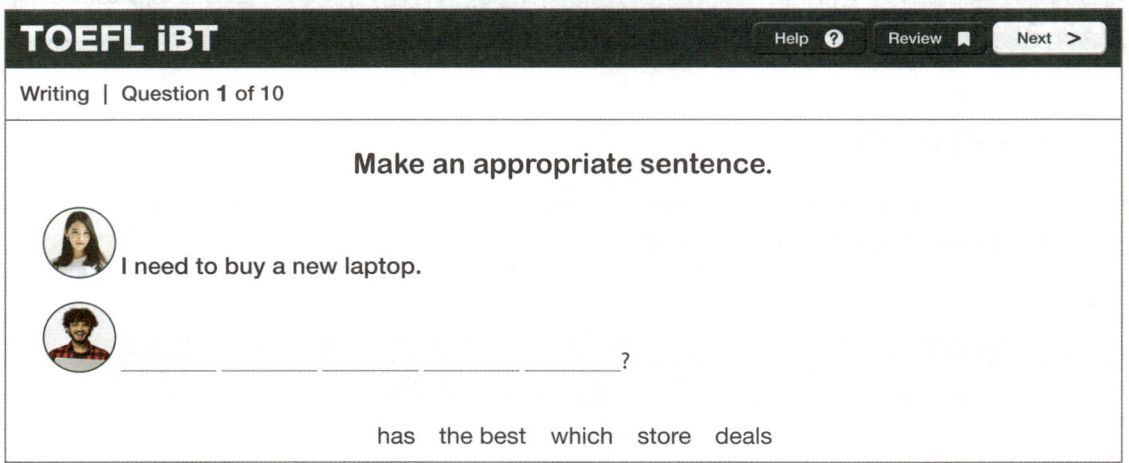

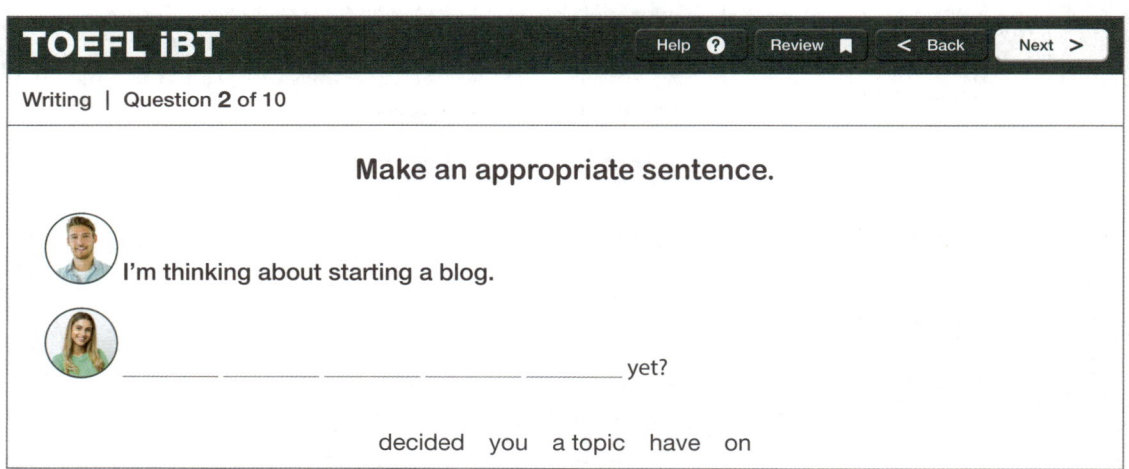

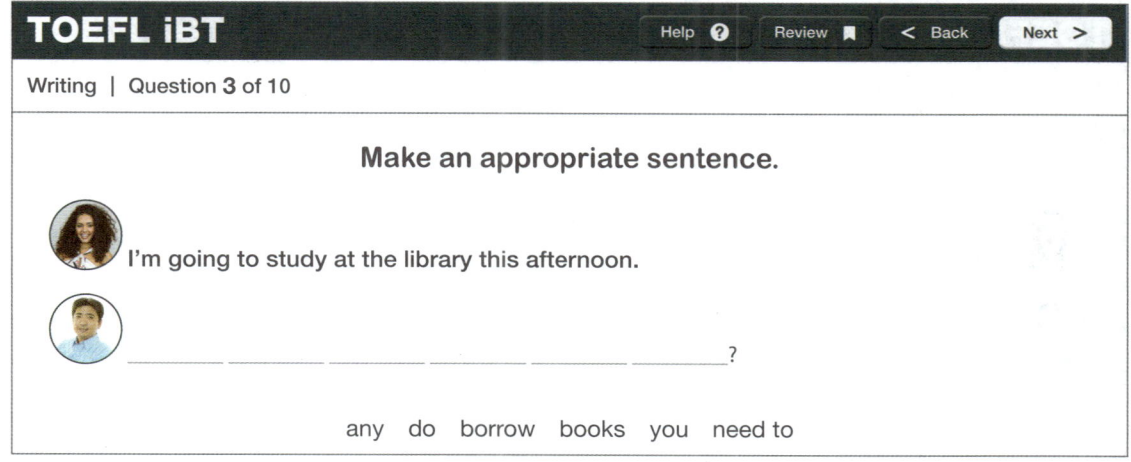

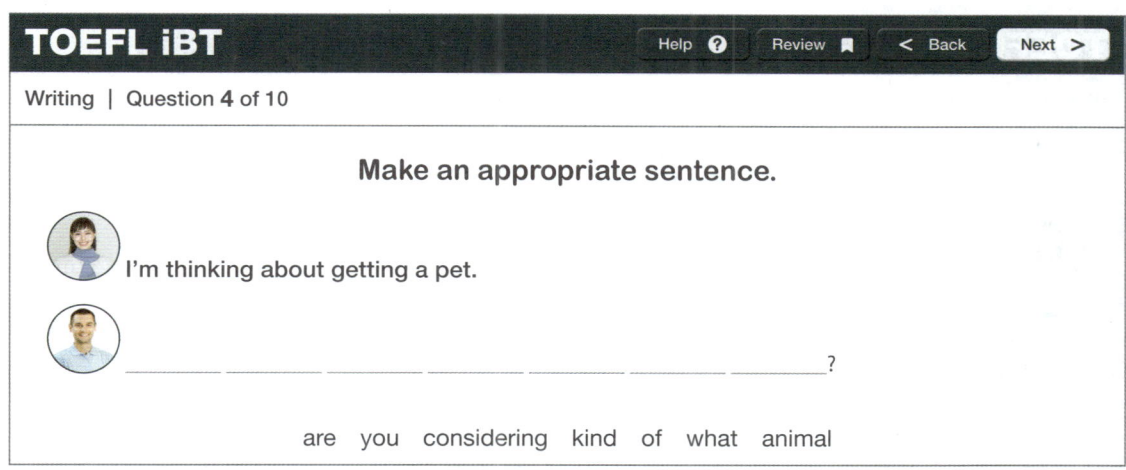

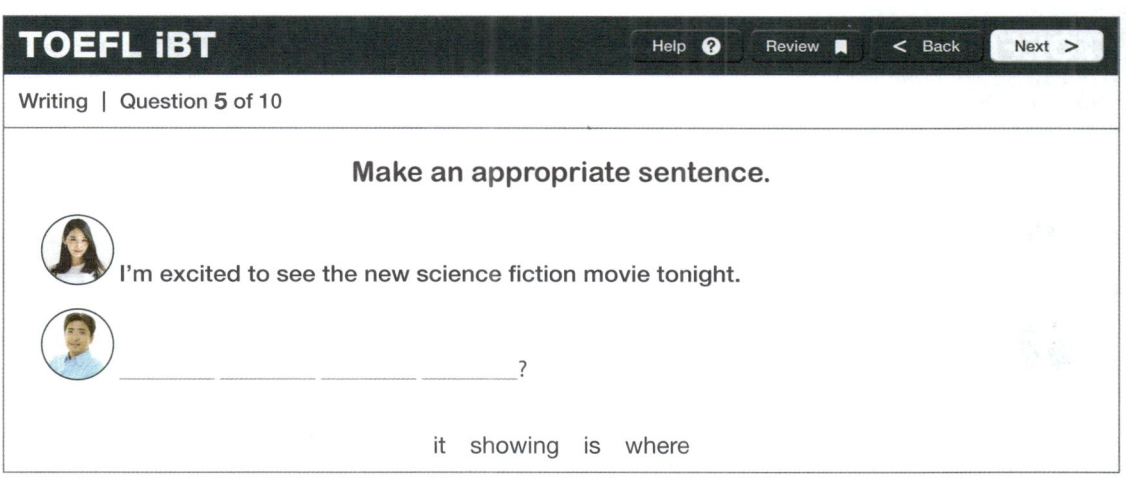

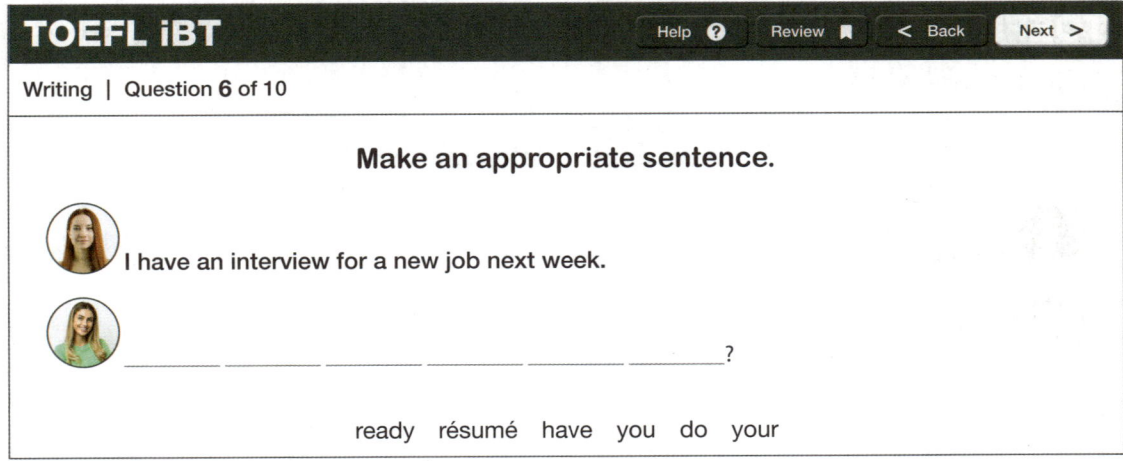

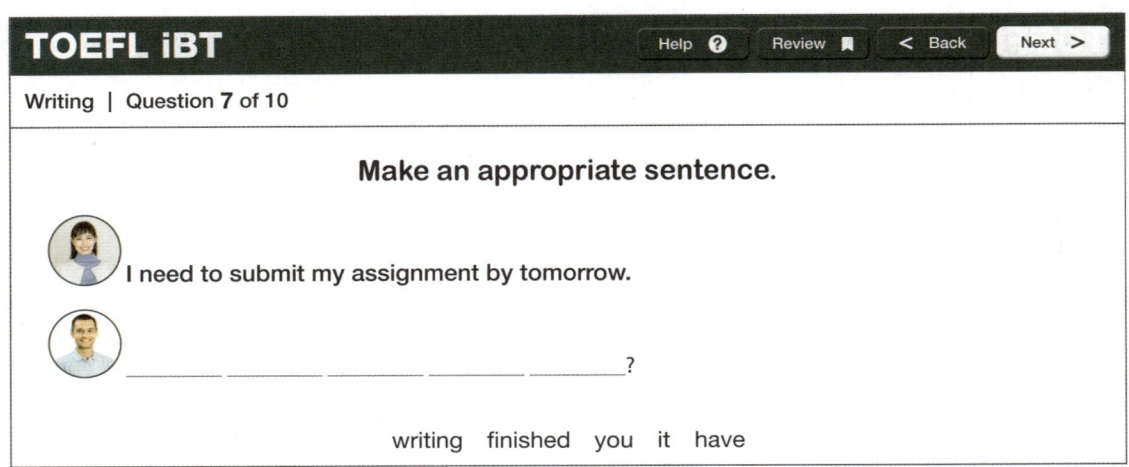

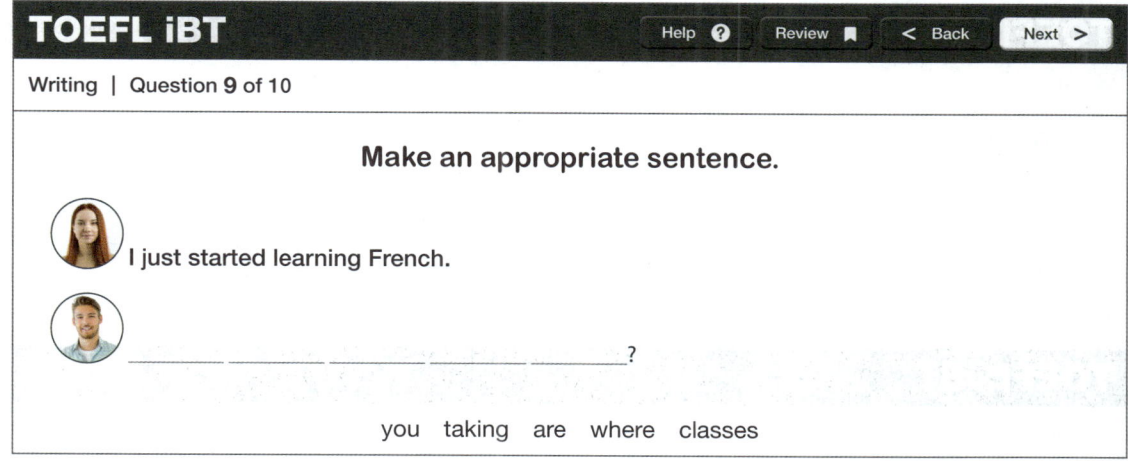

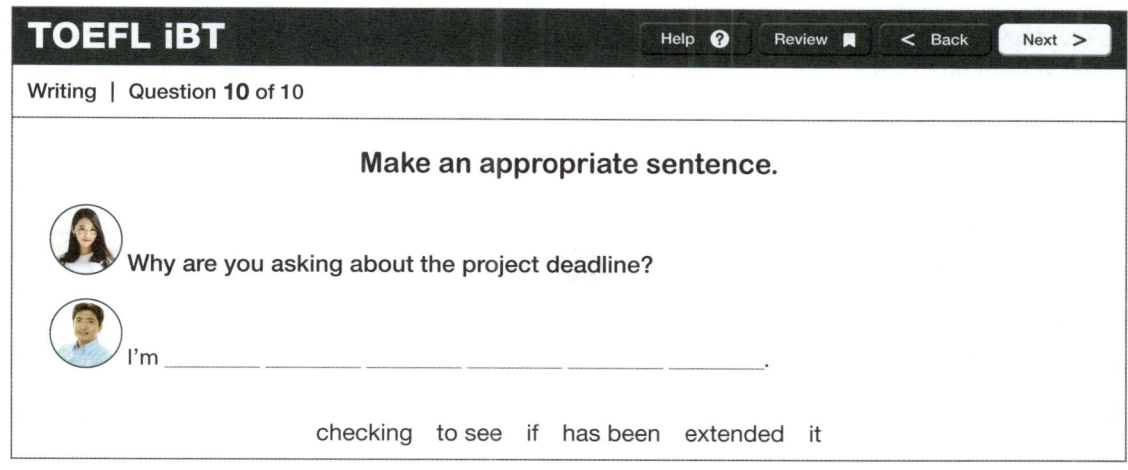

TOEFL iBT Help ? Begin >

Writing

Write an Email

You will read some information and use the information to write an email.

You will have 7 minutes to write the email.

TOEFL iBT Help ? Next >

Writing

Your coworker, Kevin, recently recommended a new restaurant for your team to visit. You took the team there, but everyone was disappointed. The food was not as good as expected, and the service was slow. You need to inform Kevin about the situation and discuss future lunch options.

Write an email to Kevin. In your email, do the following.

- Explain what was wrong with the restaurant.
- Describe the team's reaction to the visit.
- Suggest alternative lunch arrangements.

Write as much as you can and in complete sentences.

Your Response:

To: Kevin

Subject: Team Lunch Experience

Cut Paste Undo Redo Hide Word Count 0

TOEFL iBT

Writing

Write for an Academic Discussion

A professor has posted a question about a topic and students have responded with their thoughts and ideas. Make a contribution to the discussion.

You will have 10 minutes to write.

TOEFL iBT

Writing

Your professor is teaching a class on psychology. Write a post responding to the professor's question.

In your response, you should do the following:

- Express and support your opinion.
- Make a contribution to the discussion in your own words.

An effective response will contain at least 100 words.

Dr. Smith

Today we'll discuss the effects of exercise on mental health. Clearly, regular physical activity can improve mood and reduce stress. On the other hand, some people believe that mental health is primarily influenced by other factors such as genetics and the environment. Which do you believe plays a larger role in mental health? Why?

Mira

I think regular exercise has a significant positive impact on mental health. It can reduce stress, improve mood, and increase overall well-being by releasing endorphins and promoting a healthy lifestyle.

Tim

I believe that while exercise is important, other factors like genetics and environment play a larger role in mental health. A supportive environment and good mental health practices are crucial for overall well-being.

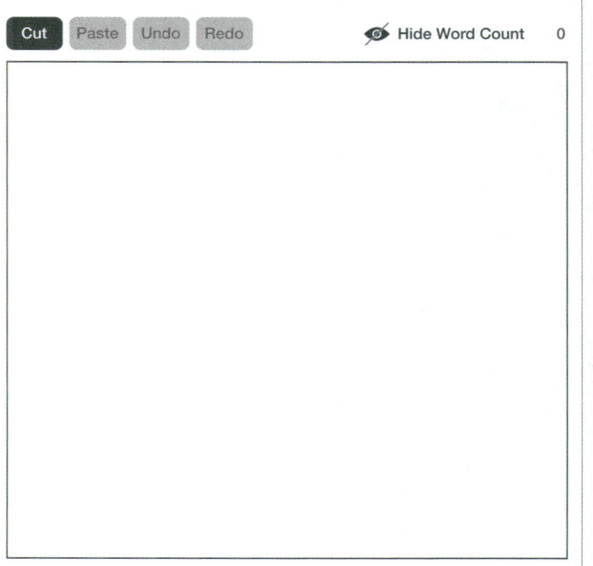

SPEAKING

TOEFL iBT

Speaking Section

In the speaking section, you will answer 11 questions to demonstrate how well you can speak English. There are two types of tasks.

Type of Task	Description
Listen and Repeat	Listen and repeat what you heard.
Take an Interview	Answer questions from the interviewer.

 p.0

TOEFL iBT

Speaking

Listen and Repeat

You will listen as someone speaks to you. Listen carefully and then repeat what you have heard. The clock will indicate how much time you have to speak.

No time for preparation will be provided.

TOEFL iBT

Speaking

You are learning how to guide new students through the campus gym. Listen to the speaker and repeat what she says. Repeat only once.

TOEFL iBT

Speaking | Question **1** of 11

T2_S_01

Listen and repeat only once.

RESPONSE TIME
00:00:08

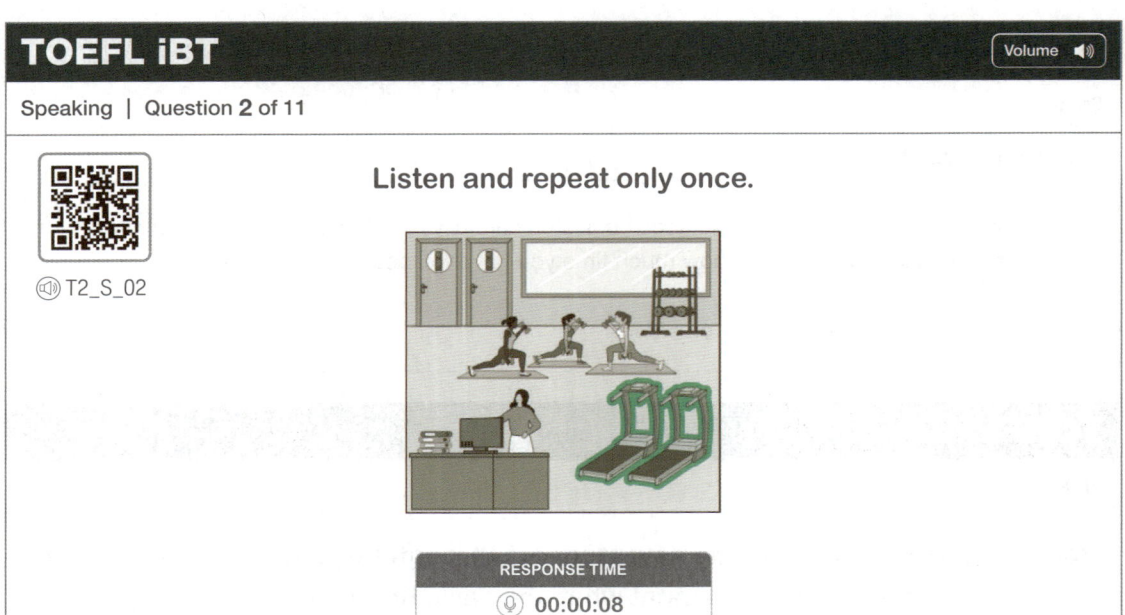

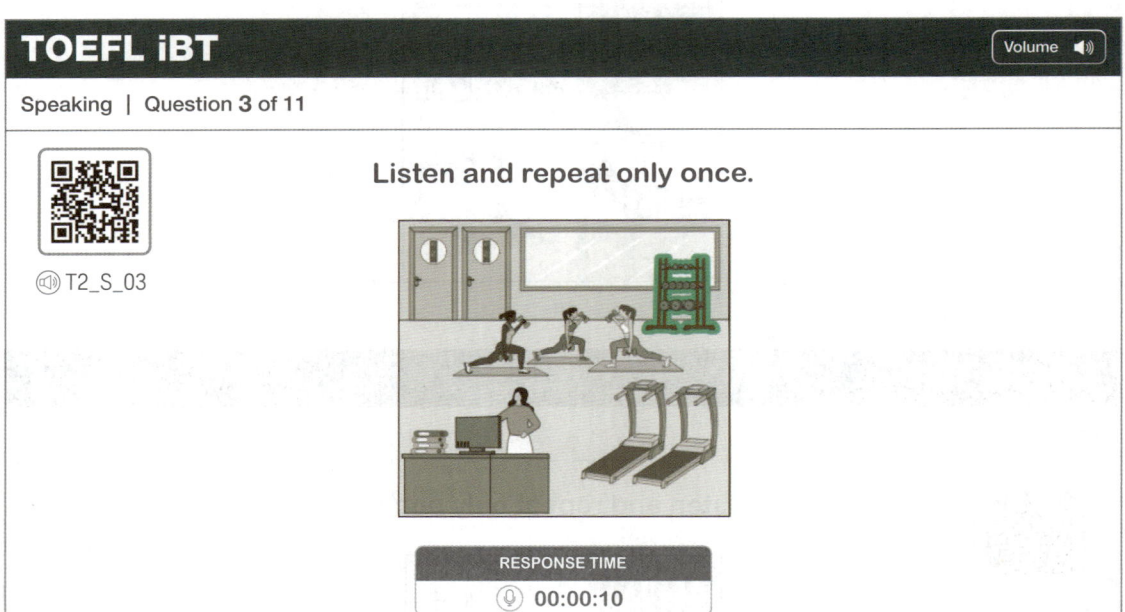

TOEFL iBT

Speaking | Question **4** of 11

T2_S_04

Listen and repeat only once.

RESPONSE TIME
00:00:10

TOEFL iBT

Speaking | Question **5** of 11

T2_S_05

Listen and repeat only once.

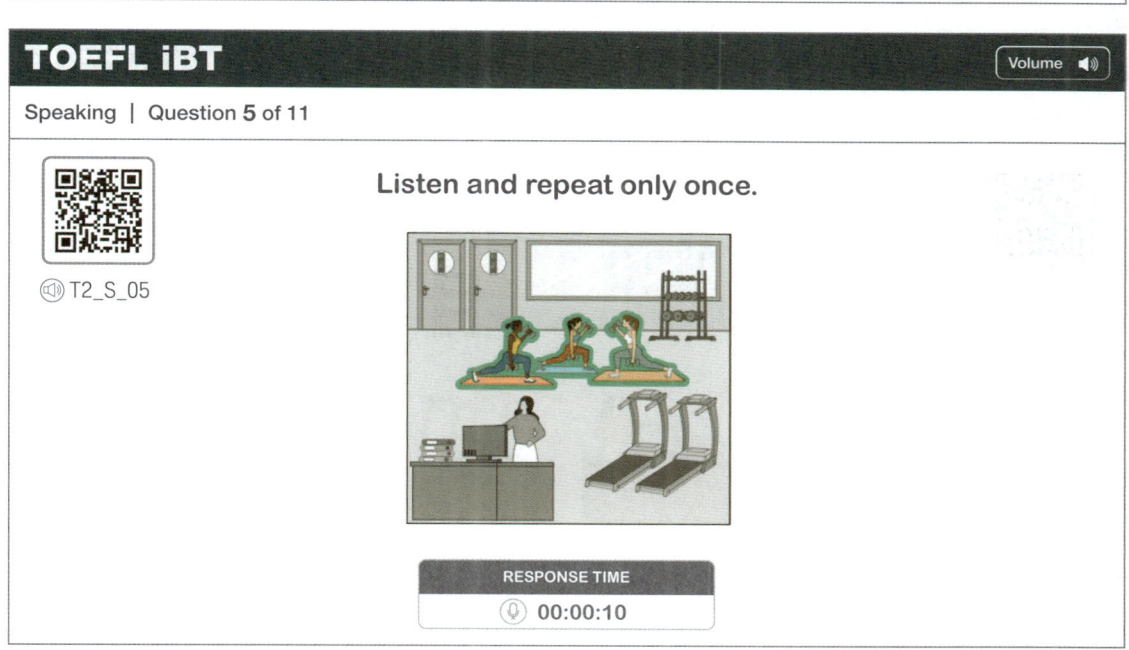

RESPONSE TIME
00:00:10

TOEFL iBT

Speaking | Question **6** of 11

🔊 T2_S_06

Listen and repeat only once.

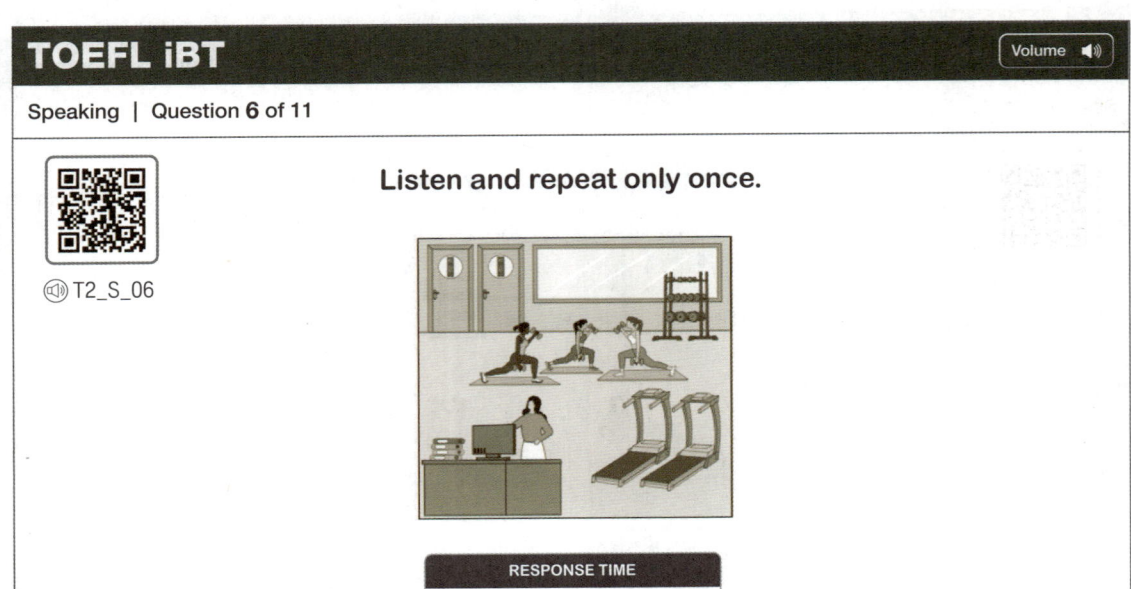

RESPONSE TIME
🎤 00:00:12

TOEFL iBT

Speaking | Question **7** of 11

🔊 T2_S_07

Listen and repeat only once.

RESPONSE TIME
🎤 00:00:12

TOEFL iBT

Speaking

Take an Interview

An interviewer will ask you questions. Answer the questions and be sure to say as much as you can in the time allowed.

No time for preparation will be provided.

TOEFL iBT

Speaking

You have volunteered for a research study about commuting habits. You will have a short online interview with a researcher. The researcher will ask you some questions.

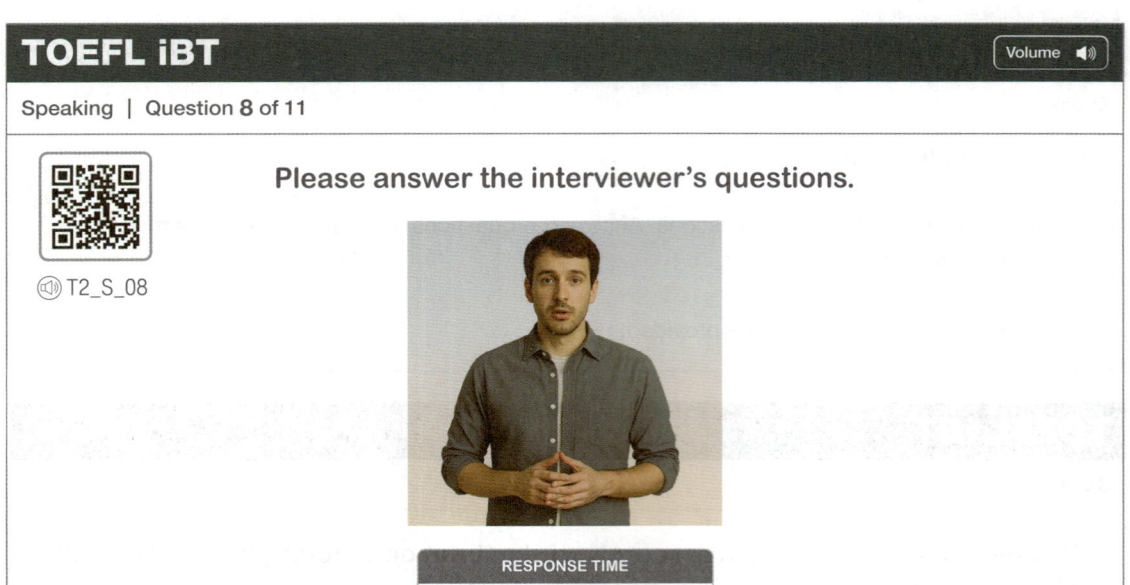

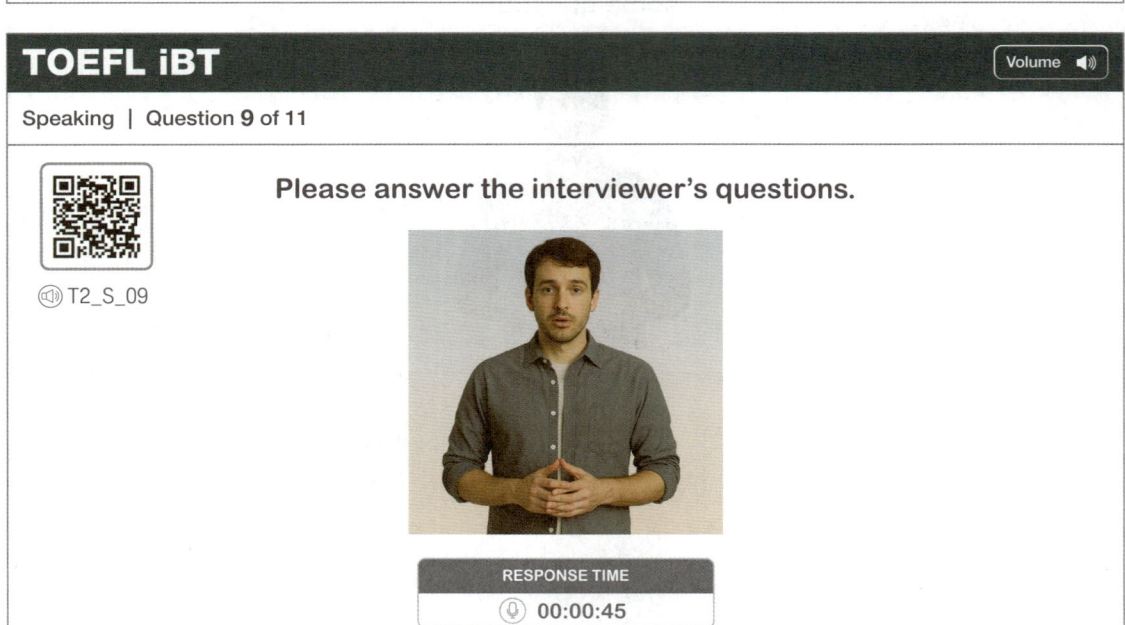

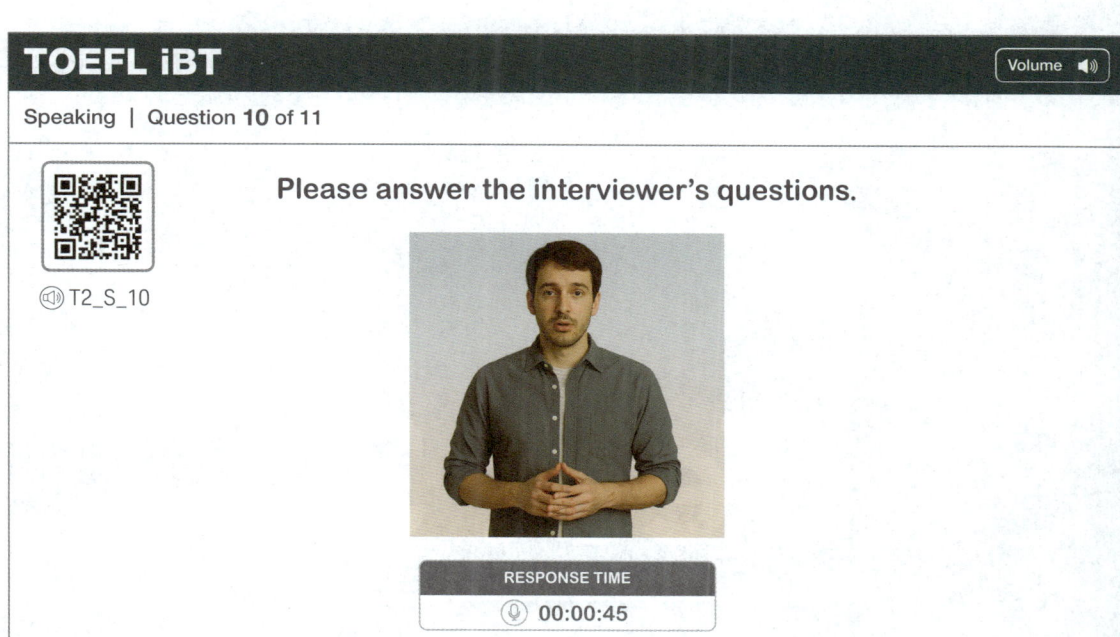

Test 3

READING

TOEFL iBT

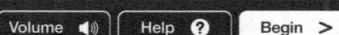

Reading Section

In the reading section, you will answer 35-48 questions to demonstrate how well you understand academic and non-academic texts in English. There are three types of tasks.

Type of Task	Description
Complete the Words	Fill in the missing letters in a paragraph.
Read in Daily Life	Answer questions about everyday reading materials.
Read an Academic Passage	Answer questions about academic passages.

Module 1

TOEFL iBT

Reading | Questions **1–10** of 20

Fill in the missing letters in the paragraph.

Early civilizations, including those in Mesopotamia, Egypt, the Indus Valley, and China, emerged around river valleys, where fertile land and water resources supported agriculture. Th_ _ developed sophis_ _ _ _ _ _ _ social struc_ _ _ _ _, written lang_ _ _ _ _, and adva_ _ _ _ technologies, wh_ _ _ allowed th_ _ to thr_ _ _ and esta_ _ _ _ _ cities, tr_ _ _ networks, and even empires. Just as important were their significant contributions to fields like art, science, and law. These developments were crucial in shaping the course of human history.

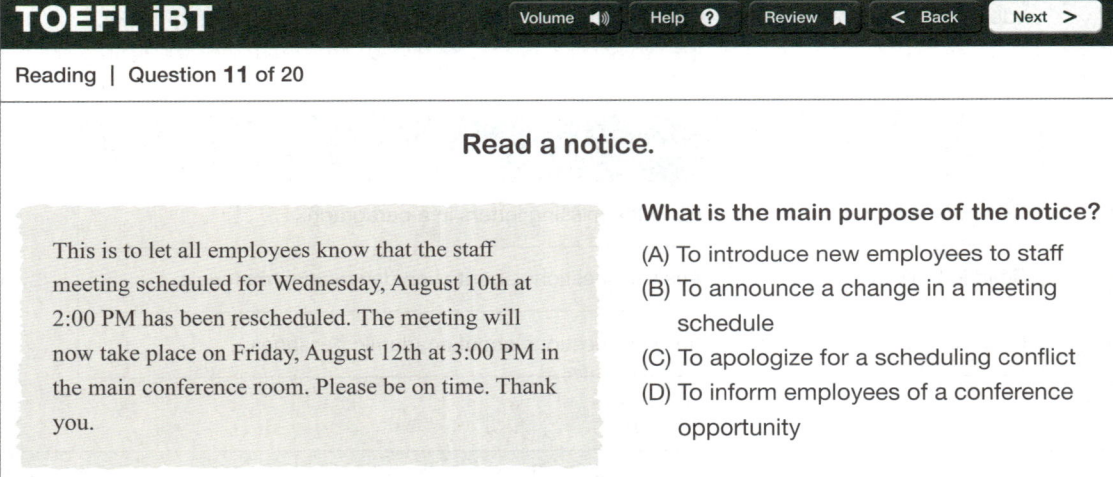

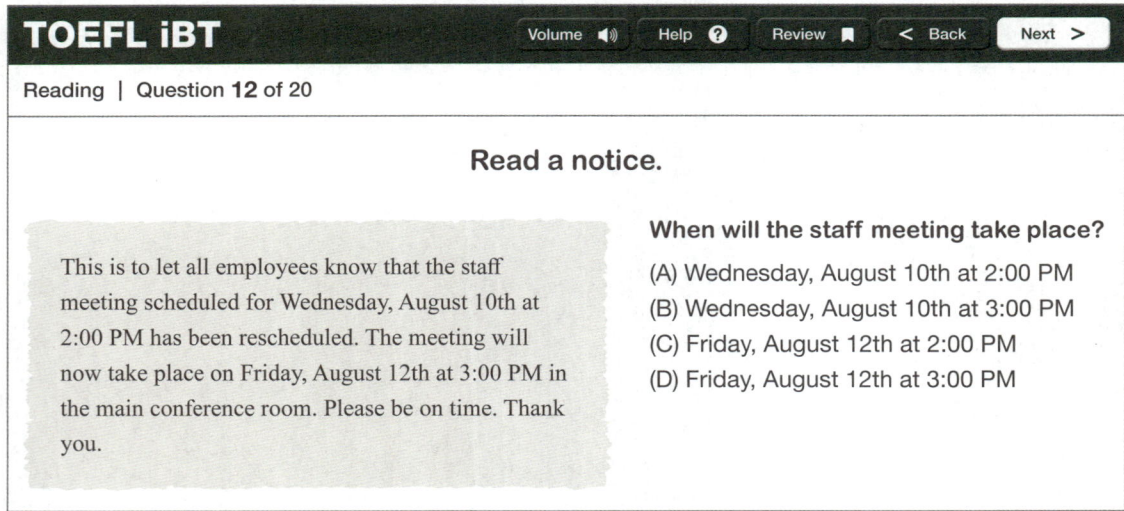

Read an email.

Subject: RE: inquiry

Dear Mr. Santiago,

We are pleased that you are considering our facility for your mother's birthday party.

Our outdoor area includes a playground and picnic tables, which can be set up to your preference. We offer a variety of dining options that suit different dietary needs. Please find the menu attached to this email.

Our team can organize activities for people of all ages, including arts and crafts, board games, and more. We do not have photographers on staff, but we have worked with external professional photographers in the past and are happy to provide you with recommendations.

To secure your date, we require a down payment of 30 percent of the total cost. If you need to cancel your booking, please notify us at least fourteen days in advance. Cancellations made outside this window will forfeit the down payment.

Regards,
Rebecca Yang

What can be inferred about Mr. Santiago?

(A) He is about to celebrate his birthday.
(B) He has used Rebecca Yang's facility in the past.
(C) He is a professional event organizer.
(D) He has requested information about Rebecca Yang's facility.

Read an email.

Subject: RE: inquiry

Dear Mr. Santiago,

We are pleased that you are considering our facility for your mother's birthday party.

Our outdoor area includes a playground and picnic tables, which can be set up to your preference. We offer a variety of dining options that suit different dietary needs. Please find the menu attached to this email.

Our team can organize activities for people of all ages, including arts and crafts, board games, and more. We do not have photographers on staff, but we have worked with external professional photographers in the past and are happy to provide you with recommendations.

To secure your date, we require a down payment of 30 percent of the total cost. If you need to cancel your booking, please notify us at least fourteen days in advance. Cancellations made outside this window will forfeit the down payment.

Regards,
Rebecca Yang

Rebecca Yang's team does NOT include

(A) Cooks
(B) Professional photographers
(C) People who can facilitate children's games
(D) People who can set up picnic tables

Read an email.

Subject: | RE: inquiry

Dear Mr. Santiago,

We are pleased that you are considering our facility for your mother's birthday party.

Our outdoor area includes a playground and picnic tables, which can be set up to your preference. We offer a variety of dining options that suit different dietary needs. Please find the menu attached to this email.

Our team can organize activities for people of all ages, including arts and crafts, board games, and more. We do not have photographers on staff, but we have worked with external professional photographers in the past and are happy to provide you with recommendations.

To secure your date, we require a down payment of 30 percent of the total cost. If you need to cancel your booking, please notify us at least fourteen days in advance. Cancellations made outside this window will forfeit the down payment.

Regards,
Rebecca Yang

What information is being provided along with the email message?

(A) Food choices
(B) Types of arts and crafts activities
(C) Dates available for booking
(D) Contact information of photographers

The Effects of Urbanization on Bird Populations

Urbanization has had a profound impact on bird populations worldwide. As cities expand, natural habitats are replaced with buildings, roads, and other infrastructure. This leads to a significant reduction in the availability of nesting sites and food sources for birds.

Some species, such as pigeons and sparrows, have adapted well to urban environments, taking advantage of the new resources and structures. However, many other species struggle to survive in these altered landscapes. Therefore, it is imperative to find solutions that help birds adapt to city life. One notable effect of urbanization is the change in bird song. Birds living in cities often sing at higher pitches and volumes than their rural counterparts. This adaptation helps them communicate over the noise of traffic and human activity. Additionally, the artificial lighting in cities can disrupt the natural circadian (daily time-related) rhythms of birds, affecting their breeding and feeding behaviors.

Conservationists are working to mitigate the negative effects of urbanization on birds. Initiatives such as creating urban green spaces, constructing bird-friendly buildings, and reducing light pollution are being implemented. These efforts aim to create a more hospitable environment for birds, allowing them to coexist with humans in urban settings.

The word "mitigate" in the passage is closest in meaning to

(A) understand
(B) analyze
(C) communicate
(D) reduce

The Effects of Urbanization on Bird Populations

Urbanization has had a profound impact on bird populations worldwide. As cities expand, natural habitats are replaced with buildings, roads, and other infrastructure. This leads to a significant reduction in the availability of nesting sites and food sources for birds.

Some species, such as pigeons and sparrows, have adapted well to urban environments, taking advantage of the new resources and structures. However, many other species struggle to survive in these altered landscapes. Therefore, it is imperative to find solutions that help birds adapt to city life. One notable effect of urbanization is the change in bird song. Birds living in cities often sing at higher pitches and volumes than their rural counterparts. This adaptation helps them communicate over the noise of traffic and human activity. Additionally, the artificial lighting in cities can disrupt the natural circadian (daily time-related) rhythms of birds, affecting their breeding and feeding behaviors.

Conservationists are working to mitigate the negative effects of urbanization on birds. Initiatives such as creating urban green spaces, constructing bird-friendly buildings, and reducing light pollution are being implemented. These efforts aim to create a more hospitable environment for birds, allowing them to coexist with humans in urban settings.

Which of the following is NOT mentioned as an effect of urbanization on birds in the passage?

(A) Reduced availability of nesting sites
(B) Changes in bird song
(C) Increased food sources
(D) Disrupted circadian rhythms

The Effects of Urbanization on Bird Populations

Urbanization has had a profound impact on bird populations worldwide. As cities expand, natural habitats are replaced with buildings, roads, and other infrastructure. This leads to a significant reduction in the availability of nesting sites and food sources for birds.

Some species, such as pigeons and sparrows, have adapted well to urban environments, taking advantage of the new resources and structures. However, many other species struggle to survive in these altered landscapes. Therefore, it is imperative to find solutions that help birds adapt to city life. One notable effect of urbanization is the change in bird song. Birds living in cities often sing at higher pitches and volumes than their rural counterparts. This adaptation helps them communicate over the noise of traffic and human activity. Additionally, the artificial lighting in cities can disrupt the natural circadian (daily time-related) rhythms of birds, affecting their breeding and feeding behaviors.

Conservationists are working to mitigate the negative effects of urbanization on birds. Initiatives such as creating urban green spaces, constructing bird-friendly buildings, and reducing light pollution are being implemented. These efforts aim to create a more hospitable environment for birds, allowing them to coexist with humans in urban settings.

Why does the author mention pigeons and sparrows?

(A) To identify birds that struggle to survive in urban environments
(B) To give examples of birds that have adjusted to living in urban settings
(C) To highlight the diversity of urban bird species
(D) To suggest that all birds can adapt to cities

The Effects of Urbanization on Bird Populations

Urbanization has had a profound impact on bird populations worldwide. As cities expand, natural habitats are replaced with buildings, roads, and other infrastructure. This leads to a significant reduction in the availability of nesting sites and food sources for birds.

Some species, such as pigeons and sparrows, have adapted well to urban environments, taking advantage of the new resources and structures. However, many other species struggle to survive in these altered landscapes. Therefore, it is imperative to find solutions that help birds adapt to city life. One notable effect of urbanization is the change in bird song. Birds living in cities often sing at higher pitches and volumes than their rural counterparts. This adaptation helps them communicate over the noise of traffic and human activity. Additionally, the artificial lighting in cities can disrupt the natural circadian (daily time-related) rhythms of birds, affecting their breeding and feeding behaviors.

Conservationists are working to mitigate the negative effects of urbanization on birds. Initiatives such as creating urban green spaces, constructing bird-friendly buildings, and reducing light pollution are being implemented. These efforts aim to create a more hospitable environment for birds, allowing them to coexist with humans in urban settings.

What is one initiative mentioned in the passage to help birds in urban areas?

(A) Introducing new bird species to urban areas
(B) Providing human-made food sources to birds
(C) Creating urban green spaces
(D) Decreasing the amount of noise made by traffic

The Effects of Urbanization on Bird Populations

Urbanization has had a profound impact on bird populations worldwide. As cities expand, natural habitats are replaced with buildings, roads, and other infrastructure. This leads to a significant reduction in the availability of nesting sites and food sources for birds.

Some species, such as pigeons and sparrows, have adapted well to urban environments, taking advantage of the new resources and structures. However, many other species struggle to survive in these altered landscapes. Therefore, it is imperative to find solutions that help birds adapt to city life. One notable effect of urbanization is the change in bird song. Birds living in cities often sing at higher pitches and volumes than their rural counterparts. This adaptation helps them communicate over the noise of traffic and human activity. Additionally, the artificial lighting in cities can disrupt the natural circadian (daily time-related) rhythms of birds, affecting their breeding and feeding behaviors.

Conservationists are working to mitigate the negative effects of urbanization on birds. Initiatives such as creating urban green spaces, constructing bird-friendly buildings, and reducing light pollution are being implemented. These efforts aim to create a more hospitable environment for birds, allowing them to coexist with humans in urban settings.

What can be inferred about the impact artificial lighting in cities has on birds?

(A) It disrupts the natural behaviors of birds.
(B) It allows birds to find food at night.
(C) It helps birds to adapt to urban environments.
(D) It increases the population of urban birds.

Module 2

Reading | Questions 1–10 of 20

Fill in the missing letters in the paragraph.

Consciousness is the state of being aware of and able to think about one's own existence, thoughts, and surroundings. Wh_ _ you lo_ _ in a mir_ _ _ and recognize your_ _ _ _ , you exh_ _ _ _ self-awareness, wh_ _ _ is n_ _ unique t_ humans b_ _ is al_ _ found in dolphins and great apes. Consciousness is not to be confused with cognition. The latter refers to mental processes involved in gaining knowledge and solving problems, like thinking, judging, and remembering.

Reading | Question 11 of 20

Read an email.

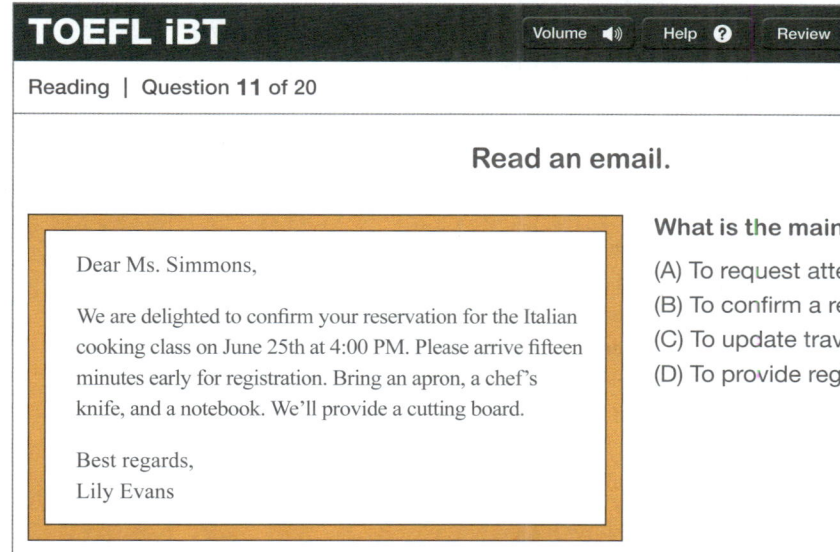

Dear Ms. Simmons,

We are delighted to confirm your reservation for the Italian cooking class on June 25th at 4:00 PM. Please arrive fifteen minutes early for registration. Bring an apron, a chef's knife, and a notebook. We'll provide a cutting board.

Best regards,
Lily Evans

What is the main purpose of the e-mail?

(A) To request attendance at a class
(B) To confirm a reservation for a class
(C) To update travel plans
(D) To provide registration instructions

Reading | Question 12 of 20

Read an email.

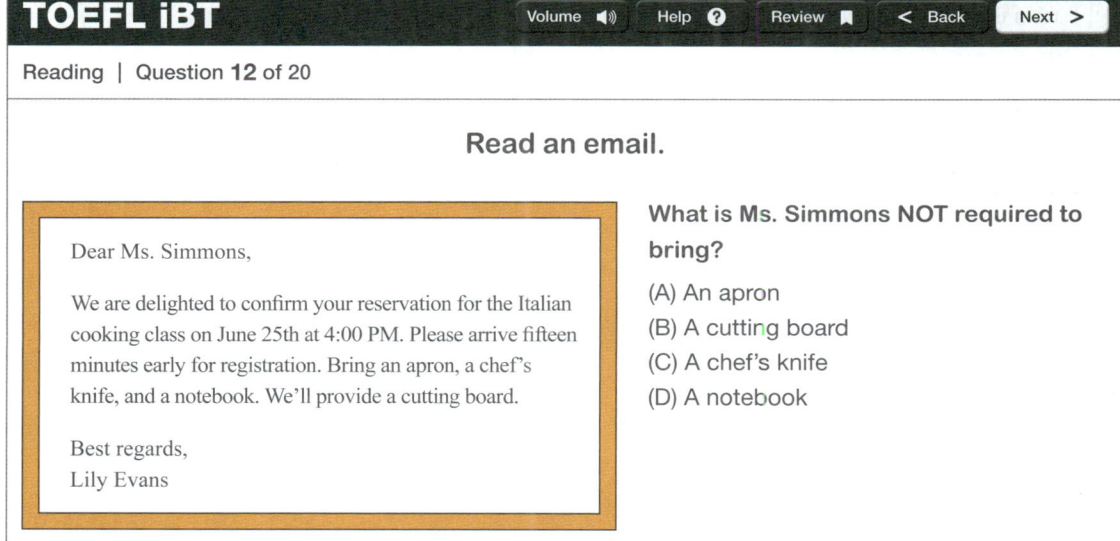

Dear Ms. Simmons,

We are delighted to confirm your reservation for the Italian cooking class on June 25th at 4:00 PM. Please arrive fifteen minutes early for registration. Bring an apron, a chef's knife, and a notebook. We'll provide a cutting board.

Best regards,
Lily Evans

What is Ms. Simmons NOT required to bring?

(A) An apron
(B) A cutting board
(C) A chef's knife
(D) A notebook

Read an email.

Subject: Annual conference

Dear Ms. Adams,

We are pleased to invite you to the annual educational psychology conference taking place on October 13-15.

This year's conference theme is "Emotions and Psychological Processes." The keynote speaker will be Dr. Jane Smith. We will also organize four panel discussions with leading scholars as well as interactive workshops. More details will be forthcoming.

We are excited to announce the return of poster sessions this year, where graduate students and early career researchers will present their work. If you would like to present your research in the poster session, please submit an extended abstract for review by the conference committee by August 31.

Breakfast and lunch will be provided for a nominal fee with a variety of options to accommodate different dietary needs. Additionally, all attendees will receive a conference packet, including materials from the sessions and a certificate of participation.

Regards,
Michael Brown

What is the main purpose of the email?

(A) To request information about Ms. Adams' research
(B) To invite Ms. Adams to speak at a conference
(C) To provide details about an event
(D) To announce participants of the poster sessions

Read an email.

Subject: Annual conference

Dear Ms. Adams,

We are pleased to invite you to the annual educational psychology conference taking place on October 13-15.

This year's conference theme is "Emotions and Psychological Processes." The keynote speaker will be Dr. Jane Smith. We will also organize four panel discussions with leading scholars as well as interactive workshops. More details will be forthcoming.

We are excited to announce the return of poster sessions this year, where graduate students and early career researchers will present their work. If you would like to present your research in the poster session, please submit an extended abstract for review by the conference committee by August 31.

Breakfast and lunch will be provided for a nominal fee with a variety of options to accommodate different dietary needs. Additionally, all attendees will receive a conference packet, including materials from the sessions and a certificate of participation.

Regards,
Michael Brown

Dr. Jane Smith will

(A) lead panel discussions
(B) organize interactive workshops
(C) talk about research about emotions
(D) present her research in the poster session

Read an email.

Subject: Annual conference

Dear Ms. Adams,

We are pleased to invite you to the annual educational psychology conference taking place on October 13-15.

This year's conference theme is "Emotions and Psychological Processes." The keynote speaker will be Dr. Jane Smith. We will also organize four panel discussions with leading scholars as well as interactive workshops. More details will be forthcoming.

We are excited to announce the return of poster sessions this year, where graduate students and early career researchers will present their work. If you would like to present your research in the poster session, please submit an extended abstract for review by the conference committee by August 31.

Breakfast and lunch will be provided for a nominal fee with a variety of options to accommodate different dietary needs. Additionally, all attendees will receive a conference packet, including materials from the sessions and a certificate of participation.

Regards,
Michael Brown

What can be inferred about the poster session?

(A) It has been part of the conference in the past.
(B) It is for leading scholars of the field.
(C) It is open to the public.
(D) It will be held on August 31.

The History of Photography

The history of photography is marked by significant technological progress and artistic innovation. It began in the early nineteenth century with the invention of the camera obscura, a device that projected images onto a surface. The first permanent photograph was created by Joseph-Nicéphore Niépce in 1826 using a process called heliography, which required several hours of exposure to light.

Photography quickly evolved with the development of daguerreotypes, introduced by Louis Daguerre in 1839. This method produced detailed images on silver-plated copper, but daguerreotypes needed delicate handling, and the exposure times required, although much shorter, still remained impractical for recording images of moving objects. The invention of the calotype by William Henry Fox Talbot in the 1840s allowed for multiple copies of an image to be made from a single negative, revolutionizing the field.

In the late nineteenth and early twentieth centuries, the introduction of film and roll cameras made photography more accessible to the public. George Eastman's establishment of the Kodak company in 1888 played a crucial role in this democratization, as his cameras were simple to use and affordable. Today, digital photography has further transformed the medium, allowing instant image capture and sharing.

The word "innovation" in the passage is closest in meaning to

(A) success
(B) advancement
(C) activity
(D) expression

The History of Photography

The history of photography is marked by significant technological progress and artistic innovation. It began in the early nineteenth century with the invention of the camera obscura, a device that projected images onto a surface. The first permanent photograph was created by Joseph-Nicéphore Niépce in 1826 using a process called heliography, which required several hours of exposure to light.

Photography quickly evolved with the development of daguerreotypes, introduced by Louis Daguerre in 1839. This method produced detailed images on silver-plated copper, but daguerreotypes needed delicate handling, and the exposure times required, although much shorter, still remained impractical for recording images of moving objects. The invention of the calotype by William Henry Fox Talbot in the 1840s allowed for multiple copies of an image to be made from a single negative, revolutionizing the field.

In the late nineteenth and early twentieth centuries, the introduction of film and roll cameras made photography more accessible to the public. George Eastman's establishment of the Kodak company in 1888 played a crucial role in this democratization, as his cameras were simple to use and affordable. Today, digital photography has further transformed the medium, allowing instant image capture and sharing.

What is suggested about daguerreotypes?

(A) They were introduced by Joseph-Nicéphore Niépce.
(B) They allowed for multiple copies of an image.
(C) They required shorter exposure times than heliographs did.
(D) They made it unnecessary to use silver-plated copper.

The History of Photography

The history of photography is marked by significant technological progress and artistic innovation. It began in the early nineteenth century with the invention of the camera obscura, a device that projected images onto a surface. The first permanent photograph was created by Joseph-Nicéphore Niépce in 1826 using a process called heliography, which required several hours of exposure to light.

Photography quickly evolved with the development of daguerreotypes, introduced by Louis Daguerre in 1839. This method produced detailed images on silver-plated copper, but daguerreotypes needed delicate handling, and the exposure times required, although much shorter, still remained impractical for recording images of moving objects. The invention of the calotype by William Henry Fox Talbot in the 1840s allowed for multiple copies of an image to be made from a single negative, revolutionizing the field.

In the late nineteenth and early twentieth centuries, the introduction of film and roll cameras made photography more accessible to the public. George Eastman's establishment of the Kodak company in 1888 played a crucial role in this democratization, as his cameras were simple to use and affordable. Today, digital photography has further transformed the medium, allowing instant image capture and sharing.

How did the calotype revolutionize photography?

(A) By enabling instant image capture
(B) By reducing the need for delicate handling
(C) By providing detailed images on silver-plated copper
(D) By allowing multiple copies from a single negative

The History of Photography

The history of photography is marked by significant technological progress and artistic innovation. It began in the early nineteenth century with the invention of the camera obscura, a device that projected images onto a surface. The first permanent photograph was created by Joseph-Nicéphore Niépce in 1826 using a process called heliography, which required several hours of exposure to light.

Photography quickly evolved with the development of daguerreotypes, introduced by Louis Daguerre in 1839. This method produced detailed images on silver-plated copper, but daguerreotypes needed delicate handling, and the exposure times required, although much shorter, still remained impractical for recording images of moving objects. The invention of the calotype by William Henry Fox Talbot in the 1840s allowed for multiple copies of an image to be made from a single negative, revolutionizing the field.

In the late nineteenth and early twentieth centuries, the introduction of film and roll cameras made photography more accessible to the public. George Eastman's establishment of the Kodak company in 1888 played a crucial role in this democratization, as his cameras were simple to use and affordable. Today, digital photography has further transformed the medium, allowing instant image capture and sharing.

Why does the author mention George Eastman's establishment of the Kodak company?

(A) To highlight the role of Kodak in making photography accessible to the public
(B) To criticize the challenges of early photographic methods
(C) To explain how film was invented
(D) To suggest that Kodak introduced digital photography

The History of Photography

The history of photography is marked by significant technological progress and artistic innovation. It began in the early nineteenth century with the invention of the camera obscura, a device that projected images onto a surface. The first permanent photograph was created by Joseph-Nicéphore Niépce in 1826 using a process called heliography, which required several hours of exposure to light.

Photography quickly evolved with the development of daguerreotypes, introduced by Louis Daguerre in 1839. This method produced detailed images on silver-plated copper, but daguerreotypes needed delicate handling, and the exposure times required, although much shorter, still remained impractical for recording images of moving objects. The invention of the calotype by William Henry Fox Talbot in the 1840s allowed for multiple copies of an image to be made from a single negative, revolutionizing the field.

(A) In the late nineteenth and early twentieth centuries, the introduction of film and roll cameras made photography more accessible to the public. **(B)** George Eastman's establishment of the Kodak company in 1888 played a crucial role in this democratization, as his cameras were simple to use and affordable. **(C)** Today, digital photography has further transformed the medium, allowing instant image capture and sharing. **(D)**

There are four locations (A, B, C, and D) in the passage that indicate where the following sentence could be added.

These developments have rendered the use of film and many types of cameras obsolete.

Where would the sentence best fit? Select a location where the sentence could be added to the passage.

(A) Option A
(B) Option B
(C) Option C
(D) Option D

LISTENING

TOEFL iBT

Listening Section

In the listening section, you will answer 35 to 45 questions to demonstrate how well you understand spoken English. There are three types of tasks.

Type of Task	Description
Listen and Choose a Response	Select the best response to the question or statement.
Conversations	Answer questions about short conversations.
Announcements and Academic Talks	Answer questions about announcements and academic talks.

You WILL NOT be able to return to previous questions.

Module 1

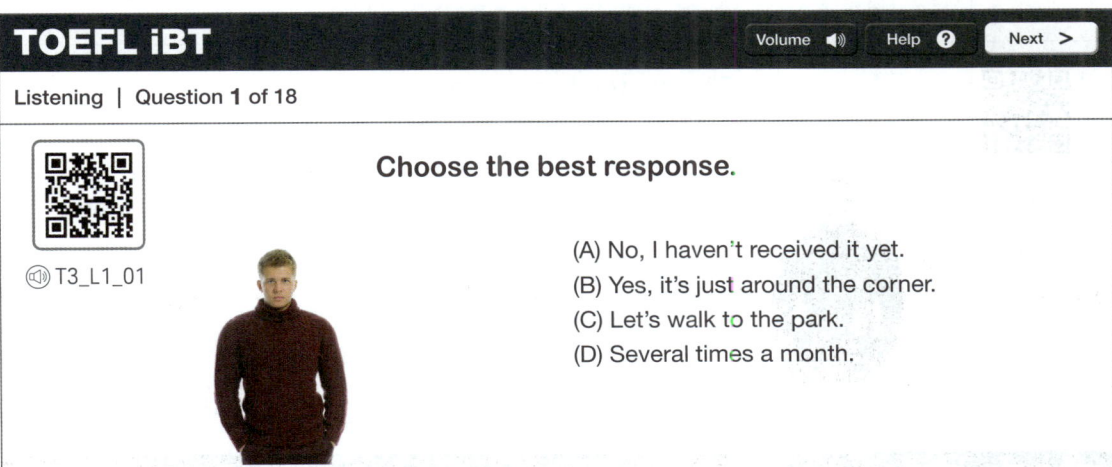

TOEFL iBT

Listening | Question **1** of 18

🔊 T3_L1_01

Choose the best response.

(A) No, I haven't received it yet.
(B) Yes, it's just around the corner.
(C) Let's walk to the park.
(D) Several times a month.

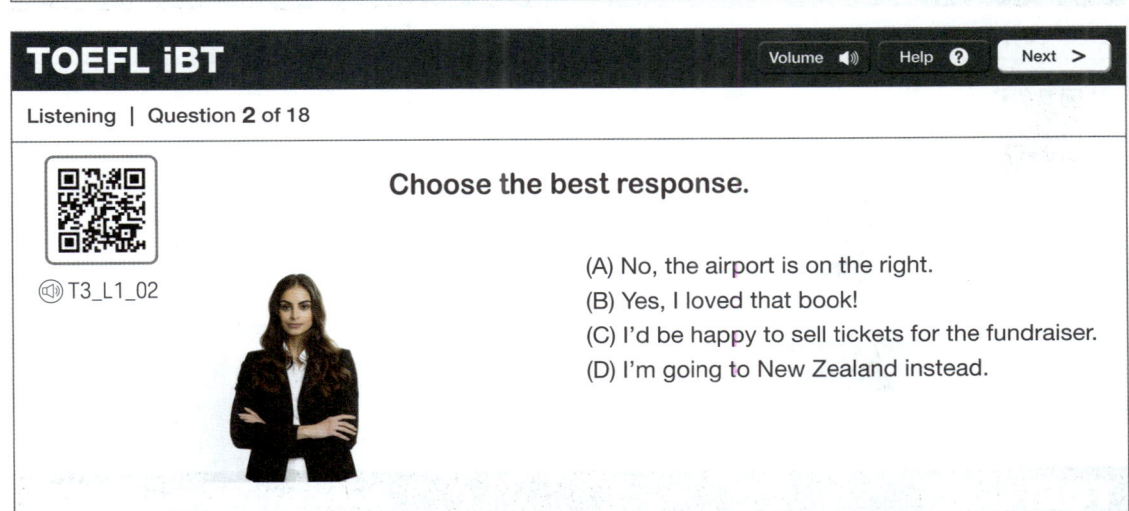

TOEFL iBT

Listening | Question **2** of 18

🔊 T3_L1_02

Choose the best response.

(A) No, the airport is on the right.
(B) Yes, I loved that book!
(C) I'd be happy to sell tickets for the fundraiser.
(D) I'm going to New Zealand instead.

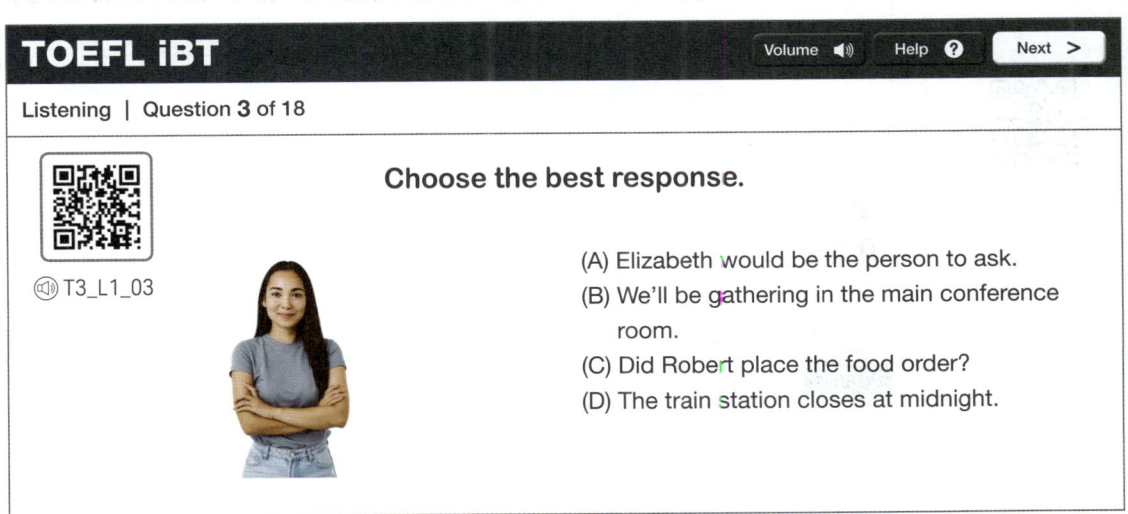

TOEFL iBT

Listening | Question **3** of 18

🔊 T3_L1_03

Choose the best response.

(A) Elizabeth would be the person to ask.
(B) We'll be gathering in the main conference room.
(C) Did Robert place the food order?
(D) The train station closes at midnight.

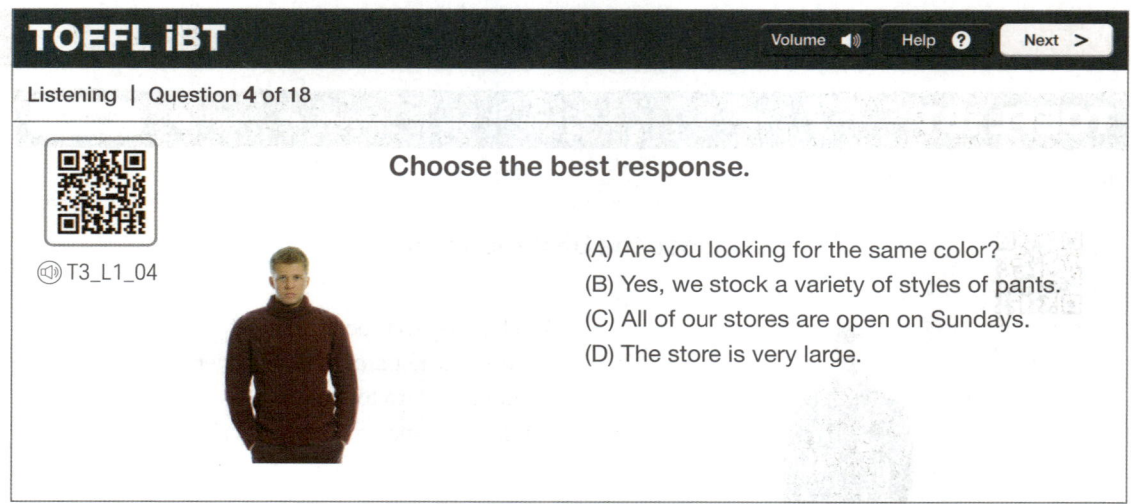

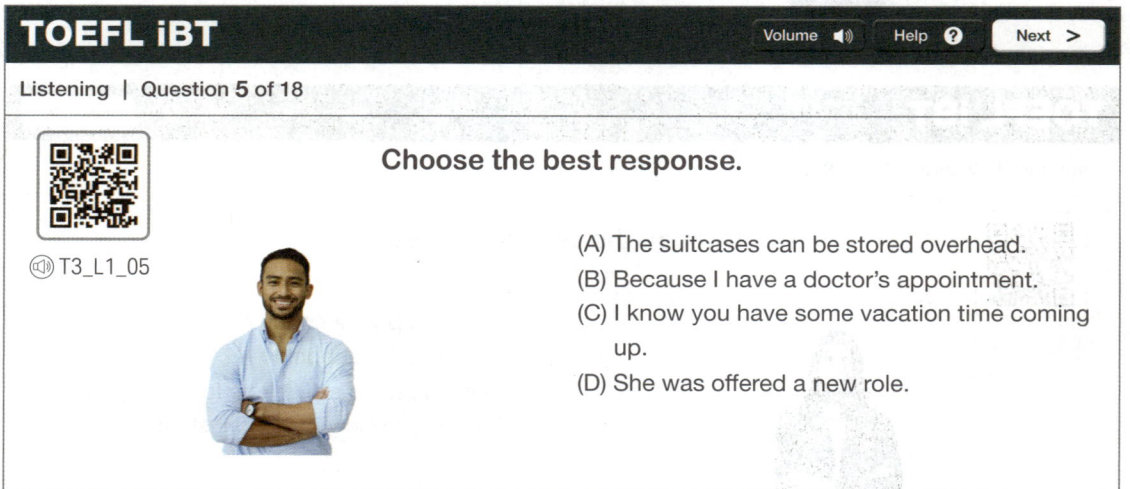

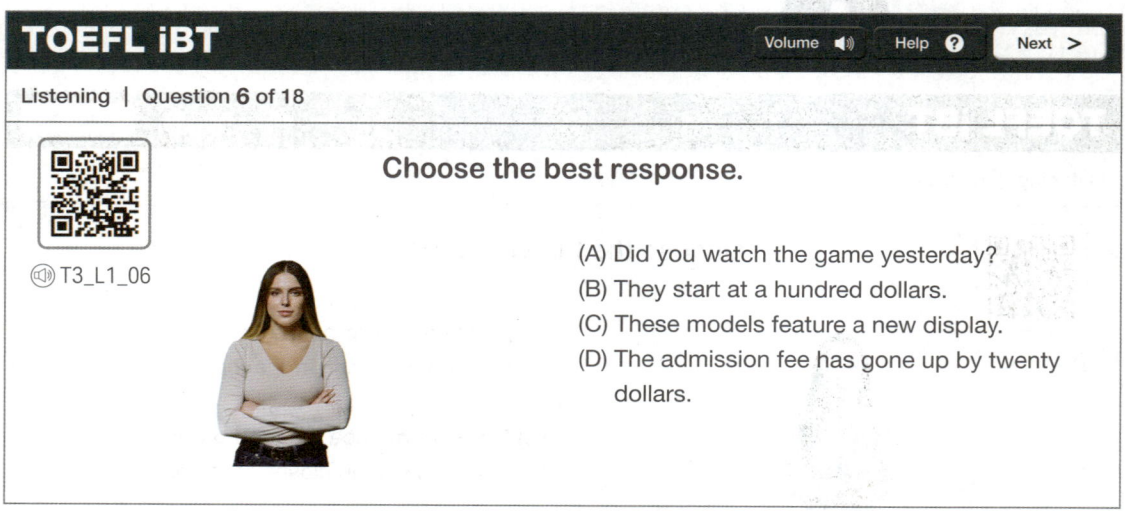

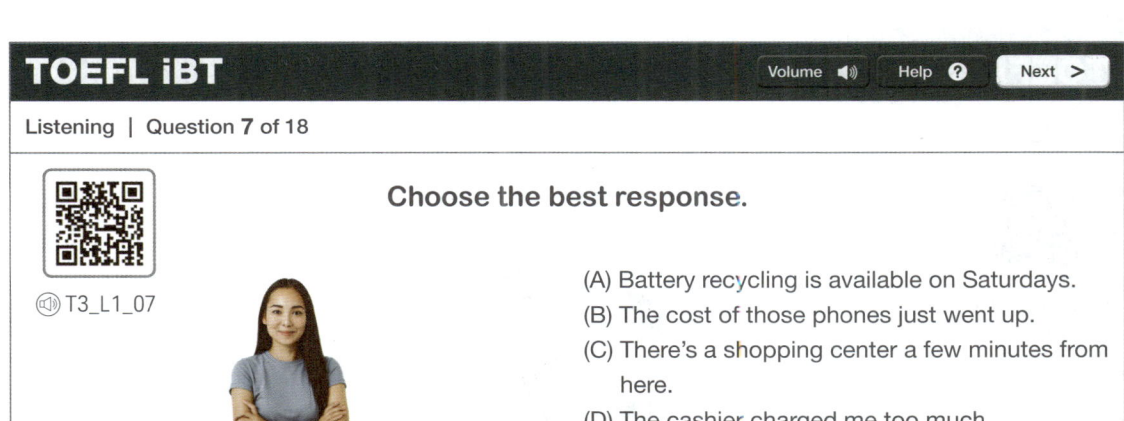

Choose the best response.

(A) Battery recycling is available on Saturdays.
(B) The cost of those phones just went up.
(C) There's a shopping center a few minutes from here.
(D) The cashier charged me too much.

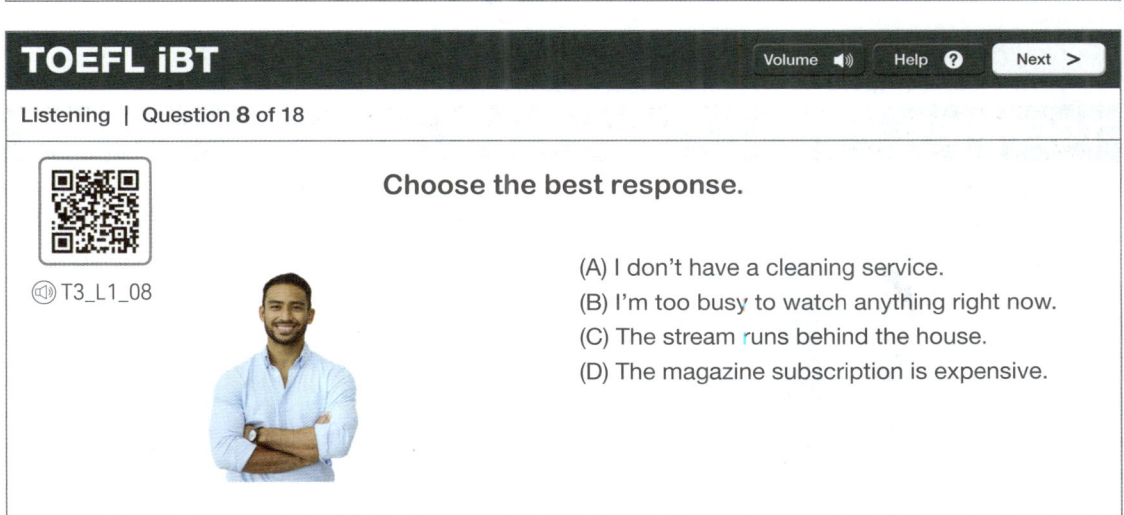

Choose the best response.

(A) I don't have a cleaning service.
(B) I'm too busy to watch anything right now.
(C) The stream runs behind the house.
(D) The magazine subscription is expensive.

Listen to a conversation.

T3_L1_0910

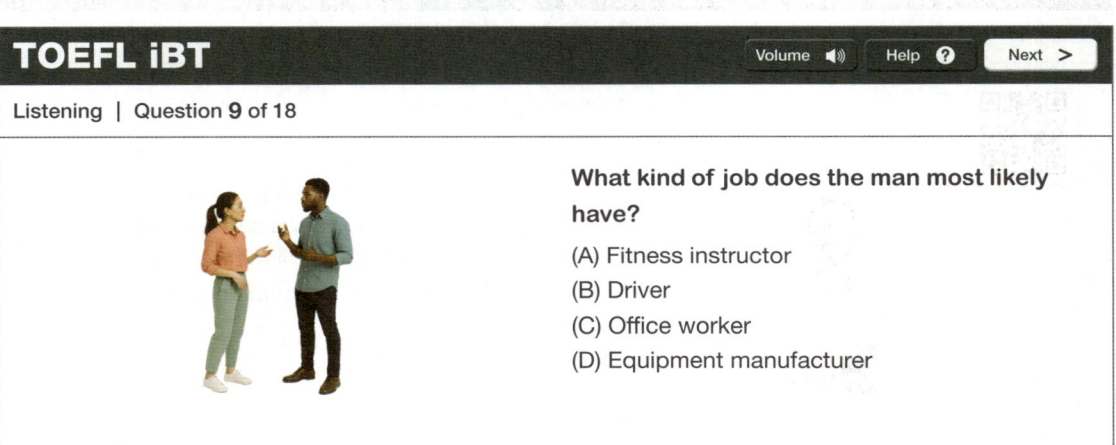

Question 9 of 18

What kind of job does the man most likely have?

(A) Fitness instructor
(B) Driver
(C) Office worker
(D) Equipment manufacturer

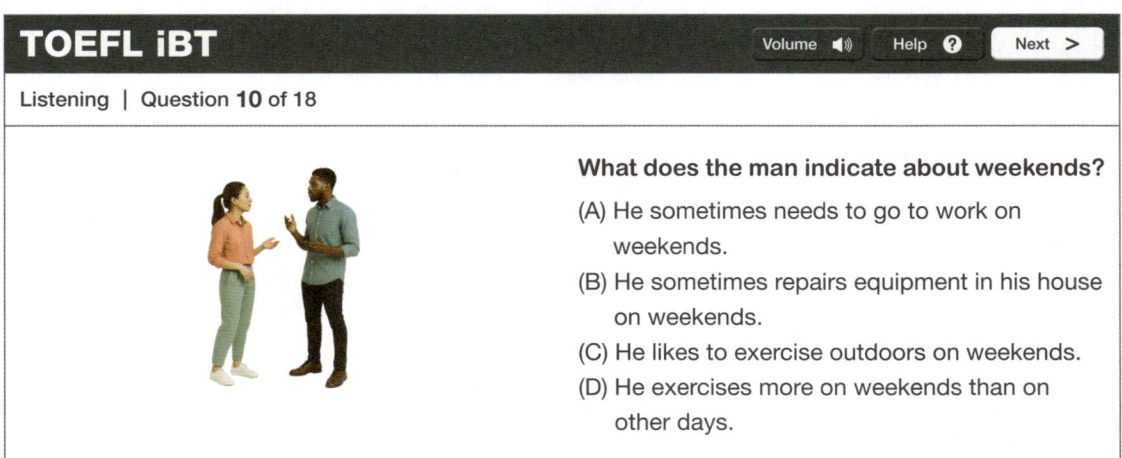

Question 10 of 18

What does the man indicate about weekends?

(A) He sometimes needs to go to work on weekends.
(B) He sometimes repairs equipment in his house on weekends.
(C) He likes to exercise outdoors on weekends.
(D) He exercises more on weekends than on other days.

Listening | Questions 11–12 of 18

Listen to a conversation.

T3_L1_1112

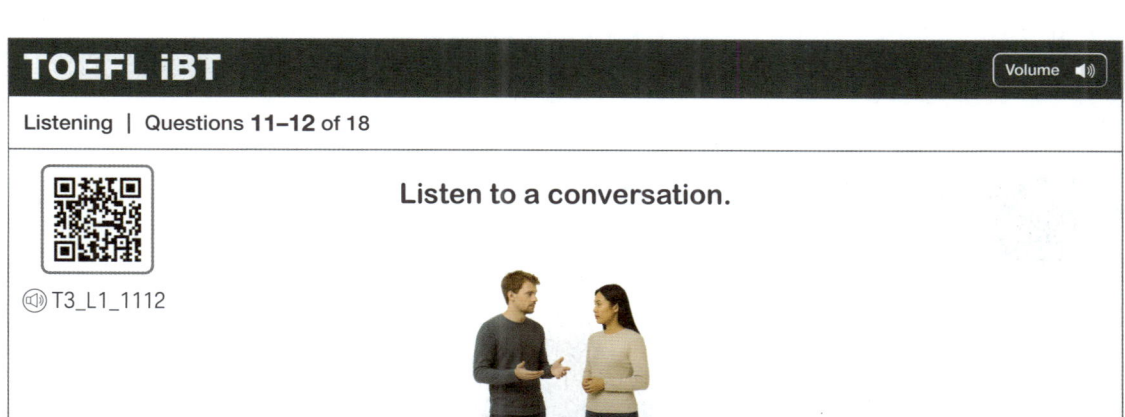

Listening | Question 11 of 18

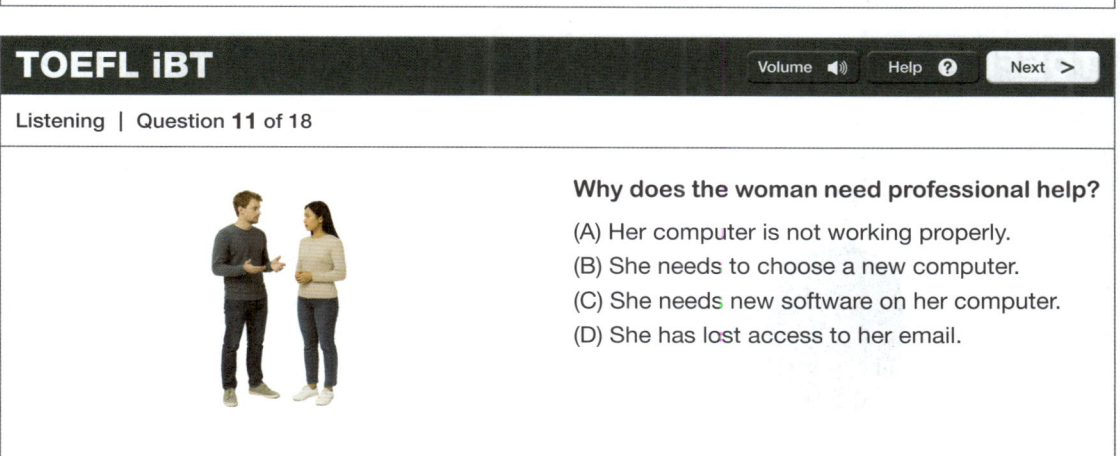

Why does the woman need professional help?

(A) Her computer is not working properly.
(B) She needs to choose a new computer.
(C) She needs new software on her computer.
(D) She has lost access to her email.

Listening | Question 12 of 18

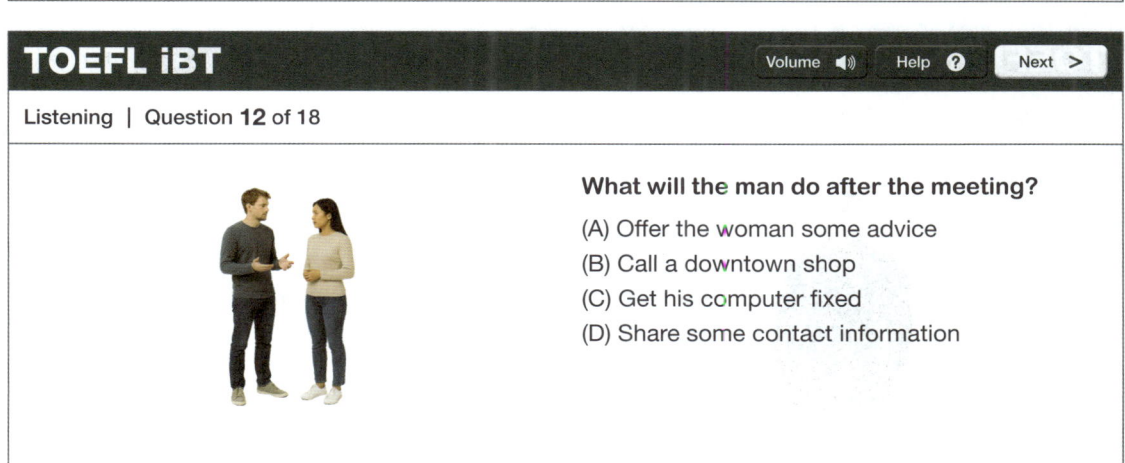

What will the man do after the meeting?

(A) Offer the woman some advice
(B) Call a downtown shop
(C) Get his computer fixed
(D) Share some contact information

TOEFL iBT

Listening | Questions 13–14 of 18

Listen to an announcement on the campus radio station.

T3_L1_1314

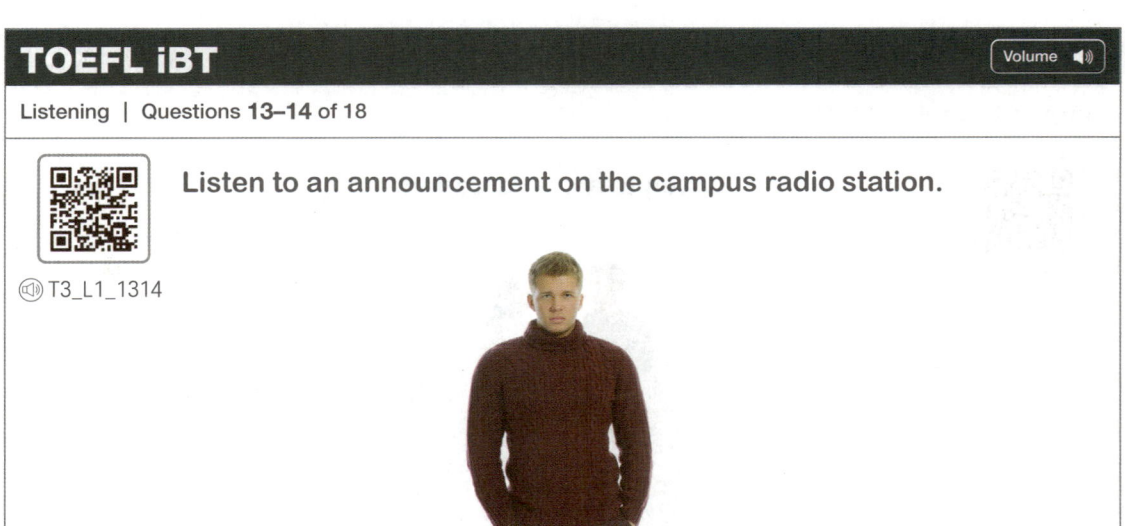

TOEFL iBT

Listening | Question 13 of 18

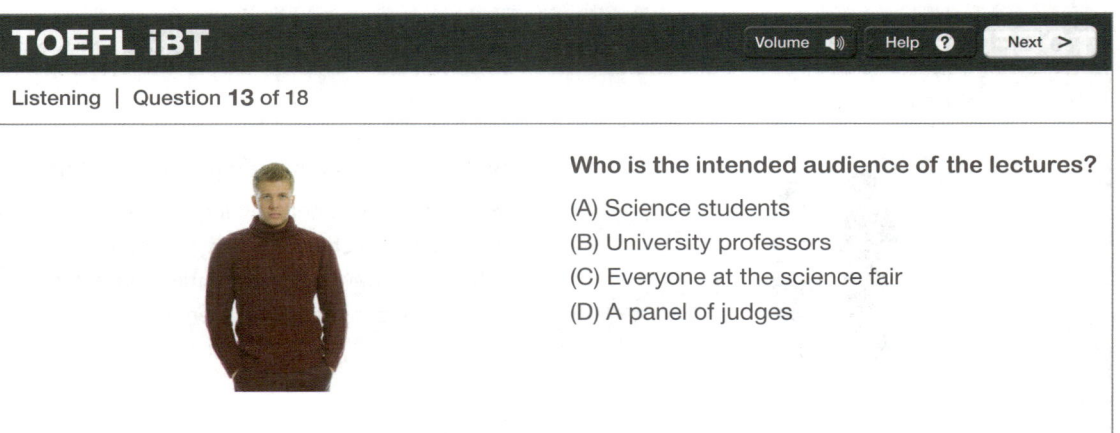

Who is the intended audience of the lectures?

(A) Science students
(B) University professors
(C) Everyone at the science fair
(D) A panel of judges

TOEFL iBT

Listening | Question 14 of 18

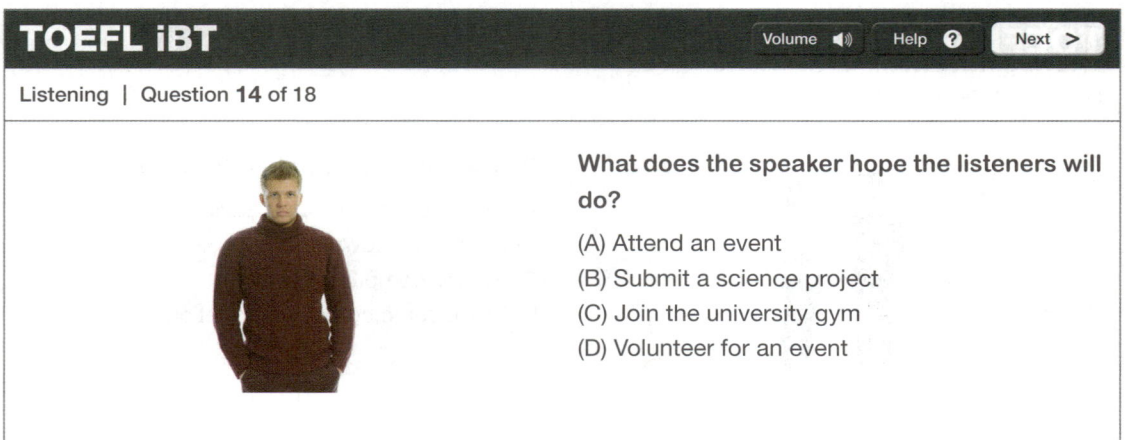

What does the speaker hope the listeners will do?

(A) Attend an event
(B) Submit a science project
(C) Join the university gym
(D) Volunteer for an event

TOEFL iBT

Listening | Questions 15–18 of 18

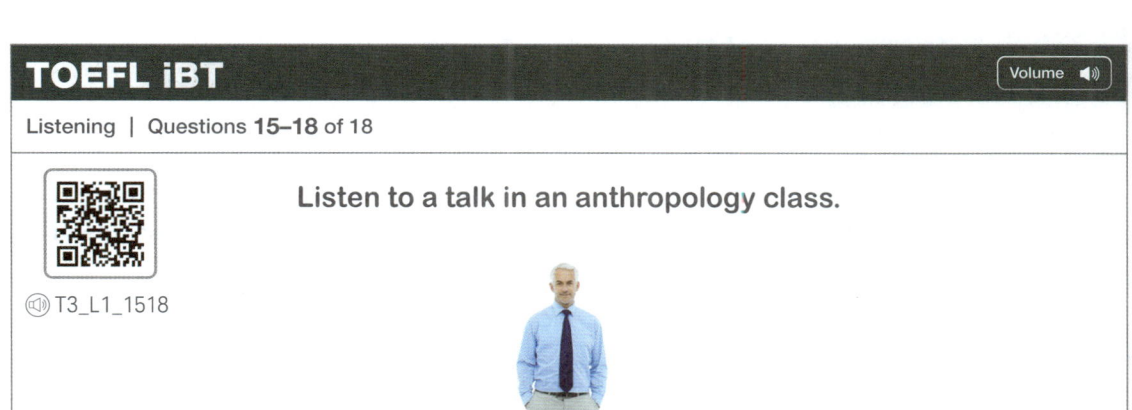

Listen to a talk in an anthropology class.

T3_L1_1518

TOEFL iBT

Listening | Question 15 of 18

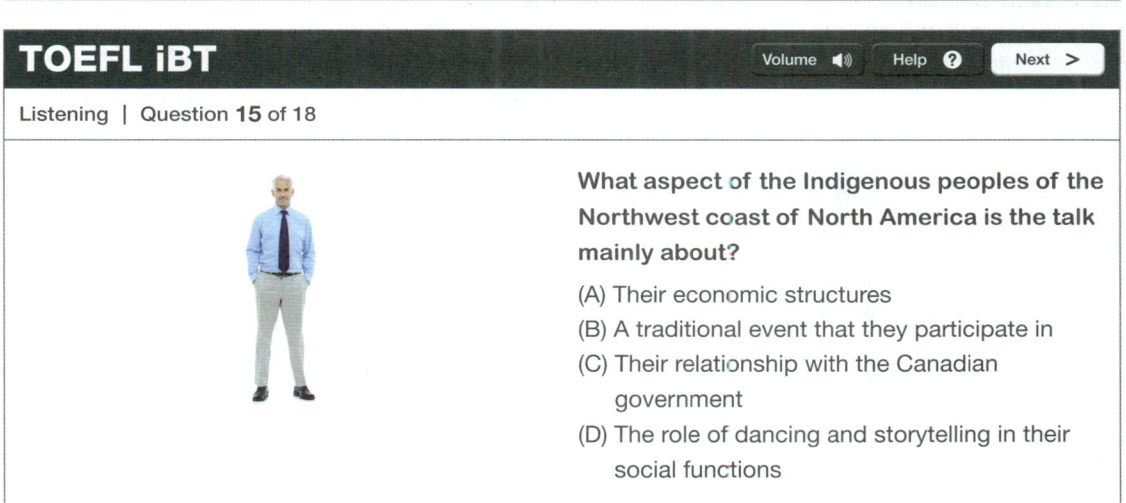

What aspect of the Indigenous peoples of the Northwest coast of North America is the talk mainly about?

(A) Their economic structures
(B) A traditional event that they participate in
(C) Their relationship with the Canadian government
(D) The role of dancing and storytelling in their social functions

TOEFL iBT

Listening | Question 16 of 18

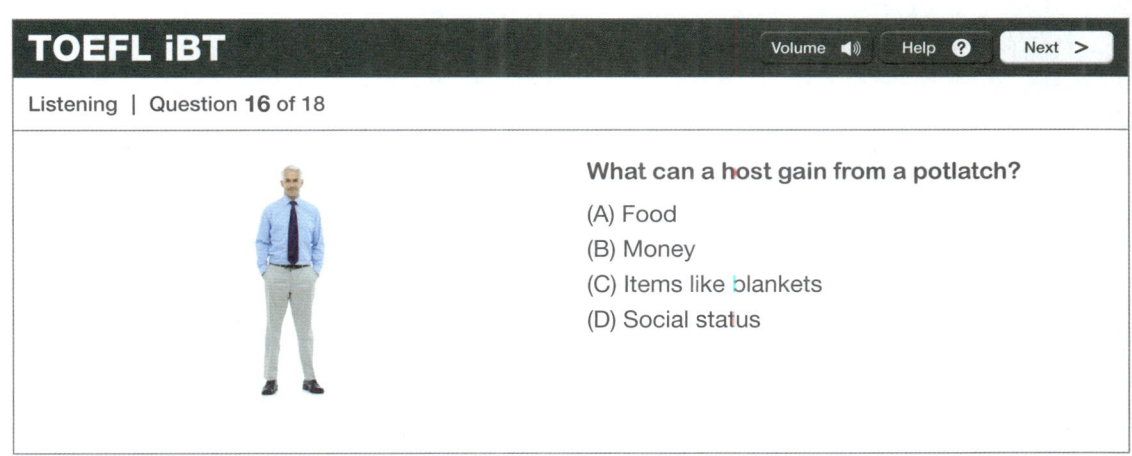

What can a host gain from a potlatch?

(A) Food
(B) Money
(C) Items like blankets
(D) Social status

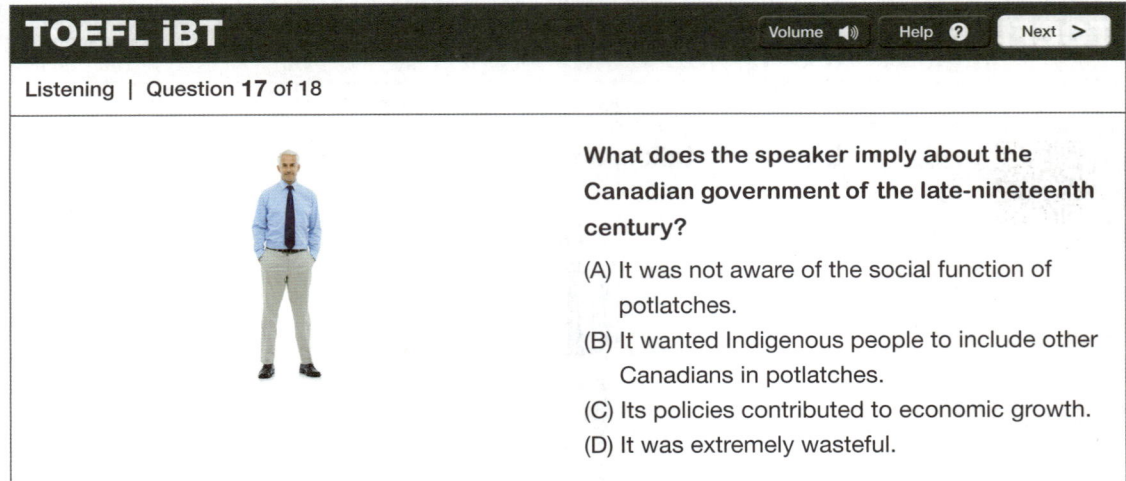

What does the speaker imply about the Canadian government of the late-nineteenth century?

(A) It was not aware of the social function of potlatches.
(B) It wanted Indigenous people to include other Canadians in potlatches.
(C) Its policies contributed to economic growth.
(D) It was extremely wasteful.

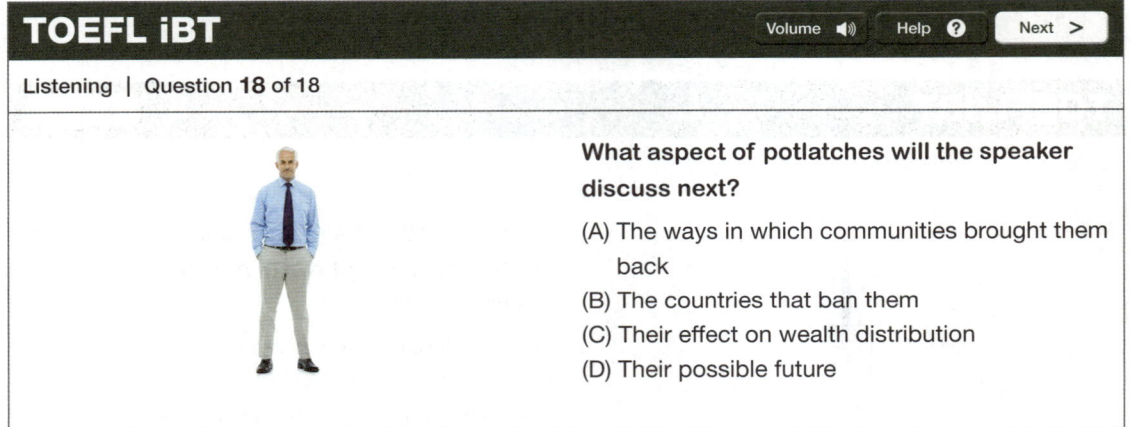

What aspect of potlatches will the speaker discuss next?

(A) The ways in which communities brought them back
(B) The countries that ban them
(C) Their effect on wealth distribution
(D) Their possible future

Module 2

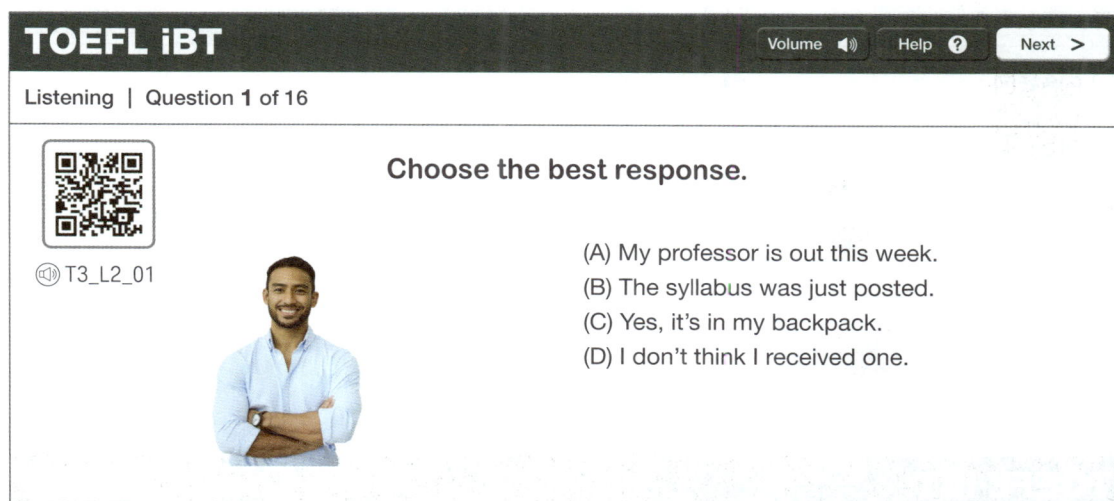

Listening | Question 1 of 16

T3_L2_01

Choose the best response.

(A) My professor is out this week.
(B) The syllabus was just posted.
(C) Yes, it's in my backpack.
(D) I don't think I received one.

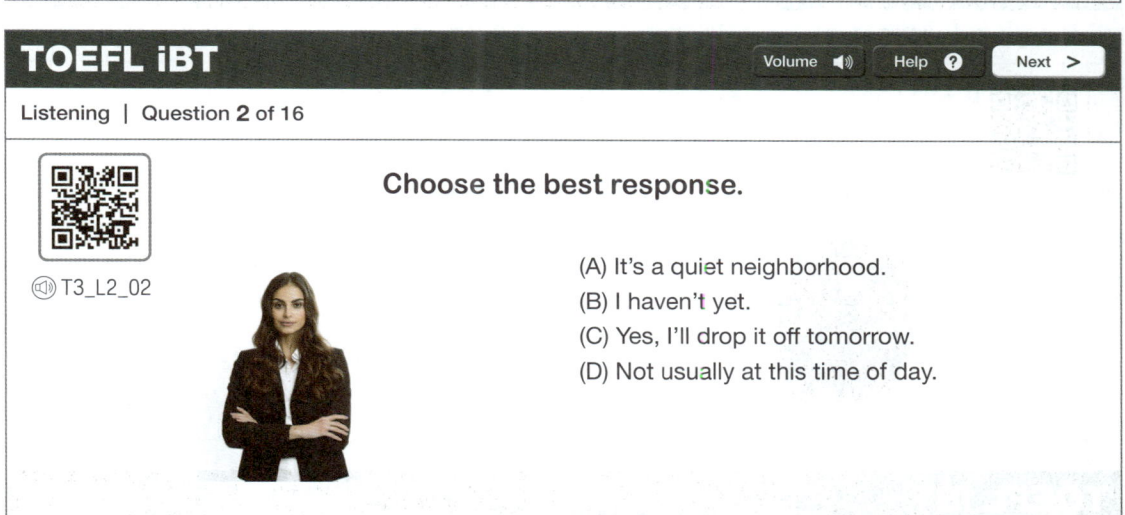

Listening | Question 2 of 16

T3_L2_02

Choose the best response.

(A) It's a quiet neighborhood.
(B) I haven't yet.
(C) Yes, I'll drop it off tomorrow.
(D) Not usually at this time of day.

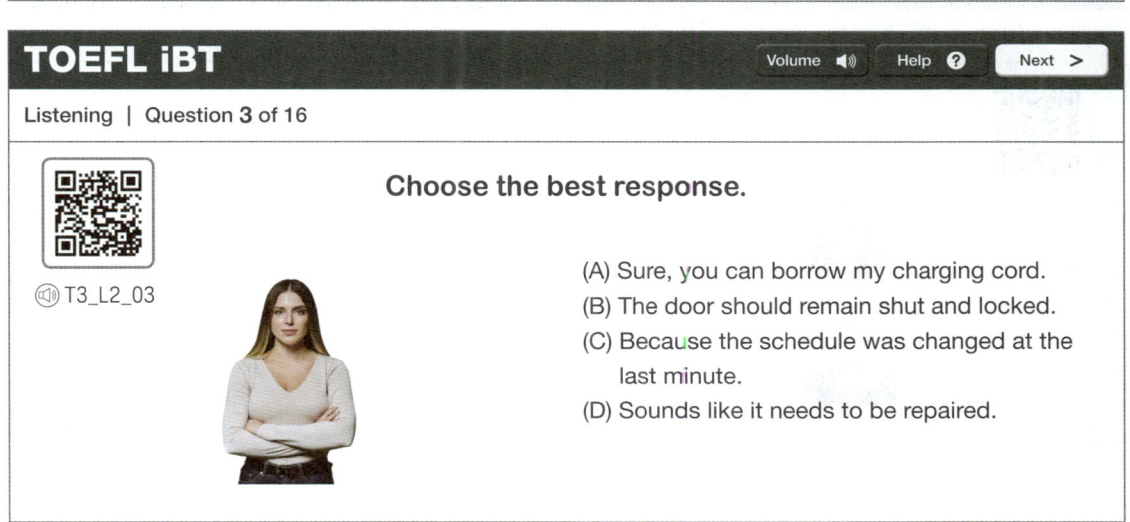

Listening | Question 3 of 16

T3_L2_03

Choose the best response.

(A) Sure, you can borrow my charging cord.
(B) The door should remain shut and locked.
(C) Because the schedule was changed at the last minute.
(D) Sounds like it needs to be repaired.

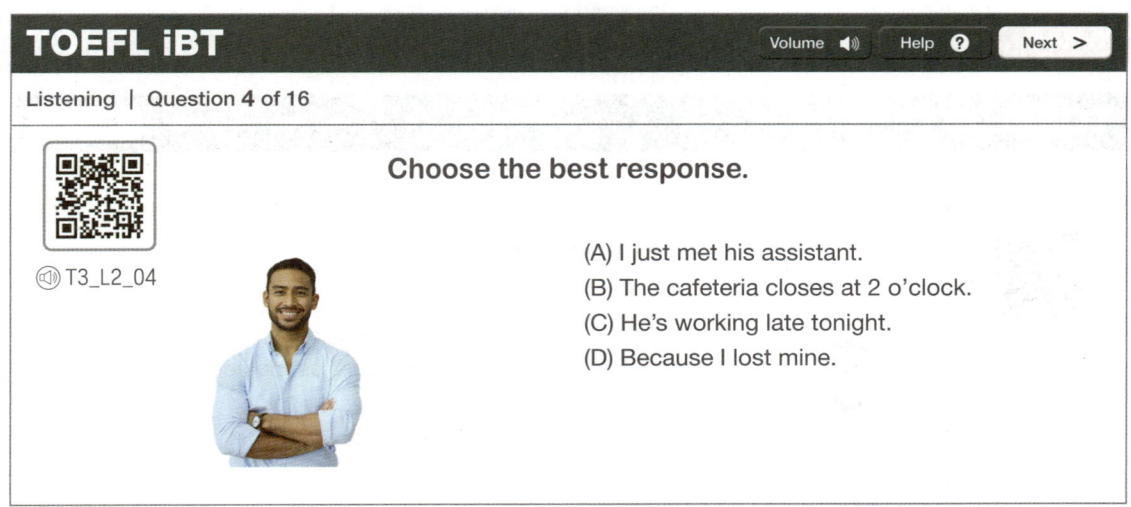

Choose the best response.

(A) I just met his assistant.
(B) The cafeteria closes at 2 o'clock.
(C) He's working late tonight.
(D) Because I lost mine.

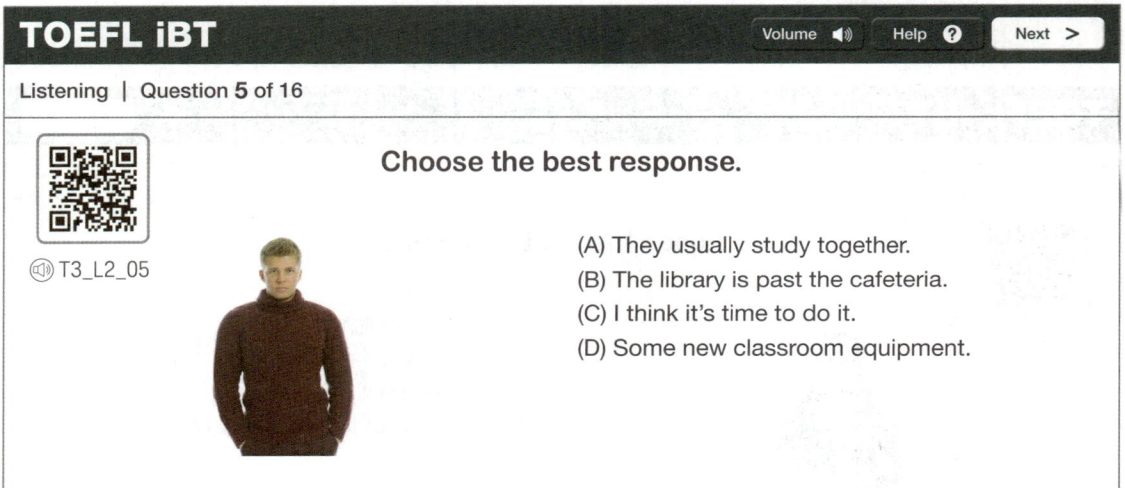

Choose the best response.

(A) They usually study together.
(B) The library is past the cafeteria.
(C) I think it's time to do it.
(D) Some new classroom equipment.

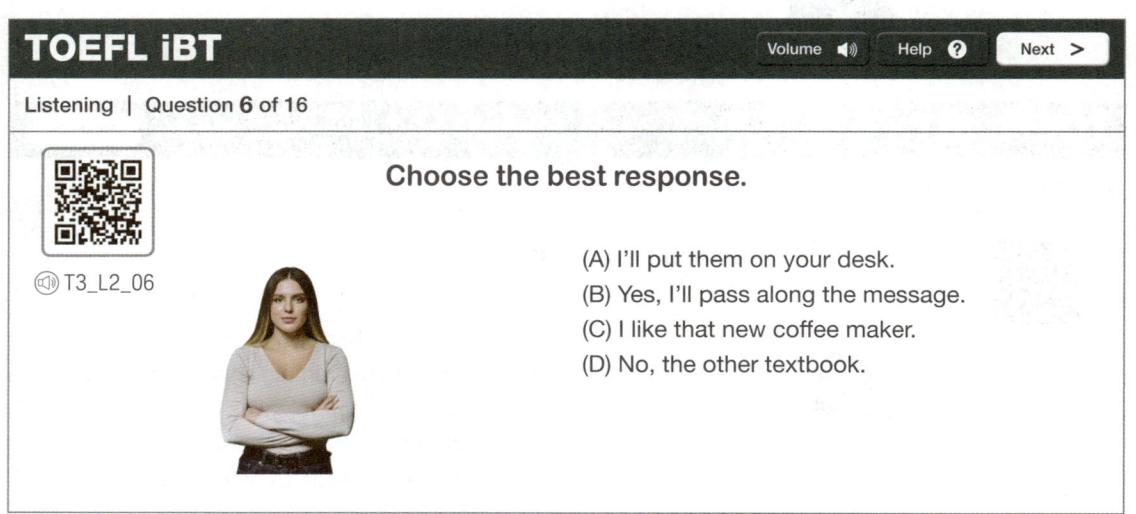

Choose the best response.

(A) I'll put them on your desk.
(B) Yes, I'll pass along the message.
(C) I like that new coffee maker.
(D) No, the other textbook.

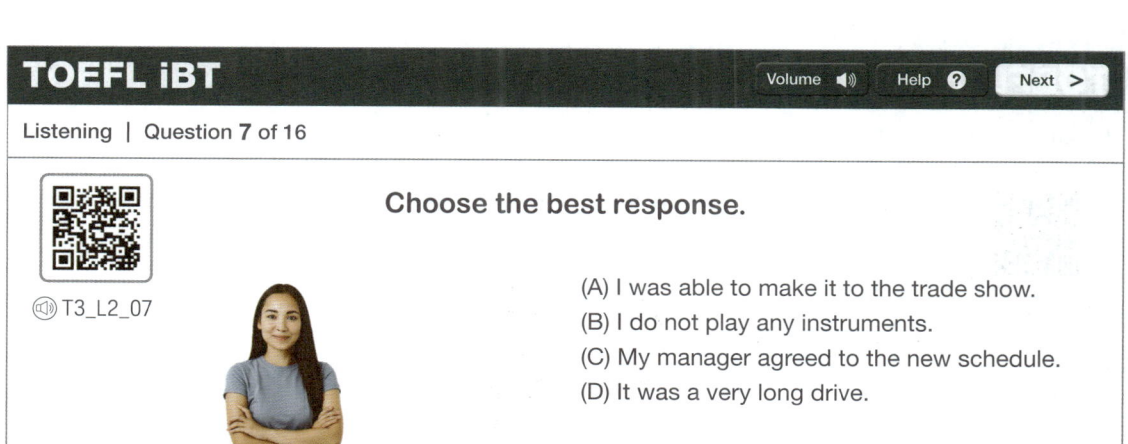

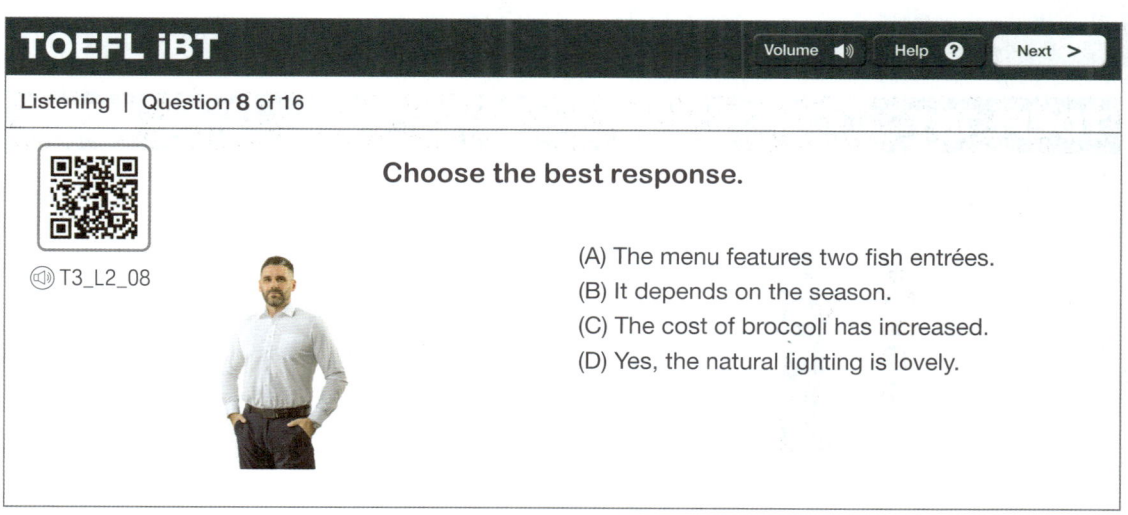

Listen to a conversation.

T3_L2_0910

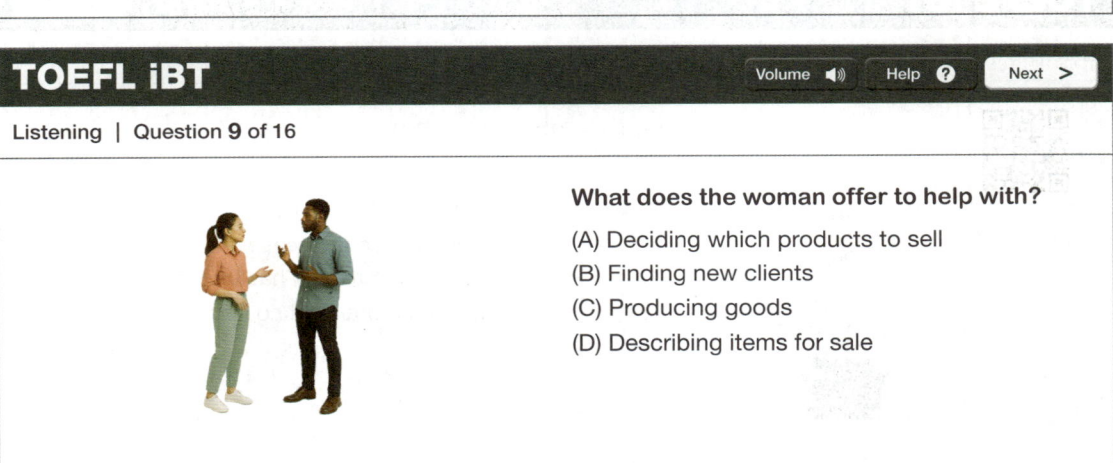

What does the woman offer to help with?

(A) Deciding which products to sell
(B) Finding new clients
(C) Producing goods
(D) Describing items for sale

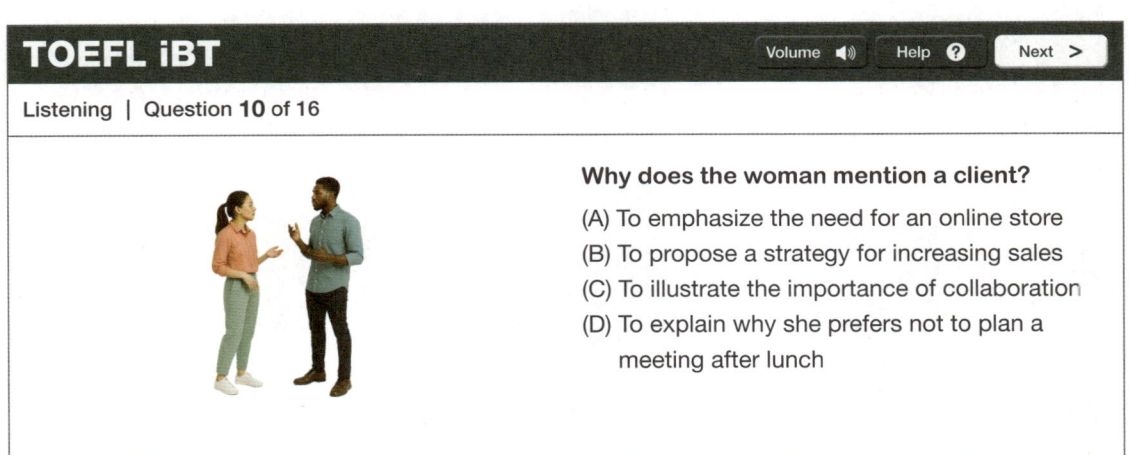

Why does the woman mention a client?

(A) To emphasize the need for an online store
(B) To propose a strategy for increasing sales
(C) To illustrate the importance of collaboration
(D) To explain why she prefers not to plan a meeting after lunch

TOEFL iBT

Listening | Questions 11–12 of 16

Listen to an announcement in a classroom.

T3_L2_1112

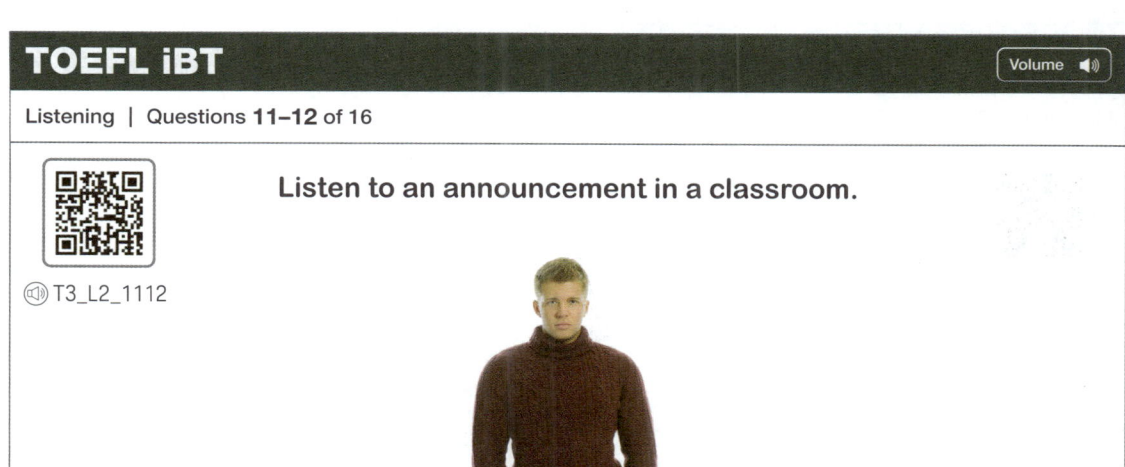

TOEFL iBT

Listening | Question 11 of 16

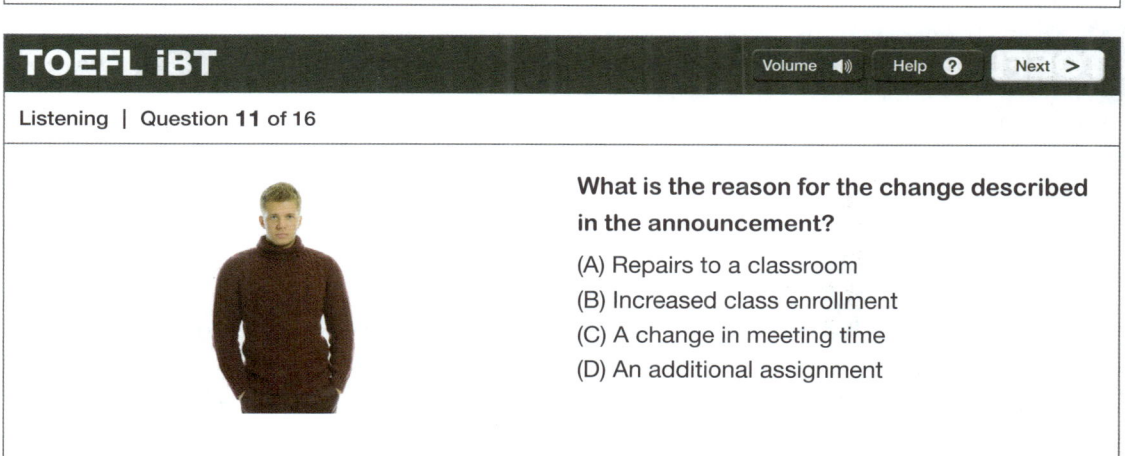

What is the reason for the change described in the announcement?

(A) Repairs to a classroom
(B) Increased class enrollment
(C) A change in meeting time
(D) An additional assignment

TOEFL iBT

Listening | Question 12 of 16

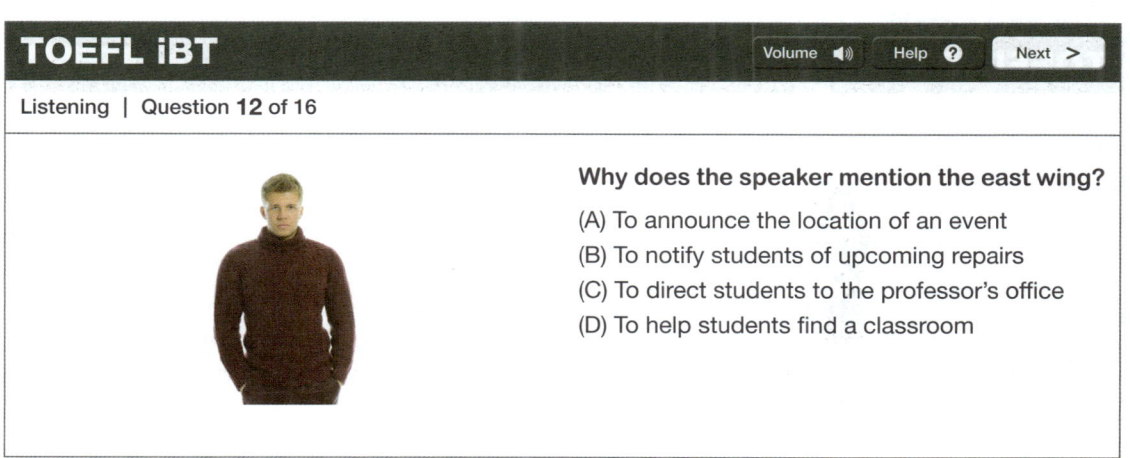

Why does the speaker mention the east wing?

(A) To announce the location of an event
(B) To notify students of upcoming repairs
(C) To direct students to the professor's office
(D) To help students find a classroom

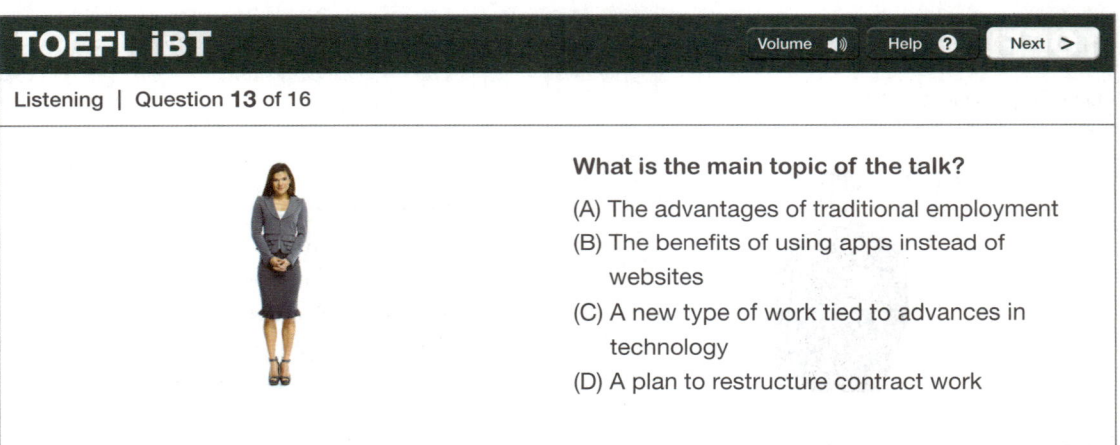

What is the main topic of the talk?

(A) The advantages of traditional employment
(B) The benefits of using apps instead of websites
(C) A new type of work tied to advances in technology
(D) A plan to restructure contract work

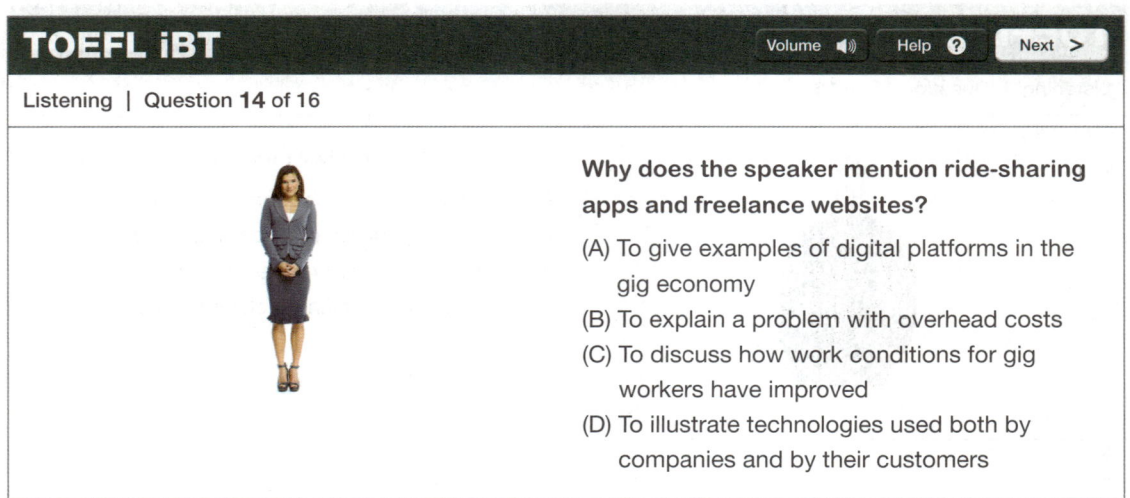

Why does the speaker mention ride-sharing apps and freelance websites?

(A) To give examples of digital platforms in the gig economy
(B) To explain a problem with overhead costs
(C) To discuss how work conditions for gig workers have improved
(D) To illustrate technologies used both by companies and by their customers

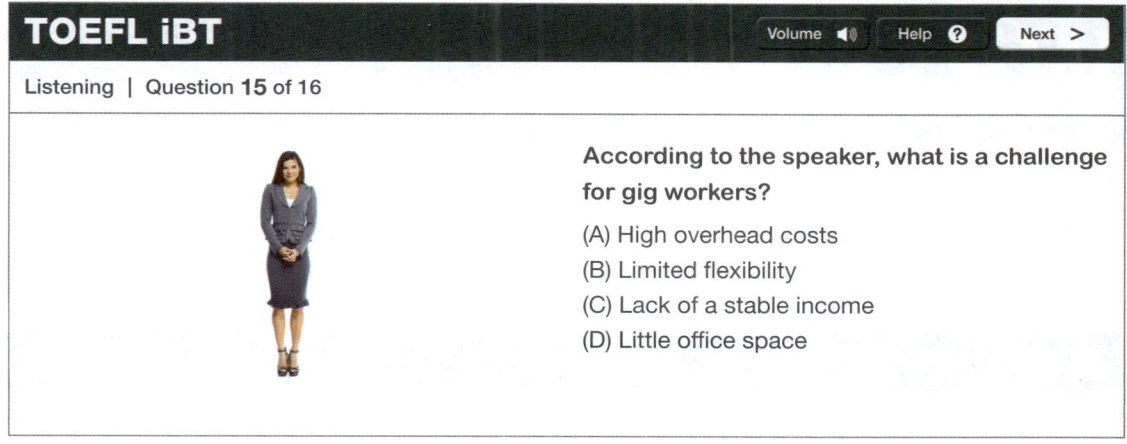

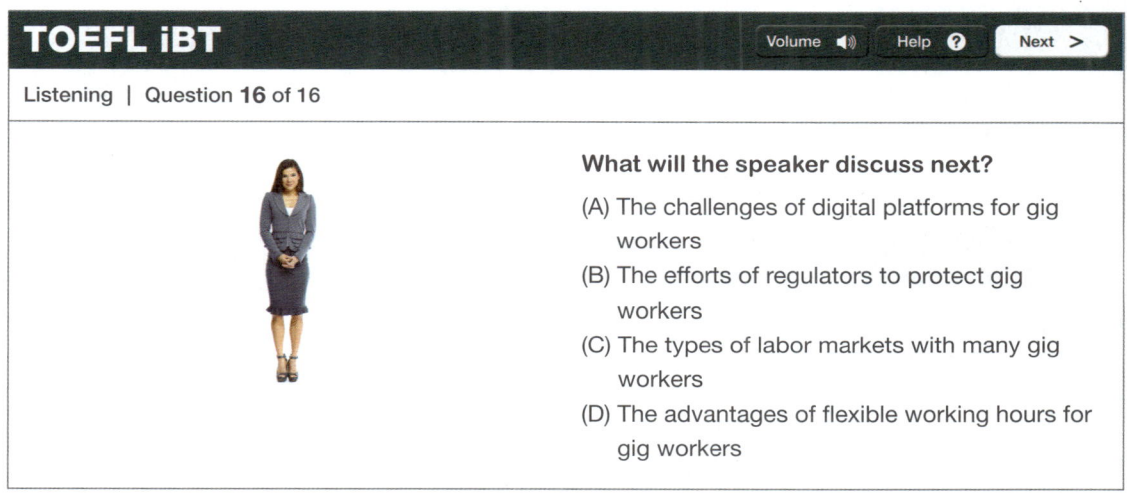

WRITING

TOEFL iBT

Writing Section

In the writing section, you will answer 12 questions to demonstrate how well you can write in English. There are three types of tasks.

Type of Task	Description
Build a Sentence	Create a grammatical sentence.
Write an Email	Write an email using information provided.
Write for an Academic Discussion	Participate in an online discussion.

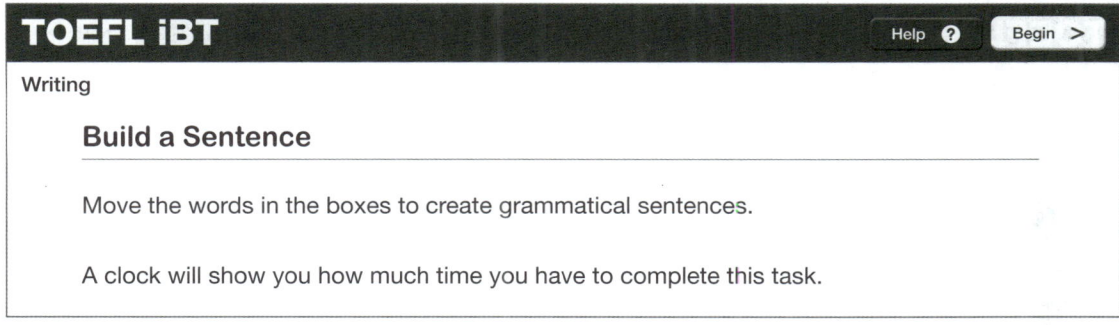

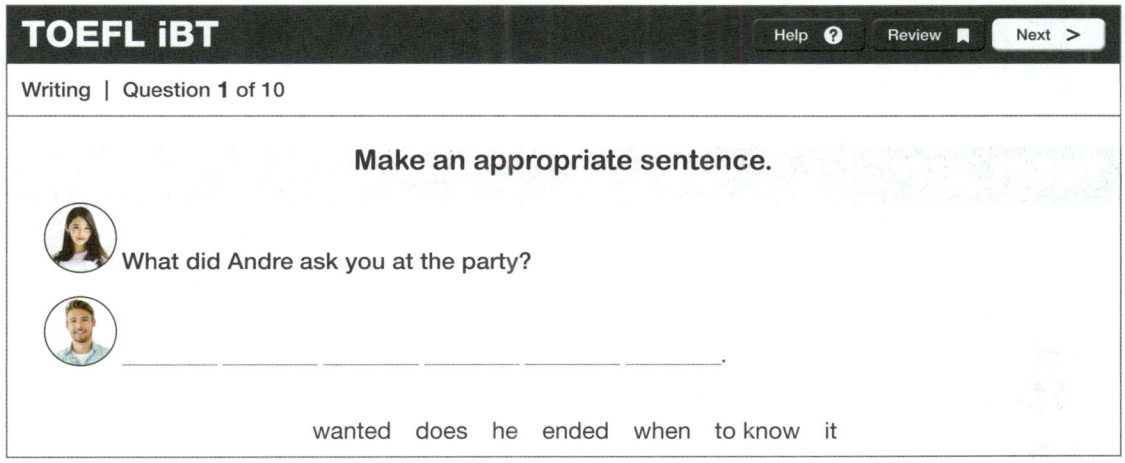

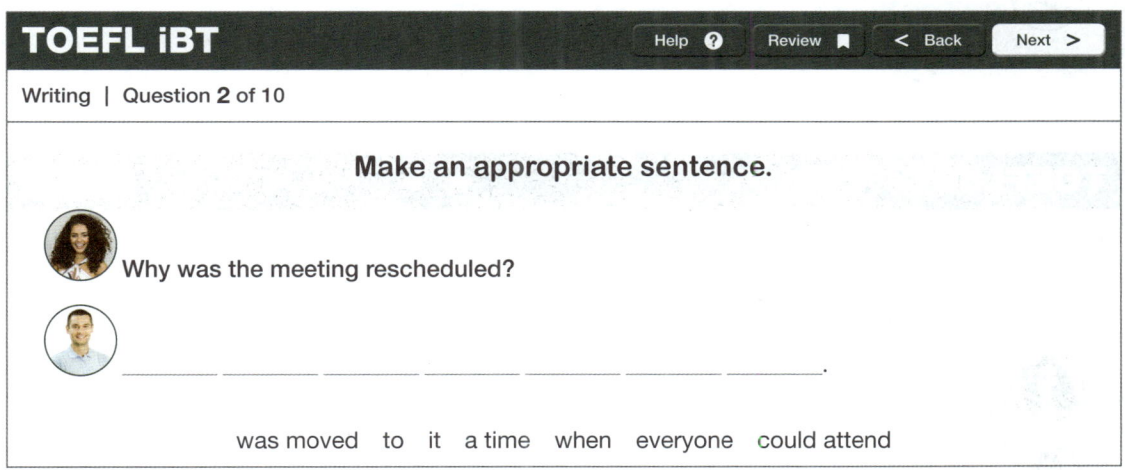

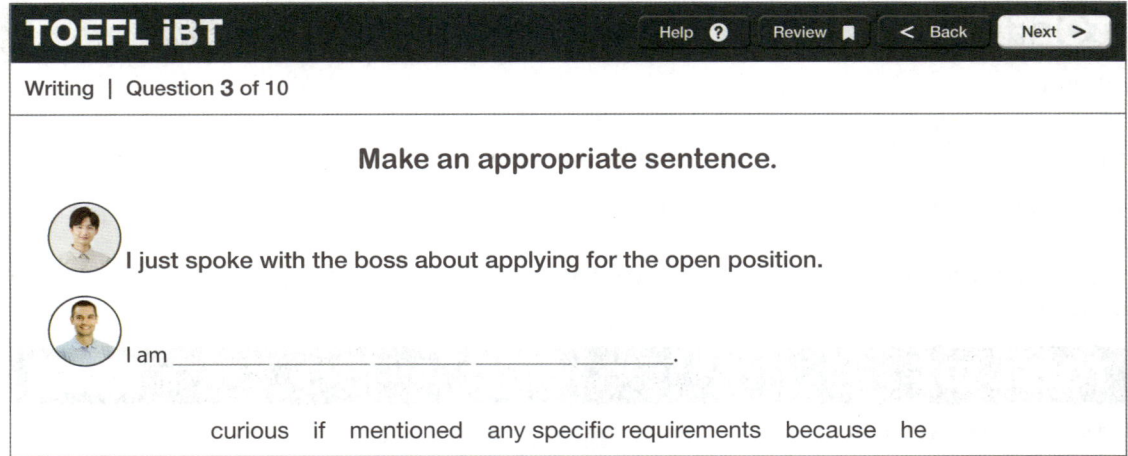

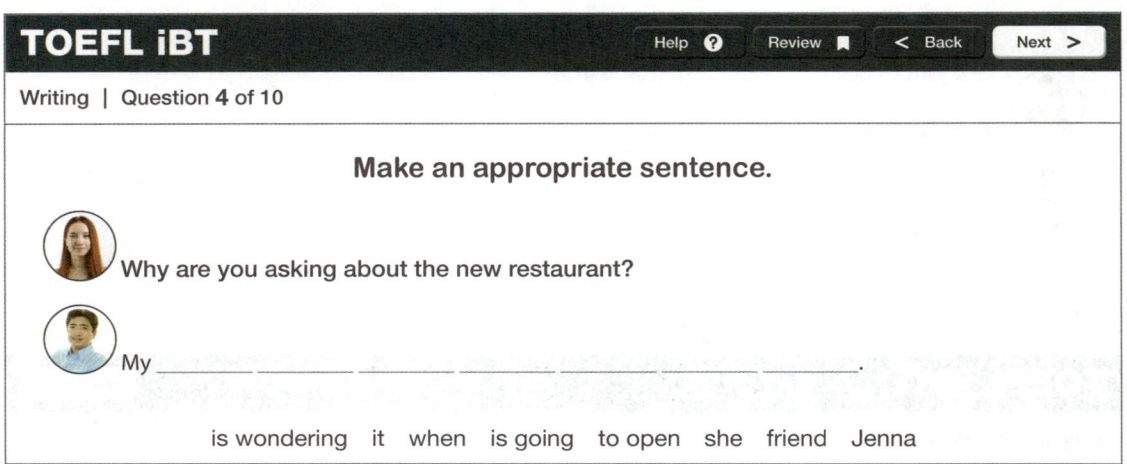

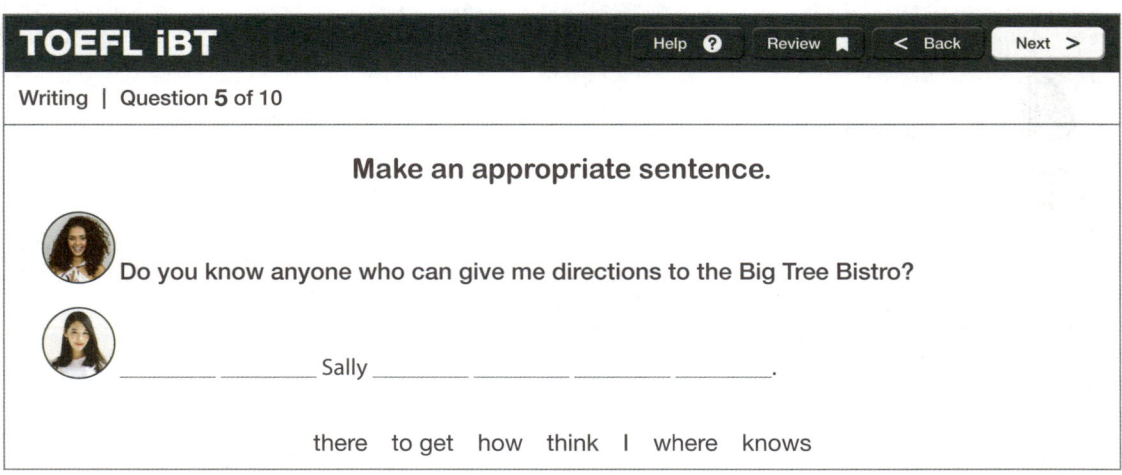

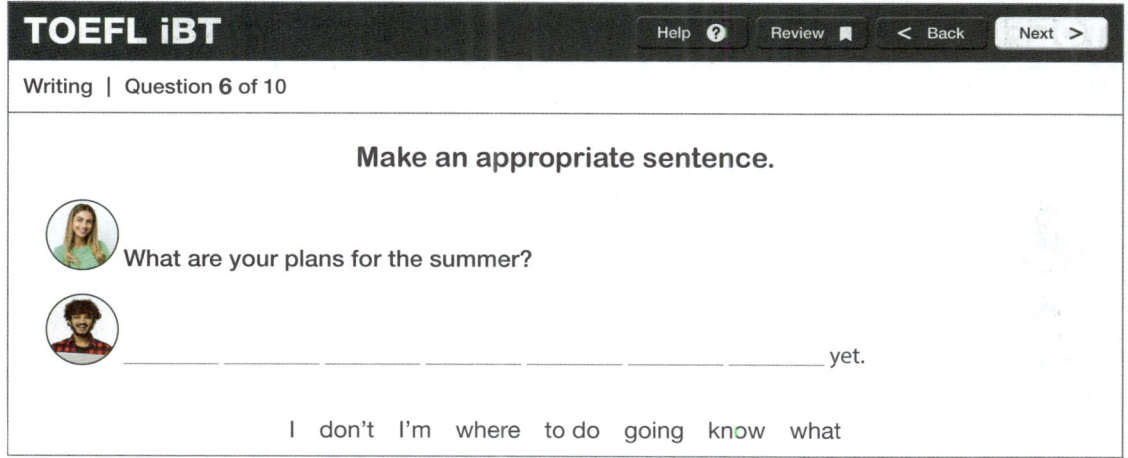

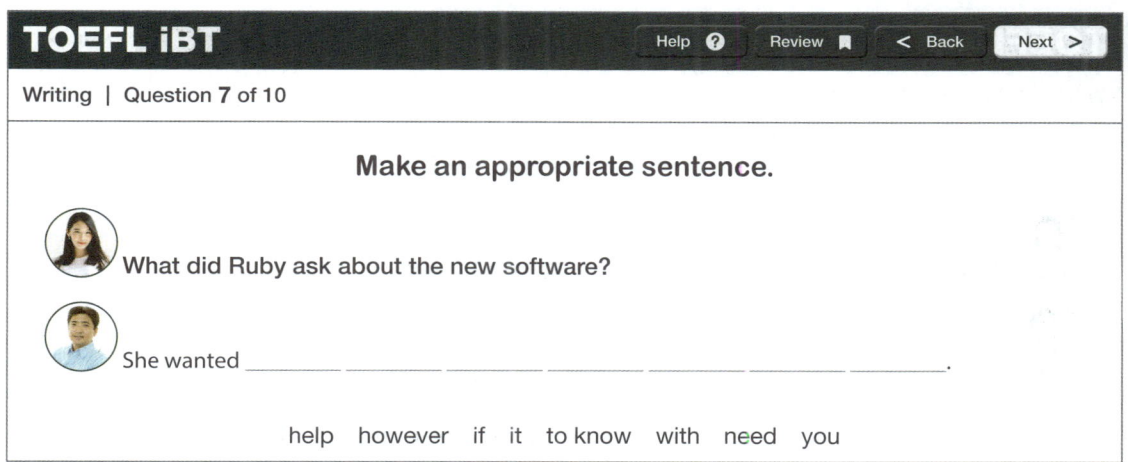

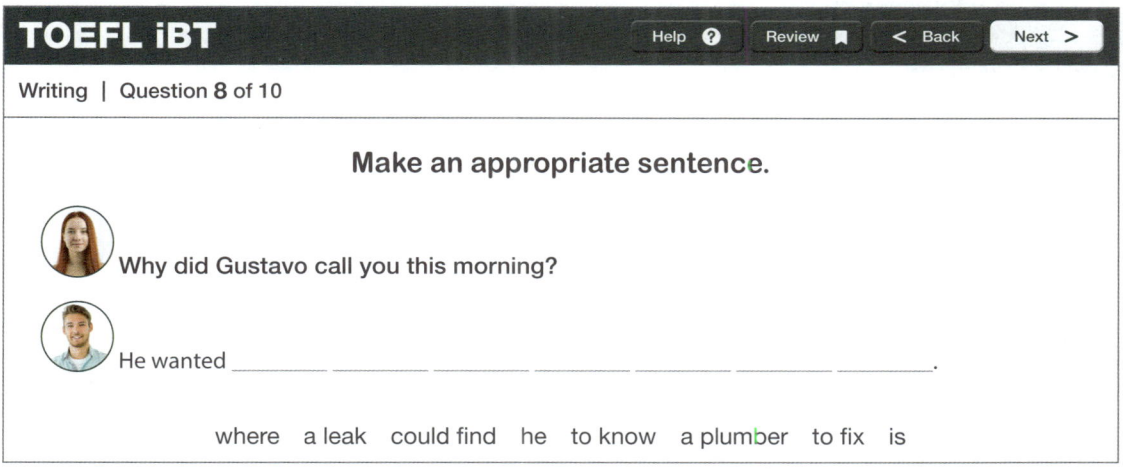

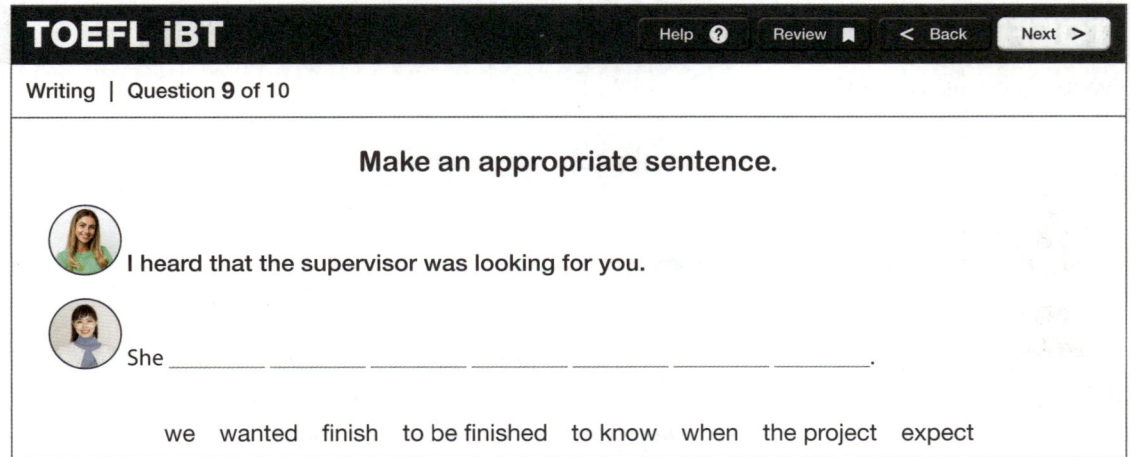

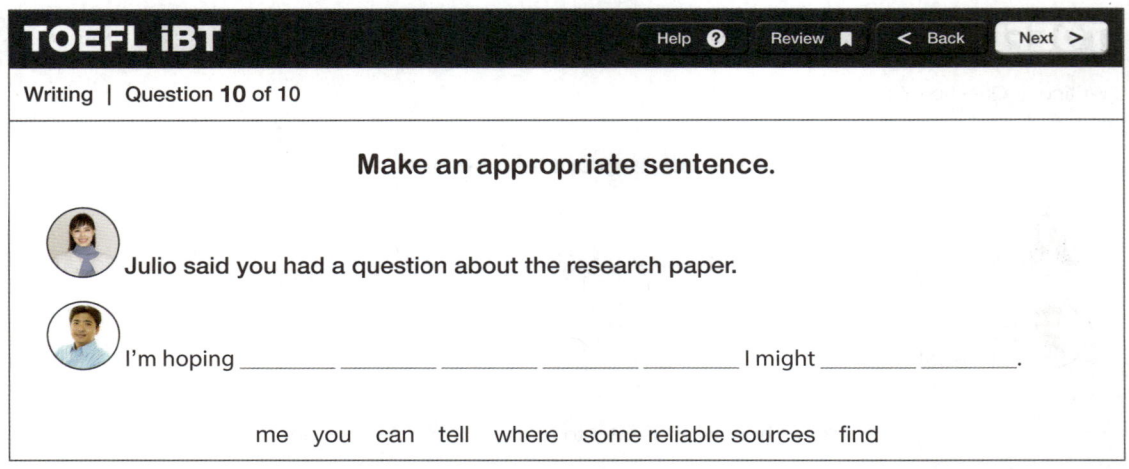

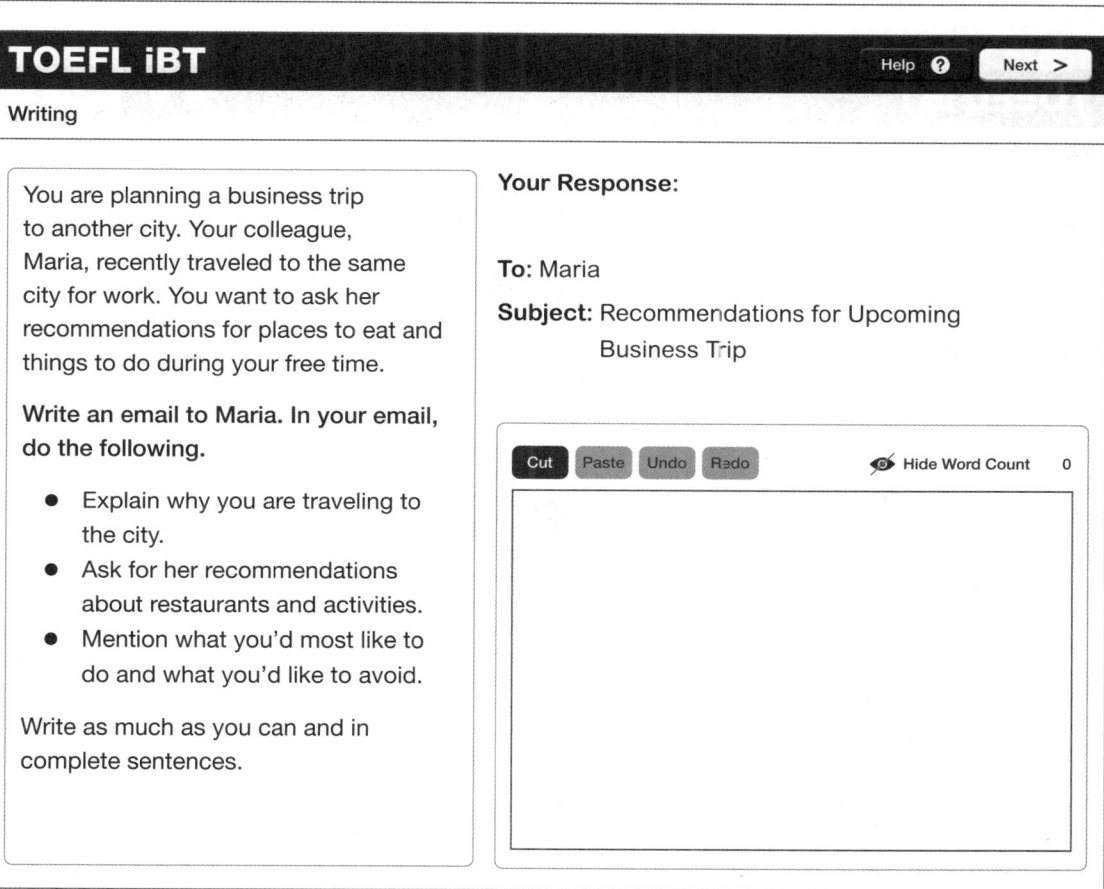

TOEFL iBT

Writing

Write for an Academic Discussion

A professor has posted a question about a topic and students have responded with their thoughts and ideas. Make a contribution to the discussion.

You will have 10 minutes to write.

TOEFL iBT

Writing

Your professor is teaching a course on labor studies. Write a post responding to the professor's question.

In your response, you should do the following:

- Express and support your opinion.
- Make a contribution to the discussion in your own words.

An effective response will contain at least 100 words.

Dr. Johns

More and more people can work remotely on portable electronic devices rather than in a dedicated office. These workers often have more flexibility regarding when and where they work, allowing them to become what are known as "digital nomads"—that is, workers who travel regularly and work from different locations, both inside and outside their own countries. Do you think digital nomadism is likely to continue increasing? Why or why not?

Claire

While digital nomadism does offer unparalleled freedom, it's important to note that it heavily relies on strong Internet connectivity. This requirement can significantly limit the destinations one can choose to work from, so digital nomadism probably won't increase globally as much as some people think.

Daniel

While Claire makes a good point, Internet technologies and speed are always improving, so I think digital nomadism will continue to grow. Why work in a stuffy city office building just so you can afford to travel to someplace beautiful once or twice a year when you could work from such places all year round?

SPEAKING

TOEFL iBT

Speaking Section

In the speaking section, you will answer 11 questions to demonstrate how well you can speak English. There are two types of tasks.

Type of Task	Description
Listen and Repeat	Listen and repeat what you heard.
Take an Interview	Answer questions from the interviewer.

TOEFL iBT

Speaking

Listen and Repeat

You will listen as someone speaks to you. Listen carefully and then repeat what you have heard. The clock will indicate how much time you have to speak.

No time for preparation will be provided.

TOEFL iBT

Speaking

You are training to assist visitors at a university orientation event. Listen to the speaker and repeat what he says. Repeat only once.

TOEFL iBT

Speaking | Question **1** of 11

T3_S_01

Listen and repeat only once.

RESPONSE TIME
00:00:08

TOEFL iBT

Speaking | Question **2** of 11

T3_S_02

Listen and repeat only once.

RESPONSE TIME
00:00:08

TOEFL iBT

Speaking | Question **3** of 11

T3_S_03

Listen and repeat only once.

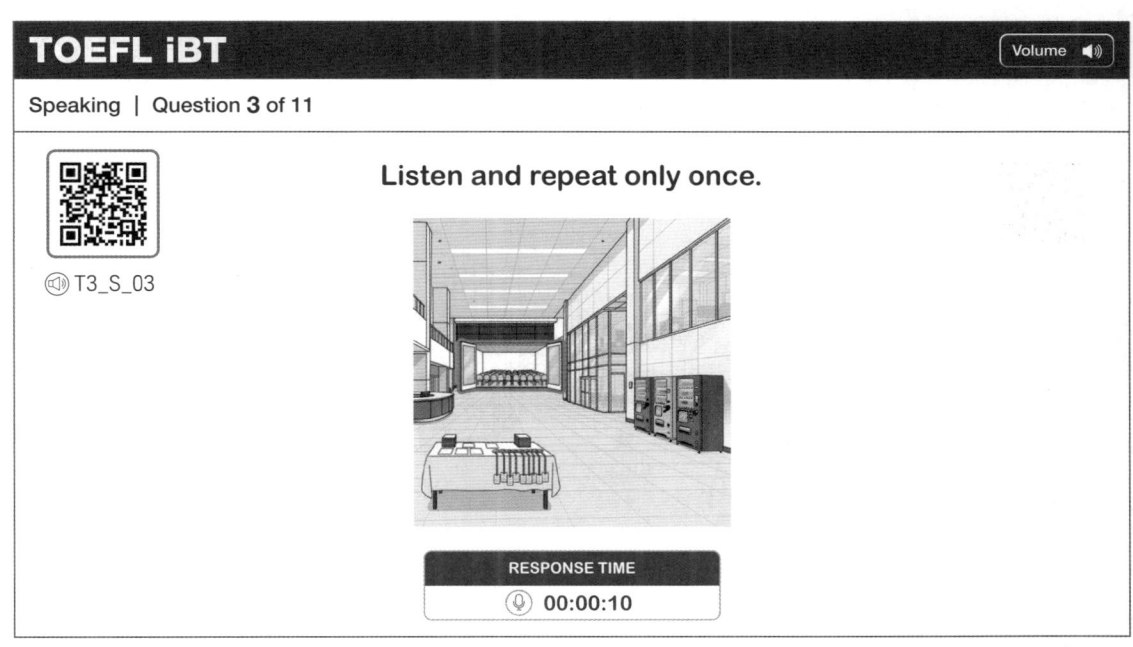

RESPONSE TIME
00:00:10

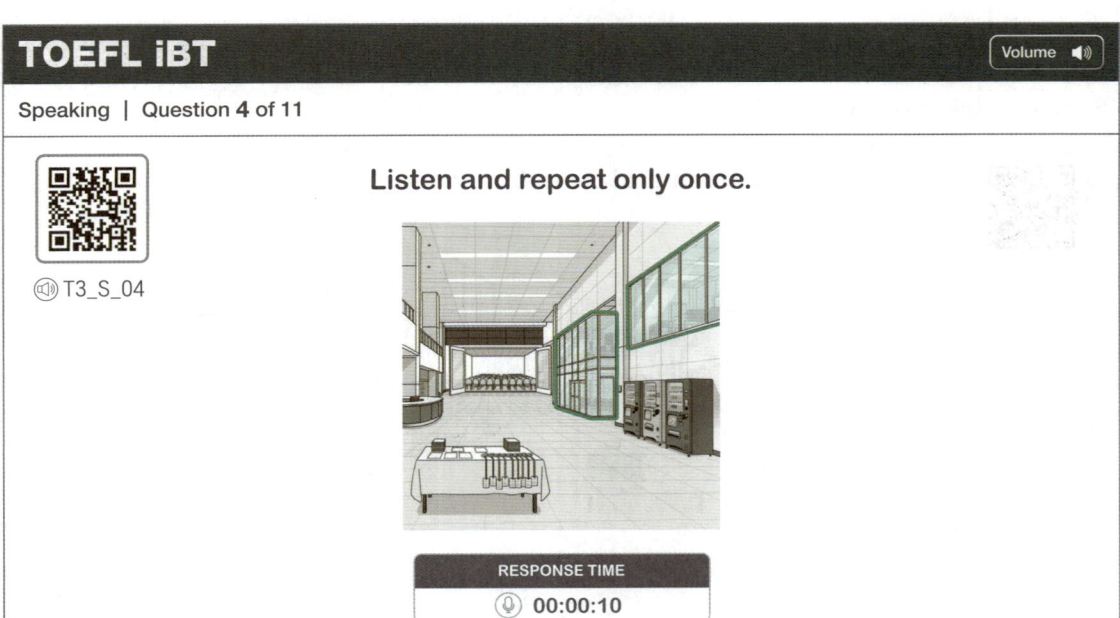

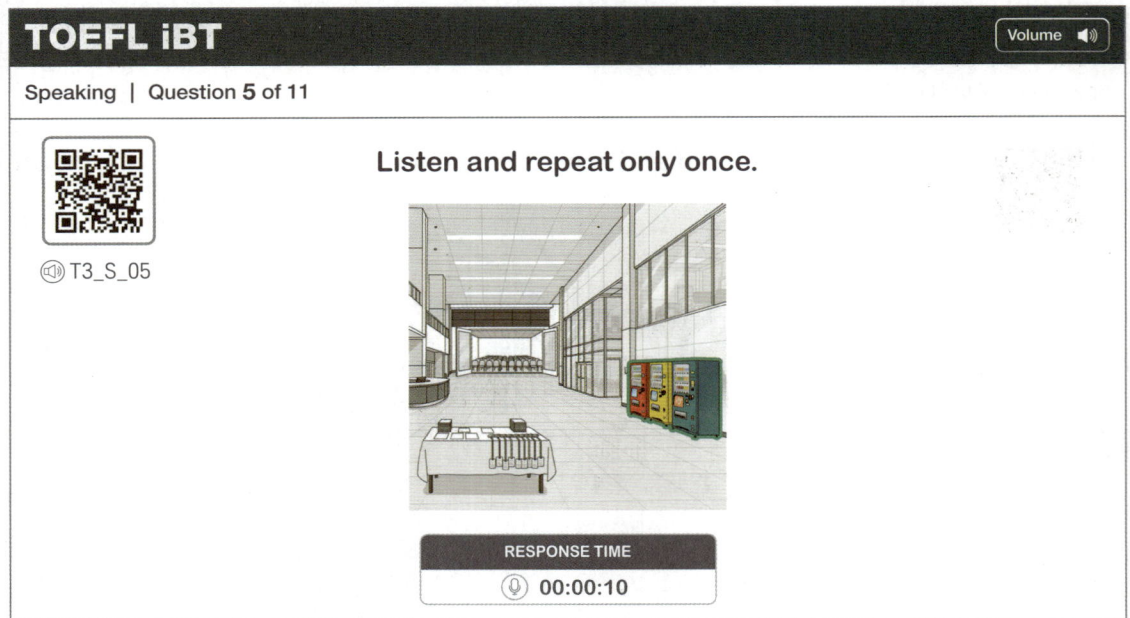

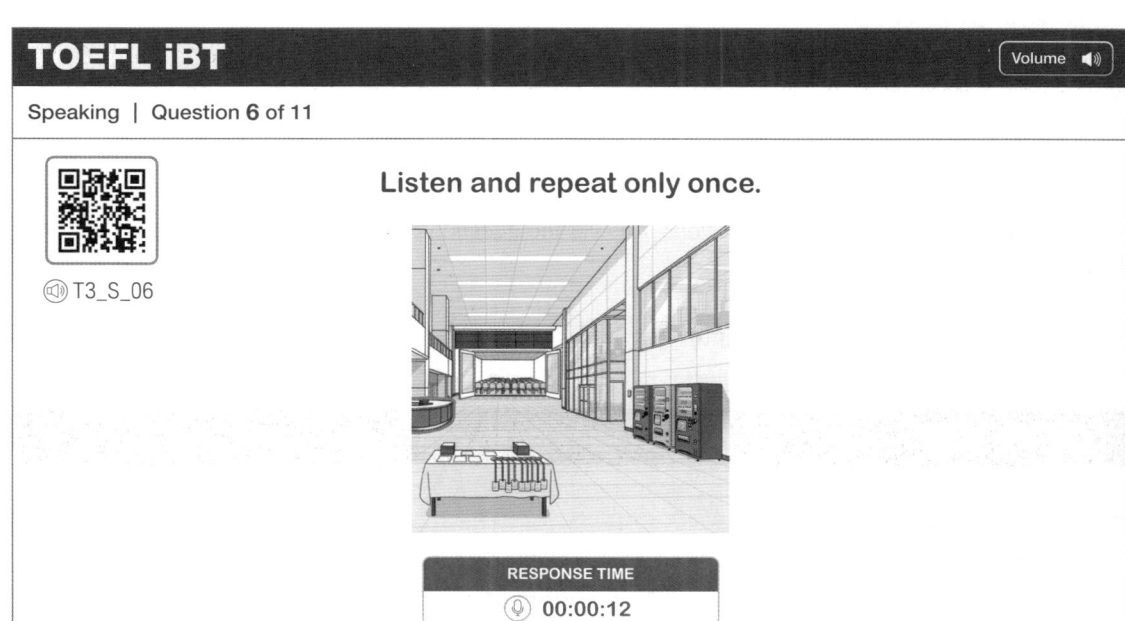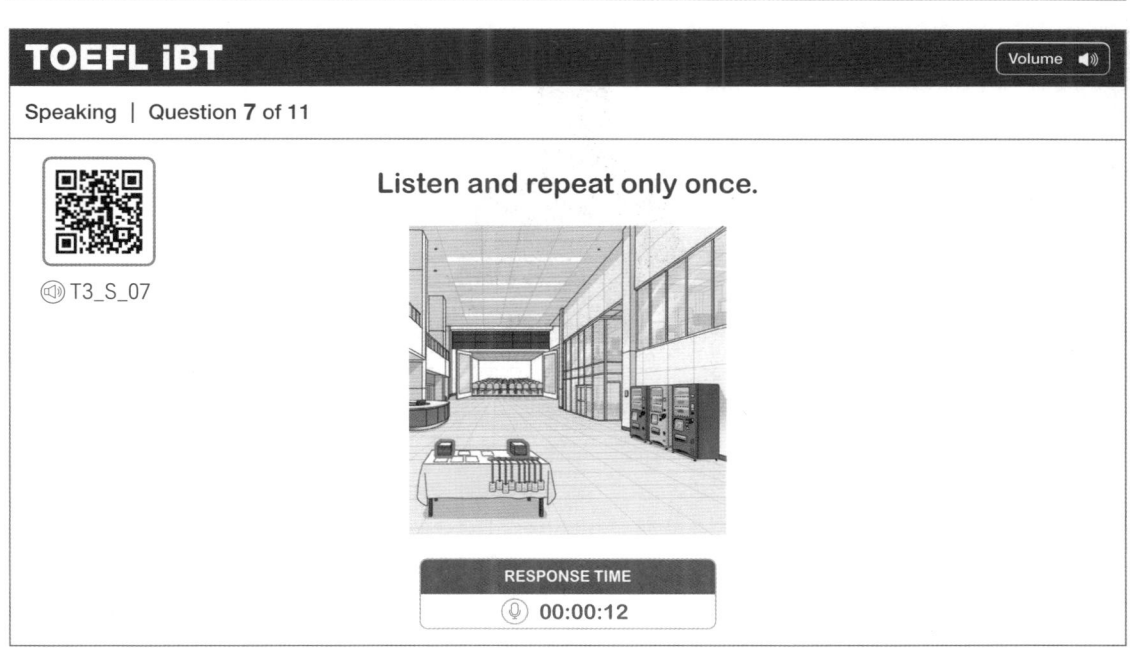

TOEFL iBT

Speaking

Take an Interview

An interviewer will ask you questions. Answer the questions and be sure to say as much as you can in the time allowed.

No time for preparation will be provided.

TOEFL iBT

Speaking

You have volunteered for a research study about work-life balance. You will have a short online interview with a researcher. The researcher will ask you some questions.

TOEFL iBT

Speaking | Question **8** of 11

Please answer the interviewer's questions.

T3_S_08

RESPONSE TIME
00:00:45

TOEFL iBT

Speaking | Question **9** of 11

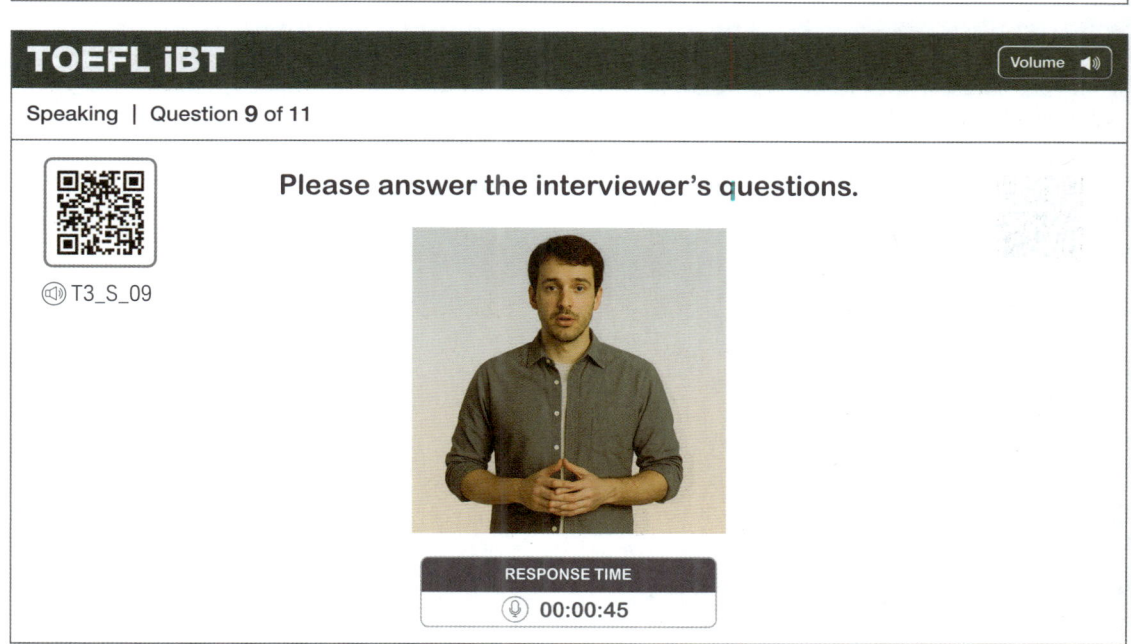

Please answer the interviewer's questions.

T3_S_09

RESPONSE TIME
00:00:45

TOEFL iBT

Speaking | Question **10** of 11

T3_S_10

Please answer the interviewer's questions.

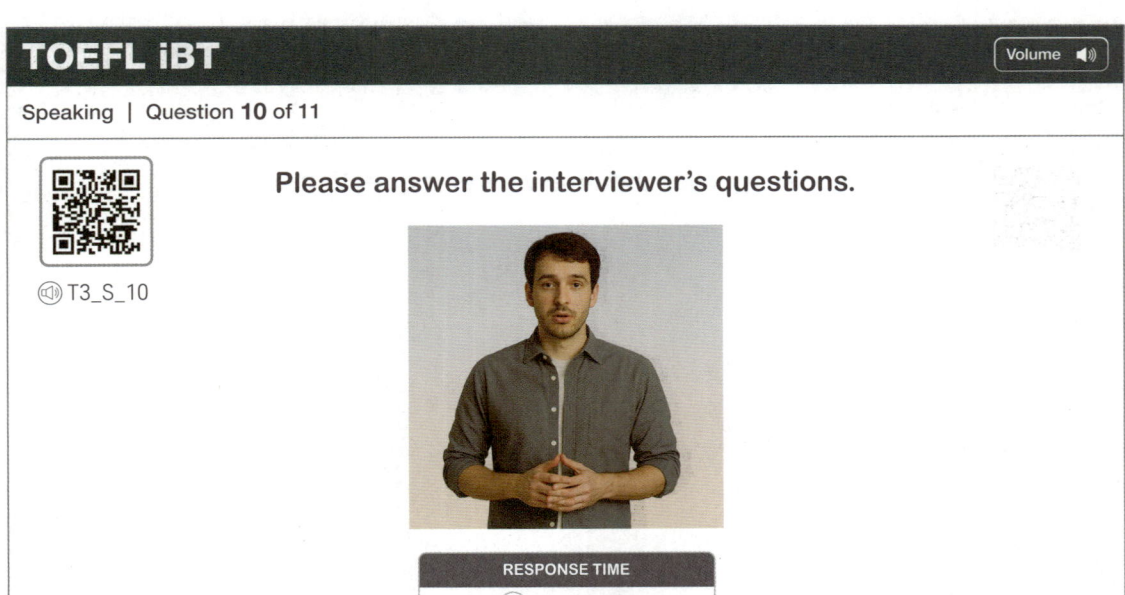

RESPONSE TIME
00:00:45

TOEFL iBT

Speaking | Question **11** of 11

T3_S_11

Please answer the interviewer's questions.

RESPONSE TIME
00:00:45

TOEFL
Complete Guide

Answers

Reading
Complete the Words

예시
ieve, tery, ed, ore, ins, ems, at, yed, jor, n

다음 문단에서 빠진 글자를 채우시오.

역사학자들은 초기 인류가 점토 항아리와 용기를 만드는 데 능숙했음을 밝히는 도구들을 고대 정착지에서 발견했다. 고고학자들은 이 도자기류가 액체, 곡물들 및 물품들을 보관하는 데 사용되었으며, 요리 및 무역에서 중요한 역할을 했다 고 믿는다. 수십 년에 걸쳐 디자인은 더욱 복잡해졌으며, 이는 예술적 표현과 문화적 교류를 반영하였다. 이러한 유물들은 종종 그들 공동체의 가치관과 신념을 반영하는 패턴으로 장식되었다.

어휘 및 표현
historian 역사학자 **tool** 도구 **ancient** 고대 **settlement** 정착지 **reveal** ~을 밝히다, 드러내다 **clay** 점토 **jar** 항아리, 단지 **container** 용기 **archaeologist** 고고학자 **pottery** 도자기(류) **store** ~을 저장하다, 보관하다 **liquid** 액체 **grain** 곡물 **item** 물품 **play a role in** ~에서 역할을 하다 **trade** 무역, 교역 **intricate** 복잡한 **artistic** 예술적인 **expression** 표현 **artifact** 유물 **decorate** ~을 장식하다 **reflect** ~을 반영하다 **communities** 공동체

Practice

1-10 ture, as, king, ying, vide, ot, ts, itors, lk, other

근린공원은 사람들이 휴식을 취하고, 놀며, 야외에서 시간을 보낼 수 있는, 따뜻하게 맞아주는 장소이다. 근린공원은 산책과 놀이를 할 수 있는 넓은 공간을 갖추고 있다. 나무는 더운 날 그늘을 제공하고, 벤치는 방문객들이 앉아 서로 이야기를 나눌 수 있게 한다. 화단은 봄과 여름에 색감을 더해주고 향기로운 냄새를 풍긴다. 자원봉사자들은 종종 청소 활동을 도와 모두가 공원을 즐길 수 있도록 한다. 이러한 공동의 공간들은 이웃을 더 친근하게 만들고, 가족들이 함께 편안하게 활동할 수 있는 방법을 제공한다.

어휘 및 표현
community park 근린공원 **welcoming** 따뜻하게 맞아주는 **feature** ~을 갖추다, ~을 특징으로 하다 **shade** 그늘 **let** ~을 하게 하다 **flower bed** 화단 **volunteer** 자원봉사자 **cleanup** 청소

11-20 rally, ious, es, bining, to, rated, rmation, ldren, cess, sual

12세 이하의 아이들은 시각 정보를 성인들과 다르게 인식하는데, 나이가 어린 사람들은 많은 감각 정보를 온전히 통합하는 능력이 부족하기 때문이다. 성인들은 일반적으로 하나의 통합된 정보 묶음으로 결합시켜 다양한 시각 신호를 처리한다. 하지만, 아이들은 더 작은 다수의 시각 정보 묶음으로 받아들여 이러한 시각 신호를 처리하는 경향이 있다. 이는 아이들이 한 가지 이미지의 더 미세한 상세 정보를 알아차릴 수 있는 반면, 성인들은 완전한 이미지에 대해 더 종합적으로 이해하도록 한다.

어휘 및 표현
perceive ~을 인식하다 **visual** 시각의 **lack** ~가 부족하다 **integrate** ~을 통합하다 **sensory information**

감각 정보 generally 일반적으로 process ~을 처리하다 cue 신호 combine ~을 결합하다 finer 더 미세한
comprehensive 종합적인, 포괄적인 complete 완전한

21-30   cause, itats, ited, ch, ey, port, tain, all, imals, ch

자연에서 생존하기 위해, 동물들은 반드시 물과 먹이 같은 자원에 대해 충분한 공급 기회를 얻어야 한다. 하지만, 서식지들에는 이러한 자원 공급이 제한되어 있기 때문에, 그것들은(서식지들은) 각 종의 동물들에 대해 작은 숫자만 지원하고 유지할 수 있다. 주어진 서식지 내에서 생존할 수 있는 한 가지 특정 동물 종의 최대 숫자를 환경 수용력이라고 일컫는다. 가령 한 가지 종과 서식지 사이의 관계를 변화시키는 방해 요소가 존재하지 않는다면, 환경 수용력과 개체수는 균형을 이룬 채로 유지될 것이다.

어휘 및 표현

have access to ~을 이용하다, ~에 접근하다 habitat 서식지 sustain ~을 살아가게 하다, 지속시키다 be referred to as ~라고 일컬어지다 carrying capacity 환경 수용력 assuming (that) 가령 ~한다면 disruption 방해, 지장 alter ~을 변경하다, 바꾸다 population (생물의) 개체수, 집단

31-40   rms, rgy, dered, inable, sil, ause, o, se, ural, r

전 세계적으로 에너지 수요가 지속적으로 증가함에 따라, 태양, 바람, 물 등 재생 가능 에너지원에 대한 관심이 높아지고 있다. 이러한 형태의 에너지는 천연 자원을 고갈시키거나 대기를 오염시키지 않기 때문에 화석 연료보다 지속 가능하다고 여겨진다. 예를 들어 태양광 패널은 광전 효과라는 과정을 통해 햇빛을 전기로 변환한다. 한편, 풍력 터빈은 움직이는 공기의 운동 에너지를 포착하여 사용 가능한 전력으로 변환한다.

어휘 및 표현

demand 수요 renewable 재생 가능한 source 원천 form 형태 sustainable 지속 가능한 fossil fuel 화석 연료 use up 고갈시키다 natural 천연의 pollute ~을 오염시키다 atmosphere 대기 solar panel 태양광 패널 convert ~을 전환하다 photovoltaic 광전의 kinetic 운동의

41-50   fts, ind, o, ps, sh, ough, sure, lt, icles, oved

부유식 담수화 뗏목은 해수를 식수로 전환하기 위해 바다에 배치된다. 이 뗏목들은 해수를 밀어 막에 통과시키는 펌프를 구동하기 위해 풍력 터빈을 이용한다. 압력이 상승함에 따라, 염분과 입자들이 제거되어, 식수가 남게 된다. 엔지니어들은 막힘을 방지하고 필터 수명을 연장하기 위해 온도와 유속을 모니터링한다.

어휘 및 표현

floating 부유의, 물에 뜨는 desalination 담수화(바닷물 염분 제거) raft 뗏목 deploy ~을 배치하다 convert ~을 전환하다 drinkable 마실 수 있는 power ~을 구동하다, ~에 동력을 공급하다 membrane 막 pressure 압력 build 높아지다, 고조되다 particle 입자 remove ~을 제거하다 potable 마실 수 있는 engineer 엔지니어, 기술자, 공학자 monitor ~을 지켜보다, 모니터링하다 temperature 온도 flow rate 유속 prevent ~을 막다 clogging 막힘 extend ~을 연장하다

51-60 ies, lvement, ree, hant, iliate, tomer, keting, ghly, cause, eads

제휴 마케팅은 제휴 업체가 다른 회사의 제품을 마케팅하는 것에 대해 수수료나 특전을 얻는 과정이다. 이것은 세 당사자, 즉 상인과 제휴 업체, 그리고 고객의 관여에 의존한다. 제휴 마케팅이 대단히 효과적인데, 제품 마케팅의 책임을 다수의 당사자에게 확대해주기 때문이다. 이는 더욱 효과적인 마케팅 전략을 만들어낼 수 있도록 해당 상인에게 다양한 제휴 업체의 능력을 활용할 수 있게 해준다.

어휘 및 표현
affiliate 제휴, 제휴 업체 **commission** (위탁 등으로 얻는) 수수료 **perk** 특혜, 특전 **involvement** 참여, 관여 **party** 당사자 **merchant** 상인 **spread** ~을 확대하다 **responsibility** 책임 **allow** ~하도록 하다, ~하게 해주다 **take advantage of** ~을 활용하다, 이용하다

Reading

Read in Daily Life

예시

(B), (D)

공지문을 읽으시오.

> **리버사이드 유틸리티 협동조합**
> **전자 청구서로 친환경을 실천하세요!**
>
> 우편함을 건너뛰고 나무를 절약하세요. 리버사이드 유틸리티 협동조합 회원들은 이제 월별 전기 요금 고지서를 이메일로 받을 수 있습니다. 가입은 빠르고 안전합니다— 온라인 계정에 로그인하거나 리버사이드 유틸리티 모바일 앱을 다운로드한 후 '청구 설정'으로 이동하세요. 가입 후 참가자들은 $5 크레딧을 받게 됩니다.

이 공지문의 주요 목적은?
(A) 결제 기한 변경을 알리기 위해
(B) 고객들이 전자 청구서를 사용하도록 장려하기 위해
(C) 새로운 공공요금 요금제를 소개하기 위해
(D) 전기 서비스에서 정전을 보고하기 위해

고객에게 제공되는 인센티브는?
(A) 월별 할인
(B) 에너지 평가
(C) 전자 기기
(D) 금전적 크레딧

어휘 및 표현

utility (수도·전기·가스 같은) 공익사업 cooperative 협동조합 go green 친환경적이 되다 e-billing 전자 청구 skip ~을 건너뛰다 electricity 전기 statement 고지서 sign up 가입하다 secure 안전한 log into ~에 로그인하다 participant 참가자 enroll 등록하다 deadline 기한 encourage ~을 장려하다 electronic 전자의 pricing plan 요금제 outage 정전 assessment 평가 financial 금전의, 재정의

Practice

1-2 (C), (B)

이메일을 읽으시오.

> **날짜:** 2025년 8월 8일
> **제목:** 도보 투어 등록 확정
>
> 친애하는 조나스 씨께,
>
> 베이사이드 역사 도보 투어에 등록해 주셔서 감사합니다. 10월 17일 예정된 투어에 대한 당신의 자리가 확정되었습니다. 투어는 오전 10시 정각에 헤리티지 박물관 앞에서 시작됩니다. 편안한 신발을 착용하시고 재사용 가능한 물병을 지참해

언제 도보 투어가 진행되는지?
(A) 10월 8일
(B) 10월 10일
(C) 10월 17일
(D) 10월 27일

주시기 바랍니다. 체크인 데스크에서 인쇄된 지도와 투어 가이드를 제공해 드립니다.

그곳에서 뵙기를 기대하겠습니다!

감사합니다,

마틴 김
베이사이드 역사 행사 코디네이터

조나스 씨가 투어에 가져가야 하는 것은?
(A) 도시 지도
(B) 음료 용기
(C) 결제 증명서
(D) 등록 양식

어휘 및 표현
subject 제목 registration 등록 confirmation 확인, 확정 spot 자리 refillable 리필이 가능한 container 용기 proof 증명서 payment 결제

3-4 (B), (A)

이메일을 읽으시오.

수신: amir.haddad@email.com
발신: tickets@mariner-museum.org
날짜: 2025년 7월 9일
제목: 시간대별 입장권 수령 안내 — 오전 시간대

친애하는 하닷 씨께,

귀하의 '얼음 가장자리 항해' 체험의 시간대 지정 입장권은 7월 15일 오전 10시부터 오후 12시까지 하버 홀 안내 데스크에서 수령하실 수 있습니다. 정부 발급 사진이 부착된 신분증을 지참해 주시기 바랍니다. 입장권은 주문서에 기재된 구매자에게만 발급됩니다.

감사합니다.
방문객 서비스팀 K. 두아르테

하다드 씨가 입장권을 수령할 수 있는 가장 이른 시간은?
(A) 오전 9시
(B) 오전 10시
(C) 오전 11시
(D) 오후 12시

하다드 씨가 사진이 부착된 신분증을 지참해야 하는 이유는?
(A) 구매자로 명시된 본인임을 확인하기 위해
(B) 별도의 입장료를 지불하기 위해
(C) 박물관 회원으로 가입하기 위해
(D) 시간대를 변경하기 위해

어휘 및 표현
timed-entry pass 시간대 지정 입장권 government-issued 정부 발급의 photo ID 사진이 부착된 신분증 purchaser 구매자 order 주문(서)

5-7 (B), (C), (C)

인터넷 게시물을 읽으시오.

짐 니콜슨

일요일 오후를 즐겁게 보낼 방법을 찾고 있나요? 메도우뷰 커뮤니티 로봇 박람회에 들러 보세요! 가족 단위로 참여하기 좋은 이 행사에는 체험형 전시물, 기술 시연, 초보자도 쉽게 참여할 수 있는 코딩 워크숍이 가득합니다.

가장 인기 있는 전시물 중 하나는 리지웨이 로봇 동아리가 주최하는 "배틀 봇 아레나"입니다. 학생들이 직접 제작한 로봇들이 친선 경기를 펼치며, 창의적인 디자인과 인상적인 엔지니어링으로 유명합니다. 경기는 오전 중으로 진행되며 좌석이 빠르게 매진됩니다—좋은 자리를 원하면 일찍 오세요!

지역 기술 기업들도 체험형 기기를 전시한 부스를 운영하며, STEM 분야 진로에 대한 질문에 답변해 줄 담당자들이 상주합니다. 심지어 집으로 가져갈 수 있는 소형 태양광 동력 기계를 만들 수 있는 '나만의 로봇 만들기' 부스도 마련되어 있습니다.

기술 애호가든 단순한 호기심이든, 이 박람회는 배우고, 즐기고, 영감을 받을 수 있는 최적의 장소입니다. 푸드트럭, 음악, 그리고 지역 사회 모두가 함께 즐길 수 있는 흥미진진한 기술 체험을 만끽하세요!

👍 좋아요   💬 댓글

이 인터넷 게시물의 주요 목적은?
(A) 로봇공학의 역사를 설명하기 위해
(B) 지역 기술 행사에서 제공되는 활동을 설명하기 위해
(C) 지역 내 다양한 공과대학을 비교하기 위해
(D) 로봇 동아리 창설에 대한 조언을 제공하기 위해

리지웨이 로봇 동아리 전시가 인기 있는 이유는?
(A) 초보자를 위한 튜토리얼을 제공한다.
(B) 참가 비용이 저렴하다.
(C) 독특한 로봇 디자인을 선보인다.
(D) 전국 대회에서 우승했다.

방문객들이 한 전시회에 일찍 도착하도록 권장되는 이유는?
(A) 워크숍에 등록하기 위해
(B) 무료 다과를 받기 위해
(C) 최적의 좌석을 확보하기 위해
(D) 입장료를 내지 않기 위해

어휘 및 표현

robotics 로봇공학 **fair** 박람회 **packed with** ~로 가득찬 **interactive** 상호작용의, 체험의 **exhibit** 전시물 **tech** 기술 **demonstration** 시연 **host** ~을 주최하다 **club** 동아리 **compete** 경쟁하다, 시합하다 **match** 시합, 경기 **known** 알려진 **creative** 창의적인 **impressive** 인상적인 **engineering** 공학기술, 엔지니어링 **fill up** 꽉 차다 **hands-on** 체험의 **gadget** 기기 **representative** 직원, 담당자 **enthusiast** 애호가 **inspire** ~에 영감을 주다

8-10 (A), (A), (C)

이메일을 읽으시오.

수신: janebookaddict@gmail.com
발신: events@greenleaflibrary.org
제목: 초대합니다 – 그린리프의 도서관 야간 행사에 함께해요!

친애하는 부커 씨께,

이번 금요일 오후 6시에 메이플 애비뉴 18번지에 위치한 새롭게 단장한 그린리프 도서관의 재개관을 기념하는 특별한 저녁 행사에 꼭 참석해 주시기 바랍니다. 이번 행사는 새롭게 단장한 독서실, 새로운 멀티미디어 센터, 확장된 어린이 코너를 둘러보실 수 있는 좋은 기회입니다.

정기 이용자 분들을 위해 마련된 이번 축하 행사에서는 가이드 투어, 생생한 스토리텔링, 인터랙티브 독서 구역, 무료 다과가 제공됩니다. 그린리프의 공동체 정신을 느끼고 책에 대한 사랑을 나누기에 안성맞춤인 행사입니다.

동반자도 환영합니다! 참석자 전원께는 도서관 상품 할인 쿠폰(당일 한정)과 가을 작가 강연 일정 사전 안내권이 제공됩니다.

문의사항이나 참석 예약은 행사 담당자(555-0198)에게 연락주시기 바랍니다.

감사합니다.
엘렌 하트
그린리프 공공도서관

이 이메일의 주요 목적은?

(A) 도서관 기념 행사에 누군가를 초대하기 위해
(B) 어린이를 위한 새로운 도서 시리즈를 홍보하기 위해
(C) 도서관 리모델링을 위한 기부금을 요청하기 위해
(D) 지역 사회 구성원들에게 새로운 사서를 소개하기 위해

부커 씨와 도서관의 관계에 대해 추론할 수 있는 것은?

(A) 그녀는 자주 방문하거나 기존 회원이다.
(B) 그녀는 지역 공립학교에서 근무한다.
(C) 그녀는 도서관 리모델링 작업을 도왔다.
(D) 그녀는 작가 강연 일정을 기획 중이다.

행사 참석자들에게 권장되는 행동은?

(A) 웹사이트 방문
(B) 책 추천
(C) 친구 동반
(D) 양식 작성

어휘 및 표현

reopening 재개장, 재개관 explore ~을 탐험하다, 둘러보다 expanded 확장된 celebration 축하 행사
interactive 상호작용의, 체험의 station 구역, 위치 complimentary 무료의 refreshment 다과 occasion 행사, 의식, 축하 attendee 참석자 merchandise 상품 author 작가 talk 강연 RSVP 참석 여부를 회답하다
coordinator 행사 담당자 donation 기부(금) librarian 사서, 도서관 직원 frequent 빈번한, 자주 가는 existing 기존의

Reading
Read an Academic Passage

예시

(A), (D)

화석

화석은 과거의 지질학적 연대에 살았던 생물체가 보존된 유해 또는 흔적이다. 주로 거대한 공룡 뼈로 인식되고 있는 화석은 발자국과 기타 눌린 자국 또는 고대 미생물의 미세한 돌 자국도 포함한다. 화석은 고대의 삶에 대한 매우 흥미로운 **통찰력**을 제공해 줄뿐만 아니라, 지질학적 연대를 구성하는 데 도움이 되기도 한다. 처음에, 지질학자들은 지층 또는 암석 층들을 분류하는 것이 지구의 지질 역사에 대한 정확한 그림을 제공해 줄 수 있기를 바랐다. 그러나 더 많은 지층을 연구하고 더 많은 층을 비교할수록, 지역마다 상관 관계가 있을 것으로 짐작되었던 지층의 암석 종류가 일치하지 않는다는 점이 명확해졌다. 전 세계에서 여러 분리된 지역들에 걸쳐 지층을 맞춰보기 위한 시도는 과거의 시대를 보여주지 못했다. 설사 여러 지역에 걸쳐 지층 속 암석의 종류가 동일하다고 해도, 여전히 결정적인 결과물을 만들어 내기 어려웠다. 시간이 흐를수록 부패하는 유기 물질과 달리, 암석은 동일한 상태로 남아 있다. 예를 들어, 석영은 홍적세에 형성된 것이든, 아니면 캄브리아기에 형성된 것이든 상관없이 원자 구성상 동일하다.

지문의 단어 "insight"에 가장 가까운 의미는?

(A) 이해
(B) 상상
(C) 관점
(D) 증거

암석 지층에서 얻은 정보가 지질학적 연대표를 확립하는 데 사용될 수 없는 이유는?

(A) 암석 지층의 동일한 층들이 멀리 떨어져 있었기 때문에
(B) 암석 속의 유기 물질이 너무 빨리 부패했기 때문에
(C) 암석 지층에서 충분한 데이터가 수집될 수 없었기 때문에
(D) 서로 일치한다고 여겨지는 암석층이 지역마다 달랐기 때문에

어휘 및 표현

remains 유해 **organism** 생물체 **geological** 지질학의 **impression** 눌린 자국 **imprint** 흔적, 자국 **microbe** 미생물 **insight** 통찰력 **catalog** ~을 분류하다 **strata** 지층(stratum의 복수형) **layer** 층, 겹, 막 **presumably** 짐작하기에 **correlating** 상관 관계에 있는 **denote** ~을 보여주다, 나타내다 **identical** 동일한 **conclusive** 결정적인 **finding** 결과(물) **quartz** 석영 **atomically** 원자 구성상 **Pleistocene** 홍적세 **Cambrian** 캄브리아기 **decay** 부패하다

Practice

1-5 (B), (C), (D), (C), (C)

깃털 코딩 프로젝트

과학자들은 오랫동안 새들의 의사소통 체계에 매료되어 왔다. 인간이 복잡한 메시지를 전달하기 위해 언어를 사용하는 반면, 많은 새 종들은 노래, 지저귐, 깃털 장식 등에 의존한다. 조류 연구에서 가장 흥미로운 발견 중 하나는 깃털 무늬가 미적 목적이나 짝짓기 이상의 기능을 할 수 있다는 가능성이다. 심지어 시각 언어와 유사한 정보를 암호화할 수도 있다는 것이다.

이 이론을 검증하기 위해 연구진은 '깃털 코딩 프로젝트'를 시작했다. 그들은 종달새 종인 '페인티드 라크'의 날개 무늬를 연구했다. 안전한 임시 염료로 무늬를 신중하게 변형시키면서 다른 새들의 행동 변화를 관찰했다. 일부 실험에서 특정 무늬를 가진 종달새는 무리 내 다른 새들에게 환영받거나 회피당했는데, 이는 시각적 단서에 기반한 인식이나 의사소통을 시사했다.

최근 연구 결과는 앵무새와 찌르레기로 확대되었다. 앵무새는 무늬 변화에 중간 정도의 반응을 보인 반면, 찌르레기는 특히 민감하게 반응하여 무리 행동을 크게 바꿨다. 이는 깃털 무늬를 통한 시각적 신호 전달이 이전에 알려진 것보다 더 **보편적이고** 정교할 수 있음을 시사한다.

추가 연구에서 이러한 관찰이 확인된다면, 특히 복잡한 사회 구조로 알려지지 않은 종에서 비언어적 동물 의사소통에 대한 과학적 이해를 완전히 바꿀 수 있을 것이다.

지문의 주요 내용은?

(A) 깃털이 새를 포식자로부터 보호하는 방법
(B) 새 깃털의 무늬를 연구하는 프로젝트
(C) 새의 비행 기술 진화
(D) 철새 종을 추적하는 데 사용되는 방법

새 깃털에 임시 염료를 바른 목적은?

(A) 새를 더 쉽게 촬영하기 위해
(B) 자외선으로부터 보호하기 위해
(C) 시각적 단서가 사회적 행동에 어떻게 영향을 미치는지 테스트하기 위해
(D) 연구 장소에 인간의 존재를 알리기 위해

지문에 따르면, 페인티드 라크에 대해 다음 중 사실이 아닌 것은?

(A) 깃털 코딩 프로젝트의 일부이다.
(B) 날개 무늬 변화에 반응했다.
(C) 무늬가 변한 다른 새들을 피했다.
(D) 고도의 언어적 의사소통을 보였다.

지문의 단어 "prevalent"에 가장 가까운 의미는?

(A) 특이한
(B) 일시적인
(C) 널리 퍼진
(D) 위험한

저자가 찌르레기를 언급한 이유는?

(A) 앵무새로부터 행동을 배운다는 점을 설명하기 위해서
(B) 패턴 변화를 무시한 새의 사례를 제시하기 위해서
(C) 시각적 신호에 매우 민감한 종을 강조하기 위해서
(D) 다른 새들보다 훈련시키기 쉽다는 점을 시사하기 위해서

어휘 및 표현

feather 깃털 coding 암호화, 부호화 fascinated 매료된 convey ~을 전달하다 complex 복잡한 chirp 지저귐 plumage 깃털 intriguing 흥미로운 pattern 패턴, 무늬 aesthetics 미적 mating 짝짓기 encode ~을 암호화하다 investigate ~을 조사하다 theory 이론 launch ~을 시작하다 lark 종달새 alter ~을 변경하다 marking 무늬, 표시 temporary 임시의 dye 염료 observe ~을 관찰하다 flock 무리, 떼, 떼로 모이다 suggest ~을 시사하다, 암시하다 recognition 인식 cue 단서 findings 연구 결과 parrot 앵무새 starling 찌르레기 moderate 중간의 particularly 특히 sensitive 민감한 significantly 크게, 상당히 prevalent 만연한, 보편적인 sophisticated 정교한 previously 이전에 observation 관찰 nonverbal 비언어적 social structure 사회 구조 ultraviolet light 자외선 illustrate ~을 설명하다 responsive 민감한, 즉각 반응하는

6-10 (A), (B), (A), (B), (A)

방음 도시: 조용한 포장도로와 차분한 거리

도시 계획가들은 교통 소음을 줄이기 위해 다공성 아스팔트와 고무화 콘크리트 시험을 시작했다. 이 표면들은 타이어 진동을 흡수하고 소리를 분산시켜, 추가 방음벽 없이도 주변 소음 수준을 낮춘다. 초기 시도들은 크지 않은 감소를 보이는데 긴 도로에 적용 시 유의미하게 된다.

하지만, 소음을 약화시키는 재료는 예측 불가능하게 노후화될 수 있다. 막힌 구멍들은 성능을 저하시키고, 겨울철 동결–해동 주기는 콘크리트를 분해할 수 있다. 이는 도로 청소, 배수 설계, 교체 주기가 아스팔트 자체만큼 중요함을 의미한다. 화물 운송로에 가장 가까운 지역이 가장 큰 혜택을 보지만, 동시에 가장 심한 마모에도 직면한다.

결과들을 평가하기 위해, 엔지니어들은 이동식 마이크를 배치하고 출퇴근 시간대와 심야 시간대의 교통 스펙트럼(분광) 지문을 분석한다. 국제 워크숍은 도로 관리 기관들이 유지 관리 전략을 공유하고 수명 주기 비용을 모델링하도록 모은다. 이러한 협력들은 조용한 거리가 화학적 작용만큼이나 정책과 유지 관리에 달려있음을 드러낸다.

지문의 단어 "absorb"에 가장 가까운 의미는?

(A) 흡수하다
(B) 증폭하다
(C) 모방하다
(D) 반영하다

어떤 상황에서 재료의 성능이 저하되는가?

(A) 긴 도로를 재포장할 때
(B) 시간이 지나며 구멍들이 막힐 때
(C) 차량에 마이크를 장착할 때
(D) 화물 운송 경로가 주거 지역을 우회할 때

2문단과 3문단의 관계는?

(A) 3문단은 2문단에서 언급된 문제점을 측정하는 방법을 설명한다.
(B) 3문단은 2문단의 유지보수 문제를 반박한다.
(C) 3문단은 2문단의 사례를 반복한다.
(D) 3문단은 관련 없는 주제를 소개한다.

워크숍은 기관들이 무엇을 하는 데 도움을 주는가?

(A) 화물 교통을 완전히 금지하기
(B) 유지 관리 전략과 비용 모델을 공유하기
(C) 소음 지도를 군중 조사로 대체하기
(D) 전 세계적으로 하나의 콘크리트 제조법을 표준화하기

저자가 스펙트럼 지문을 언급하는 이유는?

(A) 교통 패턴을 구별하는 방법을 보여주기 위해
(B) 방음벽이 불필요하다는 점을 주장하기 위해
(C) 음악 녹음과 고속도로를 비교하기 위해
(D) 마이크가 야간에 작동하지 않는 이유를 설명하기 위해

어휘 및 표현

soundproof 방음의 pavement 포장도로 urban planner 도시 계획가 porous 다공성의, 구멍이 많은 asphalt 아스팔트 rubberized 고무화된 concrete 콘크리트 surface 표면 absorb ~을 흡수하다 vibration 진동, 떨림 scatter ~을 분산하다 ambient 주변의 erect ~을 세우다 barrier 장벽 trial 시도 modest 적당한, 크지 않은 reduction 감축 significant 중대한, 유의미한 apply 적용하다 roadway 도로, 차도 material 자재 dampen ~을 약화시키다 age 노후화되다 unpredictably 예측 불가능하게 clogged 막힌 pore 구멍 performance 성능 freeze-thaw cycle 동결-해동 주기 break down ~을 분해하다 sweeping 쓸기, 청소 drainage 배수 replacement 교체 neighborhood 동네, 지역 freight 화물 운송 wear 마모 evaluate ~을 평가하다 deploy ~을 배치하다 mobile 이동식 microphone 마이크 analyze ~을 분석하다 spectral 스펙트럼의, 분광의 fingerprint 지문, 현저한 특징 agency 기관 bring together ~을 모으다, ~을 접촉시키다 maintenance 유지 관리 strategy 전략 model ~을 모델로하다, ~을 모델링하다, ~을 설계하다 lifecycle 수명 주기 cost 비용 policy 정책 upkeep 유지 관리 chemistry 화학, 화학적 작용 take in ~을 흡수하다 amplify ~을 증폭하다 imitate ~을 모방하다 reflect ~을 반영하다 bypass ~을 우회하다

11-15 (B), (C), (B), (D), (C)

주변 소음이 창의성에 미치는 영향

심리학 및 신경과학 분야의 최근 연구에 따르면 적당한 수준의 배경 소음이 창의적 사고를 실제로 향상시킬 수 있다고 한다. 고요함이 종종 집중력과 생산성과 연관되지만, 혁신과 추상적 사고가 필요한 작업에는 완전한 정적이 항상 이상적인 것은 아닐 수 있다. 연구자들은 카페, 주변에 속삭임이 들리는 도서관, 또는 부드럽게 웅웅거리는 에어컨과 같은 적당한 주변 소음이 있는 환경에서 작업하는 것이 창의적인 문제 해결을 자극하는 수준의 산만함을 촉진할 수 있음을 발견했다.

한 대학에서 진행된 실험에서 참가자들은 일상 가정용품의 새로운 용도를 발명하는 등 일련의 창의적 과제를 수행했다. 참가자들이 중간 수준의 소음(약 70데시벨)에 노출되었을 때, 조용한 환경(약 50데시벨)이나 높은 소음 환경(약 85

다음 중 지문의 주요 내용을 가장 잘 나타낸 것은?

(A) 완전히 조용한 환경에서 창의적 사고가 향상된다.
(B) 적당한 주변 소음이 창의성을 높일 수 있다.
(C) 사람들은 지속적인 소음이 있는 장소에서 가장 잘 일한다.
(D) 배경 소음이 있으면 생산성은 항상 감소한다.

지문에 언급된 대학 실험의 결과 중 하나는?

(A) 참가자들이 사실 정보를 더 쉽게 기억해냈다.
(B) 높은 소음 수준이 참가자들의 기억력을 향상시켰다.

데시벨)에서 작업한 참가자들에 비해 성과가 현저히 향상되었다. 적당한 소음은 집중력을 완전히 저해하지 않으면서도 추상적 사고를 촉진할 만큼의 적절한 산만함을 제공하는 것으로 보인다.

이러한 현상은 배경 소음이 적당할 때 정상적인 사고 과정에 약간의 방해를 주기 때문으로 여겨진다. 이러한 방해는 개인이 덜 관습적인 방식으로 생각하도록 유도하여 인지 처리 범위를 넓히고 더 독창적인 아이디어로 이어질 수 있다. 하지만, 소음이 너무 커지면, 뇌가 생각을 효과적으로 처리하는 능력을 압도하여 창의성과 생산성이 떨어지게 된다.

이러한 연구 결과는 작업 공간, 교실, 창작 스튜디오 설계에 영향을 준다. 완벽한 정적을 추구하기보다는 혁신을 촉진하기 위해 부드러운 배경음 환경을 도입하는 것이 유리할 수 있다. 기업과 교육자 모두, 특히 창의적 사고가 필수적인 상황에서 음향 환경이 성과에 미치는 영향을 고려해볼 필요가 있다.

(C) 적당한 소음 수준이 더 창의적인 응답을 이끌어냈다.
(D) 완전한 침묵이 참가자들의 집중력을 높이는 데 도움이 되었다.

저자가 지문에서 가정용품을 언급한 이유는?
(A) 심리학 실험에서 흔히 발생하는 문제의 예를 들기 위해
(B) 창의성을 테스트하는 데 사용되는 과제 유형을 보여주기 위해
(C) 가정용 도구가 새로운 발명을 촉발할 수 있음을 시사하기 위해
(D) 소음 수준이 쇼핑 행동에 미치는 영향을 보여주기 위해

지문의 단어 "disruption"에 가장 가까운 의미는?
(A) 지연
(B) 증가
(C) 반복
(D) (주의나 집중) 방해

직장에서 배경음 사용에 대해 추론할 수 있는 것은?
(A) 집중력을 떨어뜨려 생산성을 저하시킬 수 있다.
(B) 사람들이 더 많이 대화하고 협력하도록 장려할 수 있다.
(C) 혁신을 향상시킬 수 있다.
(D) 근로자들의 불만족 수준을 높인다.

어휘 및 표현

ambient 주변의 creativity 창의성 psychology 심리학 neuroscience 신경과학 moderate 적당한 enhance ~을 강화하다, 향상시키다 creative thinking 창의적 사고 silence 고요함, 정적 be associated with ~와 연관되다 focus 집중력 productivity 생산성 complete 완전한 quiet 고요함, 정적 task 업무, 작업 innovation 혁신 abstract 추상적인 murmur 속삭임, 소곤거림 distraction 산만함 stimulate ~을 자극하다, 촉진하다 experiment 실험 impair ~을 저해하다, 해치다 mild 온화한, 적당한 slight 약간의 disruption 방해 prompt ~을 촉진하다, 유도하다 individual 개인 conventional 관습적인 broaden ~을 넓히다 cognitive 인지의 process 처리 drop 하락 findings 연구 결과 have implications for ~에 영향을 주다 foster ~을 촉진하다 alike 둘 다, 똑같이 acoustic 음향의

Listening

Listen and Choose a Response

예시

(D)

가장 알맞은 답변을 선택하시오.

How much is the entry ticket for the technology expo?
테크놀로지 엑스포 입장권이 얼마지?

(A) 새로운 장소로 옮겨졌어.
(B) 난 지난달에 두 번 갔어.
(C) 그래, 일요일에는 무료 입장이야.
(D) 가격을 확인해 볼게.

어휘 및 표현
entry ticket 입장권 venue 장소 admission 입장

Practice

1 (D)

If you'd like to know more about the software, speak with Mr. Torres.
그 소프트웨어에 대해 더 알고 싶으면, 토레스 씨와 이야기해 봐.

(A) 비밀번호는 어떻게 변경하지?
(B) 몇 시에 회의가 있지?
(C) 난 언제든지 도와줄 수 있어.
(D) 그에게 연락할게.

2 (A)

Where's the nearest bike rental station?
가장 가까운 자전거 대여소는 어디에 있지?

(A) 빵집 바로 맞은편에 있어.
(B) 나는 보통 차를 타고 다녀.
(C) 출퇴근 시간에만 운영해.
(D) 이미 반납했어.

3 (B)

How do I reset the tablet's password?
태블릿 비밀번호를 어떻게 재설정하지?

(A) 그래, 언제든지 반품할 수 있어.

(B) 설명서에 있는 지침을 따르는 게 어때?
(C) 좋은 생각이야.
(D) 아니, 내 건 다른 브랜드야.

4 (B)

I don't think I'll be able to attend the book club.
북 클럽에 참석하기 어려울 것 같아.
(A) 우리는 격주로 만나.
(B) 내가 대신 메모를 해줄까?
(C) 그 카페 커피가 정말 맛있어.
(D) 그래, 내 책을 가져갈게.

5 (B)

How can I access my account?
내 계정에 어떻게 접속하지?
(A) 난 왜 그런지 기억이 안 나.
(B) 리사가 알 거야.
(C) 일정 좀 확인해 볼게.
(D) 이 커피 한번 마셔봐.

6 (A)

If you need help organizing the files, let me know.
파일 정리에 도움이 필요하면 알려줘.
(A) 난 아직 네 전화번호를 갖고 있지 않아.
(B) 아니, 난 수업에 등록하지 않았어.
(C) 그녀는 점심 먹고 곧 돌아올 거야.
(D) 궁금한 점 있니?

7 (A)

Is the ice rink open throughout the weekend?
주말 내내 아이스링크가 열려 있니?
(A) 그래, 하지만 오전에만 열려.
(B) 아니, 이미 친구들과 약속이 있어.
(C) 초과근무 수당을 지급해 주길 원해.
(D) 보통 일요일이 더 나아.

8 (A)

So did you end up seeing the photography exhibition?
사진 전시회는 보러 갔니?
(A) 시간이 없었어.
(B) 그래, 다음 달에 시작해.

(C) 약 3시간 정도 걸릴 거야.
(D) 카메라 가져갈게.

9 (B)

Who's presenting at the science fair this year?
올해 과학 박람회에서 누가 발표하지?

(A) 그는 어제 신청했어.
(B) 아직 확정되지 않았어.
(C) 과학 박람회에 참석하자.
(D) 박람회는 5월에 열릴 예정이야.

10 (A)

What's the deadline for the group project?
그룹 프로젝트 마감일이 언제야?

(A) 잠깐만—달력 확인해 볼게.
(B) 네가 원하는 날짜로 정해.
(C) 난 이미 다 끝냈어.
(D) 응, 벌써 마쳤던 것 같은데.

11 (C)

I'm going to the bookstore after class.
난 수업 끝나고 서점에 갈 거야.

(A) 매 학기마다.
(B) 공책 할인 중이래.
(C) 같이 갈래?
(D) 수업은 다섯 시에 시작해.

12 (B)

I'd like to know your opinion on the new class schedule.
새 수업 시간표에 대한 너의 의견을 듣고 싶어.

(A) 나는 전공을 바꾸려고 해.
(B) 나중에 만나서 이야기하자.
(C) 그녀가 그 수업을 포기했어.
(D) 그래, 그건 필수 과목이야.

어휘 및 표현

bike rental station 자전거 대여소 instructions 지침 manual 설명서 take notes 메모하다 account 계정 organize ~을 정리하다 overtime rate 초과근무 수당 exhibition 전시회 run out of time 시간이 없다 fair 박람회 deadline 마감일 semester 학기 major 전공 drop ~을 포기하다 required course 필수 과목

Listening

Listen to a Conversation

예시

(B)

대화를 들으시오.

> W: Hey, do you need anything from the electronics store?
> 헤이, 전자제품 가게에서 뭐 필요해?
>
> M: Huh? Aren't you giving a guitar lesson in a few minutes?
> 어? 너 몇 분 뒤에 기타 레슨 안 해?
>
> W: That's not until tomorrow morning.
> 그건 내일 아침이야.
>
> M: Oh wow, I completely lost track of the days. What are you planning to get from the store?
> 오, 와우, 날짜를 완전히 놓쳤네. 뭘 사려고?
>
> W: Just some new earbuds, and if they're on sale, maybe a USB drive too. Do you need anything?
> 그냥 새 이어폰 좀 사고, 할인 중이면 USB 드라이브도 살까 봐. 너 필요한 거 있어?
>
> M: No, but thanks!
> 아니, 그래도 고마워!

남자가 "날짜를 완전히 놓쳤네"라고 말한 이유는?

(A) 가게에서 필요한 물건을 잊어버렸다.
(B) 수업 일정에 대해 혼란스러웠다.
(C) 요일이 무엇인지 확신하지 못했다.
(D) 전자제품 가게가 영업 중인지 몰랐다.

어휘 및 표현

electronics 전자제품 lose track of ~을 놓치다 earbuds 이어폰

Practice

1-2 (A), (B)

> M: Did the library staff say when the printer would be fixed?
> 도서관 직원들이 언제 프린터가 수리될지 알려줬니?
>
> W: Yes, I checked with them earlier. They said the technician is already on the way.
> 응, 아까 확인해봤어. 기술자가 이미 오는 중이라고 하더라고.

M: That's good. I need to print some forms before my next class.
다행이네. 다음 수업 전에 서류 좀 출력해야 하는데.

W: I understand. I reported the problem as soon as it jammed. With any luck, it'll be working again soon. In the meantime, why don't you grab a snack from the café? You might have time before it's repaired.
알아. 종이가 걸리자마자 바로 신고했어. 운이 좋으면 금방 고쳐질 거야. 그동안 카페에서 간식 좀 사 먹는 거 어때? 고쳐지기 전에 시간이 좀 남을 거야.

여자가 도서관 직원에게 연락한 이유는?
(A) 프린터가 작동하지 않고 있었다.
(B) 컴퓨터가 없어졌다.
(C) 전화선이 끊겼다.
(D) 스캐너에 오류가 발생했다.

여자가 남자에게 하도록 제안하는 것은?
(A) 일찍 수업에 돌아가기
(B) 먹을 것을 사기
(C) 다른 프린터를 사용하기
(D) 문제를 다시 신고하기

어휘 및 표현
technician 기술자 on the way 오는 중 jam (종이 등이 걸려서) 움직이지 않다 grab a snack 간식을 사 먹다

3-4 (B), (C)

M: I'm thinking about joining either the photography club or the hiking club. What do you think?
사진 동아리와 등산 동아리 중 하나에 들어갈까 생각 중이야. 어떻게 생각해?

W: Well, it depends on your interests. If you enjoy exploring nature and being outdoors, the hiking club might be a better fit.
음, 네 관심사에 따라 다르겠네. 자연 탐험과 야외 활동을 즐긴다면 등산 동아리가 더 잘 맞을 거야.

M: That's a good point. But I've always wanted to learn how to take better pictures.
그건 맞는 말이야. 하지만 난 항상 사진 찍는 법을 더 잘 배우고 싶었거든.

W: In that case… maybe photography is the way to go.
그렇다면… 사진 동아리가 더 나을지도 모르겠네.

M: Hmm. I'll have to give it more thought.
흠. 좀 더 생각해봐야겠네.

남자가 결정하려고 하는 것은?
(A) 그림 수업과 하이킹 여행

(B) 사진 동아리와 하이킹 동아리
(C) 글쓰기 모임과 미술 동아리
(D) 요리 수업과 피트니스 수업

여자가 자신의 제안을 하는 이유는?

(A) 활동 비용이 더 저렴하기 때문이다.
(B) 모임이 더 자주 열린다.
(C) 남성이 야외 활동을 즐긴다.
(D) 회원 수가 더 많다.

어휘 및 표현
club 동아리 better fit 더 잘 맞는

5-6 (D), (C)

> W: My clarinet keeps going out of tune. It's fine for a few minutes, and then it sounds terrible.
> 내 클라리넷이 자꾸 음정이 틀어져. 몇 분 동안은 괜찮다가 갑자기 엉망이 돼.
>
> M: That's frustrating. Did you try swapping the reed with a new one?
> 정말 짜증나겠네. 리드를 새 거로 바꿔보려고 했니?
>
> W: I tried. I think the cork is warped—I'll have an expert inspect it.
> 해봤어. 코르크가 휘어진 것 같아—전문가에게 점검받으러 갈 거야.
>
> M: Good call. The music shop in town will be able to reseal it quickly.
> 잘 생각했어. 동네 악기점에서 재밀봉을 빨리 해줄 거야.
>
> W: I'll swing by after lunch.
> 점심 이후 들를거야.

여자가 클라리넷으로 겪고 있는 문제는?

(A) 분실되었다.
(B) 실수로 파손되었다.
(C) 부품이 일부 없다.
(D) 음정이 유지되지 않는다.

여자가 다음에 가장 할 것 같은 행동은?

(A) 새 악기를 사기
(B) 다른 리드를 구입하기
(C) 악기 수리를 맡기기
(D) 음악 공연을 하기

어휘 및 표현
out of tune 음정이 맞지 않는 terrible 엉망인, 끔찍한 frustrating 짜증나는, 불만스러운 swap ~을 바꾸다 reed

리드(악기의 얇은 울림 판) **adjust** ~을 조정하다 **cork** (관과 관의 연결 부분에 사용되는) 코르크 **warped** 휘어진 **good call** 잘 생각했어, 좋은 판단이야, 맞는 말이야 **music shop** 악기점 **reseal** 재밀봉하다 **swing by** 잠깐 들르다

7-8 (D), (B)

> M: Are you passing by the print shop today?
> 오늘 인쇄소 지나가?
>
> W: I hadn't planned on it. What's the problem?
> 그럴 생각 없었는데. 무슨 일인데?
>
> M: I wanted to make some color posters for the charity event we are hosting this Saturday, but I'm really short on time.
> 이번 주 토요일에 우리가 주최하는 자선 행사용 컬러 포스터를 만들고 싶은데 시간이 정말 촉박해.
>
> W: I've got nothing on. What exactly do you need?
> 나 할 일 없는데. 정확히 뭐가 필요해?
>
> M: That's a relief—could you take these files to the print shop and have about 20 color posters made?
> 다행이네—이 파일들 인쇄소에 가져가서 컬러 포스터 20장 정도 만들어 줄 수 있어?
>
> W: Sure thing.
> 알았어.

남자가 언급한 문제는?

(A) 인쇄소를 찾을 수 없다.
(B) 행사에 참석할 수 없다.
(C) 인쇄물을 분실했다.
(D) 작업을 완료할 시간이 없다.

여성이 "나 할 일 없는데"라고 말할 때 암시하는 것은?

(A) 행사 포스터를 디자인하겠다.
(B) 남성을 도울 수 있다.
(C) 돈이 부족하다.
(D) 행사를 건너뛰고 싶다.

어휘 및 표현

pass by 지나가다 **print shop** 인쇄소 **charity** 자선 **host** ~을 주최하다 **short on** ~이 부족한

Listening
Listen to an Announcement

예시

(C)

대학 행사에서 공지사항을 들으시오.

> Good afternoon, everyone. We're excited to share that the university's yearly charity auction is scheduled for next Friday at 6 P.M. in the main hall. All funds raised will benefit local charities. We look forward to your participation and appreciate your support.
>
> 안녕하세요, 여러분. 대학의 연례 자선 경매가 다음 주 금요일 오후 6시 본관 강당에서 열릴 예정임을 알려드리게 되어 기쁩니다. 모금된 모든 기금은 지역 자선 단체에 기부될 예정입니다. 여러분의 참여를 기대하며, 여러분의 지원에 감사드립니다.

공지사항의 주요 주제는?

(A) 장소 변경
(B) 기부금 모금 운동
(C) 자선 경매
(D) 연말 행사

어휘 및 표현

yearly 연례 charity 자선 auction 경매 main hall 본관 강당 raise funds 기금을 모으다, 자금을 조달하다 benefit ~에게 이익이 되다 participation 참여 appreciate ~에 감사하다 venue 장소 donation 기부금 drive 모금 운동 year-end 연말 ceremony 행사

Practice

1-2 (A), (C)

대학 구내식당에서 공지사항을 들으시오.

> Attention, everyone. The cafeteria will close early tomorrow at 2:00 P.M. for a scheduled deep cleaning. This is part of our monthly sanitation procedures. We apologize for the inconvenience and encourage you to visit the student café in the East Hall or the vending machines near the library. Thank you for your understanding.
>
> 여러분, 주목해 주세요. 내일 오후 2시에 예정된 대청소를 위해 구내식당이 조기 폐쇄됩니다. 이는 월간 위생 절차의 일환입니다. 불편에 대해 사과드리며 동관 학생 카페나 도서관 근처 자판기 이용을 권장합니다. 양해해 주셔서 감사합니다.

공지사항의 주요 목적은?

(A) 학생들에게 청소 일정을 알리기 위해

(B) 새로운 식당 메뉴를 홍보하기 위해
(C) 새로운 캠퍼스 카페를 소개하기 위해
(D) 학생들에게 식량 부족을 경고하기 위해

폐쇄 기간 동안 학생들이 해야 하는 것은?

(A) 식당에서 일찍 점심을 먹기
(B) 자판기 사용을 피하기
(C) 근처 다른 음식점을 이용하기
(D) 식당 청소를 돕기

어휘 및 표현

cafeteria 구내식당 deep cleaning 대청소 sanitation 위생 procedure 절차 apologize for ~에 대해 사과하다 inconvenience 불편 encourage ~을 권장하다 vending machine 자판기 shortage 부족

3-4 (C), (C)

대학 동아리 모임에서 공지사항을 들으시오.

> Good evening, amateur inventors and innovators! I'd like to remind you all that the theme of our Inventors Club summer contest is "Everyday Frictions." You are all encouraged to invent things that reduce stress in everyday life, like being stuck in traffic jams or losing your keys. Upload design proposals by July 28 through the club portal. And remember, look at the notes from our previous club meetings to find inspiration!
>
> 안녕하세요, 아마추어 발명가 및 혁신가 여러분! 발명가 동아리 여름 콘테스트의 주제가 "일상 속 마찰"임을 다시 한번 알려드립니다. 교통 체증에 갇히거나 열쇠를 잃어버리는 등 일상생활의 스트레스를 줄여주는 발명품을 만들어 보세요. 7월 28일까지 동아리 포털을 통해 설계안을 업로드하세요. 영감을 얻기 위해 지난 동아리 모임들의 노트를 참고하는 것도 잊지 마세요!

화자가 교통 체증을 언급한 이유는?

(A) 회의에 늦은 이유를 설명하기 위해
(B) 청중에게 일찍 출발하라고 조언하기 위해
(C) 스트레스 받는 상황의 예를 들기 위해
(D) 환경 문제를 강조하기 위해

참가자들에게 권장되는 행동은?

(A) 온라인 프로필 생성하기
(B) 이전 작업물 제출하기
(C) 모임 노트 검토하기
(D) 강좌 등록하기

어휘 및 표현

amateur 아마추어 inventor 발명가 innovator 혁신가 theme 주제 friction 마찰 encourage ~을 장려하다

be stuck in ~에 갇히다 proposal 제안서 previous 이전의, 지난 inspiration 영감 submit ~을 제출하다 review ~을 검토하다 register for ~을 등록하다

5-6 (B), (A)

대학 행사에서 공지사항을 들으시오.

> Attention, everyone. Tomorrow at 7 P.M., the university cinema club will host an outdoor movie night in the central plaza. Admission is free, and blankets and chairs are welcome. Refreshments will be sold at the concession stand. Bring your family or friends and enjoy the show!
>
> 주목해 주세요, 여러분. 내일 저녁 7시, 대학 영화 동아리가 중앙 광장에서 야외 영화의 밤을 개최합니다. 입장료는 무료이며, 담요와 의자를 가져오셔도 좋습니다. 매점에서 간식을 판매할 예정입니다. 가족이나 친구와 함께 오셔서 영화를 즐기세요!

공지사항의 주요 목적은?
(A) 강연 시리즈를 광고하기 위해
(B) 영화의 밤 행사를 홍보하기 위해
(C) 공원 리모델링을 알리기 위해
(D) 새로운 자원봉사자를 모집하기 위해

행사에 대해 언급된 내용은?
(A) 야외에서 진행된다.
(B) 티켓을 미리 구매해야 한다.
(C) 무료 간식이 제공된다.
(D) 다음 주로 연기되었다.

어휘 및 표현

plaza 광장 admission 입장료 blanket 담요 refreshment 간식 concession stand 매점 volunteer 자원봉사자 take place 발생하다, 일어나다, 진행되다 postpone ~을 연기하다

7-8 (A), (D)

교실에서 공지사항을 들으시오.

> Hello, everyone. I wanted to let you know that next Wednesday at 11 A.M. in Dalton Hall, Chef Marco Lazzari will be giving a culinary demonstration. Chef Lazzari has worked in award-winning restaurants around the world and specializes in sustainable cooking practices. He'll be sharing techniques and recipes that emphasize locally sourced ingredients. Seats are limited, so I encourage you to arrive early to get a good spot.
>
> 안녕하세요, 여러분. 다음 주 수요일 오전 11시, 달튼 홀에서 마르코 라자리 셰프의 요리 시연이 있을 예정임을

> 알립니다. 라자리 셰프는 전 세계 수상 경력에 빛나는 레스토랑에서 근무한 경력이 있으며 지속 가능한 요리법을 전문으로 합니다. 현지에서 조달한 재료를 강조하는 기술과 요리법을 공유할 예정입니다. 좌석이 한정되어 있으니 좋은 자리를 잡으려면 일찍 오길 권합니다.

공지사항은 무엇에 관한 것인가?

(A) 특별 요리 시연회
(B) 학생 대상 요리 경연대회
(C) 수업 일정 변경
(D) 지역 레스토랑 견학

화자가 라자리 셰프의 경력을 언급한 이유는?

(A) 학생들이 요리를 더 진지하게 받아들이도록 권유하기 위해
(B) 참석이 필수인 이유를 설명하기 위해
(C) 학생들에게 요리 관련 진로를 고려하도록 제안하기 위해
(D) 초청 연사로서의 자격을 강조하기 위해

어휘 및 표현

culinary 요리 demonstration 시연 award-winning 수상 specialize in ~에 전문이다 sustainable 지속 가능한 recipe 요리법 seat 좌석 attendance 참석 mandatory 필수의, 의무의 qualification 자격

Listening
Listen to an Academic Talk

예시

(D)

미술 수업에서의 강연을 들으시오.

Today's talk is about Impressionism in painting. Its history begins in France during the late nineteenth century. It emerged first in Paris, blending elements of earlier artistic traditions with new approaches to light, color, and brushwork. One of the key characteristics of Impressionism is its emphasis on capturing spontaneous visual impressions rather than precise, detailed representation.

Artists often painted scenes quickly, with loose brushstrokes and shifting colors, making each canvas unique and filled with a sense of immediacy. This contrasts with earlier academic art, where compositions were typically planned and executed with careful precision. Impressionist painters also explored the effects of natural light at different times of day, often using broken color and visible strokes to create an unexpected and vibrant atmosphere.

In the 1870s and 1880s, Impressionism gained wider recognition and spread beyond Paris to other parts of Europe. During this period, artists such as Claude Monet, Pierre-Auguste Renoir, and Edgar Degas became leading figures, and exhibitions of Impressionist works began to flourish as important cultural events.

Over time, Impressionism continued to evolve, by inspiring movements like Post-Impressionism and influencing modern art around the world. Today, it remains a celebrated style, admired for its creativity, expressive power, and its revolutionary break from traditional painting. Next, we will look at the impact of Impressionism on later art movements and how it has shaped contemporary visual culture.

오늘의 주제는 회화에서의 인상주의입니다. 그 역사는 19세기 후반 프랑스에서 시작됩니다. 인상주의는 파리에서 처음 등장했으며, 기존의 예술적 전통 요소와 빛, 색채, 붓놀림에 대한 새로운 접근법을 혼합했습니다. 인상주의의 핵심 특징 중 하나는 정밀하고 세부적인 묘사보다는 즉흥적인 시각적 인상을 포착하는 데 중점을 둔다는 점입니다.

화가들은 느슨한 붓질과 변화하는 색채로 장면을 빠르게 그려 각 캔버스를 독특하고 생생한 현장감으로 가득 채웠습니다. 이는 구도가 전형적으로 계획되고 정밀한 정확성이 실행되었던 이전의 학구적 예술과 대조를 이룹니다. 인상주의 화가들은 또한 하루 중 다양한 시간대의 자연광 효과를 탐구하며, 종종 분할된 색채와 붓 자국이 드러나는 기법을 사용해 예상치 못한 생동감 넘치는 분위기를 창조했습니다.

1870년대와 1880년대에 들어 인상주의는 더 넓은 인정을 받으며 파리를 넘어 유럽 전역으로 확산되었습니다. 이 시기 클로드 모네, 피에르 오귀스트 르누아르, 에드가 드가 같은 화가들이 주도적 인물로 부상했으며, 인상주의 작품 전시회가 중요한 문화 행사로 번성하기 시작했습니다.

시간이 흐르며 인상주의는 포스트 인상주의 같은 운동에 영감을 주고 전 세계 현대 미술에 영향을 미치며 계속 진화했습니다. 오늘날에도 이 양식은 창의성과 표현력, 전통 회화와의 혁명적 단절로 높이 평가받는 스타일로 남아 있습니다. 다음으로, 인상주의가 후대 예술 운동에 미친 영향과 어떻게 현대 시각 문화를 형성하였는지 살펴보겠습니다.

강연의 주요 주제는?
(A) 현대 예술에서 인상주의의 역할
(B) 파리에서 인상주의의 인기
(C) 유명한 인상주의 화가들
(D) 시간에 따른 인상주의의 발달

어휘 및 표현

Impressionism 인상주의 painting 회화 emerge 시작되다, 등장하다 blend ~을 혼합하다 element 요소 tradition 전통 brushwork 붓놀림 characteristic 특징 spontaneous 자연적인, 즉흥적인 visual impression 시각적 인상 precise 정확한 detailed 세부적인 representation 표현 scene 장면 loose 느슨한 brushstroke 붓질 shifting 변화하는 a sense of immediacy 생생한 현장감 contrast with ~와 대조되다 academic 학구적 composition 구성 execute ~을 실행하다 unexpected 예상치 못한 vibrant atmosphere 생동감 넘치는 분위기 recognition 인정 spread 확산되다 leading figure 주도적 인물 exhibition 전시회 flourish 번성하다 evolve 발달하다 inspire ~에 영감을 주다 movement 운동 celebrated 유명한, 명성 높은 admired 존경 받는 creativity 창의성 expressive power 표현력 revolutionary break 혁명적 단절 shape ~을 형성하다 contemporary 현대의, 동시대의

Practice

1-4 (C), (A), (D), (B)

영양에 관한 팟캐스트 강연을 들으시오.

Have you ever skipped breakfast because you were running late, and then found yourself craving snacks all day? It turns out there's a scientific explanation for that. Nutritionists talk about two types of hunger—physical hunger and hedonic hunger. Physical hunger is what you feel when your body actually needs fuel. But hedonic hunger? That's driven more by your senses—what smells good, looks delicious, or feels comforting to eat.

Let me give you an example. Yesterday morning, I skipped breakfast and had nothing until noon. That was physical hunger—I needed food. But after lunch, I passed by a bakery and smelled fresh cinnamon rolls. I wasn't really hungry, but I still wanted one. That's hedonic hunger in action.

Now, here's the interesting part. Researchers have found that hedonic hunger is often linked to habits and environment more than actual need. It activates reward centers in the brain, making you feel good temporarily. But the downside is that it can lead to overeating or making less nutritious choices.

If you're looking to manage this, try eating consistent meals, drinking enough water, and being aware of your triggers. And if you do indulge sometimes, that's okay too—awareness is the first step to balance.

지각 때문에 아침을 거르고 나서 하루 종일 간식을 먹고 싶어 한 적 있나요? 사실 이 현상에 과학적 설명이 있습니다. 영양학자들은 두 가지 유형의 배고픔을 구분합니다—물리적 배고픔과 쾌락적 배고픔이죠. 물리적 배고픔은 몸이 실제로 연료가 필요할 때 느끼는 것입니다. 하지만 쾌락적 배고픔은? 이는 감각에 의해 더 많이 유발됩니다—좋은 냄새가 나거나, 맛있어 보이거나, 먹으면 편안함을 주는 것들이죠.

예를 들어 보죠. 어제 아침 저는 아침을 거르고 점심까지 아무것도 먹지 않았습니다. 그건 신체적 배고픔이었어요—음식이 필요했죠. 하지만 점심 후 빵집을 지나가다 신선한 시나몬 롤 냄새를 맡았을 때, 저는 실제로 배고프지 않았지만 하나 먹고 싶었습니다. 바로 쾌락적 배고픔이 작용한 거죠.

이제 흥미로운 부분이 있습니다. 연구자들은 쾌락적 배고픔이 실제 필요보다 습관과 환경에 더 자주 연결된다는 사실을 발견했습니다. 이는 뇌의 보상 센터를 활성화시켜 일시적으로 기분 좋게 만듭니다. 하지만 단점은 과식이나 영양가 낮은 선택으로 이어질 수 있다는 점이죠.

이를 관리하려면 규칙적인 식사, 충분한 수분 섭취, 그리고 자신의 유발 요인에 대한 인식을 시도해 보세요. 가끔은 마음껏 하는 것도 괜찮습니다—인식이 균형 잡힌 삶의 첫걸음이죠.

강연의 주제는?
(A) 예산 내 식사 전략
(B) 배고픔이 의사 결정에 미치는 영향
(C) 두 가지 다른 배고픔 비교
(D) 일상 건강에서 아침 식사의 역할

화자가 아침 식사 거르기에 대해 말하는 것은?
(A) 음식을 갈망하게 만들었다.
(B) 나중에 더 건강하게 먹는 데 도움이 되었다.
(C) 전반적인 식욕을 감소시켰다.
(D) 그녀의 일상적인 루틴의 일부이다.

화자가 시나몬 롤을 언급한 이유는?
(A) 음식을 얼마나 빨리 준비할 수 있는지 보여주기 위해
(B) 뇌가 향기와 맛을 혼동하는 방식을 보여주기 위해
(C) 아침 식사와 관련된 습관이 어떻게 형성되는지 설명하기 위해
(D) 쾌락적 배고픔의 예를 들기 위해

화자가 쾌락적 배고픔에 대해 말하는 것은?
(A) 더 나은 에너지 수준으로 이끈다.
(B) 뇌의 보상 시스템을 활성화할 수 있다.
(C) 항상 신체적 배고픔에 뒤따른다.
(D) 운동으로 통제하기가 더 쉽다.

어휘 및 표현

running late 지각하는 crave ~을 갈망하다 snack 간식 nutritionist 영양학자 hunger 배고픔 physical 신체적 hedonic 쾌락적 fuel 연료 drive ~을 몰다, ~하게 하다 sense 감각 comforting 위로가 되는 in action 작동하는 actual 실제 activate ~을 활성화하다 reward 보상 temporarily 일시적으로 downside 단점 lead to ~로 이어지다 overeating 과식 nutritious 영양 있는 consistent meals 규칙적인 식사 aware of ~을 인지하는 trigger 유발 요인 indulge 마음껏 하다 awareness 인식 strategy 전략 on a budget 예산 내 illustrate ~을 보여주다 confuse ~을 혼동하다 scent 향기 taste 맛 form ~을 형성하다

5-8 (C), (A), (B), (C)

역사 수업에서의 강연을 들으시오.

> When we think about the earliest forms of writing, many people imagine ancient scripts carved in stone or written on parchment. But one of the most fascinating early writing systems was developed in Mesopotamia over 5,000 years ago—cuneiform. This system began as a series of pictographs—simple drawings representing objects or ideas—but gradually evolved into wedge-shaped marks made with a stylus on clay tablets.
>
> What's interesting is that cuneiform wasn't tied to just one language. It was adapted by different cultures, including the Sumerians, Akkadians, and Babylonians. This flexibility made cuneiform especially useful for trade, government administration, and recording literature. For instance, the famous *Epic of Gilgamesh* was written in cuneiform.
>
> Now, you might wonder how scholars today even know how to read it. That's thanks to a discovery called the Behistun Inscription—a large stone carving with the same text written in three languages, one of which was in cuneiform. It was key to deciphering the script, much like the Rosetta Stone was for Egyptian hieroglyphs.
>
> Understanding cuneiform gives us a window into the development of written language and communication. It also tells us a great deal about early civilizations—what they valued, how they governed, and how they saw the world. In the next part of the lecture, I'll introduce some other early writing systems, like Egyptian hieroglyphs and Chinese oracle bone script.
>
> 가장 초기의 표기 형태를 떠올릴 때, 많은 사람들은 돌에 새겨진 고대 문자나 양피지에 기록된 글씨를 상상합니다. 그러나 가장 흥미로운 초기 문자 체계 중 하나는 5,000년 전 메소포타미아에서 개발된 설형문자입니다. 이 체계는 사물이나 개념을 나타내는 단순한 그림인 일련의 그림문자로 시작되었지만, 점차 점토판에 스타일러스로 새긴 쐐기 모양의 표식으로 진화했습니다.
>
> 흥미로운 점은 설형문자가 단일 언어에만 국한되지 않았다는 것입니다. 수메르인, 아카드인, 바빌로니아인 등 다양한 문화권에서 채택되었습니다. 이러한 유연성 덕분에 설형문자는 무역, 정부 행정, 문헌 기록에 특히 유용했습니다. 예를 들어 유명한 길가메시 서사시도 설형문자로 기록되었습니다.

이제, 여러분은 현대 학자들이 어떻게 이를 해독할 수 있었을지 궁금할 것입니다. 그 해답은 '베히스툰 비문'이라는 불리는 발견물 덕분입니다. 이 거대한 석각에는 세 가지 언어로 같은 내용이 새겨져 있었는데, 그중 하나가 바로 설형문자였습니다. 이 비문은 이집트 상형문자의 해독에 로제타석이 그랬듯, 설형문자 해독의 열쇠가 되었습니다.

설형문자를 이해하는 것은 문자와 의사소통의 발전 과정을 들여다보는 창이 됩니다. 또한 초기 문명들이 무엇을 소중히 여겼는지, 어떻게 통치했는지, 세상을 어떻게 바라보았는지에 대해 많은 것을 알려줍니다. 강의의 다음 부분에서는, 이집트 상형문자나 중국 갑골문자 같은 다른 초기 문자 체계들을 소개하겠습니다.

강연의 주요 주제는?
(A) 고대 건축에서 점토판의 사용
(B) 문자 체계가 어떻게 언어 발음에 영향을 미쳤는지
(C) 설형문자 표기 체계의 역사와 중요성
(D) 메소포타미아의 구전 전통과 문헌 전통의 차이점

교수가 길가메시 서사시를 언급한 이유는?
(A) 설형문자가 유명한 이야기를 기록하는 데 사용되었음을 보여주기 위해
(B) 메소포타미아 종교의 기원을 설명하기 위해
(C) 초기 신화가 어떻게 전승되었는지 설명하기 위해
(D) 설형문자와 이집트 문자를 비교하기 위해

교수가 베히스툰 비문에 대해 말하는 것은?
(A) 바빌론의 초대 왕이 쓴 법률이 담겨 있었다
(B) 학자들이 설형문자를 번역하는 데 도움을 주기 위해 사용되었다
(C) 역사상 최초의 이중 언어 기록 사례이다
(D) 1800년대에 현지 농부들에 의해 발견되었다

교수가 다음에 논의할 가능성이 가장 높은 것은?
(A) 구전 이야기 전통이 어떻게 초기 종교에 영향을 미쳤는지
(B) 메소포타미아 무역로의 중요성
(C) 세계 각지의 다른 고대 표기 체계
(D) 후대에 설형문자가 어떻게 유럽으로 전파되었는지

어휘 및 표현

script 글씨 carve ~을 새기다 parchment 양피지(양의 생가죽을 얇게 펴서 약품 처리를 한 후에 표백하여 말린, 글을 쓰는 데 사용하는 재료) fascinating 흥미로운, 매혹적인 writing system 표기 체계 cuneiform 설형문자 pictograph 그림문자 wedge-shaped 쐐기 모양의 mark 표시 stylus 스타일러스(바늘같이 뾰족한 도구) clay tablet 점토판 adapt ~을 채택하다 flexibility 유연성 trade 무역, 교역 government administration 정부 행정 record ~을 기록하다 literature 문헌 epic 서사(시), 대작 scholar 학자 discovery 발견물 inscription 비문(비석에 새긴 글) decipher ~을 해독하다 hieroglyph 상형문자 civilization 문명 value ~을 소중히 여기다 govern 통치하다 oracle bone script 갑골문자 architecture 건축 pronunciation 발음 significance 중요성 oral 구두의 myth 신화 translate ~을 번역하다 bilingual 이중 언어

9-12 (B), (D), (A), (D)

도시계획 수업에서의 강연을 들으시오.

> Many cities are experimenting with gardens on rooftops. These "green roofs" keep buildings cooler because plants provide shade and release moisture into the air. As a result, the roof surface does not heat up as much as bare concrete or metal.
>
> Some roofs only have a thin layer of soil and small plants like grasses. These are light and easy to install, but they don't hold much rainwater. However, other roofs have deeper soil that can support bushes or even small trees. These heavier systems store more water and stay cooler for longer after a hot day.
>
> Researchers first proved the cooling effect by taking photos with special cameras that show surface temperature. Roofs with plants looked much cooler than roofs without them. Studies also suggest that if many rooftops in a city are covered with plants, summer heat waves are less intense and flooding from heavy rain is reduced. In the next part of our lecture, we'll look at what kinds of plants grow best in different regions and how much care each type of roof needs.
>
> 많은 도시들이 옥상 정원을 실험하고 있습니다. 이러한 '녹색 지붕'은 식물이 그늘을 제공하고 공기 중으로 수분을 방출하기 때문에 건물을 더 시원하게 유지합니다. 그 결과 지붕 표면은 맨 콘크리트나 금속만큼 뜨거워지지 않습니다.
>
> 일부 옥상은 얇은 흙층과 잔디 같은 작은 식물만 심습니다. 가볍고 설치가 쉽지만 빗물을 많이 수용하지는 못합니다. 하지만, 다른 옥상은 관목이나 작은 나무까지 키울 수 있는 깊은 흙층을 갖추고 있습니다. 이런 무거운 시스템은 더 많은 물을 저장하며 더운 날 이후에도 더 오래 시원함을 유지합니다.
>
> 연구진은 표면 온도를 보여주는 특수 카메라로 사진을 찍어 냉각 효과를 처음 입증했습니다. 식물이 있는 옥상은 없는 옥상보다 훨씬 시원해 보였습니다. 연구에 따르면 도시 내 다수의 지붕이 식물로 덮일 경우 여름 폭염의 강도가 약해지고 폭우로 인한 홍수도 감소한다고 합니다. 다음 강의에서는 지역별로 가장 잘 자라는 식물 종류와 각 지붕 유형이 얼마나 많은 관리를 필요로 하는지에 대해 살펴보겠습니다.

강연의 주요 초점은?

(A) 도시 공원이 어떻게 조성되는지
(B) 정원이 어떻게 열기를 줄일 수 있는지
(C) 건물이 어떻게 에너지를 절약하는지
(D) 식물이 도시에서 어떻게 생존할 수 있는지

깊은 지붕 시스템에 대한 점은?

(A) 배수에 전혀 영향을 미치지 않는다.
(B) 설치 비용이 항상 덜 나간다.
(C) 유지보수 필요성을 없앤다.
(D) 더 큰 식물을 지원하고 더 많은 물을 저장한다.

교수가 특수 카메라를 언급한 이유는?

(A) 더 시원한 표면의 증거를 보여주기 위해
(B) 폭풍이 어떻게 형성되는지 설명하기 위해
(C) 얕은 토양 시스템을 비판하기 위해
(D) 조류 조사를 설명하기 위해

교수가 다음에 논의할 가능성이 가장 높은 것은?

(A) 식물 종이 먼 거리를 어떻게 이주하는지
(B) 옥상 팬의 소음
(C) 태양광 패널의 화학 성분
(D) 다른 장소에 적합한 식물들

어휘 및 표현

experiment 실험하다 rooftop 옥상 shade 그늘 release ~을 내보내다 moisture 수분 surface 표면 bare 맨, 벌거벗은 metal 금속 thin layer 얇은 층 soil 흙, 토양 hold ~을 수용하다 rainwater 빗물 bush 관목 temperature 온도 heat wave 폭염 intense 강렬한 flooding 홍수 heavy rain 폭우 region 지역 conserve ~을 보존하다 drainage 배수 eliminate ~을 없애다 retain ~을 간직하다 shallow 얕은 migrate 이주하다, 이동하다

Writing
Build a Sentence

예시

Did she say what part she loved the best?

적절한 문장을 만드시오.
W: 제인이 네가 추천한 영화가 좋았대.
M: 그녀가 어떤 부분을 가장 좋아한다고 말했니?

Practice

1 He has not had time to watch it yet.

M: 네가 빌려준 DVD를 마크가 돌려줬니?
W: 마크가 아직 볼 시간이 없었어.

2 They wanted to know what I liked best about him.

W: 새 매니저에 대해 너희 동료들이 무엇을 물어봤어?
M: 그들은 내가 그에 대해 가장 좋아하는 점에 대해 알길 원했어.

3 Yes. I tried to explain why I had not finished the report.

M: 너 교수님께 말씀드렸니?
W: 응. 난 내가 보고서를 끝내지 못한 이유를 설명하려고 했어.

4 Did you remind her when her appointment is?

M: 페니는 아직 여기 없어.
W: 페니에게 그녀의 예약이 언제인지 상기시켜줬니?

5 The instructions were not clear to me.

W: 왜 도움이 필요해?
M: 설명이 내게 명확하지가 않았어.

6 She wanted to find out where she could apply for a part-time job.

W: 수업 후 티나가 네게 무엇을 물었니?
M: 그녀는 아르바이트를 어디에 지원할 수 있는지 알아보고 싶어 했어.

7 They just found out which ingredient was being removed.

W: 왜 모든 사람들이 회의실에 있지?

M: 그들은 방금 어떤 성분이 제거되고 있는지 알아냈어.

8 The shoe store he works at had the sneakers in stock.

M: 매튜가 어디에서 저 신발들을 구했지?
W: 그가 일하는 신발 가게이는 그 운동화가 재고로 있었어.

9 No, I can't figure out which color is the most appealing.

M: 아직 책상 주문했어?
W: 아니, 어떤 색이 가장 매력적인지 도저히 생각이 안 돼.

10 She does not respond to messages on Sundays.

M: 니콜에게 사라진 파일에 대해 물어봤어?
W: 그녀는 일요일에는 메시지에 답장을 하지 않아.

11 I found the atmosphere at this restaurant to be much more comfortable.

W: 왜 장소를 바꿨어?
M: 이 식당의 분위기가 훨씬 더 편안하다고 느꼈어.

12 I was hoping you could tell me when I can meet with the professor.

W: 어떻게 도와드릴까요?
M: 제가 교수님을 언제 뵐 수 있는지 알려주시길 바랍니다.

어휘 및 표현

appointment 예약, 약속 **instructions** 설명, 지시사항, 지시문 **find out** 알아보다, 알아내다 **apply for** ~에 지원하다 **ingredient** 성분, 재료 **sneakers** 운동화 **in stock** 재고로 **figure out** 생각해 내다, 계산해 내다, 이해하다 **appealing** 매력적인 **missing** 사라진, 없어진 **venue** 장소 **find** 느끼다 **atmosphere** 분위기 **comfortable** 편안한

Writing

Write an Email

예시

문제

최근 재택근무를 시작했지만 인터넷 신호가 매우 약하고 연결이 불안정하다는 점을 발견했다. 이 문제를 알리고 수리를 요청하기 위해, 당신은 집주인 월튼 씨에게 연락해야 한다.

월튼 씨에게 이메일을 작성하시오. 이메일에서 다음을 수행하시오:

- 인터넷 연결에서 당신이 겪고 있는 문제를 서술하시오.
- 이러한 문제가 업무에 어떤 영향을 미치는지 설명하시오.
- 수리를 요청하고 문제가 언제 해결될 수 있는지 물어보시오.

가능한 한 많이 완전한 문장으로 작성하시오.

당신의 답변:

수신인: 월튼 씨
제목: 인터넷 수리 요청

모범답안

Dear Ms. Walton,

I hope this message finds you well.

I am writing to report an issue with the internet connection in my apartment. The signal is very weak, and the connection frequently cuts off. When I try to access web pages or make video calls, I experience long delays or receive a "failed to connect" message. As I work from home, these issues are affecting my ability to complete tasks efficiently and participate in team meetings. They are also making it difficult for me to meet an important deadline. Could you please arrange for a repair as soon as possible and let me know when it is scheduled?

I look forward to your response.

Best regards,
Rumi Kim

(119 words)

월튼 씨께,

저는 이 메시지가 당신께 잘 전달되길 바랍니다.

제 아파트의 인터넷 연결 문제에 대해 알려드리기 위해 이메일을 씁니다. 신호가 매우 약하고 연결이 자주 끊깁니다. 웹 페이지를 열거나 영상 통화를 시도할 때면 지연이 심하거나 "연결 실패" 메시지가 표시됩니다. 재택근무를 하는 저로서는, 이러한 문제로 인해 업무를 효율적으로 처리하고 팀 회의에 참여하는 데 지장을 받고 있습니다. 또한 중요한 마감일을 맞추는 데도 어려움을 겪고 있습니다. 가능한 한 빨리 수리를 진행해 주시고, 일정이 예정되면 알려주시겠습니까?

당신의 답변을 기대하겠습니다.

안녕히 계세요,
루미 김

(119 단어)

어휘 및 표현

video call 화상 통화 **work from home** 재택근무하다 **affect** ~에 영향을 미치다 **arrange** ~을 마련하다, 진행하다

Practice

1

문제

당신은 대학생이며 국제학생 동아리 회원이다. 동아리는 세계 각국의 인기 음식을 축하하는 팟럭 행사를 주최하고 있다. 행사 주최자인 루이지가 회원들에게 참여를 요청했다.

루이지에게 이메일을 작성하시오. 이메일에서 다음을 수행하시오:

- 당신의 나라에서 인기 있는 요리를 만들겠다고 제안하시오.
- 그 요리가 무엇인지에 대한 세부 정보를 제공하시오.
- 행사를 위해 다른 방법으로 어떻게 도울 수 있는지 루이지에게 물어보시오.

가능한 한 많이 완전한 문장으로 작성하시오.

당신의 답변:

수신인: 루이지
제목: 팟럭을 위한 요리

모범답안

Hello Luigi,

I hope you are doing well.

I am writing to offer to contribute to the International Students' Club potluck by making a Korean dish called kimbap. Kimbap consists of bite-sized pieces of rice rolled in seaweed with various vegetables and proteins, and it is perfect as a light snack for the event. My version will include eggs, carrots, pickled radish, tuna, and spinach. It is not spicy, so it should be suitable for everyone. Is there anything else I could do to help with the event? Since I have plenty of free time, I would be happy to help in any way.

I look forward to hearing from you soon.

Best regards,
Jeremy

(115 words)

루이지에게,

잘 지내나요.

국제학생 동아리 팟럭 행사에 김밥을 만들어 기여하고자 이메일을 써요. 김밥은 김에 다양한 채소와 단백질을 넣어 말아 만든 한입 크기의 밥으로, 행사에 가벼운 간식으로 안성맞춤입니다. 제가 준비할 김밥에는 달걀, 당근, 단무지, 참치, 그리고 시금치가 들어갈 예정이에요. 매운 맛이 없어서 누구나 먹기 좋을 거예요. 행사 준비에 제가 더 도울 수 있는 일이 있을까요? 시간이 많이 남아서 어떤 일이든 기꺼이 도울게요.

곧 연락 주길 기대할게요.

잘 있어요,
제레미

(115 단어)

어휘 및 표현

potluck (여러 사람들이) 각자 음식을 조금씩 가져 와서 나눠 먹는 식사 **contribute to** ~에 기여하다 **consist of** ~을 이루다, 구성하다 **bite-sized** 한입 크기의 **seaweed** 김, 해초 **protein** 단백질 **pickled radish** 단무지 **tuna** 참치 **spinach** 시금치 **spicy** 매운 **suitable** 적합한 **plenty of** 많은

2

문제

당신은 해외 유학을 계획 중이며, 학업 중 경제적 뒷받침을 위해 아르바이트를 구하고 싶어한다. 당신은 이미 그곳에 살고 있는 친구 첼시에게 조언을 구하길 원한다.

첼시에게 이메일을 작성하시오. 이메일에서 다음을 수행하시오:

- 아르바이트를 하고 싶은 이유를 설명하시오.
- 어떤 종류의 일을 하고 싶은지 언급하시오.
- 일자리를 찾는 방법에 대한 그녀의 조언을 구하시오.

가능한 한 많이 완전한 문장으로 작성하시오.

당신의 답변:

수신인: 첼시
제목: 아르바이트 구하는 것에 대한 조언

모범답안

Hello Chelsea,

I hope you are doing well.

I am writing to ask for your advice on finding a part-time job while I am studying in New York City next month. Since you have lived there for a long time, I thought you might have valuable insights to share. I have a tight budget, so I would like to work to support myself financially while I am there. Ideally, I would like to work at a hotel, particularly at the front desk, so that I can learn more about hotel management. Could you please share any tips or recommend websites for finding part-time jobs?

I look forward to your response.

Best regards,
Terry

(113 words)

첼시에게,

잘 지내니.

다음 달 뉴욕에서 공부하는 동안 아르바이트를 구하는데 네 조언을 구하려고 이메일 써. 네가 오랫동안 그곳에서 살았으니, 공유할 귀중한 식견을 갖고 있을 것 같다고 생각했어. 난 예산이 넉넉하지 않아서, 그곳에 있는 동안 생활비를 벌고 싶어. 이상적으로, 난 호텔, 특히 프런트 데스크에서 일하고 싶은데, 호텔 경영에 대해 더 배울 수 있도록 말이야. 아르바이트 구직 팁이나 추천 웹사이트를 알려줄 수 있겠니?

답변 기대할게.

잘 있어,
테리

(113 단어)

어휘 및 표현

part-time job 아르바이트 **valuable** 귀중한, 소중한 **insight** 통찰력, 식견 **tight budget** 넉넉치 않은 예산 **particularly** 특히 **hotel management** 호텔 경영

Writing
Write for an Academic Discussion

예시

문제

교수가 마케팅 수업을 진행 중이다. 교수의 질문에 답변하는 게시글을 작성하시오.

답변에서는 다음을 수행해야 한다:

- 본인의 의견을 제시하고 뒷받침하시오.
- 토론에 본인의 표현으로 기여하시오.

효과적인 답변은 최소 100단어 이상이어야 한다.

브라운 박사: 우리는 최근 타겟팅 광고라는 새로운 광고 전략 개념에 대해 논의해 왔는데, 이는 일반 대중을 대상으로 광고를 제작하는 대신 특정 특성이나 관심사를 가진 소비자에게 광고를 전달하는 방식입니다. 일부는 타겟팅 광고가 윤리적이라고 믿습니다. 다른 이들은 사생활 침해라고 주장합니다. 이에 대한 당신의 의견은 무엇입니까?

저스틴: 저는 타겟팅 광고에 윤리적 문제가 있다고 생각하지 않습니다. 타겟팅 광고를 받고 싶지 않다면 간단히 개인정보 설정을 변경하면 됩니다. 또한 기업은 자사 제품이나 서비스와 관련된 관심사를 가진 사람들에게 접근함으로써 비용을 절감할 수 있으며, 이는 고객에게 더 낮은 가격으로 이어질 수 있습니다.

켈리: 저는 타겟팅 광고가 개인의 사생활을 침해한다고 생각합니다. 비록 효과적인 전략일 수 있지만, 웹사이트가 사람들의 개인정보를 추적하여 자신들의 목적을 위해 사용하는 것은 허용되어서는 안 됩니다. 대신, 기업들은 광범위한 대중에게 어필할 수 있는 광고를 제작해야 합니다.

모범답안

While I understand Justin's point about lower prices, I think targeted advertising is unethical and a violation of privacy. Companies that use targeted advertising collect consumers' personal data, including which websites they visit, the media they watch, and even their recent purchases, in order to analyze their behavior. This information is often used without people's awareness or consent to display ads for products that companies believe consumers are more likely to buy. Although the companies claim these actions are not illegal, they are still ethically questionable. Furthermore, it makes people feel a sense of uneasiness, as though their actions are being tracked and monitored. Therefore, targeted advertising should not be practiced, and ads should instead be aimed at a large audience.

(121 words)

저스틴의 가격 인하 주장은 이해하지만, 타겟팅 광고는 비윤리적이며 사생활 침해라고 생각합니다. 타겟팅 광고를 활용하는 기업들은 소비자의 행동을 분석하기 위해 방문한 웹사이트, 시청한 미디어, 최근 구매 내역 등 개인 데이터를 수집합니다. 이러한 정보는 기업이 소비자가 구매 가능성이 높다고 판단하는 제품 광고를 노출하는 데 소비자의 인지나 동의 없이 사용됩니다. 비록 기업들은 이러한 행위가 불법이 아니라고 주장하지만, 여전히 윤리적으로 의문스럽습니다. 더욱이, 이는 마치 자신의 행동이 추적되고 감시받는 듯한 불안감을 사람들에게 느끼게 합니다. 따라서, 타겟팅 광고는 시행되어서는 안 되며, 광고는 대신 광범위한 대중을 대상으로 해야 합니다.

(121 단어)

어휘 및 표현

strategy 전략 **audience** 관중, 청중 **ethical** 윤리적인 **violate** ~을 침해하다 **privacy** 개인 사생활 **relevant to** ~와 관련된 **lower** ~을 낮추다 **appeal** 호소하다 **unethical** 비윤리적인 **awareness** 인지, 인식 **consent** 동의 **illegal** 불법의 **questionable** 의문스러운 **uneasiness** 불안감 **track** ~을 추적하다 **monitor** ~을 감시하다 **practice** ~을 시행하다, 실행하다

Practice

1

문제

교수가 정치학 수업을 진행 중이다. 교수의 질문에 답변하는 게시글을 작성하시오.

답변에서는 다음을 수행해야 한다:

- 본인의 의견을 제시하고 뒷받침하시오.
- 토론에 본인의 표현으로 기여하시오.

효과적인 답변은 최소 100단어 이상이어야 한다.

로빈슨 박사: 우리는 수업에서 예방 가능한 질병 증가에 대한 해결책으로 건강세 개념을 논의해 왔습니다. 일부는 설탕 음료나 정크푸드 같은 건강에 해로운 제품에 세금을 부과하는 것이 공중보건 개선에 필수적이라고 주장하는 반면, 다른 이들은 효과적이지 않다고 생각합니다. 당신은 건강에 해로운 제품에 세금을 부과하는 것이 좋은 생각이라고 생각합니까? 그 이유는 무엇입니까?

줄리: 저는 건강에 해로운 제품에 세금을 부과하는 것은 좋은 생각이라고 생각합니다. 탄산음료나 간식 같은 품목의 가격이 오르면 사람들이 구매를 꺼리게 될 가능성이 더 커집니다. 시간이 지나면, 이는 더 건강한 선택을 하는 습관을 기르는 데 도움이 될 수 있습니다.

폴: 저는 건강에 해로운 제품에 세금을 부과하는 것은 효과가 없을 것이라고 생각합니다. 사람들의 취향은 바꾸기 어렵고, 가격이 높아져도 즐기는 제품을 계속 구매하는 경우가 많습니다. 당분이 많은 음료와 정크푸드는 일상 습관에 깊이 뿌리내려 있어, 세금만으로는 소비를 크게 줄일 수 없습니다.

모범답안

Even though Paul makes a valid point regarding people's tastes, I believe taxing unhealthy products is important for promoting a healthier general public. Consuming unhealthy foods and beverages is a major cause of serious diseases, including diabetes and obesity. If the government imposes health taxes, people are more likely to choose healthier alternatives, such as tea and fruit, which could reduce the number of individuals suffering from these preventable health issues. In addition, revenue from health taxes could be used to fund public health

폴이 사람들의 취향에 대해 타당한 지적을 했지만, 저는 건강에 해로운 제품에 세금을 부과하는 것이 국민 건강 증진에 중요하다고 생각합니다. 건강에 해로운 음식과 음료의 섭취는 당뇨병과 비만 등 심각한 질병의 주요 원인입니다. 정부가 건강세를 부과하면 사람들은 차나 과일처럼 더 건강한 대안을 선택할 가능성이 높아져, 이렇게 예방 가능한 건강 문제로 고통받는 사람들의 수를 줄일 수 있습니다. 또한 건강세로 조성된 재원은 공중보건 프로그램에 투자되어 병원과 진료소의 접근성을 높일 수 있습니다. 결론적으로, 정부는 예방 가능한 질병을 줄이고 의료 서비스를 개선할 수 있으므로 건강에 해로운 제품에 세금을 부과해야 합니다.

(111 단어)

programs, making hospitals and clinics more accessible for everyone. In conclusion, the government should tax unhealthy products because it can help reduce preventable diseases and improve healthcare.

(111 words)

어휘 및 표현

political science 정치학 **concept** 개념 **health tax** 건강세 **preventable** 막을 수 있는, 예방 가능한 **disease** 질병 **tax** ~에 세금을 매기다 **unhealthy** 해로운, 건강하지 않은 **sugary** 설탕의 **soda** 탄산음료 **discourage** ~을 막다 **habit** 습관 **regardless of** ~에 상관없이 **ingrained** 뿌리 깊은, 깊이 밴 **significantly** 크게, 상당히 **consumption** 소비 **valid** 타당한 **regarding** ~에 관한 **taste** 취향 **general public** 일반 대중 **beverage** 음료 **diabetes** 당뇨병 **obesity** 비만 **alternative** 대안 **revenue** 수입, 재원 **clinic** 진료소 **healthcare** 의료 서비스

2
문제

교수가 교육학 수업을 진행 중이다. 교수의 질문에 답변하는 게시글을 작성하시오.

답변에서는 다음을 수행해야 한다:

- 본인의 의견을 제시하고 뒷받침하시오.
- 토론에 본인의 표현으로 기여하시오.

효과적인 답변은 최소 100단어 이상이어야 한다.

스미스 박사: 우리는 최근 교육 분야에서 과외 활동의 개념에 대해 논의해 왔습니다. 일부는 스포츠 팀, 학생회, 종교 단체와 같은 학생 단체 및 동아리가 유익하다고 주장합니다. 다른 이들은 이러한 활동이 주의 분산 요인이 되며 대학은 주로 학습의 장이어야 한다고 믿습니다. 학생 단체에 대한 당신의 의견은 무엇입니까?

브래드: 저는 학업 성취는 대학 생활에서 가장 중요한 측면이라고 생각합니다. 그러나 일부 학생 단체들은 많은 시간과 헌신을 요구하기 때문에 동아리 활동은 종종 학생들의 학업에 방해가 되기도 합니다. 이는 소중한 공부 시간을 빼앗아 성적을 떨어뜨릴 수 있습니다.

에이프럴: 저는 과외 활동은 학생들이 대학 생활을 즐길 수 있게 해주기 때문에 유익하다고 생각합니다. 대학은 단순히 공부만 하는 곳이 아닙니다; 다양한 사람들과 우정을 쌓고 교류하는 것은 대학 경험의 핵심 부분입니다. 학생 단체와 동아리는 이를 위한 훌륭한 방법입니다.

모범답안

While I understand Brad's point about academic achievement, I believe extracurricular activities are a valuable part of attending university. They can help students in their future careers by developing skills such as teamwork,

브래드의 학업 성취에 대한 주장은 이해하지만, 저는 과외 활동이 대학 생활의 소중한 부분이라고 생각합니다. 팀워크, 리더십, 시간 관리 같은 기술을 함양함으로써 학생들의 미래 진로에 도움이 될 수 있습니다. 고용주들은 종종 학업 성적과 함께 이 같은 경험을 이력서에서 찾습니다. 더욱이, 과외 활동은 스트레스를 해소하는 데도 도움이 됩니다. 대학생들은 수업으로 인한 상당한

leadership, and time management. Employers often look for these experiences on résumés alongside academic performance. Moreover, extracurricular activities can relieve stress. University students face significant pressure from their classes, which can lead to mental health problems like anxiety and depression. Participating in clubs, sports, or art activities allows students to relax, socialize, and take a break from their studies, which improves overall well-being. In conclusion, universities should encourage students to take part in extracurricular activities because they support both personal growth and mental health.

(117 words)

압박에 직면하며, 이는 불안과 우울증 같은 정신 건강 문제로 이어질 수 있습니다. 동아리, 스포츠, 예술 활동에 참여는 학생들이 휴식을 취하고, 사교 활동을 하며, 학업에서 잠시 벗어날 수 있도록 하는데, 이는 전반적인 웰빙을 향상시킵니다. 결론적으로, 과외 활동들은 학생들의 개인적 성장과 정신 건강을 모두 지원하기 때문에, 대학은 학생들에게 과외 활동 참여를 장려해야 합니다.

(117 단어)

어휘 및 표현

extracurricular 과외의, 정규 과목 이외의 organization 단체, 조직 club 동아리 student government 학생회 religious 종교의 academic achievement 학업 성취 distract 정신을 산만하게 하다 commitment 헌신 take away 빼앗아 가다 interact with ~와 교류하다 career 진로, 경력 résumé 이력서 academic performance 학업 성적 relieve stress 스트레스를 해소하다 mental health 정신 건강 anxiety 불안 depression 우울증 take part in ~에 참여하다

Speaking

Listen and Repeat

> **예시**

당신은 대학 오리엔테이션 기간 동안 신입생들을 돕는 트레이닝을 받고 있다. 슈퍼바이저의 말을 듣고 따라 하시오. 오직 한 번만 따라 하시오.

Visit the student center to pick up your student identification cards.
학생회관에 방문해서 학생증을 수령하세요.

어휘 및 표현
pick up ~을 가져가다, 수령하다 student identification card 학생증

> **Practice**

1-7
당신은 미술관에서 방문객들을 환영하는 준비를 하고 있다. 슈퍼바이저의 말을 듣고 따라 하시오. 오직 한 번만 따라 하시오.

Our gallery features a wide range of artwork.
저희 미술관에서는 다양한 예술 작품을 특징으로 합니다.

Donated paintings are displayed in the west wing.
기증받은 그림들은 서쪽 건물에 전시되어 있습니다.

Modern sculptures and abstract pieces are located upstairs.
현대 조각품과 추상 작품들은 위층에 위치해 있습니다.

Please, no food or drinks are allowed inside the galleries.
미술관 내에서는 음식물 및 음료 반입이 금지됩니다.

Avoid touching the artwork or leaning on the display cases.
작품을 만지거나 전시 케이스에 기대지 마세요.

Families are welcome to join our weekend art classes and guided tours.
주말 미술 수업과 가이드 투어에 가족 단위로 참여하실 수 있습니다.

The information desk, located near the main lobby, can provide further details.
메인 로비 근처에 위치한 안내 데스크에서 자세한 정보를 확인하실 수 있습니다.

어휘 및 표현
feature ~을 특징으로 하다 a wide range of 다양한 artwork 예술 작품 donated 기증된 wing 부속 건물 modern 현대 sculpture 조각품 abstract 추상의 located 위치한 upstairs 위층에 lean 기대다 display case 전시 케이스 further details 자세한 정보

8-14

당신은 보관함 대여 업체에서 고객을 돕기 위한 교육을 받고 있다. 트레이너의 말을 듣고 따라 하시오. 오직 한 번만 따라 하시오.

Welcome. Please provide your personal information.
어서 오세요. 개인정보를 알려주세요.

You can choose your unit from these available spaces.
여기 사용 가능한 공간에서 보관함을 선택하실 수 있습니다.

Storage rental agreements are signed at the front desk.
보관함 대여 계약서는 프런트 데스크에서 서명합니다.

Once everything is set, look at the screen for your building access code.
모든 절차가 완료되면, 건물 출입 코드가 표시된 화면을 확인하세요.

This is where you return your storage unit keys after the rental period is over.
여기는 대여 기간이 종료된 후 보관함 열쇠를 반납하는 곳입니다.

Please check your unit for trash or any items left behind before storing your items.
물품을 보관하기 전에 보관함에 쓰레기나 남겨진 물건이 있는지 확인해 주세요.

When moving out, make sure to clean the space so that it is in the same condition as you found it.
퇴실 시에는, 처음 사용했을 때와 동일한 상태가 되도록 공간을 청소하여 주시기 바랍니다.

어휘 및 표현
unit 장비나 시설 하나, 한 대 **storage** 보관 **rental** 임대, 대여 **agreement** 계약(서) **sign** ~을 서명하다 **be set** 완료되다, 정리되다 **period** 기간 **trash** 쓰레기 **item** 물품 **store** ~을 보관하다 **so that** ~하도록

Speaking

Take an Interview

> **예시**

당신은 스포츠 활동에 관한 연구 조사에 자원했다. 당신은 연구원과 간단한 온라인 인터뷰를 진행하게 된다. 연구원이 몇 가지 질문을 할 것이다.

Thank you for taking the time to speak with me about playing sports. When you play sports, do you prefer individual sports, like tennis, or team sports, like basketball?
저와 스포츠 활동에 대해 이야기하기 위해 시간을 내주셔서 감사합니다. 당신은 스포츠를 할 때, 테니스 같은 개인 스포츠와 농구 같은 팀 스포츠 중 어느 쪽을 더 선호하시나요?

Between the two, my preference is to play sports in a team rather than alone. The main reason is that I find playing sports with team members to be more exciting. An occasion I clearly remember is playing soccer with my high school team against another school. We worked together, encouraged each other during the game, and celebrated every point together. Although we lost the match, it was still very fun thanks to my teammates. Overall, I think playing team sports is more preferable.
둘 중에서, 제가 선호하는 것은 혼자보다 팀으로 스포츠를 하는 것입니다. 가장 큰 이유는 팀원들과 함께 하는 스포츠가 더 흥미진진하다고 느끼기 때문입니다. 제가 특히 생생하게 기억하는 경험은 고등학교 시절 다른 학교와 축구 경기를 했던 것입니다. 우리는 경기 내내 서로 협력하고 격려하며, 득점할 때마다 함께 기뻐했습니다. 비록 경기에서 졌지만, 팀원들 덕분에 여전히 매우 즐거웠습니다. 전반적으로, 저는 팀 스포츠를 하는 것을 더 선호합니다.

어휘 및 표현
volunteer 자원하다 **occasion** 경우, 상황, 때, 일 **thanks to** ~ 덕분에

> **Practice**

1-4
당신은 여가로 여행을 하는 것에 대한 연구 조사에 참여하기로 동의하였다. 당신은 연구원과 간단한 온라인 인터뷰를 진행하게 된다. 연구원이 몇 가지 질문을 할 것이다.

1
Thank you for taking part in this study. Today, I'd like to ask you some questions about traveling for leisure. Where are some places your family or friends generally like to visit? For example, do they prefer museums, beaches, or other places?
이 연구에 참여해 주셔서 감사합니다. 오늘, 저는 여가로 여행을 하는 것에 대한 몇 가지 질문을 드리겠습니다. 당신의 가족이나 친구들이 주로 방문하는 장소는 어디인가요? 예를 들어, 박물관, 해변, 또는 다른 장소를 선호하나요?

I would say that my family enjoys visiting outdoor places like beaches and mountains. One experience that comes to mind is when we went to Jeju Island, a popular holiday destination known for its natural wonders. Everyone loved exploring the white sandy beaches and hiking up mountain trails for the scenic views. We also enjoy going to parks or botanical gardens because being in nature is peaceful and relaxing. Overall, my family prefers destinations where we can enjoy the beauty of the outdoors.

저희 가족은 해변이나 산 같은 야외 장소를 방문하는 것을 즐기는 편입니다. 한 가지 생각나는 경험은 경이로운 자연 경관으로 유명한 인기 휴양지인 제주도에 갔을 때입니다. 모두가 하얀 모래사장을 탐험하고 경치를 보기 위해 산길을 하이킹하는 것을 좋아했습니다. 또한 공원이나 식물원에 가는 것도 즐기는데, 자연 속에 있으면 평화롭고 편안하기 때문입니다. 전반적으로, 저희 가족은 야외의 아름다움을 즐길 수 있는 장소를 선호합니다.

2

I see. When you travel for leisure, do you prefer to travel alone, or do you like to travel with your family or friends? Why?

알겠습니다. 당신은 여가로 여행을 할 때 혼자 다니는 것을 선호하시나요, 아니면 가족이나 친구와 함께 다니는 것을 좋아하시나요? 이유는요?

Between the two, my preference is to travel with family or friends rather than alone. The main reason is that traveling with others makes the experience more fun since we can create memorable experiences together. An occasion I clearly remember is when I went camping with my friends. During the trip, we set up tents, cooked food over a campfire, and stayed up all night telling scary stories. In the end, we created unforgettable memories that we still talk about to this day.

둘 중에서, 제가 선호하는 것은 혼자보다 가족이나 친구들과 함께 여행하는 것입니다. 그 주된 이유는 다른 사람들과 함께 여행하면 여행 경험이 더 즐거운데, 함께 잊지 못할 추억을 만들 수 있기 때문입니다. 제가 생생하게 기억하는 경험은 친구들과 함께 캠핑을 갔을 때입니다. 그 여행에서, 우리는 텐트를 치고, 모닥불에 음식을 요리하며, 밤새 무서운 이야기를 나누었습니다. 결국, 우리는 지금까지도 이야기하는 잊을 수 없는 추억을 만들었습니다.

3

Interesting. Next, I'd like to get your opinion. In recent years, overtourism has become a problem, with popular destinations becoming overcrowded with visitors. Do you think this issue will become even more serious in the future? Why or why not?

흥미롭네요. 다음으로, 당신의 의견을 듣고 싶습니다. 최근 몇 년 동안, 인기 있는 여행지들이 관광객들로 넘치면서 과잉관광(overtourism)이 문제가 되고 있습니다. 당신은 이 문제가 앞으로 더 심각해질 것이라고 생각하나요? 이유는요?

It is likely that overtourism will become an even bigger problem in the future. One reason is that travel has become more accessible due to cheaper flights from budget airlines, allowing more people to travel than ever before. Another reason is that social media platforms have made it easy for people to share travel photos and experiences, which often inspires others to visit the same places. For these reasons, overtourism is a growing concern as more tourists flock to popular destinations.

과잉관광은 앞으로 더 심각한 문제가 될 가능성이 높을 것 같습니다. 한 가지 이유는 저가 항공사의 증가로 항공권이 더 저렴해져서, 이전보다 훨씬 더 많은 사람들이 여행할 수 있게 되었기 때문입니다. 또 다른 이유는 소셜 미디어 덕분에 사람들이 여행 사진과 경험을 쉽게 공유할 수 있게 되었고, 이것이 다른 사람들에게 같은 장소를 방문하도록 영감을 주기 때문입니다. 이런 이유로, 더 많은 관광객이 인기 있는 여행지로 몰리면서 과잉관광은 점점 더 큰 사회적 문제가 됩니다.

4

Good points. I just have one more question. Some people believe that traveling abroad is essential for developing cultural awareness. Do you agree or disagree with this idea? Explain why you think so.
좋은 지적이에요. 마지막으로 한 가지 더 묻고 싶습니다. 어떤 사람들은 문화적 인식을 발전시키기 위해 해외여행이 필수적이라고 믿습니다. 이 생각에 동의하나요, 아니면 동의하지 않나요? 그 이유를 설명해주세요.

I agree with the statement that traveling to other countries allows individuals to gain cultural understanding. This is because people can observe the local customs and daily life of residents, which cannot be fully learned from books or videos. However, cultural awareness can also be developed through other experiences. For instance, studying with international classmates or working with colleagues from diverse backgrounds provides opportunities to understand different perspectives. For these reasons, I think traveling abroad is valuable, but not the only path to cultural awareness.
저는 해외여행이 사람들에게 문화적 이해를 넓혀준다는 의견에 동의합니다. 이는 여행을 통해 현지 사람들의 풍습이나 일상생활을 직접 관찰할 수 있기 때문인데, 이러한 경험은 책이나 영상만으로는 완전히 배울 수 없는 것들입니다. 하지만, 문화적 인식은 다른 경험을 통해서도 발전시킬 수 있습니다. 예를 들어, 다양한 배경을 가진 외국의 급우들과 공부하거나 다양한 문화에서 온 동료들과 함께 일하는 것도 서로 다른 관점을 이해하는 좋은 기회를 제공합니다. 이런 이유로, 저는 해외여행이 문화적 인식에 도움이 되지만, 그것이 유일한 방법은 아니라고 생각합니다.

어휘 및 표현
participate in ~에 참여하다 leisure 여가 come to mind 생각이 떠오르다 holiday destination 휴양지 natural wonder 경이로운 자연 경관 mountain trail 산길 scenic view 경치 botanical garden 식물원 memorable 기억에 남는 scary 무서운 overtourism 과잉관광 overcrowded 지나치게 붐비는, 넘치는 budget airline 저가 항공사 social media 소셜미디어(SNS) inspire ~에게 영감을 주다 concern 문제, 관심사, 걱정 flock 몰리다 essential 필수적인 cultural awareness 문화적 인식 individual 개인 observe ~을 관찰하다 local customs 현지 풍습 daily life 일상생활 perspective 관점, 시각

5-8
당신은 식습관에 대한 연구 조사에 자원하였다. 당신은 연구원과 간단한 온라인 인터뷰를 진행하게 된다. 연구원이 몇 가지 질문을 할 것이다.

5
Thank you for your participation. I'd like to ask you some questions about your eating habits. First, what kind of food do you or your friends like to eat? For example, do you like seafood, fast food, or other types of food?
참여해 주셔서 감사합니다. 당신의 식습관에 대한 몇 가지 질문을 하려고 합니다. 먼저, 당신이나 당신의 친구들은 어떤 종류의 음식을 좋아하나요? 예를 들어, 해산물, 패스트푸드, 혹은 다른 종류의 음식을 좋아하나요?

There were not many chances for me to think about this, but my friends and I enjoy eating Korean barbecue. The primary reason for our preference is that it is very flavorful. We like to order different cuts of meat to grill over charcoal and eat with spicy sauces and a variety of side dishes. We enjoy it so much that we eat Korean barbecue at least once or twice a month. Overall, Korean barbecue is our top choice when we eat out.

저는 이 질문에 대해 깊이 생각해 본 적이 많지 않지만, 제 친구들과 저는 한국식 바비큐를 즐겨 먹습니다. 우리가 그것을 좋아하는 주된 이유는 맛이 매우 풍부하기 때문입니다. 우리는 여러 부위의 고기를 숯불에 구워 매운 소스와 다양한 반찬과 함께 먹는 것을 좋아합니다. 우리는 그것을 아주 즐겨서 한 달에 한두 번은 꼭 한국식 바비큐를 먹습니다. 전반적으로, 외식할 때 한국식 바비큐가 우리의 최우선 선택입니다.

6
Thank you. When you have a meal at a restaurant, do you prefer to eat alone or with other people? Why?
감사합니다. 당신은 식당에서 식사할 때, 혼자 먹는 것을 선호하나요, 아니면 다른 사람들과 함께 먹는 것을 선호하나요? 이유는요?

Given the choice, I would choose eating with others over eating by myself. This is because sharing a meal with other people is more lively and enjoyable. To give a personal example, I recently had lunch with a friend I had not seen in a long time, and I really appreciated the chance to catch up on each other's lives while enjoying good food. However, I can also see the appeal of eating alone when I am tired or busy. All in all, I prefer eating with others.

선택한다면, 저는 혼자 먹는 것보다 다른 사람들과 함께 식사하는 것을 선택하겠습니다. 이는 다른 사람들과 음식을 나누는 것이 훨씬 더 활기차고 즐겁기 때문입니다. 개인적인 예를 들자면, 최근에 오랜만에 만난 친구와 점심을 함께 했는데, 맛있는 음식을 먹으며 서로의 근황을 나눌 수 있어서 정말 좋았습니다. 하지만, 피곤하거나 바쁠 때는 혼자 식사하는 것도 괜찮다고 생각합니다. 전반적으로, 저는 다른 사람들과 함께 식사하는 것을 더 좋아합니다.

7
Interesting. Next, I'd like to get your opinion. Where I live, consuming sugar-free products is becoming increasingly popular. Do you think that in the place you live, the popularity of sugar-free food and drinks will increase in the future? Why or why not?
흥미롭네요. 다음으로, 당신의 의견을 듣고 싶습니다. 제가 사는 곳에서는, 무가당 제품을 소비하는 것이 점점 더 인기를 얻고 있습니다. 당신이 사는 곳에서도 앞으로 무가당 음식과 음료가 더 인기를 끌 것이라고 생각하나요? 이유는요?

I predict that sugar-free food and drinks will become more popular in my country. The main reason is that people are becoming more health-conscious and are paying closer attention to what they eat and drink. In fact, the demand for regular sugary drinks has decreased so much that many convenience stores now stock more sugar-free options, and numerous restaurants have started offering only sugar-free choices on their menus. To sum up, sugar-free products are likely to grow in popularity.

저는 무가당 음식과 음료가 우리나라에서 더 인기를 얻게 될 것이라고 예상합니다. 그 주된 이유는 사람들이 점점 더 건강에 관심을 가지게 되고, 자신이 먹고 마시는 것에 더 신경을 쓰기 때문입니다. 실제로, 일반적인

가당 음료의 수요가 크게 줄어들어서, 많은 편의점들이 이제는 무가당 제품을 더 많이 비치하고 있고, 수많은 식당들도 메뉴에서 무가당 옵션만 제공하기 시작했습니다. 요약하면, 무가당 제품의 인기는 앞으로 더욱 높아질 것으로 보입니다.

8
Good points. I just have one more question. Some people believe that vegetarian diets help improve health and well-being. Do you agree with this idea? Or do you think there are other dietary choices that can also contribute to health and well-being? Explain your answer.
좋은 지적이에요. 마지막으로 한 가지 질문만 더 하겠습니다. 어떤 사람들은 채식 식단이 건강과 웰빙을 향상시키는 데 도움이 된다고 믿습니다. 당신은 이 생각에 동의하나요? 아니면 건강과 웰빙에 도움이 되는 다른 식단도 있다고 생각하나요? 당신의 생각을 설명해 주세요.

I tend to think that eating a plant-based diet can help people become healthier. The reason is that eating more vegetables, fruits, and grains provides important vital nutrients to the body. However, I also believe that non-vegetarian food, such as meat and dairy, are essential for a balanced diet, as they provide other vitamins and minerals necessary for good health. In the end, a combination of vegetarian food and other types of food is important for maintaining a healthy lifestyle.
저는 식물 기반 식단이 사람들의 건강을 개선하는 데 도움이 된다고 생각하는 편입니다. 그 이유는 채소, 과일, 곡류를 많이 섭취하면 신체에 중요한 영양소를 공급하기 때문입니다. 하지만, 저는 또한 고기나 유제품 같은 비채식 음식도 균형 잡힌 식단에 꼭 필요하다고 생각하는데, 그것들이 건강에 좋은 비타민과 미네랄을 제공하기 때문입니다. 결국, 채식 음식과 다른 종류의 음식을 조화롭게 섭취하는 것이 건강한 삶을 유지하는 데 중요합니다.

어휘 및 표현
eating habits 식습관 flavorful 맛이 풍부한 cut 자른 부분, 부위 charcoal 숯불 spicy 매운 side dish 반찬 appreciate 소중히 여기다 catch up on ~을 따라잡다, 만회하다 appeal 매력 all in all 전반적으로, 전체적으로 health-conscious 건강에 관심을 갖는 diet 식단 grain 곡류 nutrient 영양소 dairy 유제품 combination 조화

ETS Practice Tests

Test 1

Reading Section, Module 1	
1	ght
2	at
3	ple
4	ly
5	sic
6	ever
7	s
8	om
9	ord
10	cing
11	D
12	C
13	B
14	C
15	B
16	B
17	A
18	B
19	D
20	A

Reading Section, Module 2	
1	s
2	to
3	ions
4	th
5	les
6	ts
7	rt
8	lved
9	itive
10	ch
11	C
12	C
13	A
14	C
15	D
16	D
17	B
18	C
19	B
20	C

Listening Section, Module 1	
1	A
2	C
3	B
4	B
5	D
6	D
7	D
8	A
9	C
10	B
11	B
12	D
13	A
14	D
15	C
16	B
17	B
18	A

Listening Section, Module 2	
1	B
2	A
3	D
4	B
5	A
6	B
7	C
8	B
9	B
10	B
11	A
12	C
13	B
14	C
15	D
16	A

		Writing Section
	1	The tour guides who showed us around the old city were fantastic.
	2	Do you know if she will be moving to a different department?
	3	Can you tell me whether the cabins will be available?
	4	What time does it start?
	5	Do you know how much the tickets will cost?
	6	What is the water temperature like this time of year?
	7	Do you have a shopping list?
	8	What recipes will you learn?
	9	She wanted to know where she could buy a copy.
	10	I used the study guide that was provided by the professor.

		Speaking Section
	1	We have a variety of wildlife.
	2	Bears, wolves, and large cats are to the right.
	3	You can find sea lions and elephants further down the path.
	4	Please, no outside food or drinks, and do not feed the animals.
	5	Avoid banging or tapping on the displays and enclosures.
	6	For those with children, we offer summer camps and educational opportunities.
	7	The visitor's center, located near the front entrance, can give you more information.

Test 2

	Reading Section, Module 1		Reading Section, Module 2
1	ow	1	nicate
2	tions	2	nds
3	ces	3	nd
4	ies	4	mals
5	nd	5	own
6	ese	6	eir
7	ides	7	ily
8	so	8	ten
9	pes	9	ch
10	mation	10	n
11	C	11	B
12	C	12	C
13	C	13	B
14	A	14	A
15	A	15	C
16	C	16	A
17	D	17	B
18	A	18	D
19	C	19	C
20	B	20	C

	Listening Section, Module 1		Listening Section, Module 2
1	B	1	B
2	B	2	C
3	D	3	C
4	A	4	A
5	A	5	C
6	A	6	B
7	A	7	A
8	D	8	C
9	C	9	B
10	C	10	A
11	C	11	D
12	B	12	A
13	C	13	D
14	A	14	C
15	B	15	A
16	D	16	D
17	A		
18	B		

	Writing Section
1	Which store has the best deals?
2	Have you decided on a topic yet?
3	Do you need to borrow any books?
4	What kind of animal are you considering?
5	Where is it showing?
6	Do you have your résumé ready?
7	Have you finished writing it?
8	Did you book your flight yet?
9	Where are you taking classes?
10	I'm checking to see if it has been extended.

	Speaking Section
1	Welcome to our campus gym.
2	Cardio machines are near the entrance.
3	Free weights are in the back.
4	All of our locker rooms are equipped with showers and towels.
5	Our fitness instructors hold exercise classes over here.
6	You can check the schedule for available classes and timings.
7	If you have any questions, please seek assistance from the attendants at the help desk.

Test 3

Reading Section, Module 1	
1	ey
2	ticated
3	tures
4	uages
5	nced
6	ich
7	em
8	ive
9	blish
10	ade
11	B
12	D
13	D
14	B
15	A
16	D
17	C
18	B
19	C
20	A

Reading Section, Module 2	
1	en
2	ok
3	ror
4	self
5	ibit
6	ich
7	ot
8	o
9	ut
10	so
11	B
12	B
13	C
14	C
15	A
16	B
17	C
18	D
19	A
20	D

Listening Section, Module 1	
1	B
2	D
3	A
4	A
5	D
6	B
7	C
8	B
9	C
10	D
11	A
12	D
13	C
14	A
15	B
16	D
17	A
18	A

Listening Section, Module 2	
1	A
2	B
3	D
4	C
5	C
6	A
7	D
8	B
9	D
10	D
11	B
12	D
13	C
14	A
15	C
16	B

Writing Section	
1	He wanted to know when it ended.
2	It was moved to a time when everyone could attend.
3	I am curious if he mentioned any specific requirements.
4	My friend Jenna is wondering when it is going to open.
5	I think Sally knows how to get there.
6	I don't know what I'm going to do yet.
7	She wanted to know if you need help with it.
8	He wanted to know where he could find a plumber to fix a leak.
9	She wanted to know when we expect the project to be finished.
10	I'm hoping you can tell me where I might find some reliable sources.

Speaking Section	
1	Welcome to our event.
2	Get your name badge at the registration desk.
3	Our event is in the auditorium.
4	For small group sessions, we will be in the breakout rooms over there.
5	Snacks can be found in the vending area throughout the event.
6	Please see the information desk if you need an agenda.
7	If you want to check session times and locations, please use the schedule provided.

MEMO

*toefl. × 시원스쿨 LAB

*toefl Complete Guide 이론서
온라인 강의

2026 NEW

시원스쿨 토플 전문강사
박주영 선생님

ETS 토플 공식 파트너 시원스쿨랩의
최신 개정 강의로 빠르게 목표 달성!

2026 개정
토플에 대한 기준을
제공

전 레벨 대상
개정 시험 정보 제공
+기본기 완벽 학습

R/L/W/S 4영역에 대한
완벽한 이론과 전략, 학습방법,
연습 문제를 **한 번에 학습!**

*toefl × 시원스쿨 LAB

2026 Updated!
개정 시험 ETS 토플 제공 컨텐츠로 최단기 목표 달성!

ETS 토플 제공 컨텐츠 학습 + 2026 개정 내용 완벽 반영 + 이론-실전까지 한 번에

ETS 토플 공식 파트너 시원스쿨랩이 쏜다!

토플 패키지
3만원 할인권
쿠폰번호 : SIWONTOEFL1

- 유효기간 : 발급일로부터 7일간
- 할인내용 : 토플 패키지 3만원 할인
- 사용방법 : 시원스쿨랩 사이트 ▶ 내강의실 ▶ 내쿠폰함 ▶ 쿠폰번호 등록 후, 결제 시 사용

토플 단과
1만원 할인권
쿠폰번호 : SIWONTOEFL2

- 유효기간 : 발급일로부터 7일간
- 할인내용 : 토플 단과 1만원 할인
- 사용방법 : 시원스쿨랩 사이트 ▶ 내강의실 ▶ 내쿠폰함 ▶ 쿠폰번호 등록 후, 결제 시 사용